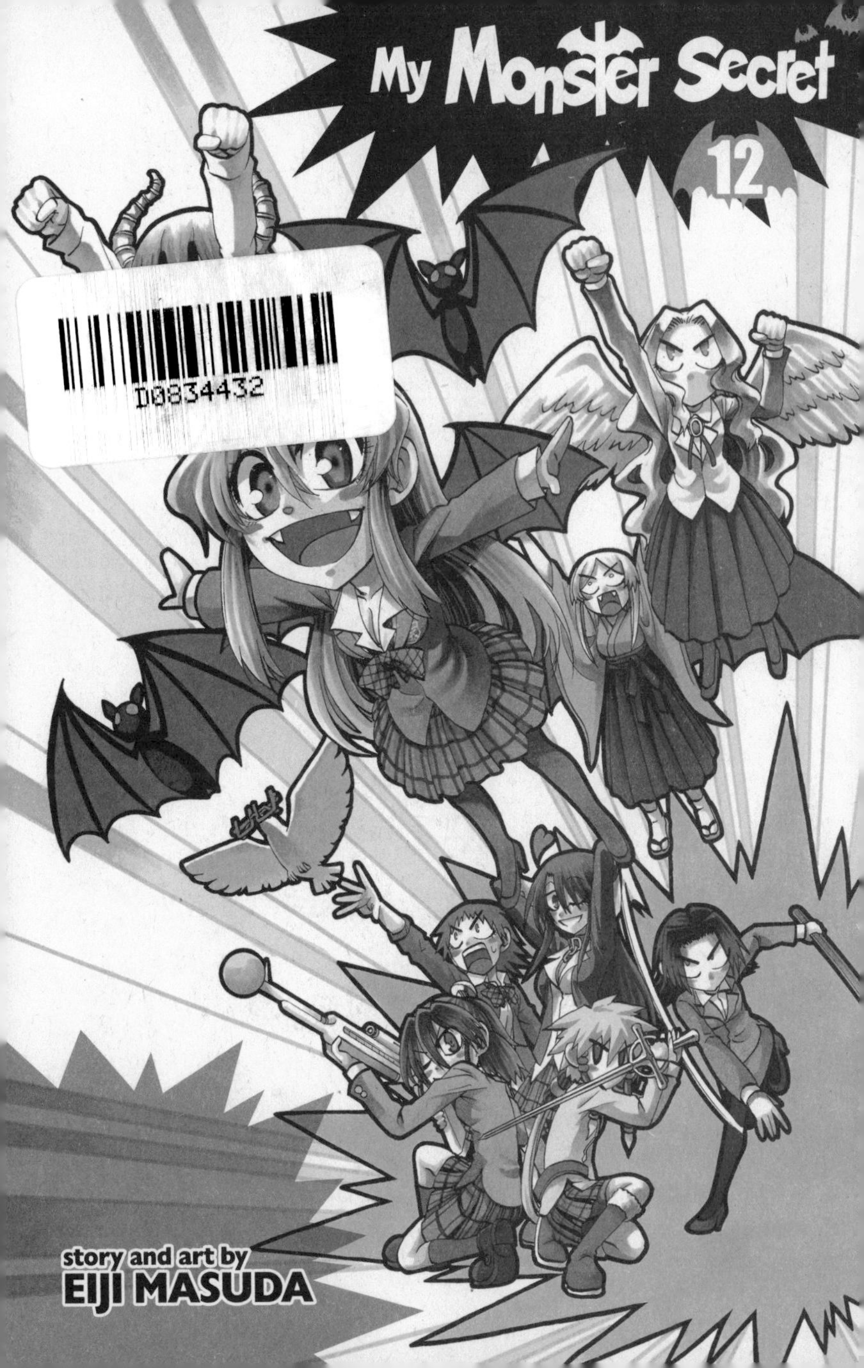
My Monster Secret
12
story and art by
EIJI MASUDA

Story & Character

After school one day, Kuromine Asahi opened the door to his classroom to confess his love to his crush Shiragami Youko...and discovered that she's actually a vampire! His goal was to tell Shiragami that he loved her, but he instead resolved to keep her secret--as a friend. It means they can continue to go to school together, but their problems are only beginning...

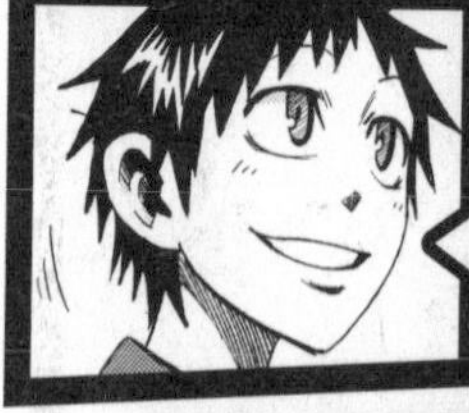

KUROMINE ASAHI

THE HOLEY SIEVE

The man with the worst poker face in the world, he's known as ***The Sieve With A Hole In It...*** because secrets slide right out of him. Now he has to hide the fact that Shiragami-san--the girl he's in love with--is a vampire.

SHIRAGAMI YOUKO

ACTUALLY A VAMPIRE

She's attending a human high school under the condition that she'll ***stop going immediately*** if her true identity is discovered. Asahi found out (whoops), but she believes him when he says he'll keep her secret, and the two are now friends.

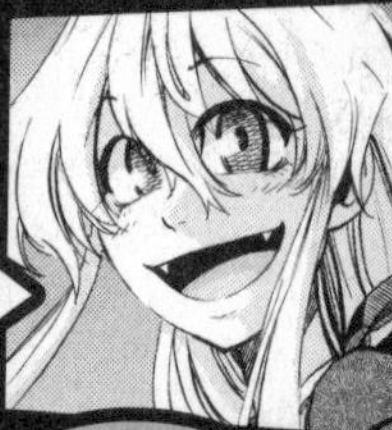

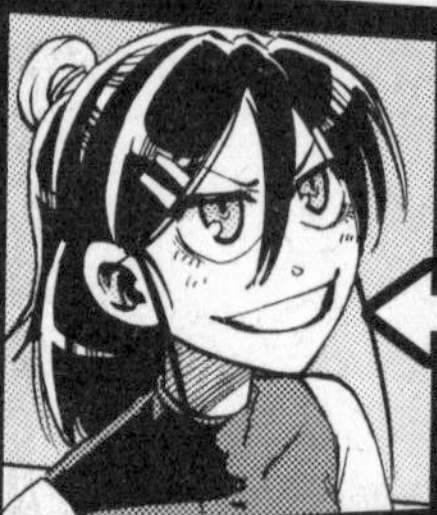

AIZAWA NAGISA

ACTUALLY AN ALIEN

Currently investigating Earth as a class representative, she once mercilessly tore Asahi to shreds before he could confess his love, but she now harbors an unrequited crush on him. Her true (tiny) form emerges from the screw-shaped cockpit on her head. Her brother **Aizawa Ryo** is also staying on Earth.

AKEMI MIKAN

THE QUEEN OF PURE EVIL

Editor-in-chief of the school newspaper and a childhood friend of Asahi's. Currently straying from the path of villainy since her favorite pair of glasses became the **Goddess of Fortune, Fuku-chan.**

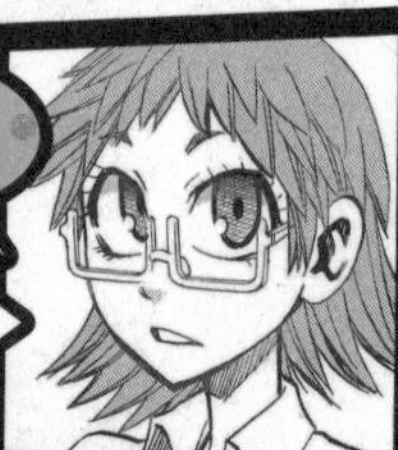

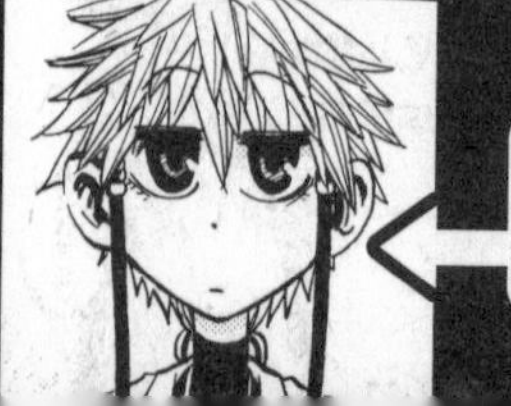

KIRYUIN RIN

ACTUALLY FROM THE FUTURE

Came from fifty years in the future to save the world from the clutches of a nympho tyrant. Now she's a refugee who can't return home because she told Asahi (among others) about the future. Asahi's granddaughter.

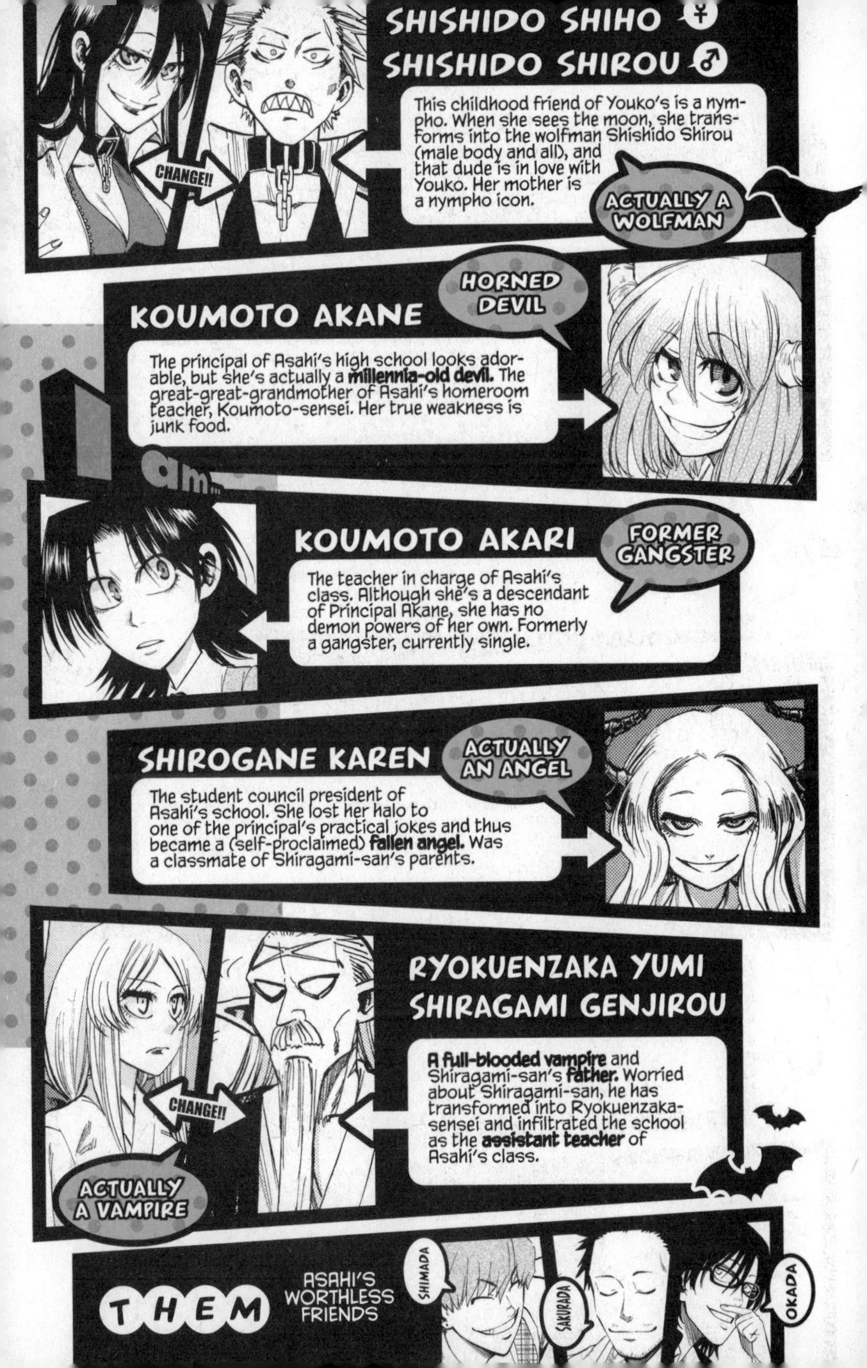
SHISHIDO SHIHO ♀
SHISHIDO SHIROU ♂
This childhood friend of Youko's is a nympho. When she sees the moon, she transforms into the wolfman Shishido Shirou (male body and all), and that dude is in love with Youko. Her mother is a nympho icon.
CHANGE!!
ACTUALLY A WOLFMAN
KOUMOTO AKANE
HORNED DEVIL
The principal of Asahi's high school looks adorable, but she's actually a **millennia-old devil.** The great-great-grandmother of Asahi's homeroom teacher, Koumoto-sensei. Her true weakness is junk food.
I am...
KOUMOTO AKARI
FORMER GANGSTER
The teacher in charge of Asahi's class. Although she's a descendant of Principal Akane, she has no demon powers of her own. Formerly a gangster, currently single.
SHIROGANE KAREN
ACTUALLY AN ANGEL
The student council president of Asahi's school. She lost her halo to one of the principal's practical jokes and thus became a (self-proclaimed) **fallen angel.** Was a classmate of Shiragami-san's parents.
RYOKUENZAKA YUMI
SHIRAGAMI GENJIROU
A full-blooded vampire and Shiragami-san's **father.** Worried about Shiragami-san, he has transformed into Ryokuenzaka-sensei and infiltrated the school as the **assistant teacher** of Asahi's class.
CHANGE!!
ACTUALLY A VAMPIRE
THEM
ASAHI'S WORTHLESS FRIENDS
SHIMADA
SAKURADA
OKADA

SEVEN SEAS ENTERTAINMENT PRESENTS

My Monster Secret
"Actually, I am..."

story and art by Eiji Masuda

VOLUME 12

TRANSLATION
Alethea and Athena Nibley

ADAPTATION
Rebecca Scoble

LETTERING AND RETOUCH
Annaliese Christman

LOGO DESIGN
Karis Page

COVER DESIGN
Nicky Lim

PROOFREADER
Shanti Whitesides
Danielle King

EDITOR
Jenn Grunigen

PRODUCTION ASSISTANT
CK Russell

PRODUCTION MANAGER
Lissa Pattillo

EDITOR IN CHIEF
Adam Arnold

PUBLISHER
Jason DeAngelis

JITSUHA WATASHIHA Volume 12
© EIJI MASUDA 2015
Originally published in Japan in 2015 by Akita Publishing Co., Ltd.
English translation rights arranged with Akita Publishing Co., Ltd.
through TOHAN CORPORATION, Tokyo.

Seven Seas books may be purchased in bulk for promotional, educational, or
business use. Please contact your local bookseller or the Macmillan Corporate
and Premium Sales Department at 1-800-221-7945, extension 5442, or by
e-mail at MacmillanSpecialMarkets@macmillan.com.

Seven Seas and the Seven Seas logo are trademarks of
Seven Seas Entertainment, LLC. All rights reserved.

ISBN: 978-1-626928-52-7

Printed in Canada

First Printing: August 2018

10 9 8 7 6 5 4 3 2 1

FOLLOW US ONLINE: *www.sevenseasentertainment.com*

READING DIRECTIONS

This book reads from *right to left*, Japanese style.
If this is your first time reading manga, you start
reading from the top right panel on each page and
take it from there. If you get lost, just follow the
numbered diagram here. It may seem backwards at
first, but you'll get the hang of it! Have fun!!

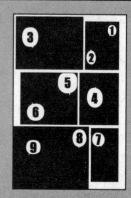

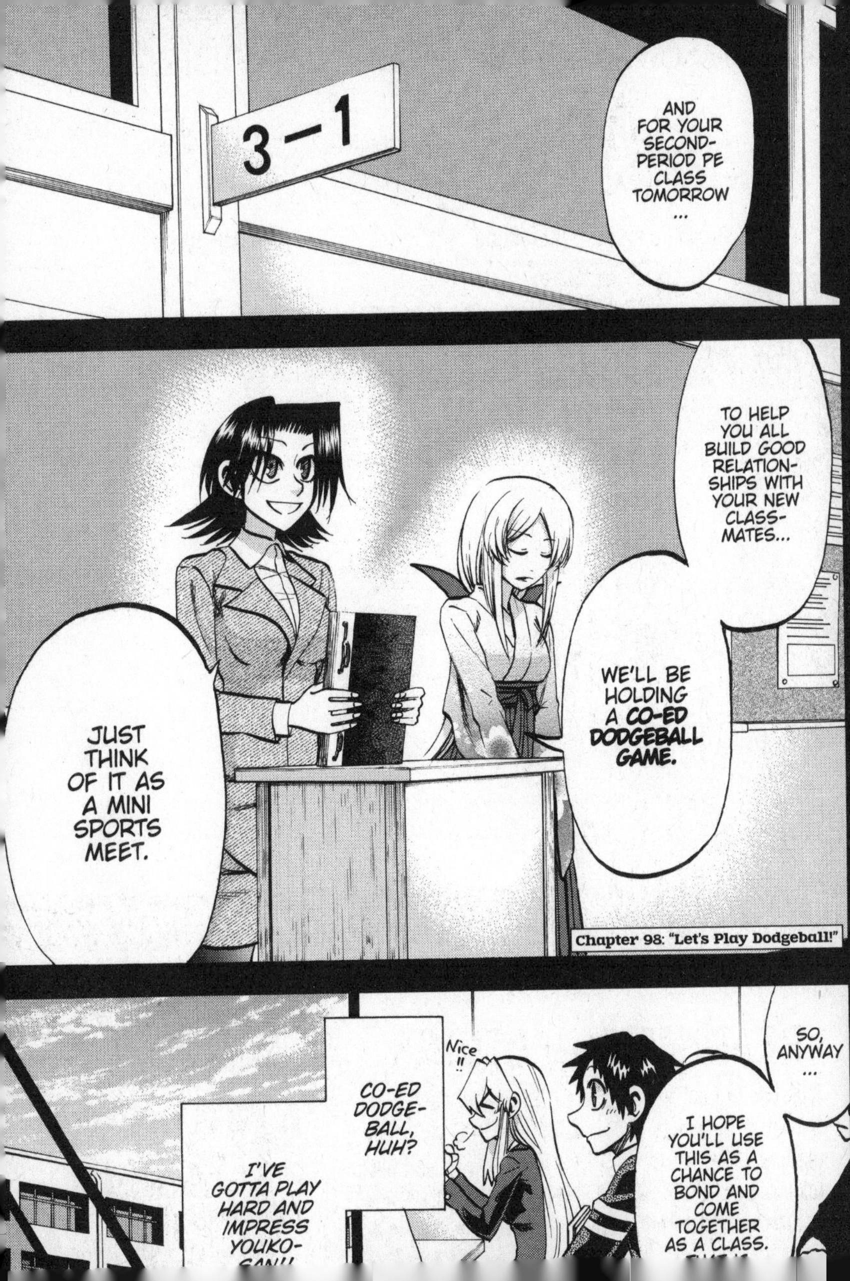
3—1
AND FOR YOUR SECOND-PERIOD PE CLASS TOMORROW ...
TO HELP YOU ALL BUILD GOOD RELATIONSHIPS WITH YOUR NEW CLASSMATES...
WE'LL BE HOLDING A CO-ED DODGEBALL GAME.
JUST THINK OF IT AS A MINI SPORTS MEET.
Chapter 98: "Let's Play Dodgeball!"
SO, ANYWAY ...
I HOPE YOU'LL USE THIS AS A CHANCE TO BOND AND COME TOGETHER AS A CLASS.
Nice!!
CO-ED DODGEBALL, HUH?
I'VE GOTTA PLAY HARD AND IMPRESS YOUKO-

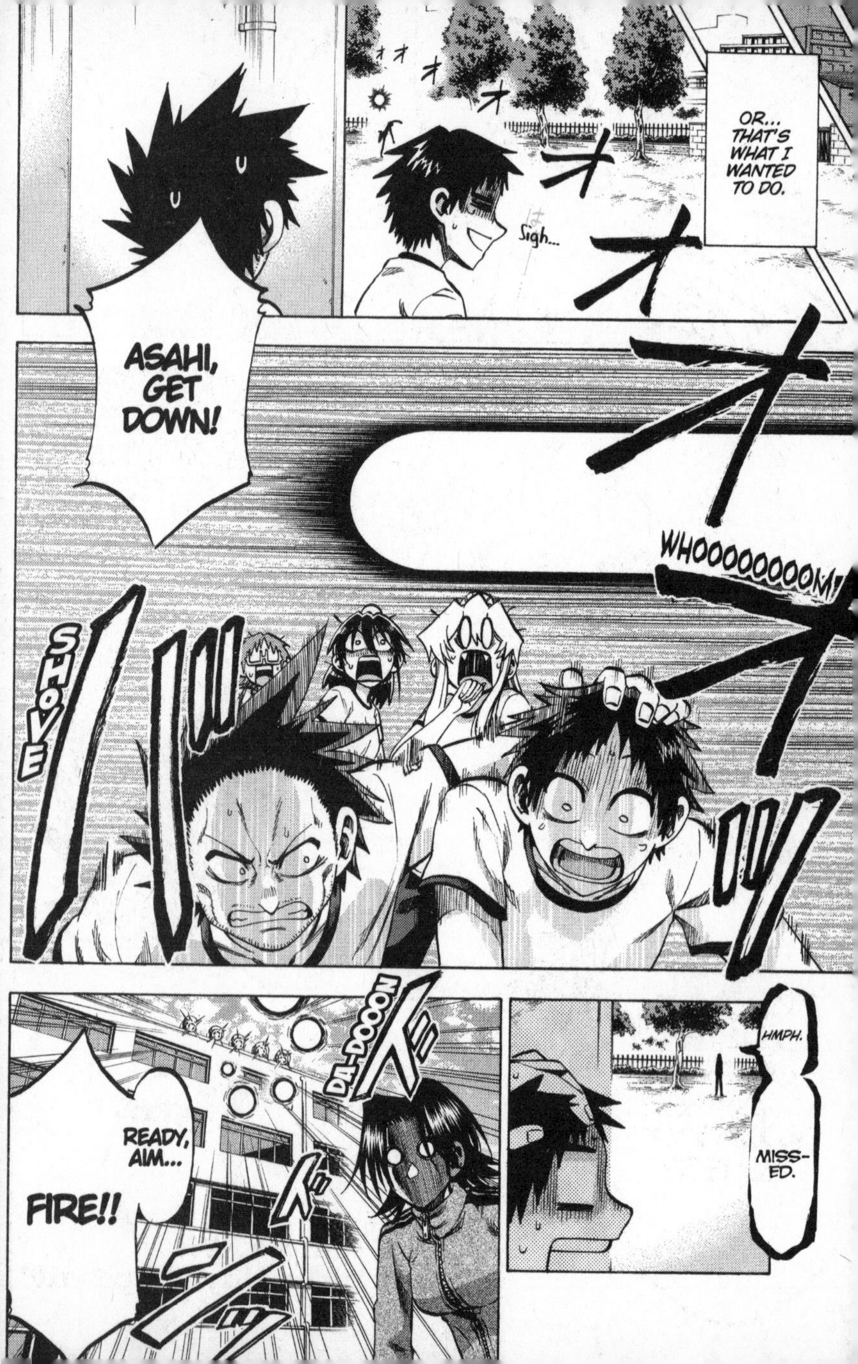
OR... THAT'S WHAT I WANTED TO DO.
Sigh...
ASAHI, GET DOWN!
WHOOOOOOOOOM!
SHOVE
HMPH.
MISS-ED.
DA-DOOON
READY, AIM...
FIRE!!

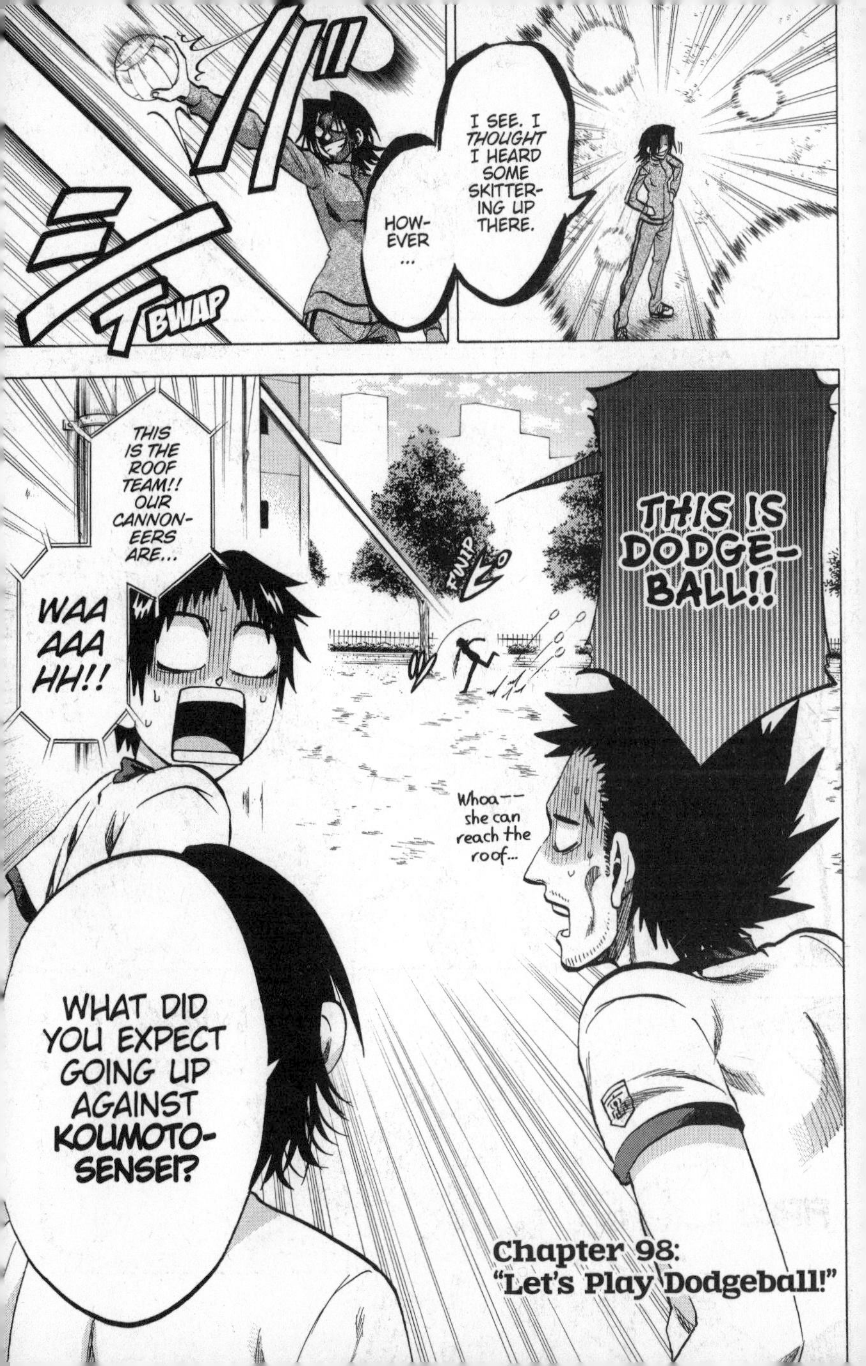
I SEE. I THOUGHT I HEARD SOME SKITTERING UP THERE.
HOWEVER...
BWAP
THIS IS DODGEBALL!!
FWIP
THIS IS THE ROOF TEAM!! OUR CANNONEERS ARE...
WAAAAAHH!!
Whoa-- she can reach the roof...
WHAT DID YOU EXPECT GOING UP AGAINST KOUMOTO-SENSEI?

Chapter 98: "Let's Play Dodgeball!"

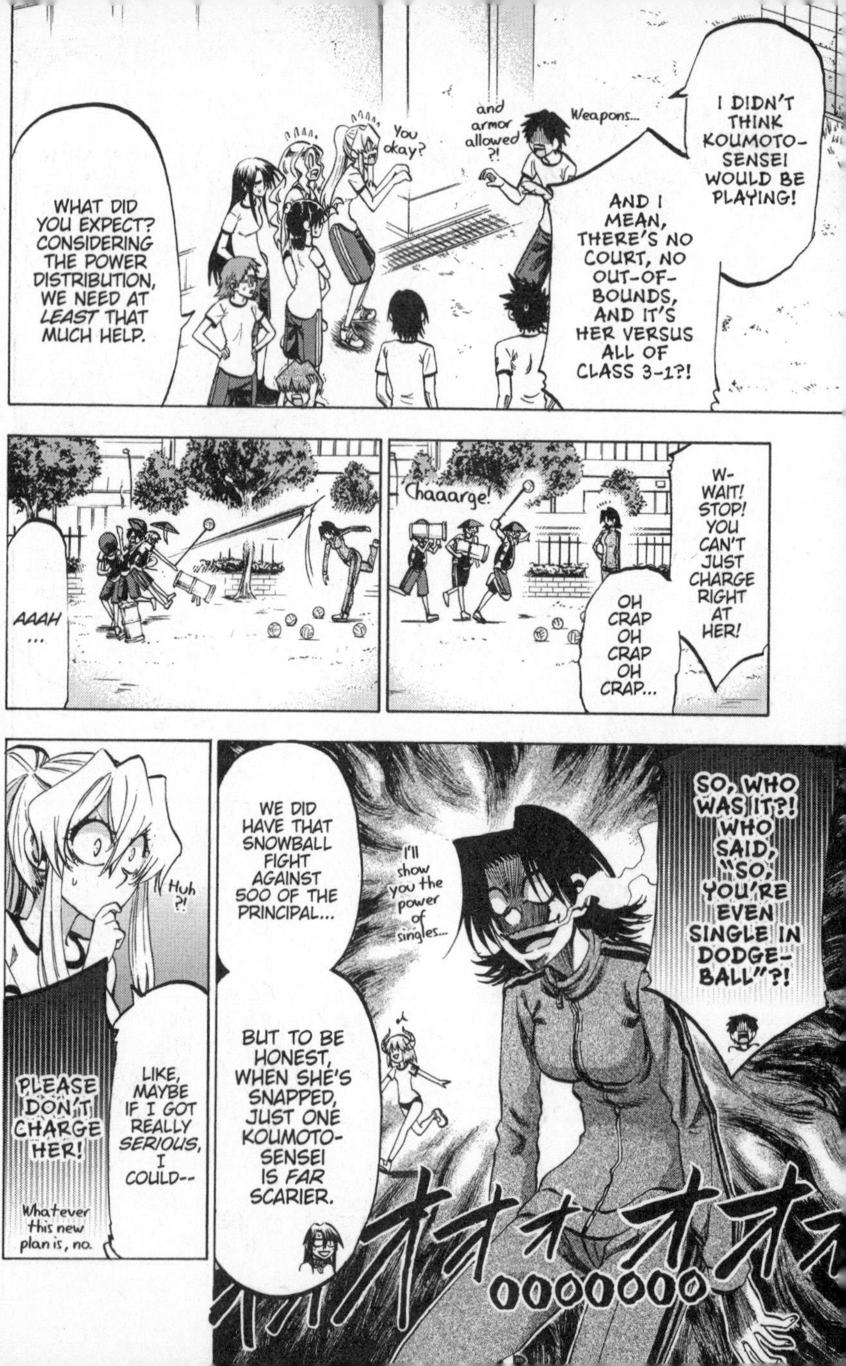
I DIDN'T THINK KOUMOTO-SENSEI WOULD BE PLAYING!
AND I MEAN, THERE'S NO COURT, NO OUT-OF-BOUNDS, AND IT'S HER VERSUS ALL OF CLASS 3-1?!
Weapons...
and armor allowed?!
You okay?
WHAT DID YOU EXPECT? CONSIDERING THE POWER DISTRIBUTION, WE NEED AT LEAST THAT MUCH HELP.
W-WAIT! STOP! YOU CAN'T JUST CHARGE RIGHT AT HER!
Chaaarge!
OH CRAP OH CRAP OH CRAP...
AAAH...
SO, WHO WAS IT?! WHO SAID, "SO, YOU'RE EVEN SINGLE IN DODGE-BALL"?!
I'll show you the power of singles...
WE DID HAVE THAT SNOWBALL FIGHT AGAINST 500 OF THE PRINCIPAL...
BUT TO BE HONEST, WHEN SHE'S SNAPPED, JUST ONE KOUMOTO-SENSEI IS FAR SCARIER.
OOOOOOO
Huh?!
LIKE, MAYBE IF I GOT REALLY SERIOUS, I COULD--
PLEASE DON'T CHARGE HER!
Whatever this new plan is, no.

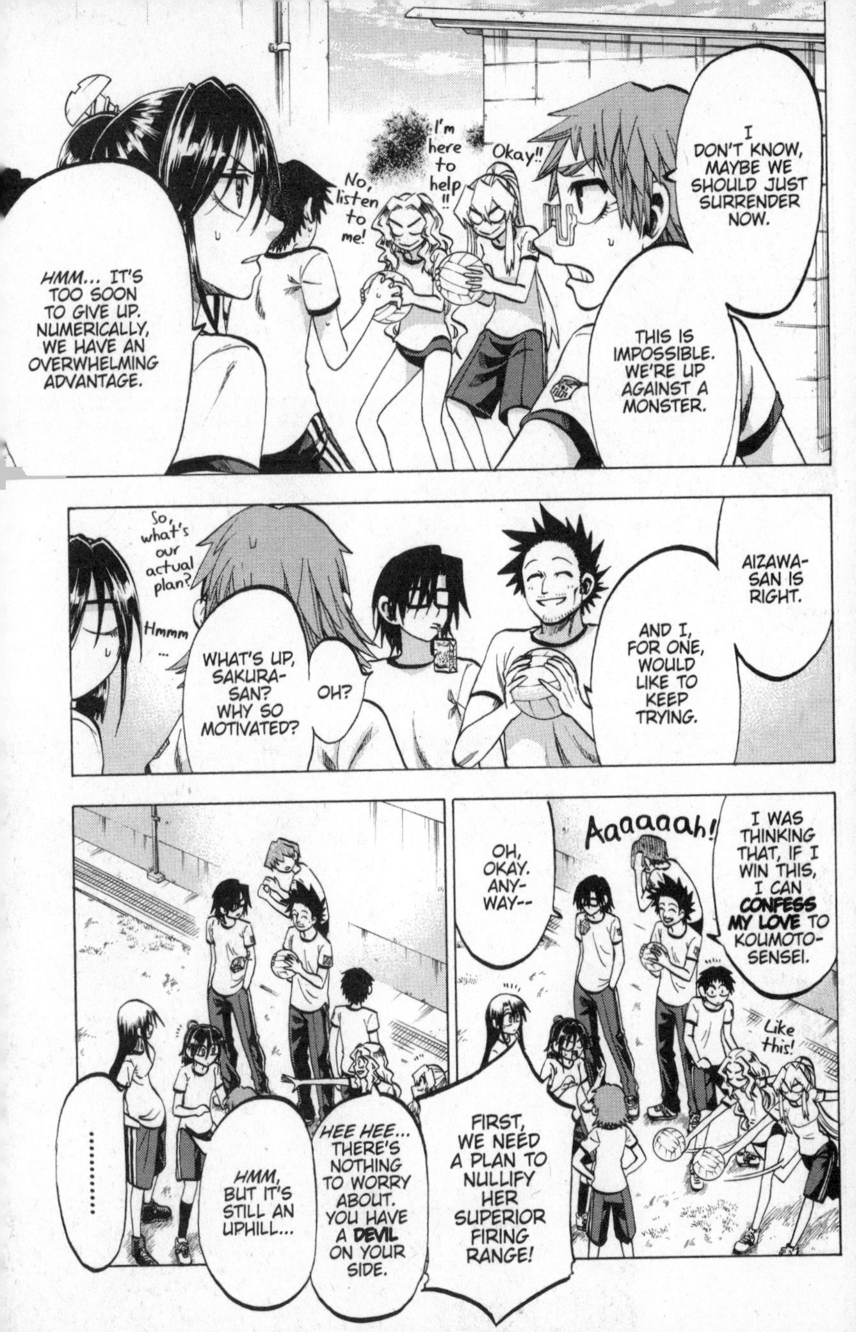
I DON'T KNOW, MAYBE WE SHOULD JUST SURRENDER NOW.
THIS IS IMPOSSIBLE. WE'RE UP AGAINST A MONSTER.
Okay!!
I'm here to help!!
No, listen to me!
HMM... IT'S TOO SOON TO GIVE UP. NUMERICALLY, WE HAVE AN OVERWHELMING ADVANTAGE.
AIZAWA-SAN IS RIGHT.
AND I, FOR ONE, WOULD LIKE TO KEEP TRYING.
OH?
WHAT'S UP, SAKURA-SAN? WHY SO MOTIVATED?
So, what's our actual plan?
Hmmm...
I WAS THINKING THAT, IF I WIN THIS, I CAN **CONFESS MY LOVE** TO KOUMOTO-SENSEI.
Aaaaaah!
OH, OKAY. ANYWAY--
Like this!
FIRST, WE NEED A PLAN TO NULLIFY HER SUPERIOR FIRING RANGE!
HEE HEE... THERE'S NOTHING TO WORRY ABOUT. YOU HAVE A **DEVIL** ON YOUR SIDE.
HMM, BUT IT'S STILL AN UPHILL...
....

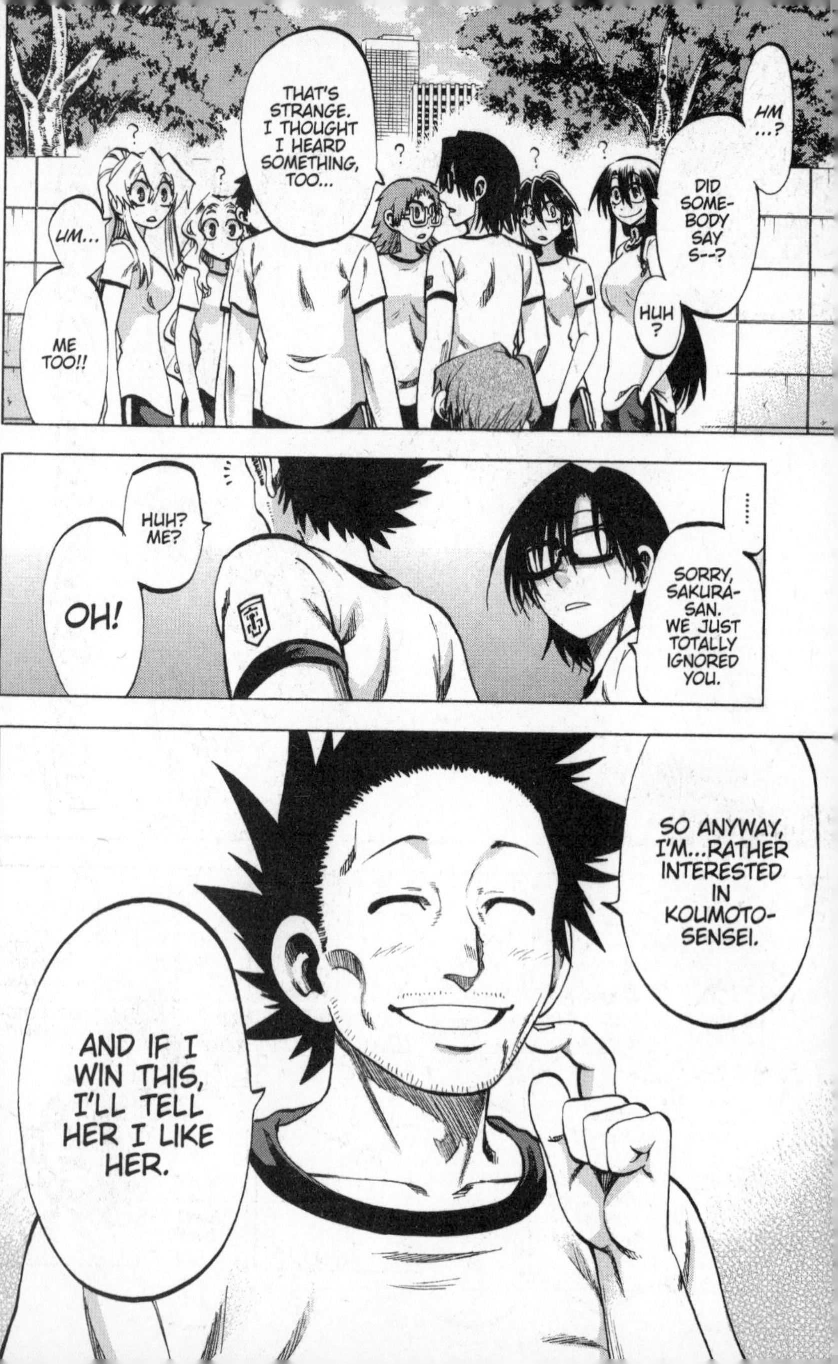
HM ...?
DID SOMEBODY SAY S--?
HUH ?
THAT'S STRANGE. I THOUGHT I HEARD SOMETHING, TOO...
UM...
ME TOO!!
......
SORRY, SAKURA-SAN. WE JUST TOTALLY IGNORED YOU.
HUH? ME?
OH!
SO ANYWAY, I'M...RATHER INTERESTED IN KOUMOTO-SENSEI.
AND IF I WIN THIS, I'LL TELL HER I LIKE HER.

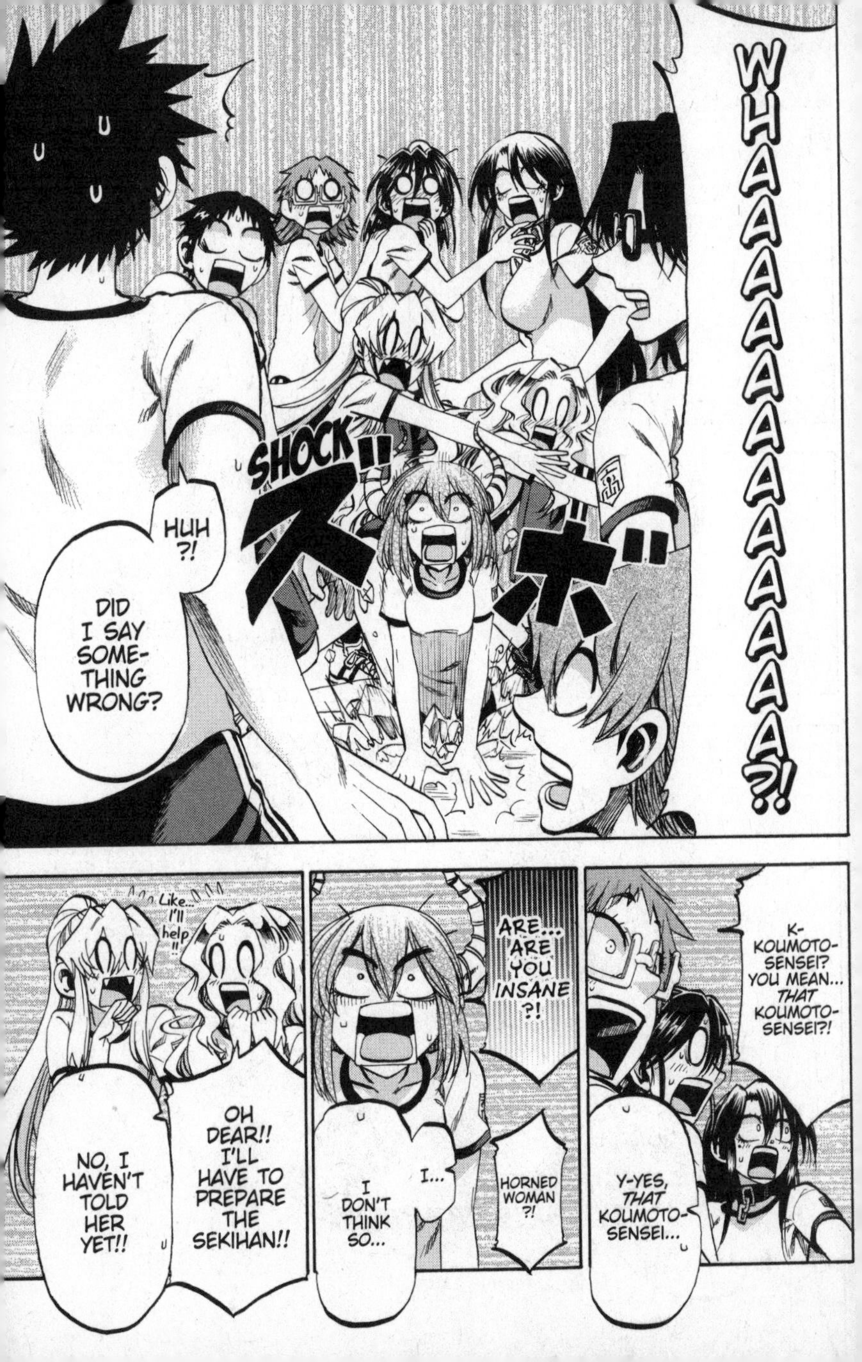
WHAAAAAAAAAAAAAA?!
SHOCK!!
HUH ?!
DID I SAY SOME-THING WRONG?
K-KOUMOTO-SENSEI? YOU MEAN... *THAT* KOUMOTO-SENSEI?!
Y-YES, *THAT* KOUMOTO-SENSEI...
ARE... ARE YOU INSANE ?!
HORNED WOMAN ?!
I...
I DON'T THINK SO...
Like... I'll help!!
OH DEAR!! I'LL HAVE TO PREPARE THE SEKIHAN!!
NO, I HAVEN'T TOLD HER YET!!

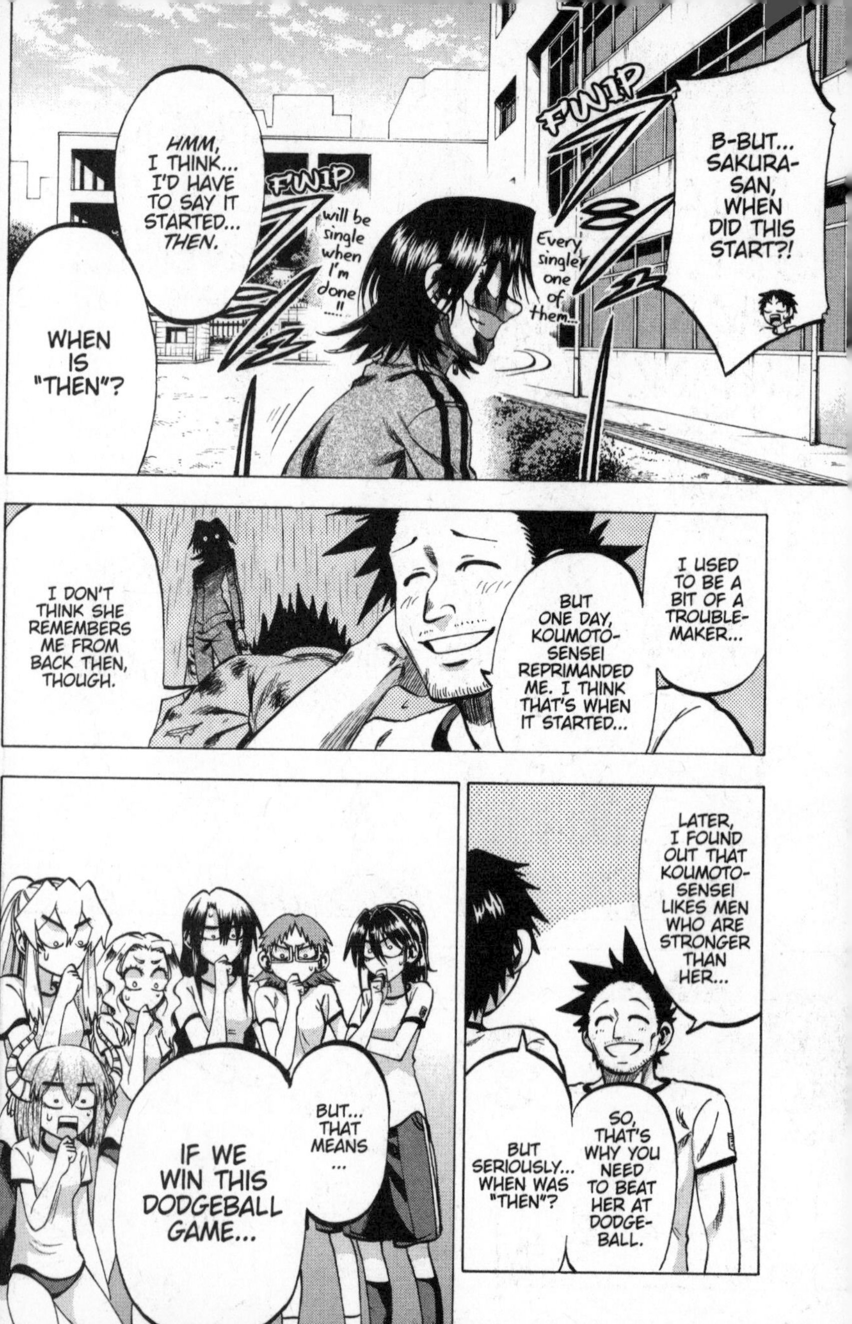
B-BUT... SAKURA-SAN, WHEN DID THIS START?!
FWIP
Every single one of them...
FWIP
will be single when I'm done .....!!
HMM, I THINK... I'D HAVE TO SAY IT STARTED... THEN.
WHEN IS "THEN"?
I USED TO BE A BIT OF A TROUBLE-MAKER...
BUT ONE DAY, KOUMOTO-SENSEI REPRIMANDED ME. I THINK THAT'S WHEN IT STARTED...
I DON'T THINK SHE REMEMBERS ME FROM BACK THEN, THOUGH.
LATER, I FOUND OUT THAT KOUMOTO-SENSEI LIKES MEN WHO ARE STRONGER THAN HER...
SO, THAT'S WHY YOU NEED TO BEAT HER AT DODGE-BALL.
BUT SERIOUSLY... WHEN WAS "THEN"?
BUT... THAT MEANS ...
IF WE WIN THIS DODGEBALL GAME...

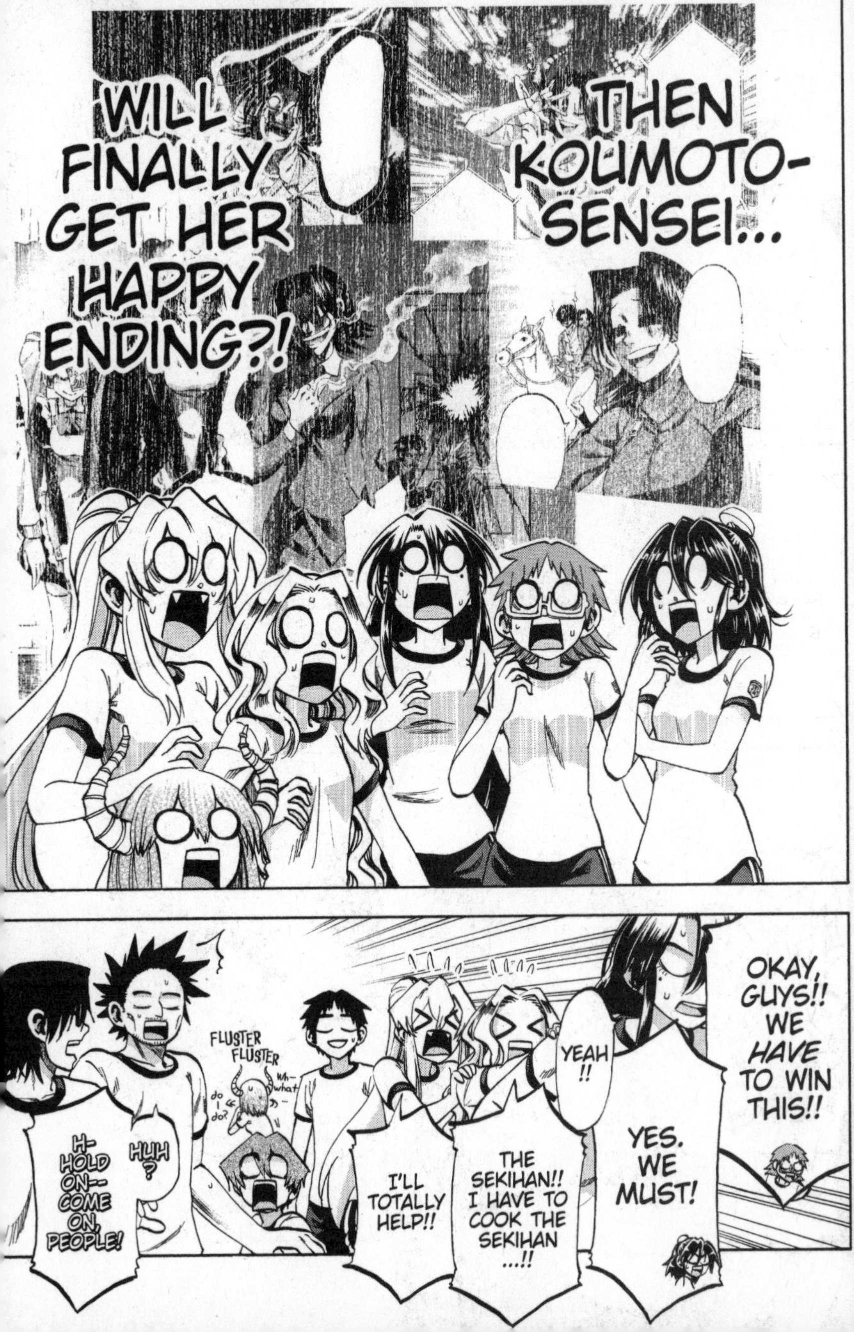
THEN KOUMOTO-SENSEI...
WILL FINALLY GET HER HAPPY ENDING?!
OKAY, GUYS!! WE HAVE TO WIN THIS!!
YEAH !!
YES. WE MUST!
THE SEKIHAN!! I HAVE TO COOK THE SEKIHAN ...!!
I'LL TOTALLY HELP!!
FLUSTER FLUSTER
HUH ?
H- HOLD ON-- COME ON, PEOPLE!

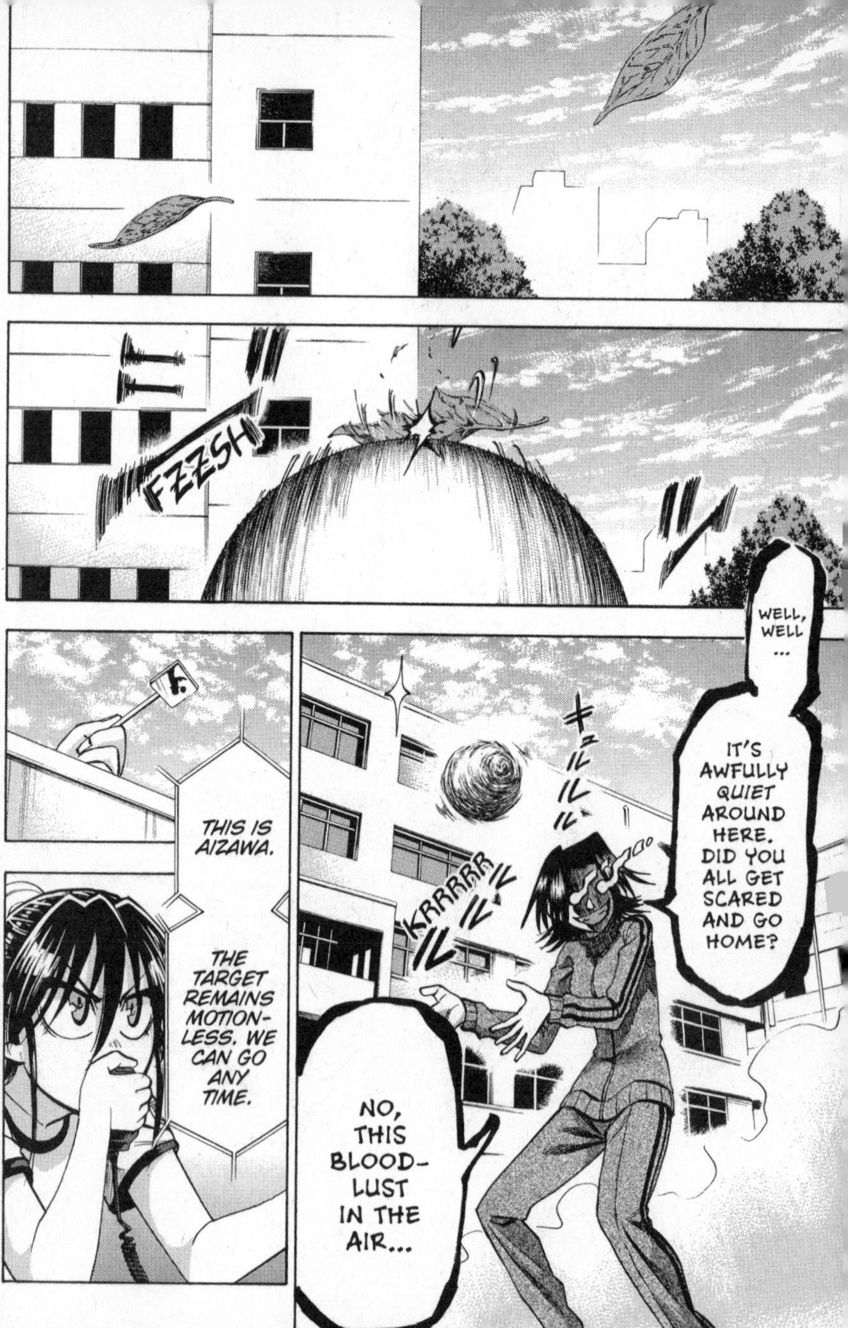
FZZSH
WELL, WELL...
IT'S AWFULLY QUIET AROUND HERE. DID YOU ALL GET SCARED AND GO HOME?
KRRRRR
NO, THIS BLOOD-LUST IN THE AIR...
THIS IS AIZAWA.
THE TARGET REMAINS MOTION-LESS. WE CAN GO ANY TIME.

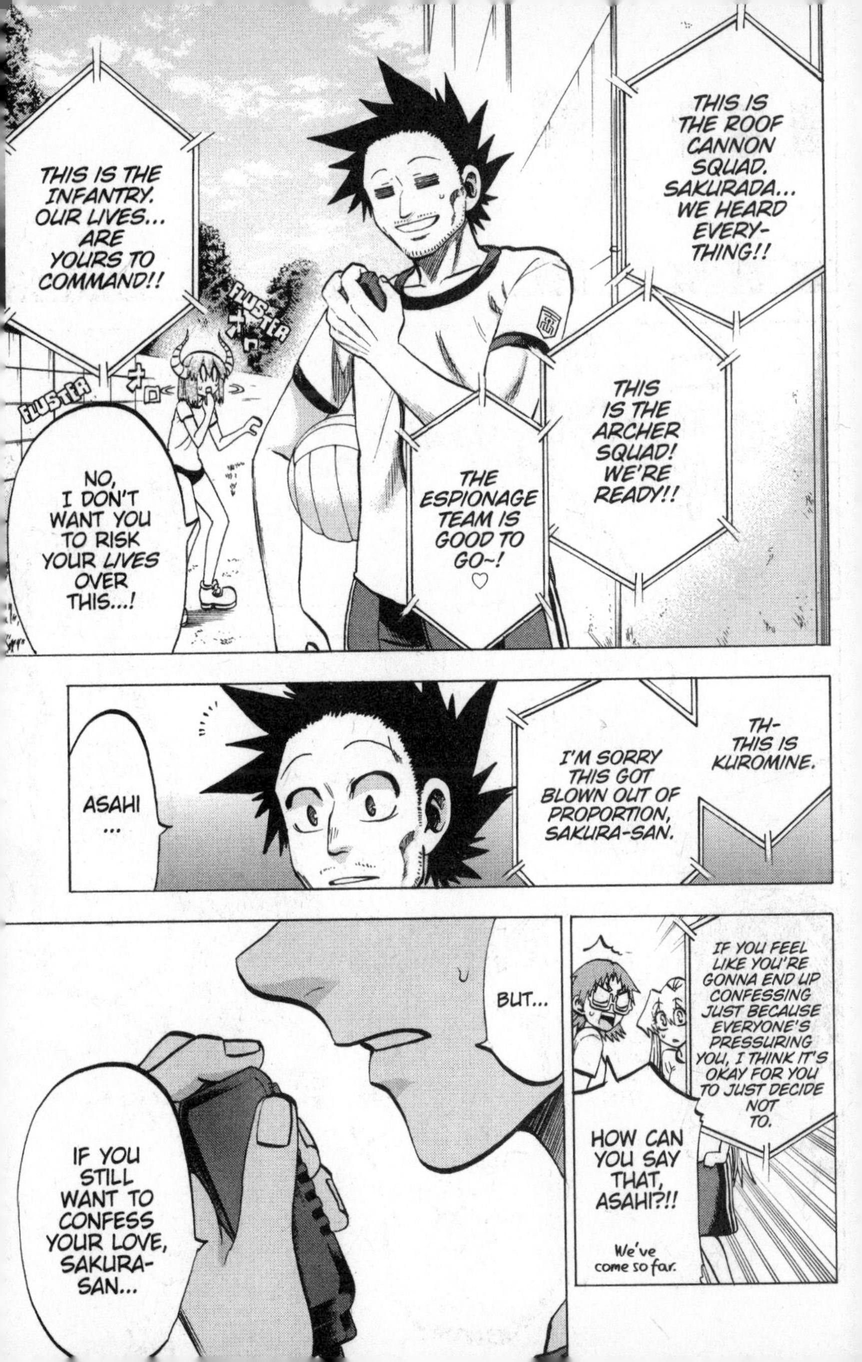
THIS IS THE ROOF CANNON SQUAD. SAKURADA... WE HEARD EVERY-THING!!
THIS IS THE INFANTRY. OUR LIVES... ARE YOURS TO COMMAND!!
THIS IS THE ARCHER SQUAD! WE'RE READY!!
THE ESPIONAGE TEAM IS GOOD TO GO~! ♡
FLUSTER
FLUSTER
NO, I DON'T WANT YOU TO RISK YOUR *LIVES* OVER THIS...!
TH- THIS IS KUROMINE.
I'M SORRY THIS GOT BLOWN OUT OF PROPORTION, SAKURA-SAN.
ASAHI ...
IF YOU FEEL LIKE YOU'RE GONNA END UP CONFESSING JUST BECAUSE EVERYONE'S PRESSURING YOU, I THINK IT'S OKAY FOR YOU TO JUST DECIDE NOT TO.
HOW CAN YOU SAY THAT, ASAHI?!!
We've come so far.
BUT...
IF YOU STILL WANT TO CONFESS YOUR LOVE, SAKURA-SAN...

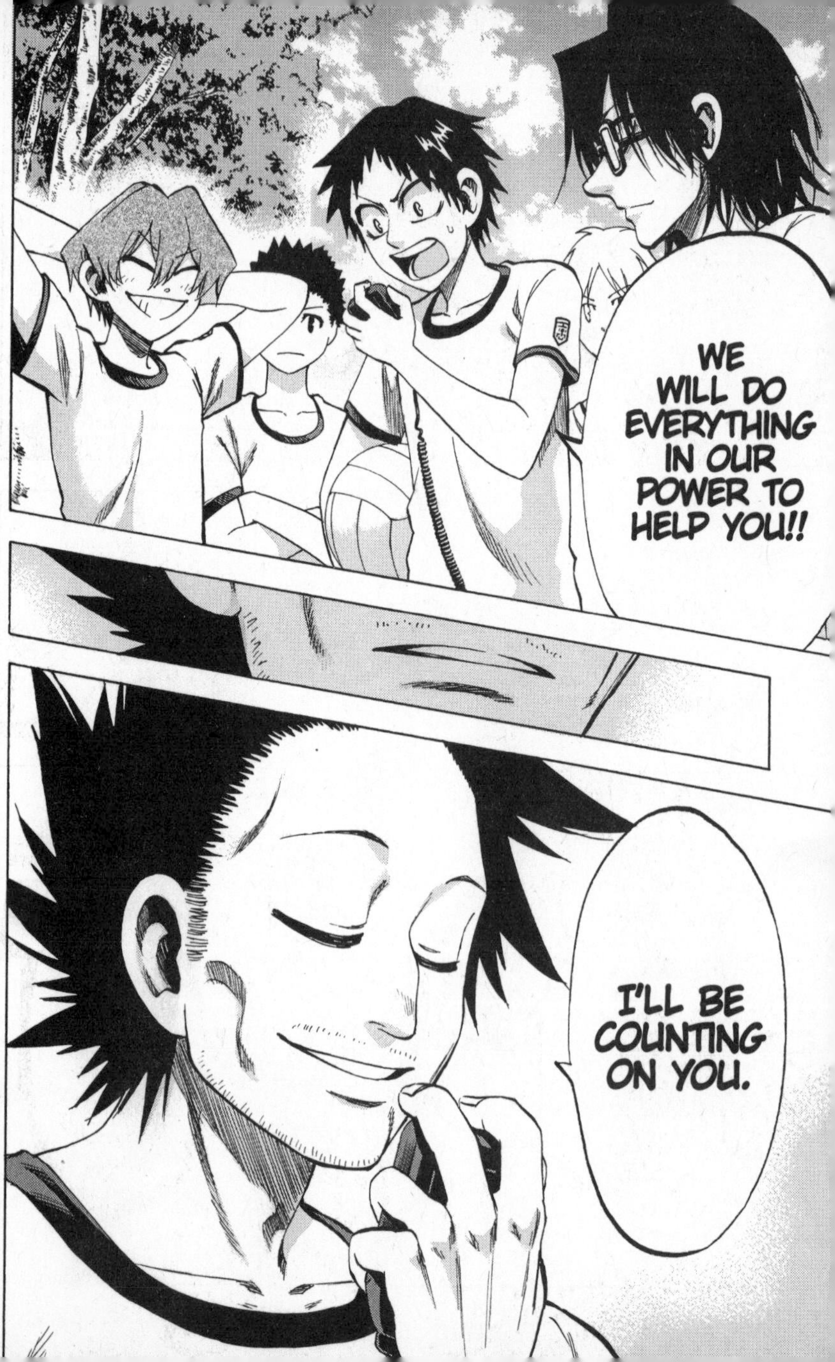
WE WILL DO EVERYTHING IN OUR POWER TO HELP YOU!!
I'LL BE COUNTING ON YOU.

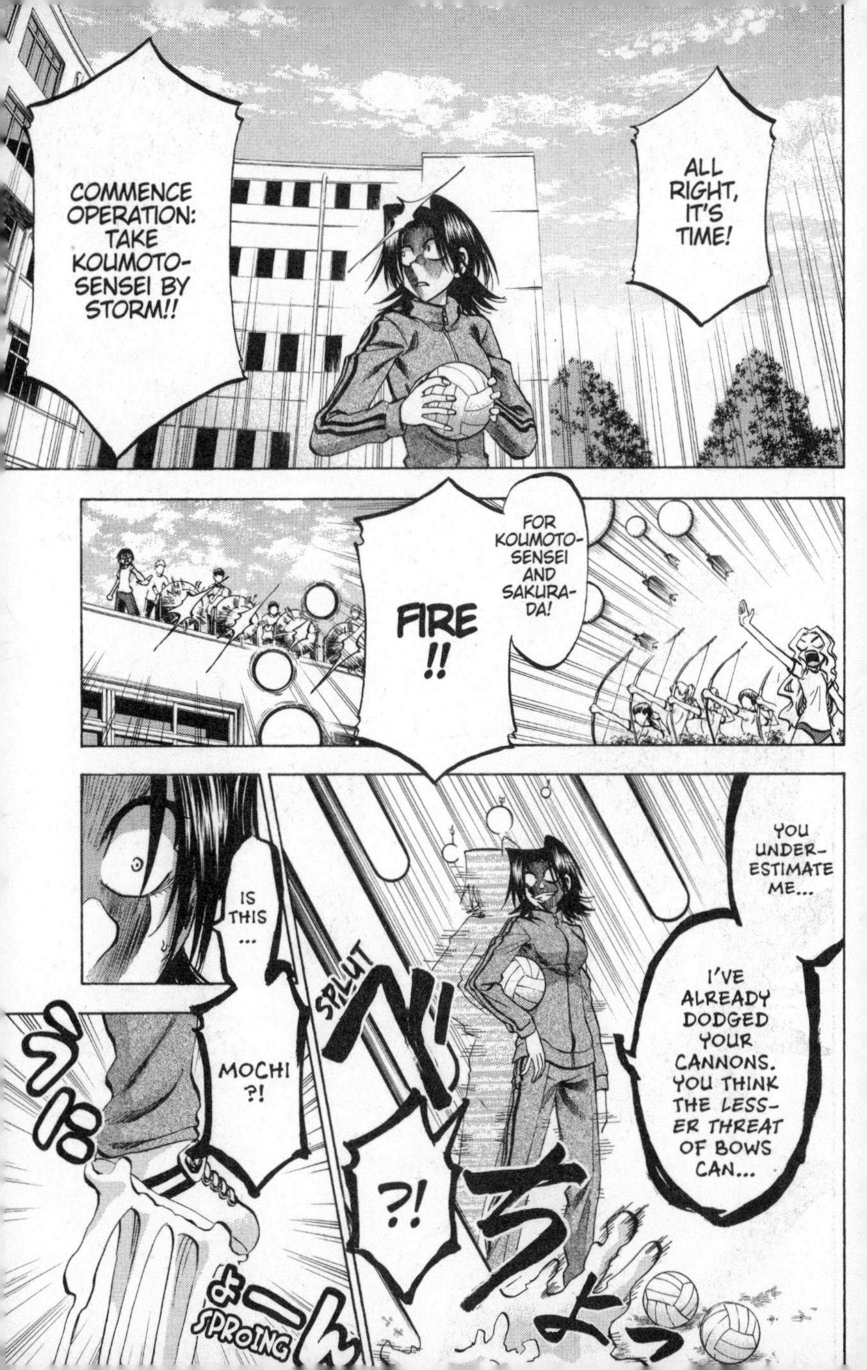
ALL RIGHT, IT'S TIME!
COMMENCE OPERATION: TAKE KOUMOTO-SENSEI BY STORM!!
FOR KOUMOTO-SENSEI AND SAKURADA!
FIRE!!
YOU UNDER-ESTIMATE ME...
I'VE ALREADY DODGED YOUR CANNONS. YOU THINK THE LESSER THREAT OF BOWS CAN...
?!
SPLUT
IS THIS ...
MOCHI ?!
SPROING

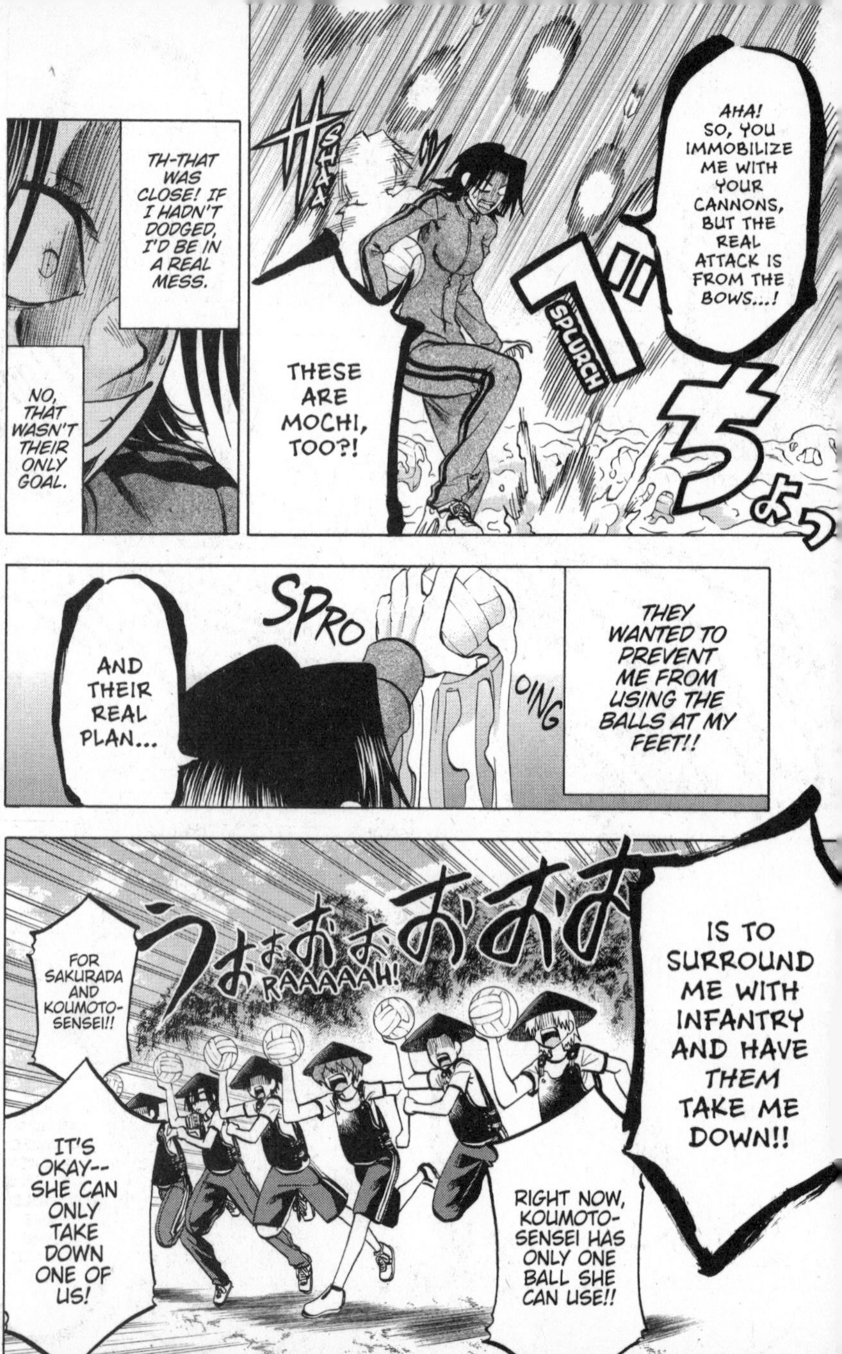
AHA! SO, YOU IMMOBILIZE ME WITH YOUR CANNONS, BUT THE REAL ATTACK IS FROM THE BOWS...!
SHAA
SPLURCH
THESE ARE MOCHI, TOO?!
TH-THAT WAS CLOSE! IF I HADN'T DODGED, I'D BE IN A REAL MESS.
NO, THAT WASN'T THEIR ONLY GOAL.
THEY WANTED TO PREVENT ME FROM USING THE BALLS AT MY FEET!!
SPROING
AND THEIR REAL PLAN...
IS TO SURROUND ME WITH INFANTRY AND HAVE THEM TAKE ME DOWN!!
RAAAAAH!
FOR SAKURADA AND KOUMOTO-SENSEI!!
RIGHT NOW, KOUMOTO-SENSEI HAS ONLY ONE BALL SHE CAN USE!!
IT'S OKAY-- SHE CAN ONLY TAKE DOWN ONE OF US!

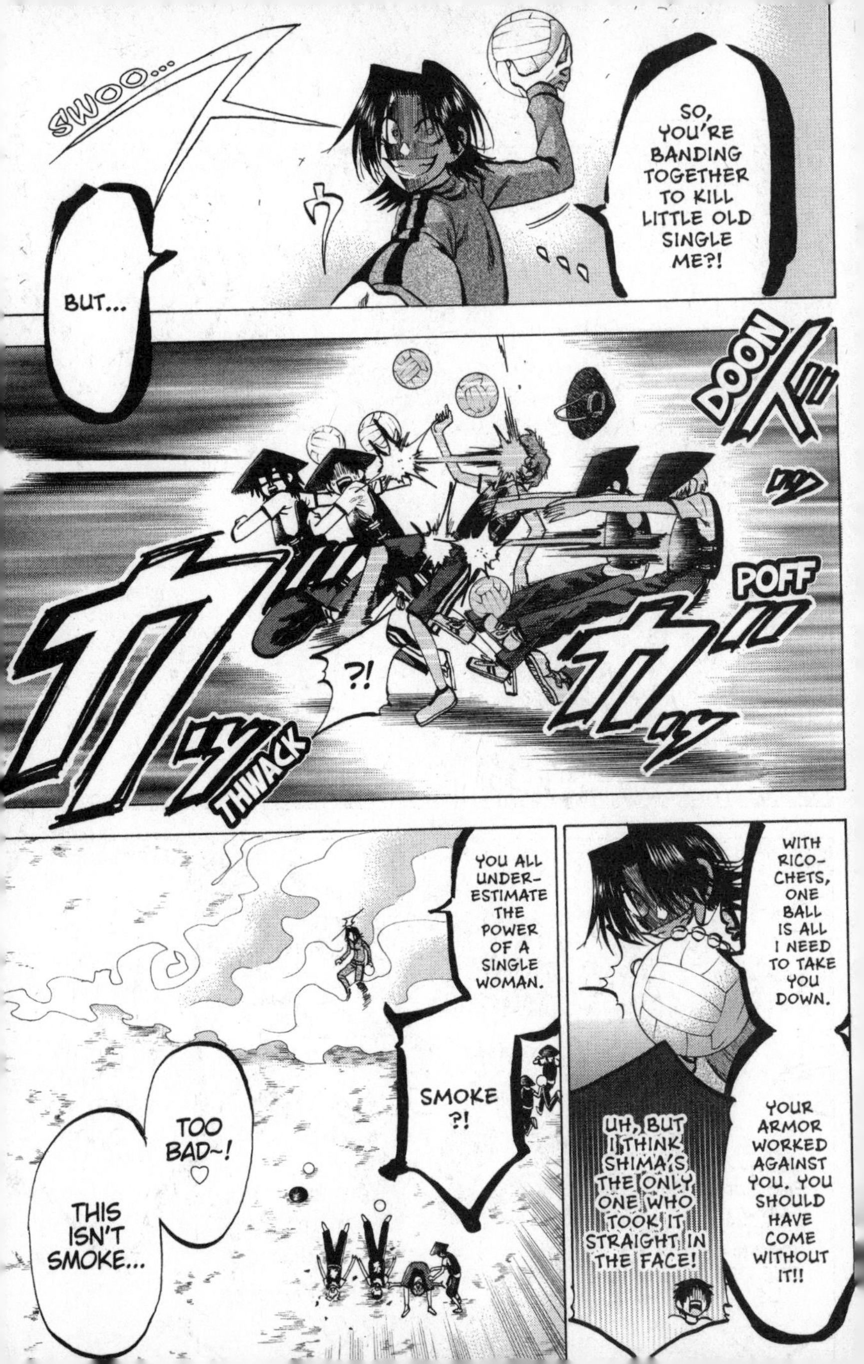
SO, YOU'RE BANDING TOGETHER TO KILL LITTLE OLD SINGLE ME?!
SWOO...
BUT...
DOON
POFF
?!
THWACK
WITH RICOCHETS, ONE BALL IS ALL I NEED TO TAKE YOU DOWN.
YOUR ARMOR WORKED AGAINST YOU. YOU SHOULD HAVE COME WITHOUT IT!!
UH, BUT I THINK SHIMA'S THE ONLY ONE WHO TOOK IT STRAIGHT IN THE FACE!
YOU ALL UNDER-ESTIMATE THE POWER OF A SINGLE WOMAN.
SMOKE ?!
TOO BAD~! ♡
THIS ISN'T SMOKE...

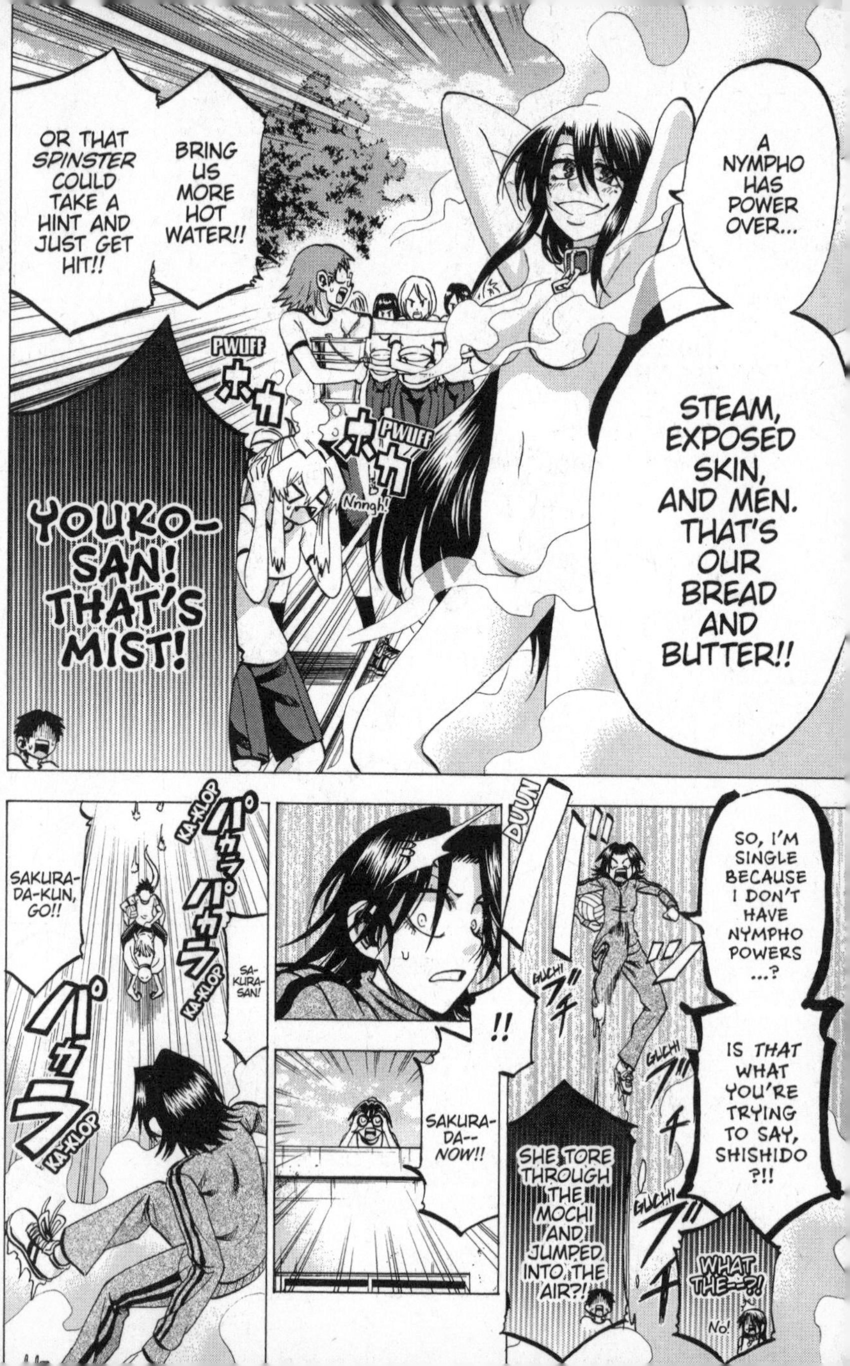
A NYMPHO HAS POWER OVER...
STEAM, EXPOSED SKIN, AND MEN. THAT'S OUR BREAD AND BUTTER!!
BRING US MORE HOT WATER!!
OR THAT SPINSTER COULD TAKE A HINT AND JUST GET HIT!!
PWUFF
PWUFF
Nnngh!
YOUKO-SAN! THAT'S MIST!
SO, I'M SINGLE BECAUSE I DON'T HAVE NYMPHO POWERS ...?
IS THAT WHAT YOU'RE TRYING TO SAY, SHISHIDO ?!!
GUCHI
GUCHI
GUCHI
SHE TORE THROUGH THE MOCHI AND JUMPED INTO THE AIR?!
WHAT THE--?!
No!
DUUN
!!
SAKURA-DA--NOW!!
KA-KLOP
KA-KLOP
SAKURA-DA-KUN, GO!!
SA-KURA-SAN!
KA-KLOP

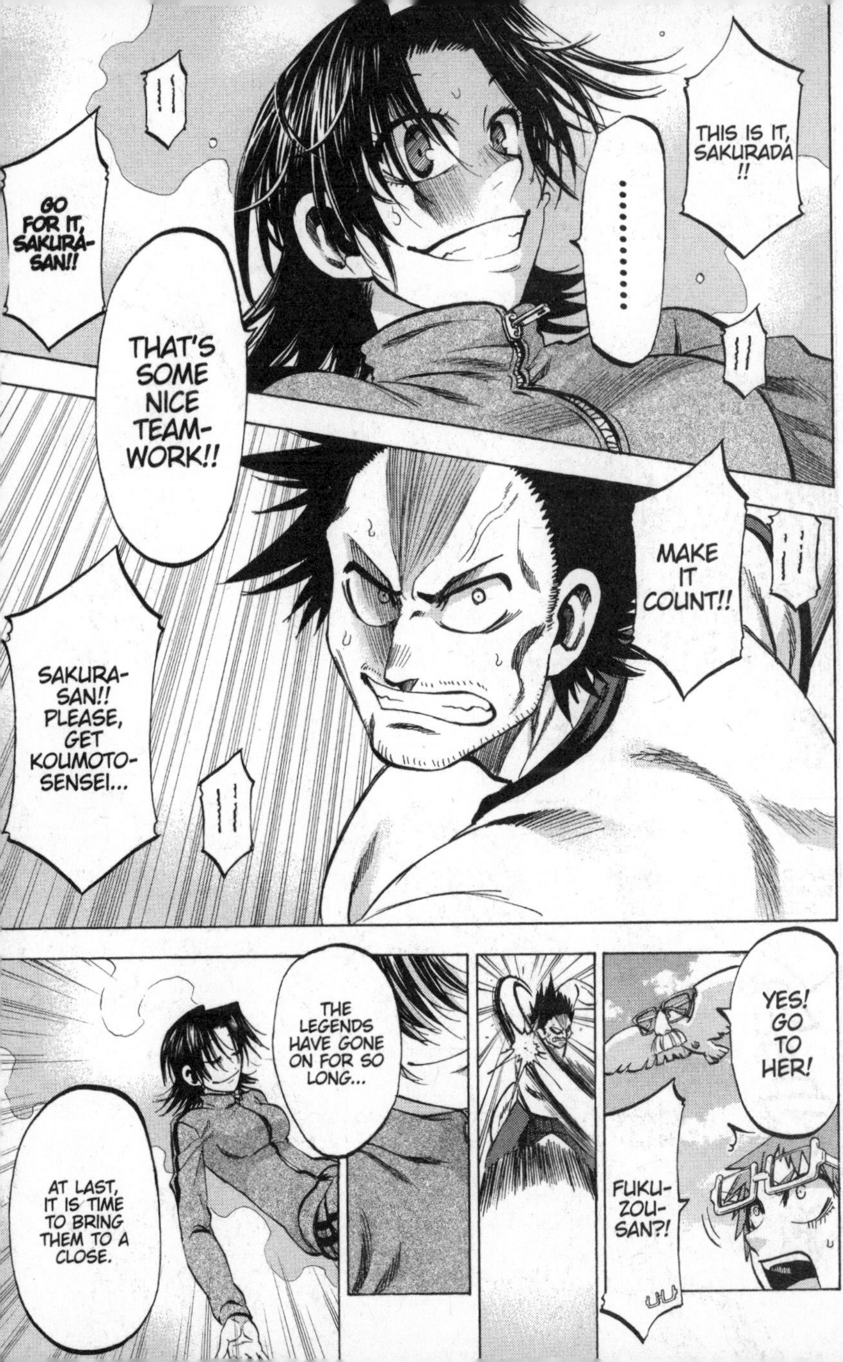
THIS IS IT, SAKURADA!!
....
!!
!!
GO FOR IT, SAKURA-SAN!!
THAT'S SOME NICE TEAM-WORK!!
!!
MAKE IT COUNT!!
SAKURA-SAN!! PLEASE, GET KOUMOTO-SENSEI...
!!
YES! GO TO HER!
FUKU-ZOU-SAN?!
THE LEGENDS HAVE GONE ON FOR SO LONG...
AT LAST, IT IS TIME TO BRING THEM TO A CLOSE.

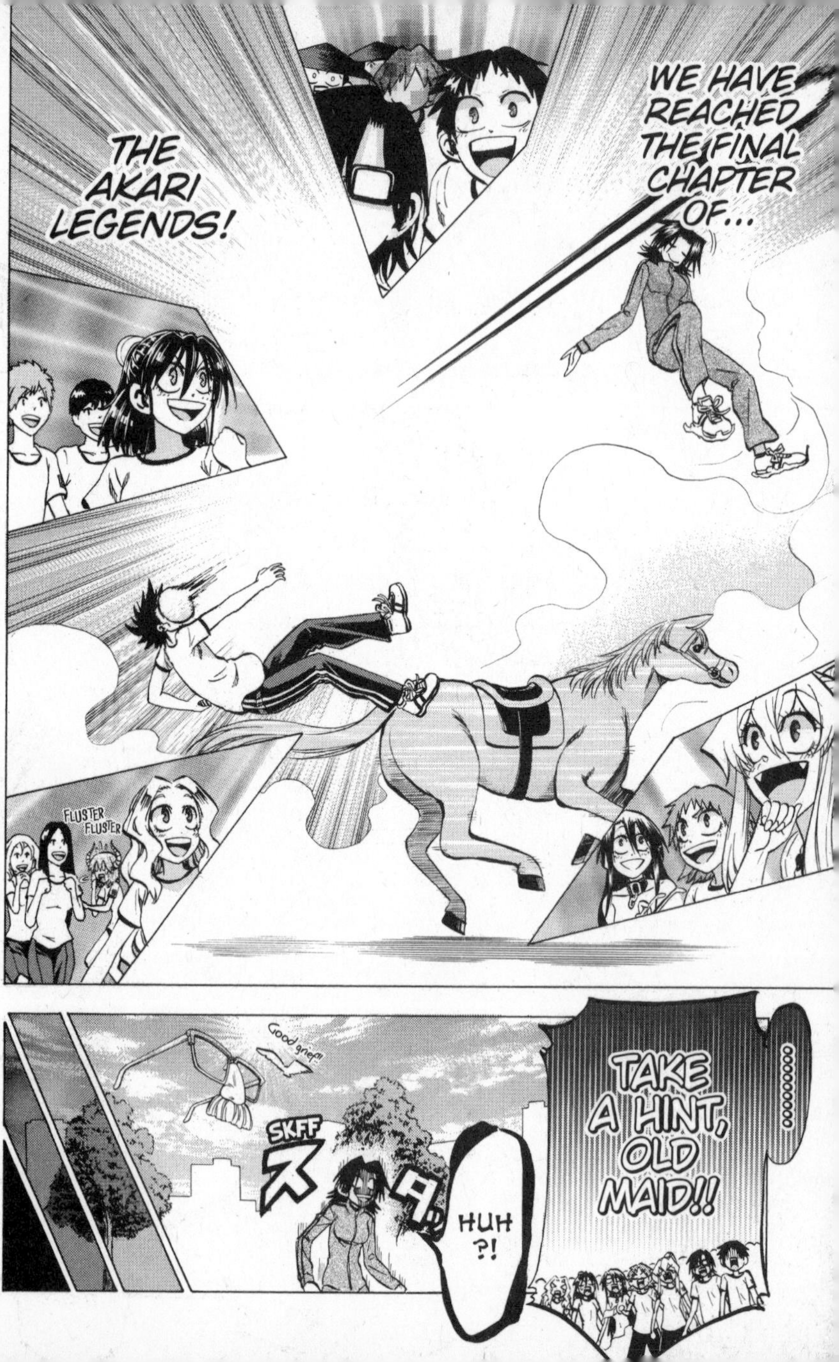
WE HAVE REACHED THE FINAL CHAPTER OF...
THE AKARI LEGENDS!
FLUSTER FLUSTER
OOOOOOOOOO
TAKE A HINT, OLD MAID!!
HUH ?!
SKFF
スタ
Good grief!!

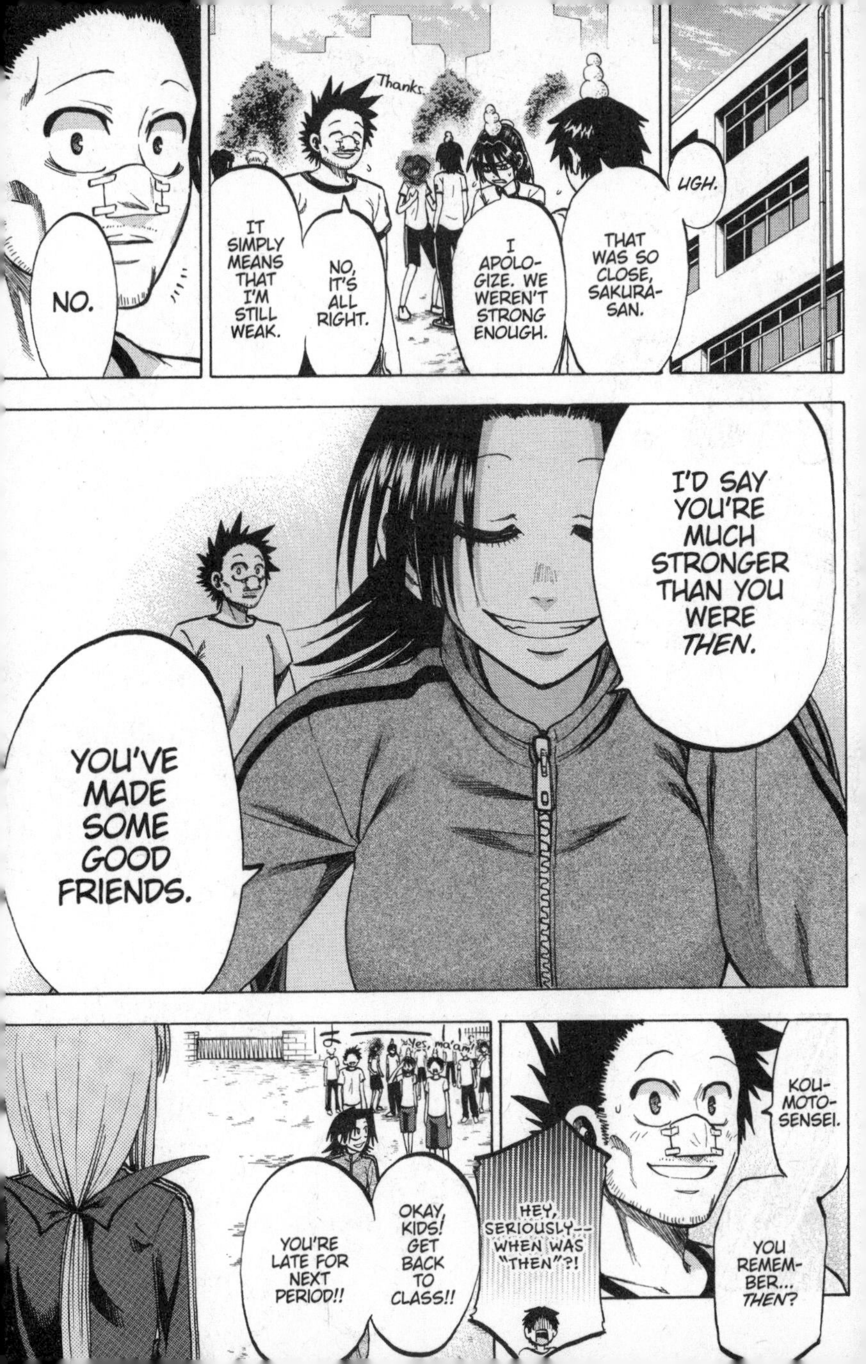
UGH.
THAT WAS SO CLOSE, SAKURA-SAN.
I APOLOGIZE. WE WEREN'T STRONG ENOUGH.
Thanks.
NO, IT'S ALL RIGHT.
IT SIMPLY MEANS THAT I'M STILL WEAK.
NO.
I'D SAY YOU'RE MUCH STRONGER THAN YOU WERE *THEN.*
YOU'VE MADE SOME GOOD FRIENDS.
KOU-MOTO-SENSEI.
YOU REMEMBER... *THEN?*
HEY, SERIOUSLY-- WHEN WAS "THEN"?!
Yes, ma'am!
OKAY, KIDS! GET BACK TO CLASS!!
YOU'RE LATE FOR NEXT PERIOD!!

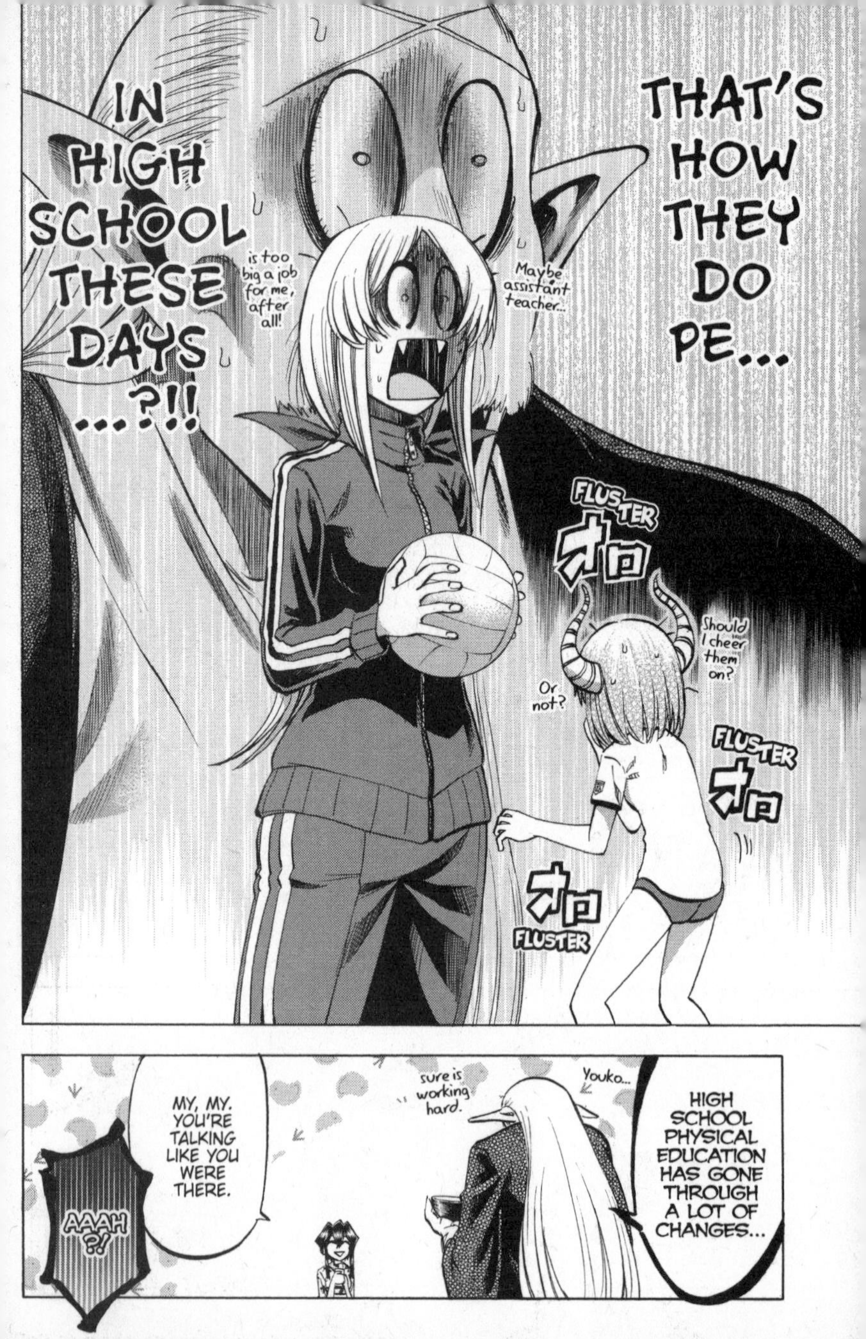
THAT'S HOW THEY DO PE...
Maybe assistant teacher...
is too big a job for me, after all!
IN HIGH SCHOOL THESE DAYS...?!!
FLUSTER オロ
Should I cheer them on?
Or not?
FLUSTER オロ
オロ FLUSTER
HIGH SCHOOL PHYSICAL EDUCATION HAS GONE THROUGH A LOT OF CHANGES...
Youko...
sure is working hard.
MY, MY. YOU'RE TALKING LIKE YOU WERE THERE.
AAAH?!

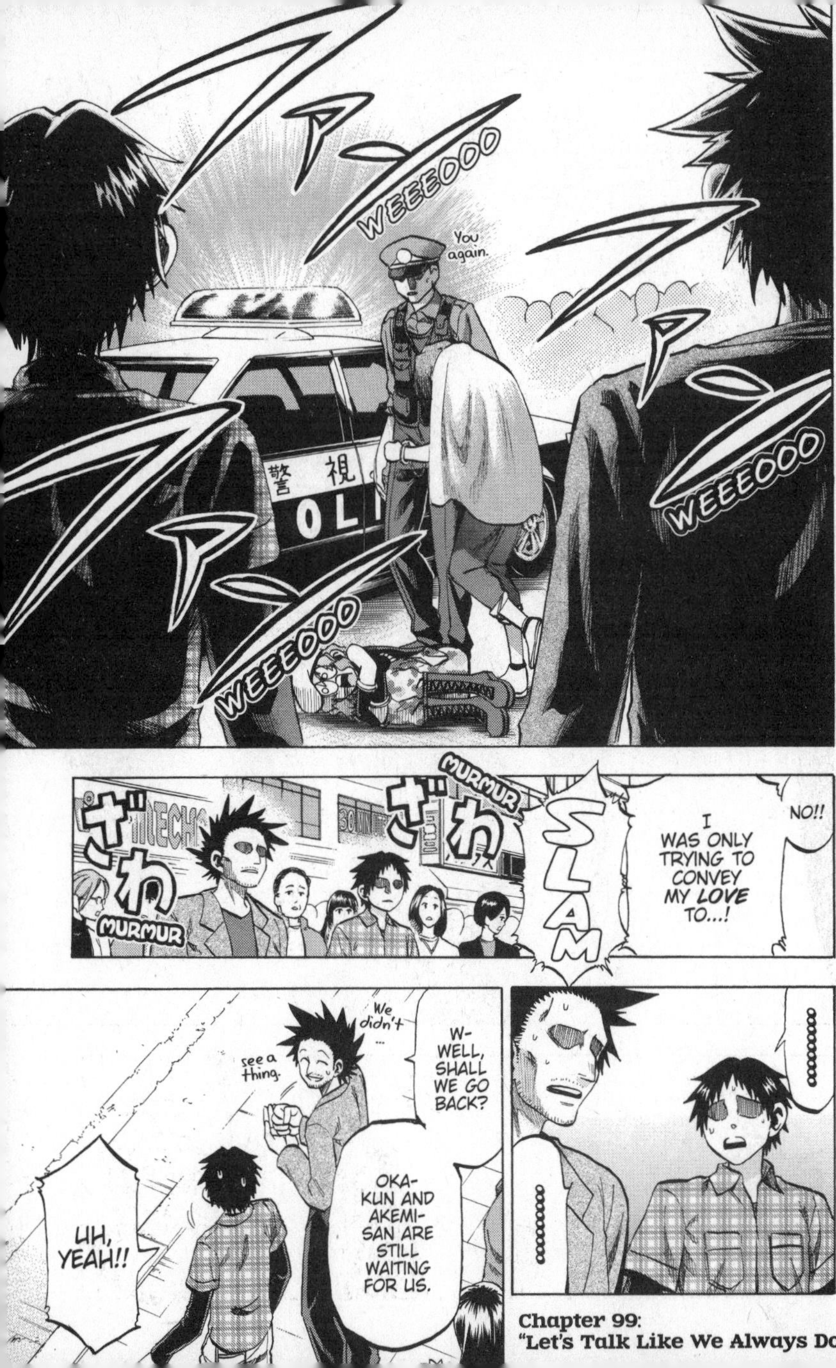
WEEEOOO
You again.
WEEEOOO
WEEEOOO
NO!!
I WAS ONLY TRYING TO CONVEY MY *LOVE* TO...!
SLAM
MURMUR
ざわ
ざわ
MURMUR
....
....
W-WELL, SHALL WE GO BACK?
We didn't ... see a thing.
OKA-KUN AND AKEMI-SAN ARE STILL WAITING FOR US.
UH, YEAH!!

Chapter 99: "Let's Talk Like We Always Do!"

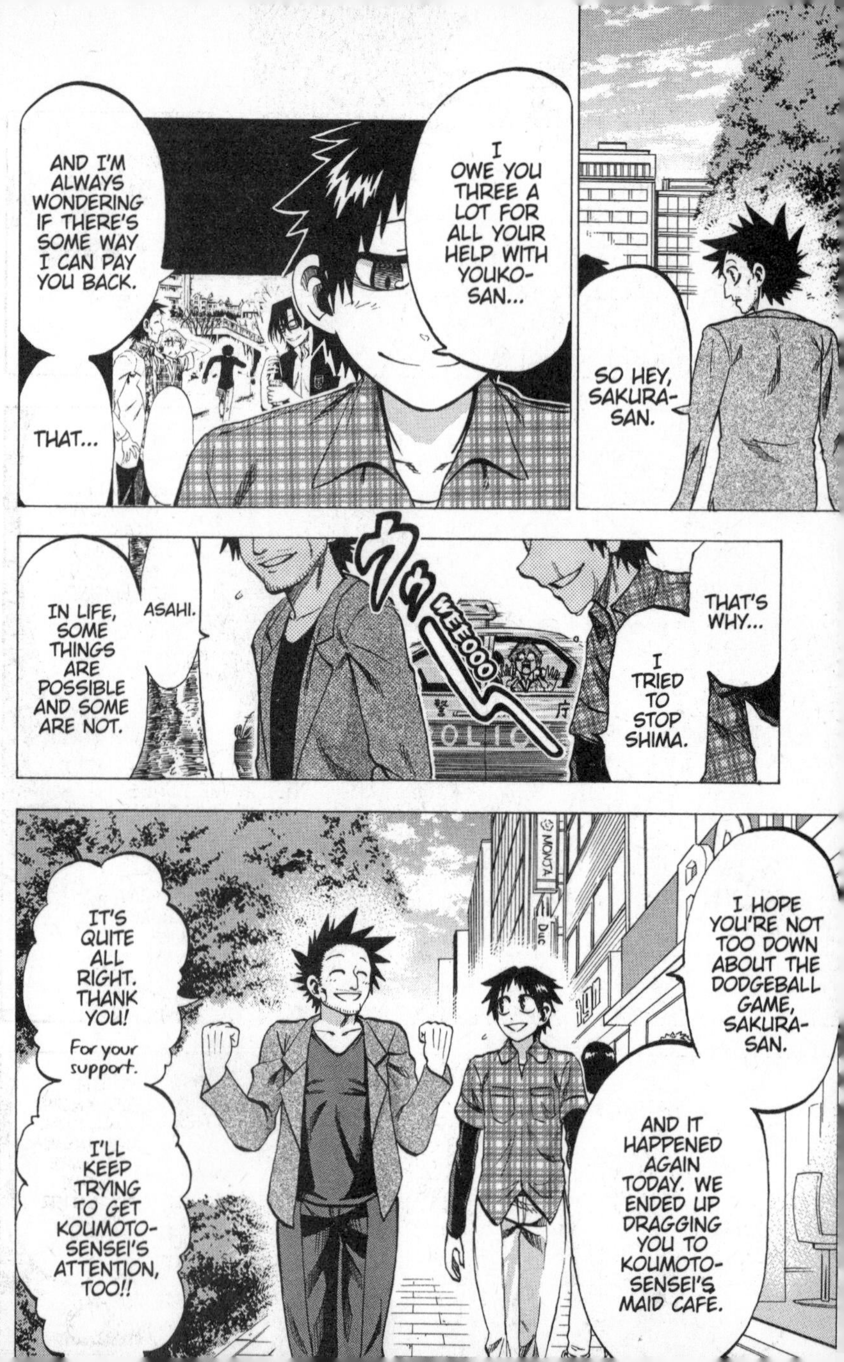
SO HEY, SAKURA-SAN.
I OWE YOU THREE A LOT FOR ALL YOUR HELP WITH YOUKO-SAN...
AND I'M ALWAYS WONDERING IF THERE'S SOME WAY I CAN PAY YOU BACK.
THAT...
THAT'S WHY...
I TRIED TO STOP SHIMA.
WEEOOO
ASAHI.
IN LIFE, SOME THINGS ARE POSSIBLE AND SOME ARE NOT.
MONJA
I HOPE YOU'RE NOT TOO DOWN ABOUT THE DODGEBALL GAME, SAKURA-SAN.
AND IT HAPPENED AGAIN TODAY. WE ENDED UP DRAGGING YOU TO KOUMOTO-SENSEI'S MAID CAFE.
IT'S QUITE ALL RIGHT. THANK YOU!
For your support.
I'LL KEEP TRYING TO GET KOUMOTO-SENSEI'S ATTENTION, TOO!!

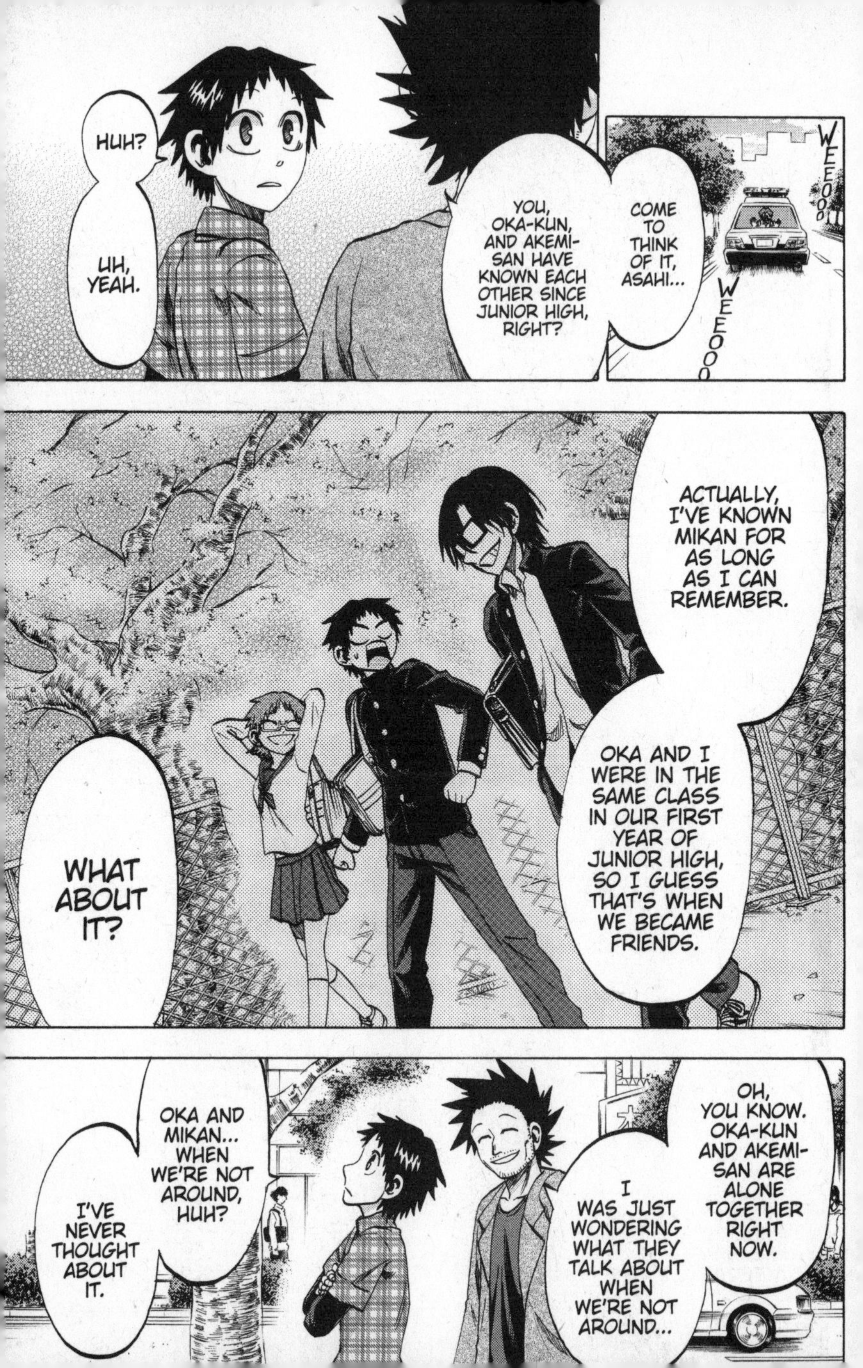
WEEOOO
WEEOOO
COME TO THINK OF IT, ASAHI...
YOU, OKA-KUN, AND AKEMI-SAN HAVE KNOWN EACH OTHER SINCE JUNIOR HIGH, RIGHT?
HUH?
UH, YEAH.
ACTUALLY, I'VE KNOWN MIKAN FOR AS LONG AS I CAN REMEMBER.
OKA AND I WERE IN THE SAME CLASS IN OUR FIRST YEAR OF JUNIOR HIGH, SO I GUESS THAT'S WHEN WE BECAME FRIENDS.
WHAT ABOUT IT?
OH, YOU KNOW. OKA-KUN AND AKEMI-SAN ARE ALONE TOGETHER RIGHT NOW.
I WAS JUST WONDERING WHAT THEY TALK ABOUT WHEN WE'RE NOT AROUND...
OKA AND MIKAN... WHEN WE'RE NOT AROUND, HUH?
I'VE NEVER THOUGHT ABOUT IT.

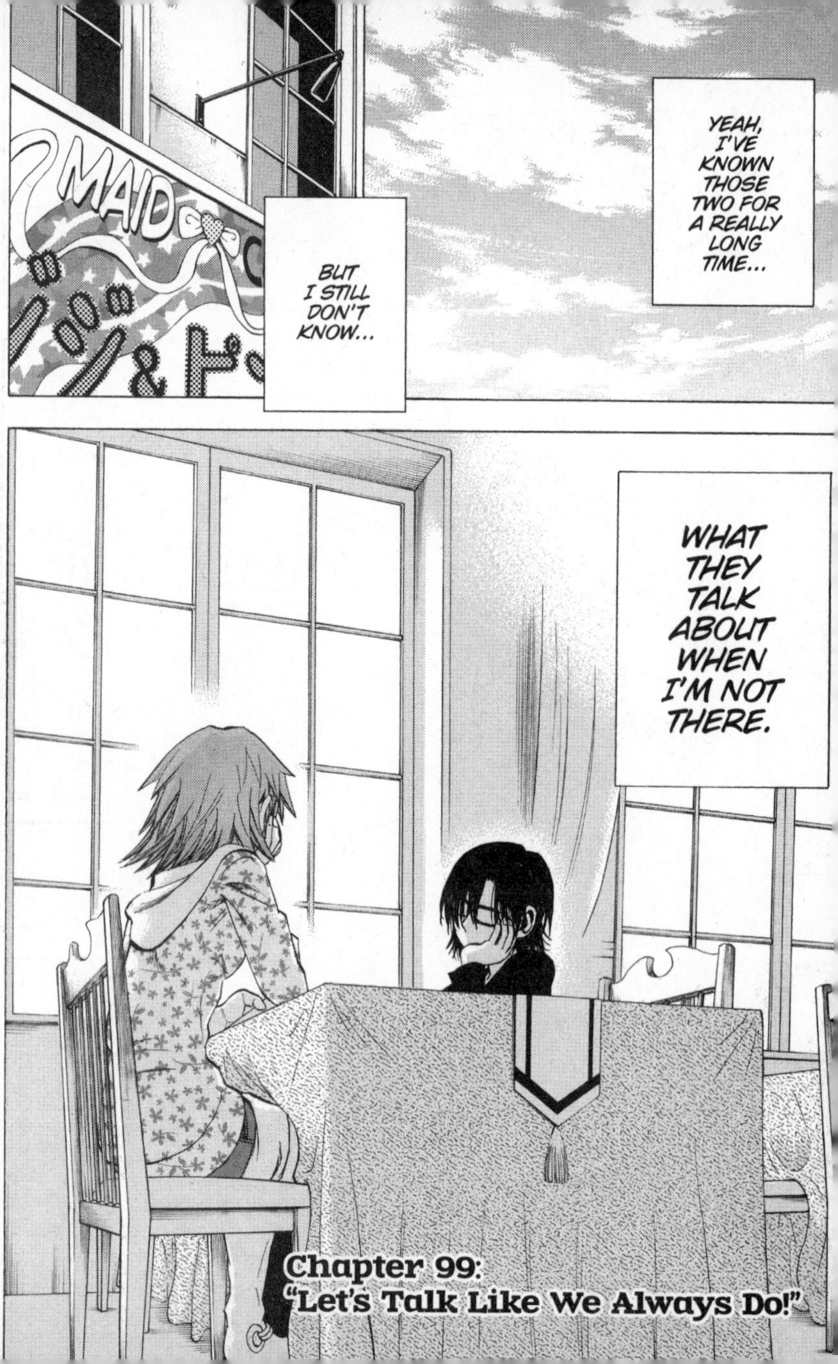
YEAH, I'VE KNOWN THOSE TWO FOR A REALLY LONG TIME...
MAID
BUT I STILL DON'T KNOW...
WHAT THEY TALK ABOUT WHEN I'M NOT THERE.
Chapter 99:
"Let's Talk Like We Always Do!"

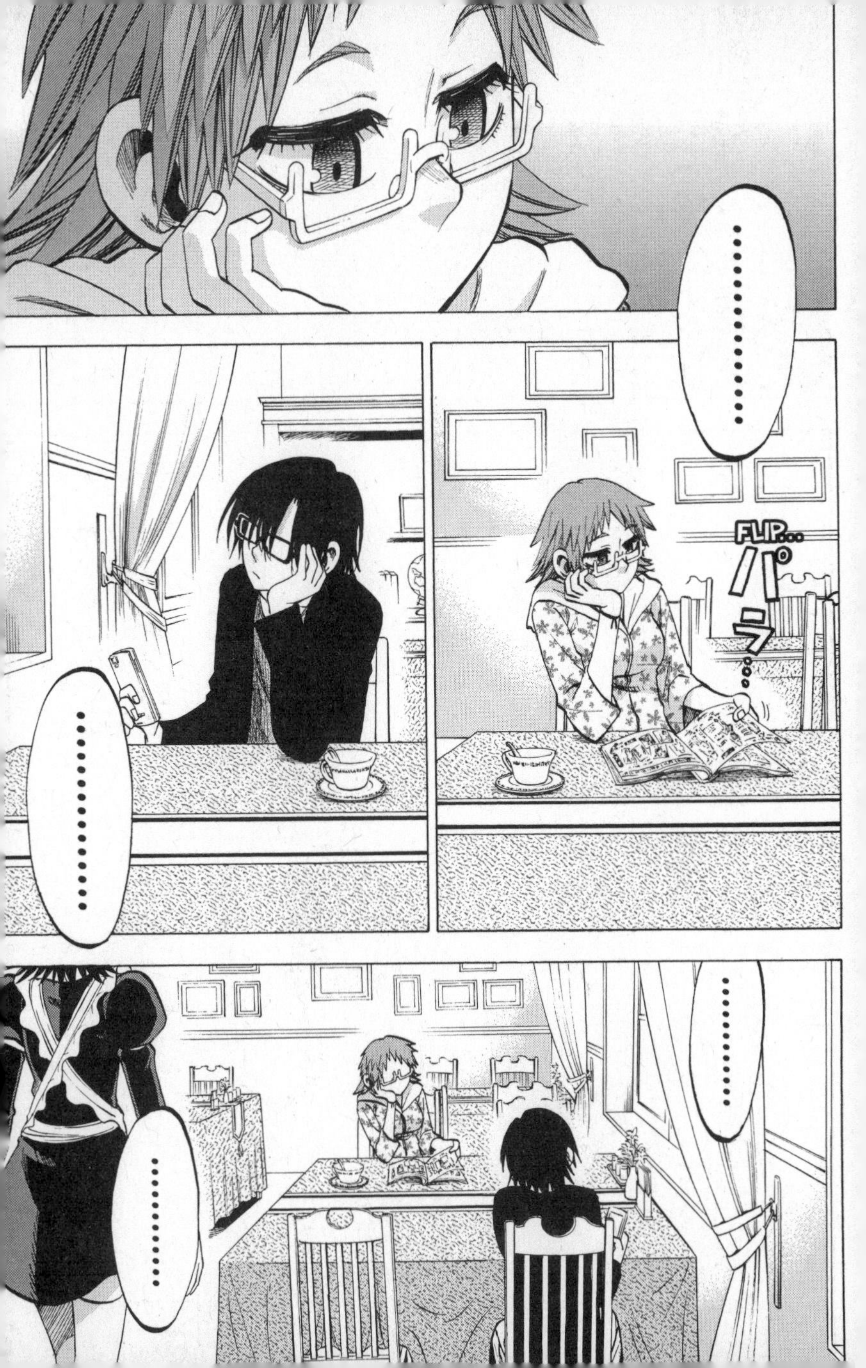

....
FLIP... パラ...
....
....
....

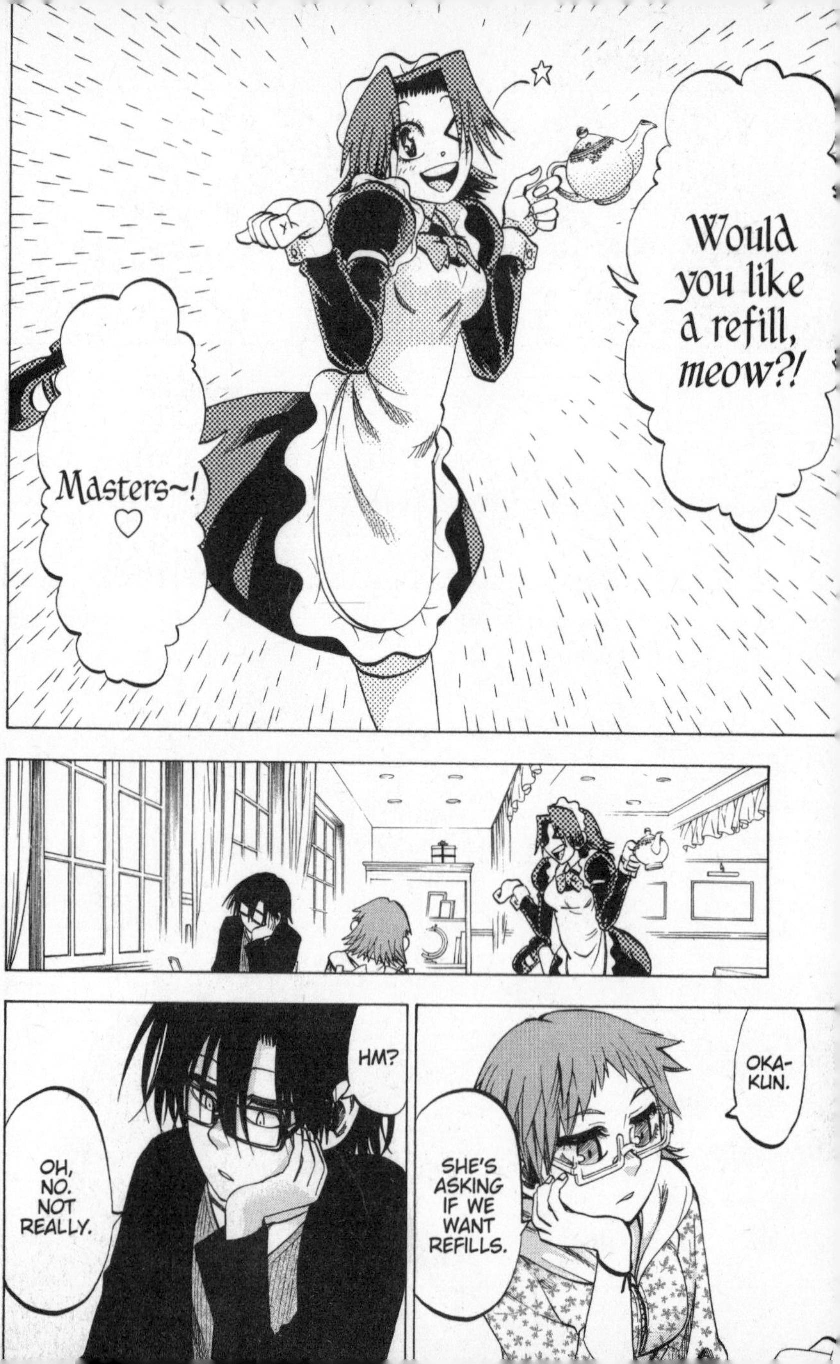
Would you like a refill, meow?!
Masters~! ♡
OKA-KUN.
SHE'S ASKING IF WE WANT REFILLS.
HM?
OH, NO. NOT REALLY.

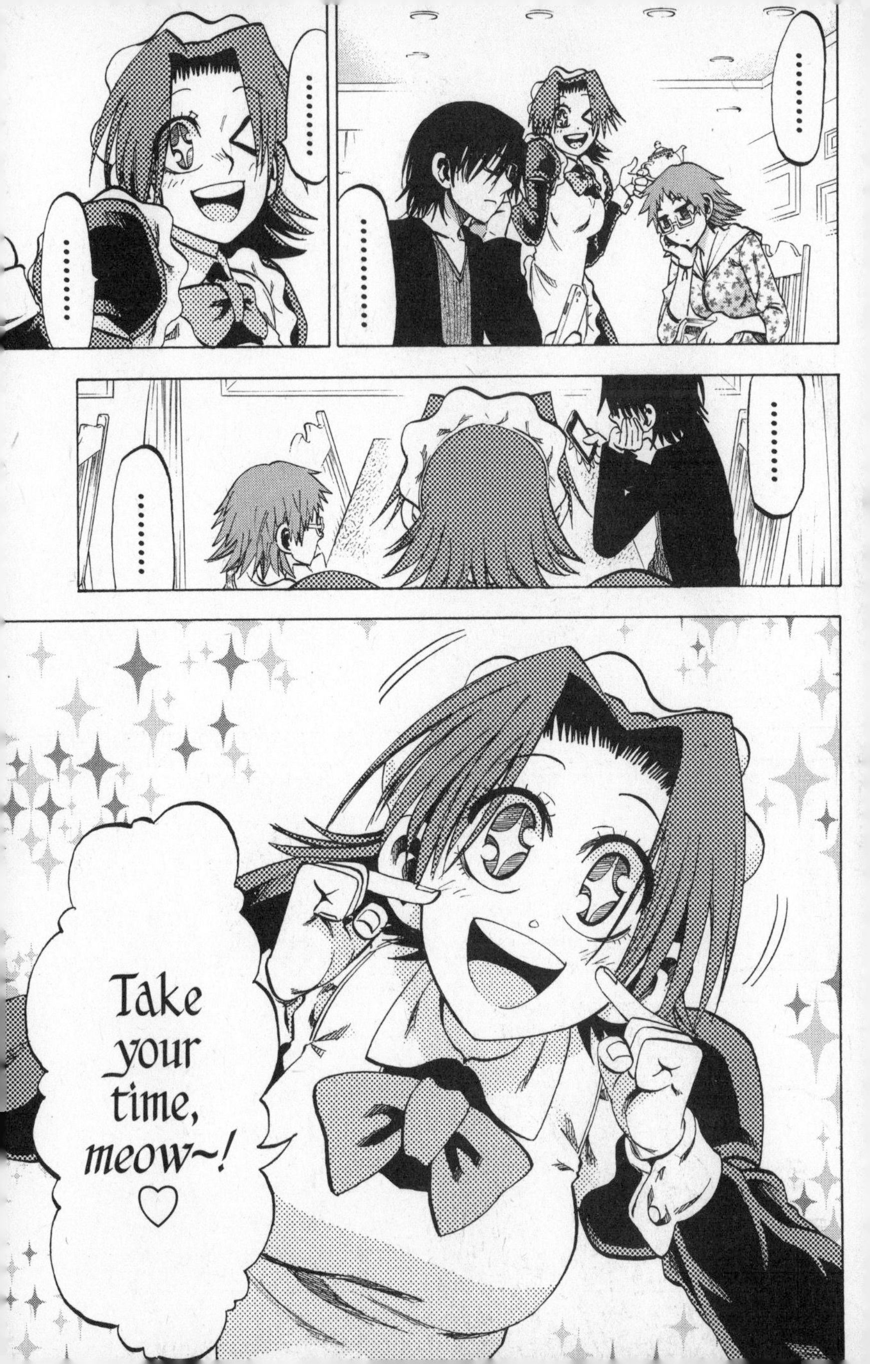
......
......
......
......
......
......
Take your time, meow~! ♡

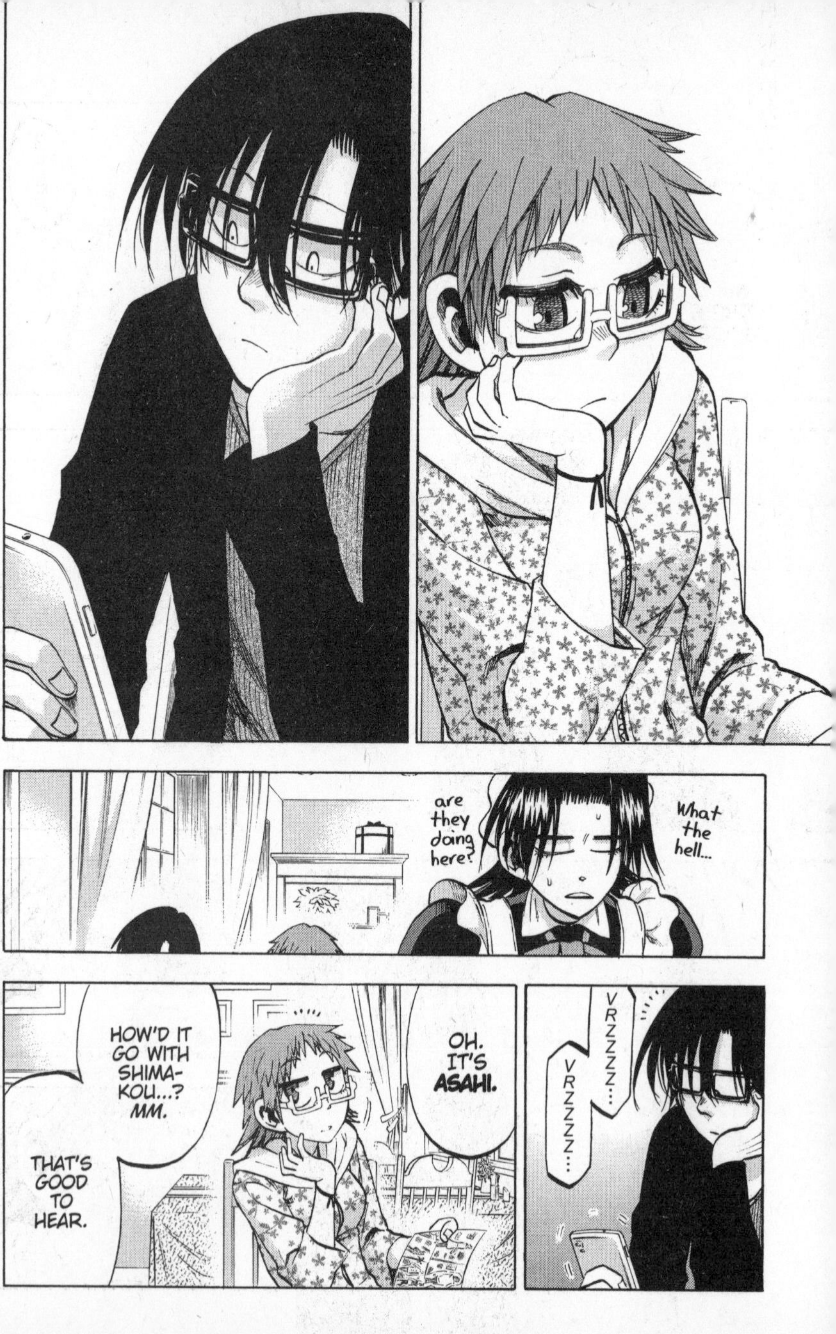
What the hell...
are they doing here?
VRZZZZ....
VRZZZZ...
OH. IT'S ASAHI.
HOW'D IT GO WITH SHIMA-KOU...? MM.
THAT'S GOOD TO HEAR.

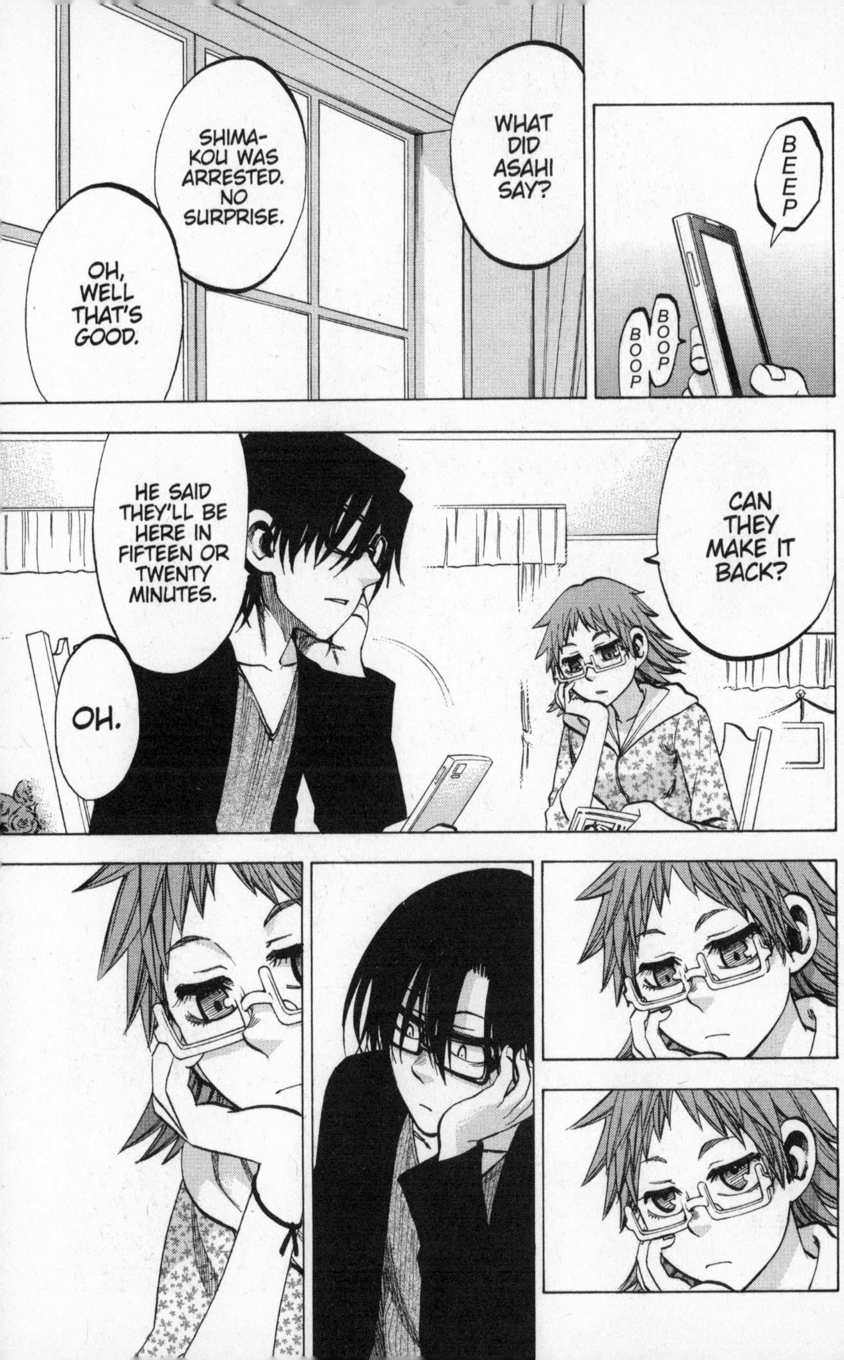
BEEP
BOOP
BOOP
WHAT DID ASAHI SAY?
SHIMA-KOU WAS ARRESTED. NO SURPRISE.
OH, WELL THAT'S GOOD.
CAN THEY MAKE IT BACK?
HE SAID THEY'LL BE HERE IN FIFTEEN OR TWENTY MINUTES.
OH.

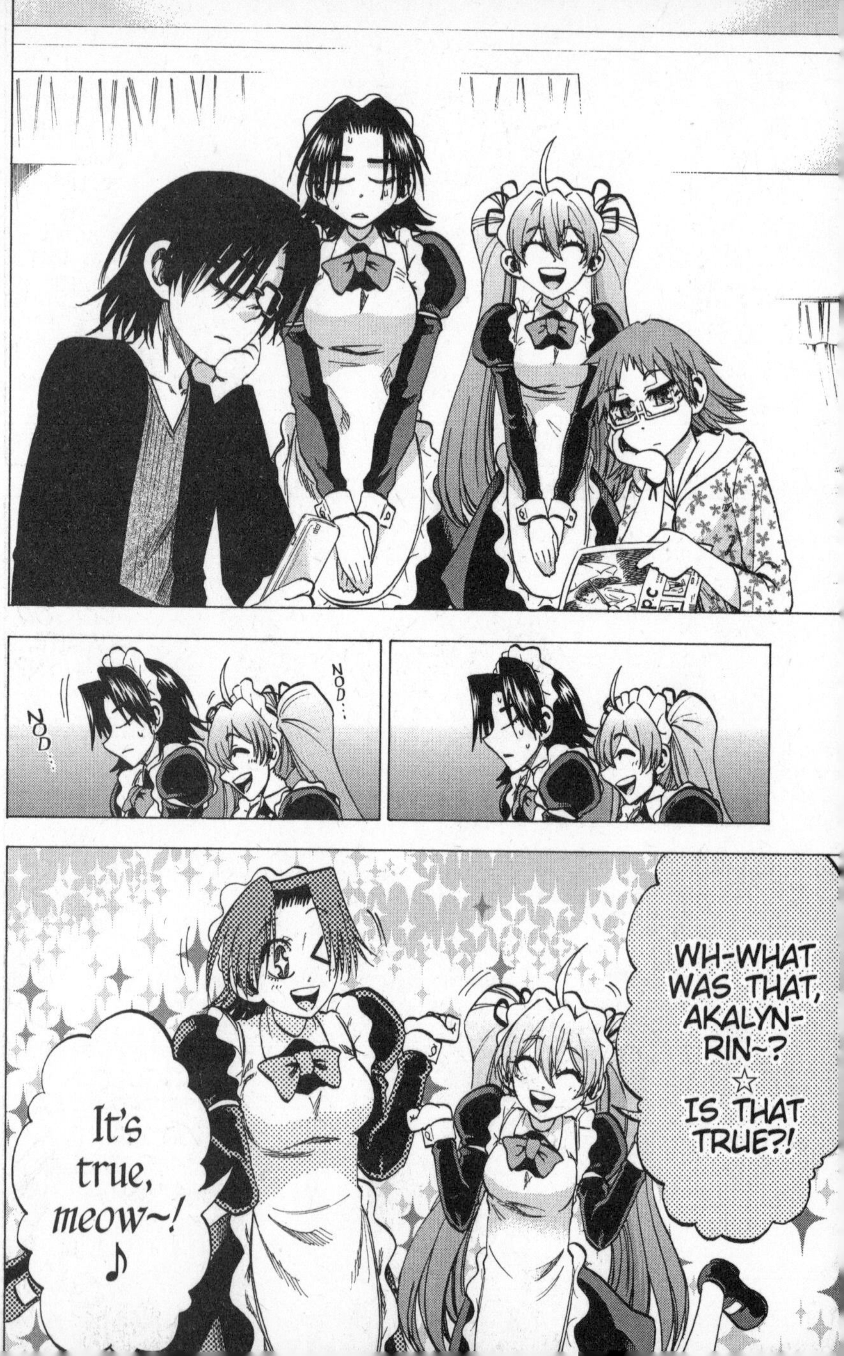
NOD...
NOD...
WH-WHAT WAS THAT, AKALYN-RIN~? ☆ IS THAT TRUE?!
It's true, meow~! ♪

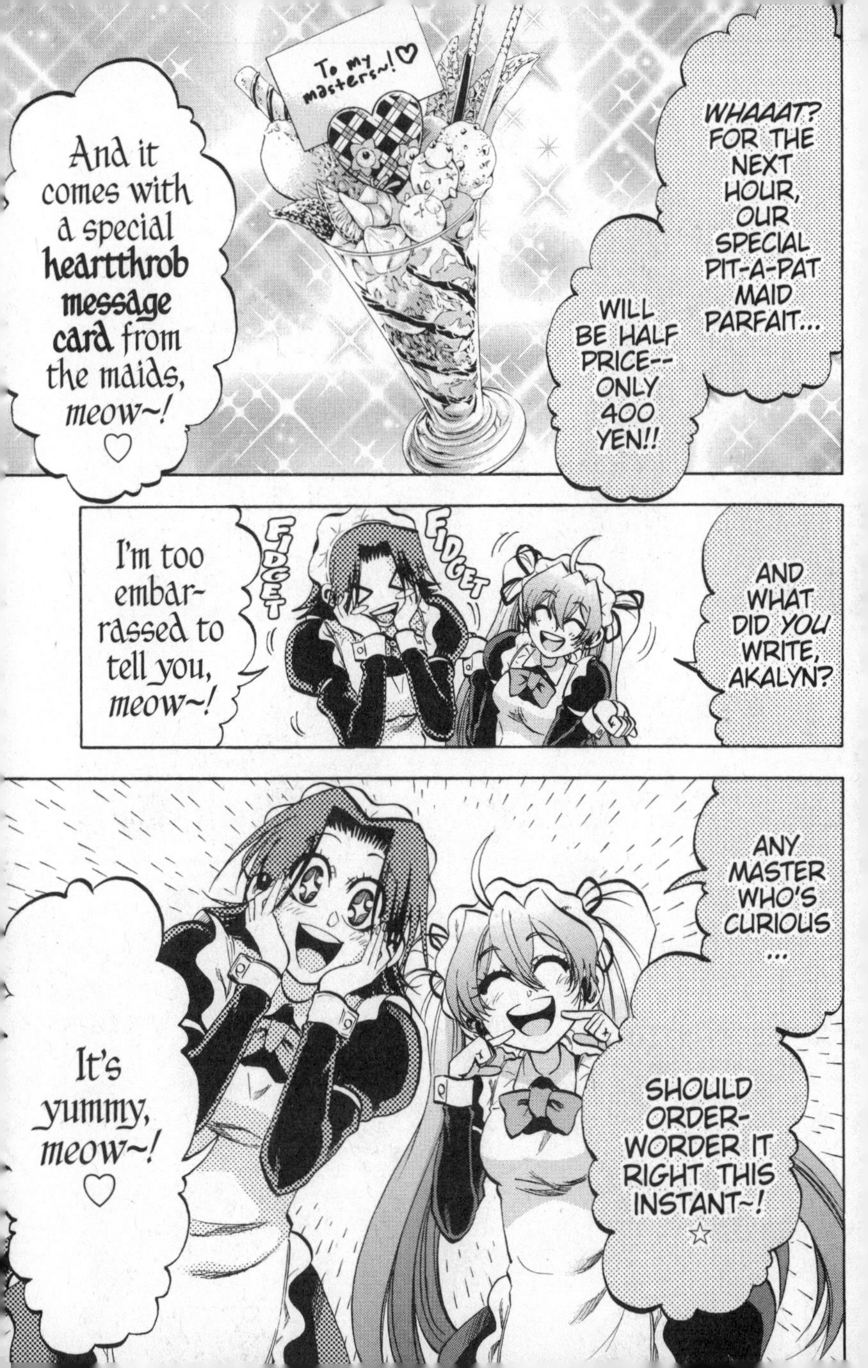
WHAAAT? FOR THE NEXT HOUR, OUR SPECIAL PIT-A-PAT MAID PARFAIT...
WILL BE HALF PRICE-- ONLY 400 YEN!!
To my masters~!♡
And it comes with a special **heartthrob message card** from the maids, *meow~!* ♡
AND WHAT DID *YOU* WRITE, AKALYN?
FIDGET
FIDGET
I'm too embar-rassed to tell you, *meow~!*
ANY MASTER WHO'S CURIOUS ...
SHOULD ORDER-WORDER IT RIGHT THIS INSTANT~! ☆
It's yummy, *meow~!* ♡

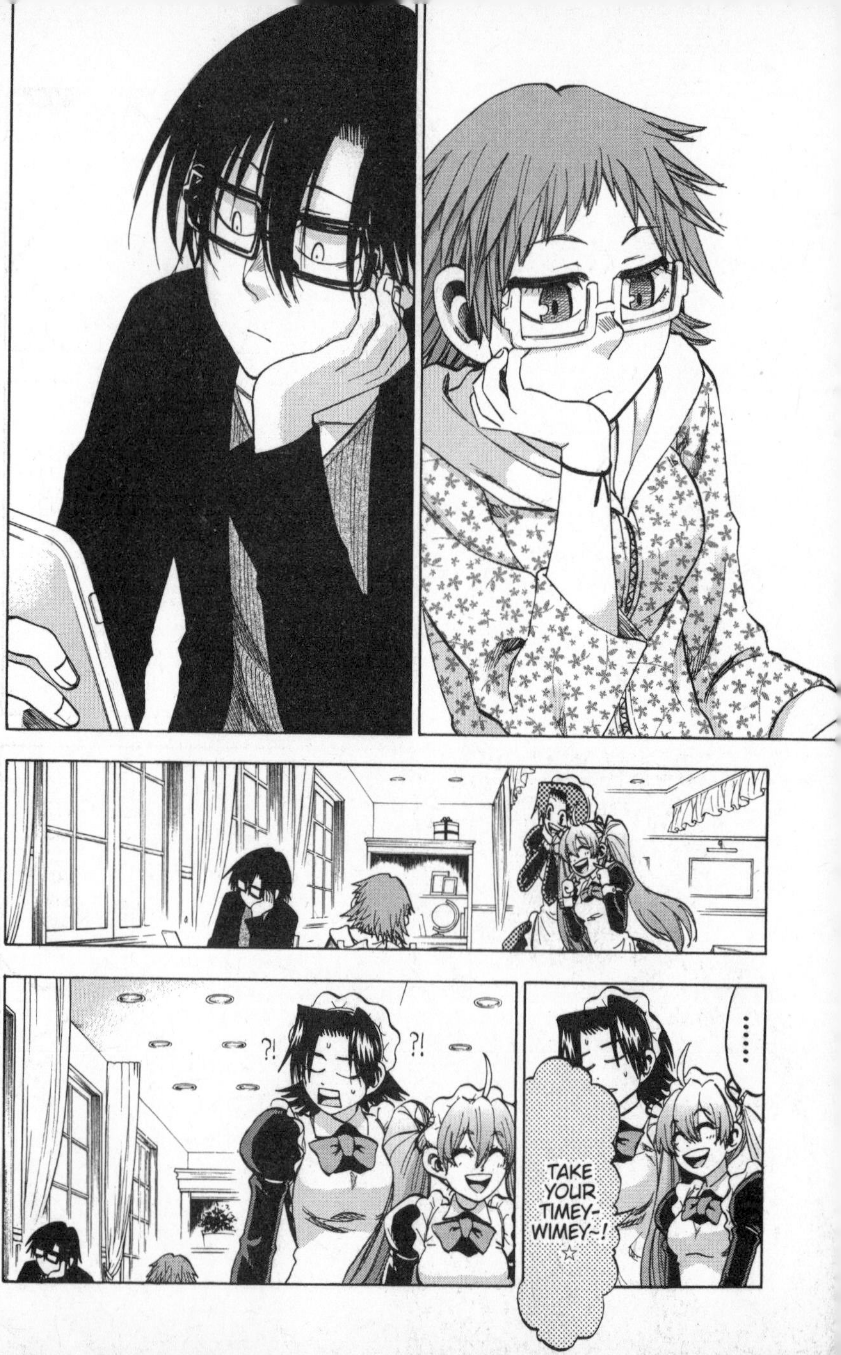
......
TAKE YOUR TIMEY-WIMEY~! ☆
?!
?!

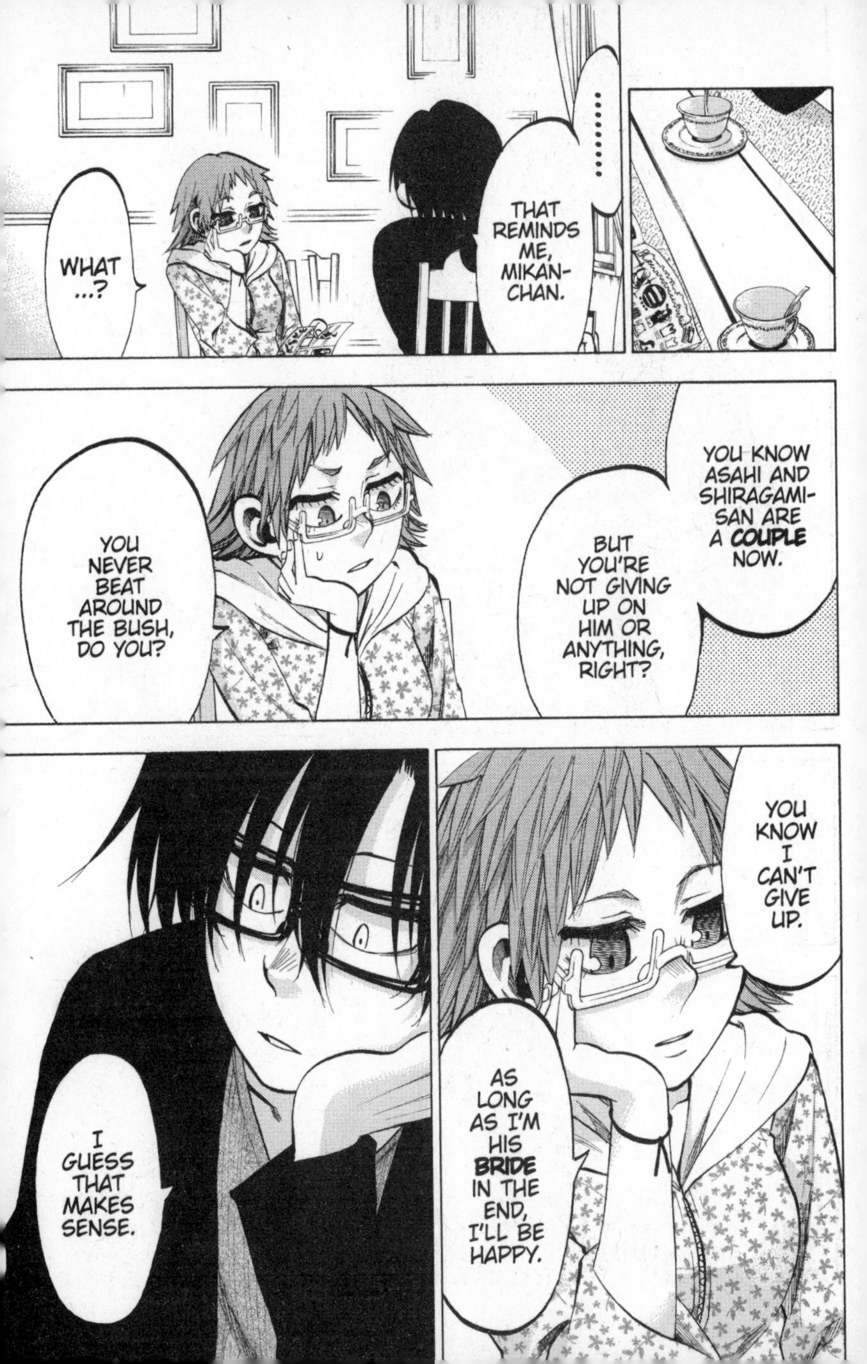
......
THAT REMINDS ME, MIKAN-CHAN.
WHAT ...?
YOU KNOW ASAHI AND SHIRAGAMI-SAN ARE A **COUPLE** NOW.
BUT YOU'RE NOT GIVING UP ON HIM OR ANYTHING, RIGHT?
YOU NEVER BEAT AROUND THE BUSH, DO YOU?
YOU KNOW I CAN'T GIVE UP.
AS LONG AS I'M HIS **BRIDE** IN THE END, I'LL BE HAPPY.
I GUESS THAT MAKES SENSE.

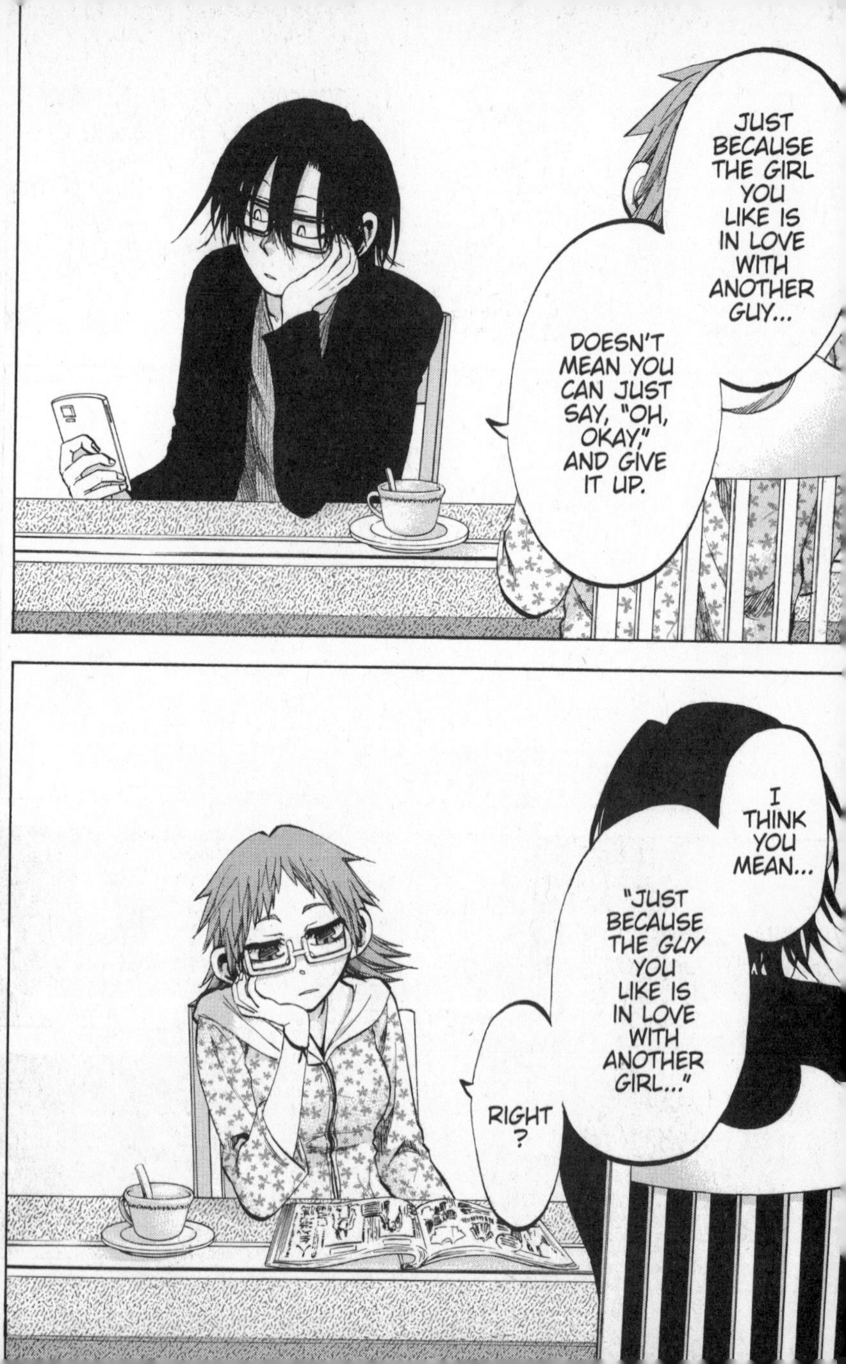
JUST BECAUSE THE GIRL YOU LIKE IS IN LOVE WITH ANOTHER GUY...
DOESN'T MEAN YOU CAN JUST SAY, "OH, OKAY," AND GIVE IT UP.
I THINK YOU MEAN...
"JUST BECAUSE THE GUY YOU LIKE IS IN LOVE WITH ANOTHER GIRL..."
RIGHT?

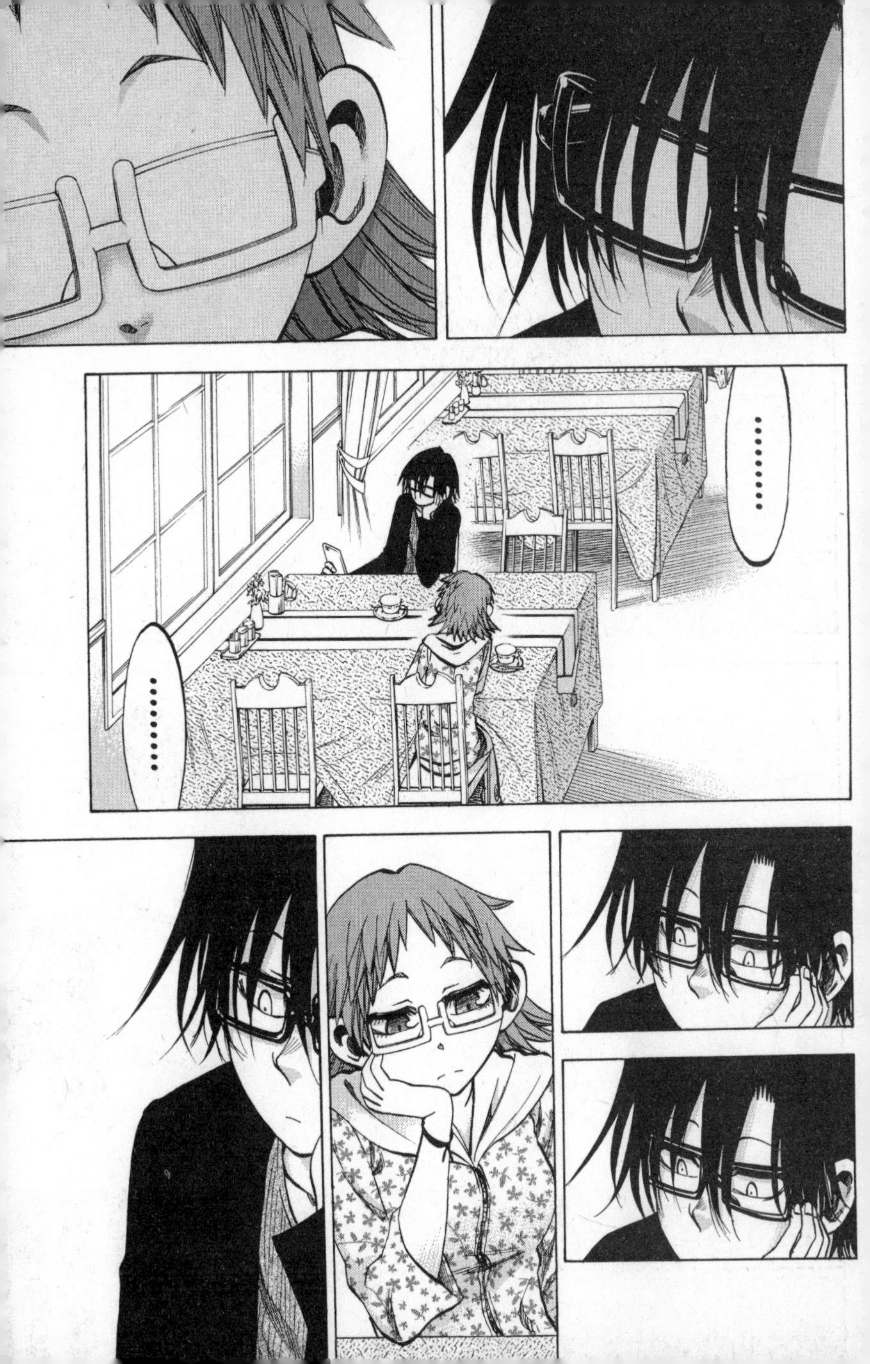
....
....

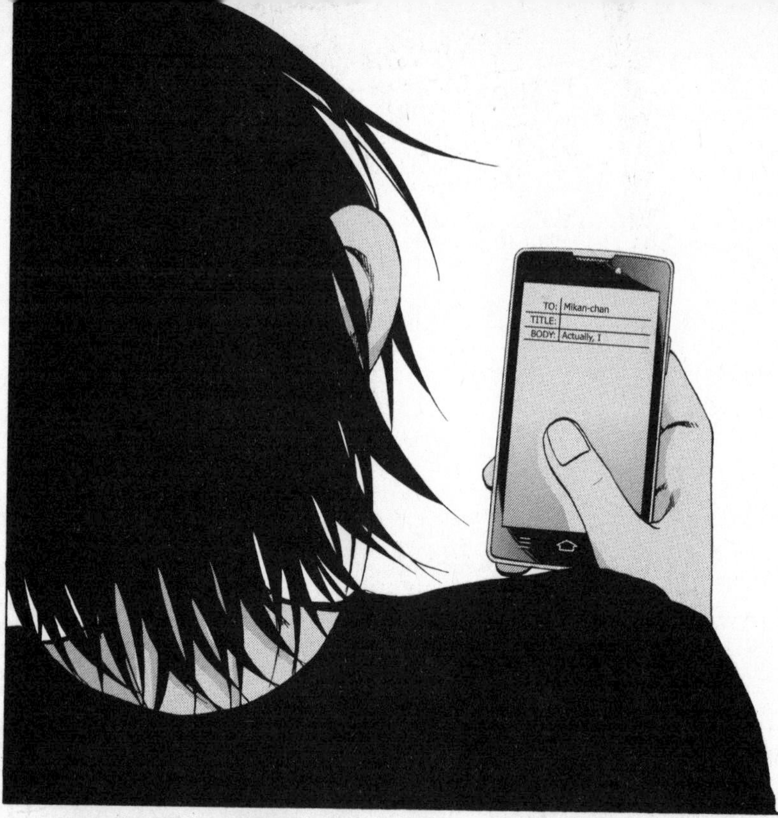
TO: Mikan-chan
TITLE:
BODY: Actually, I

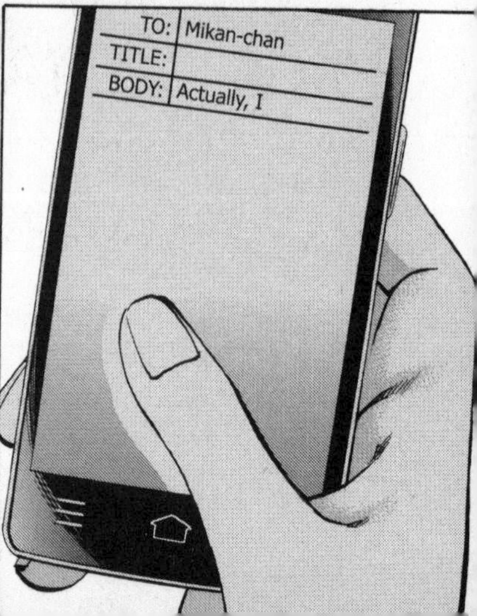
TO: Mikan-chan
TITLE:
BODY: Actually, I

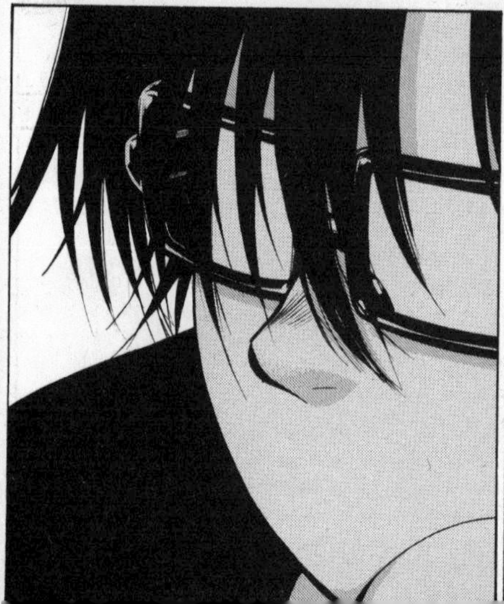

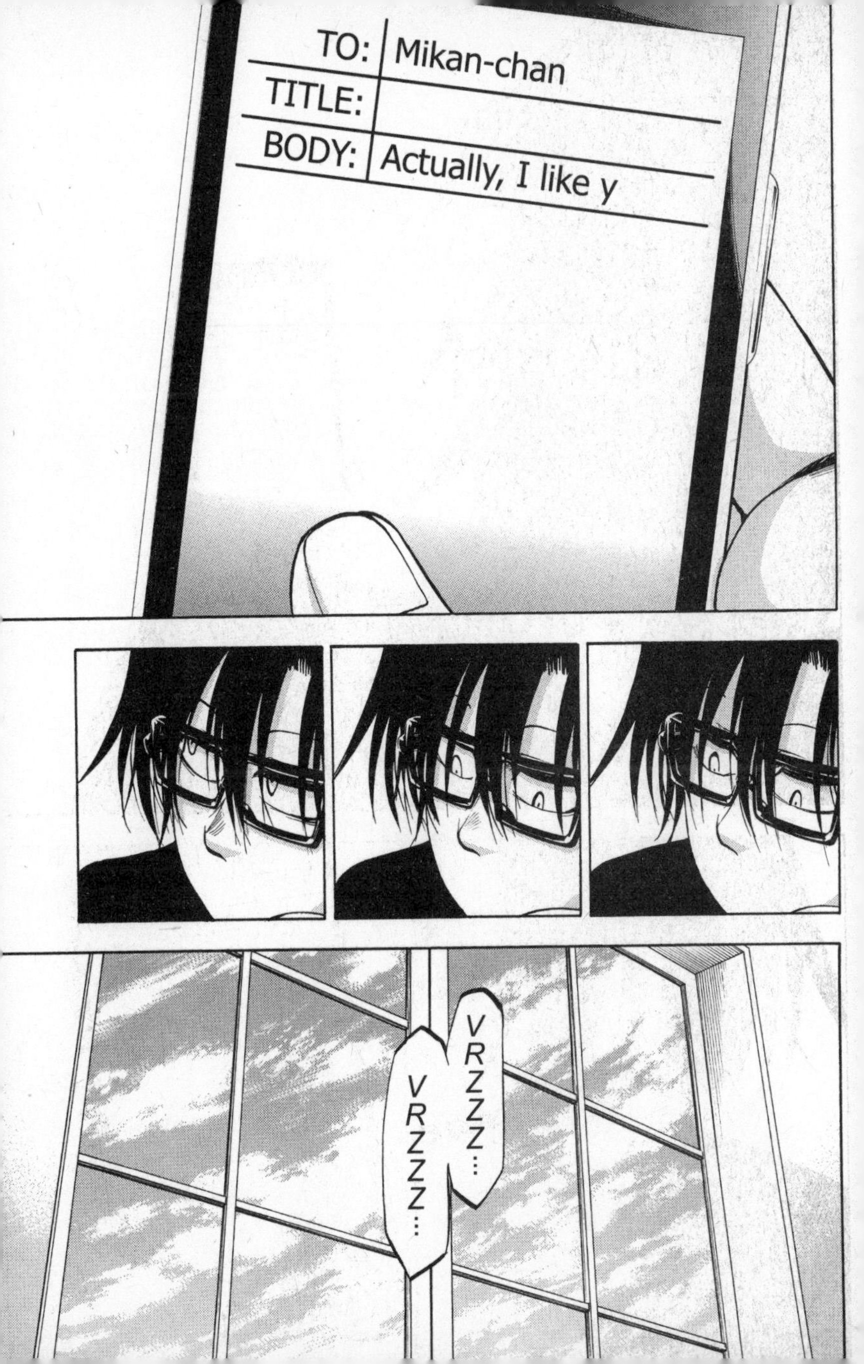
TO: Mikan-chan
TITLE:
BODY: Actually, I like y
VRZZZ...
VRZZZ...

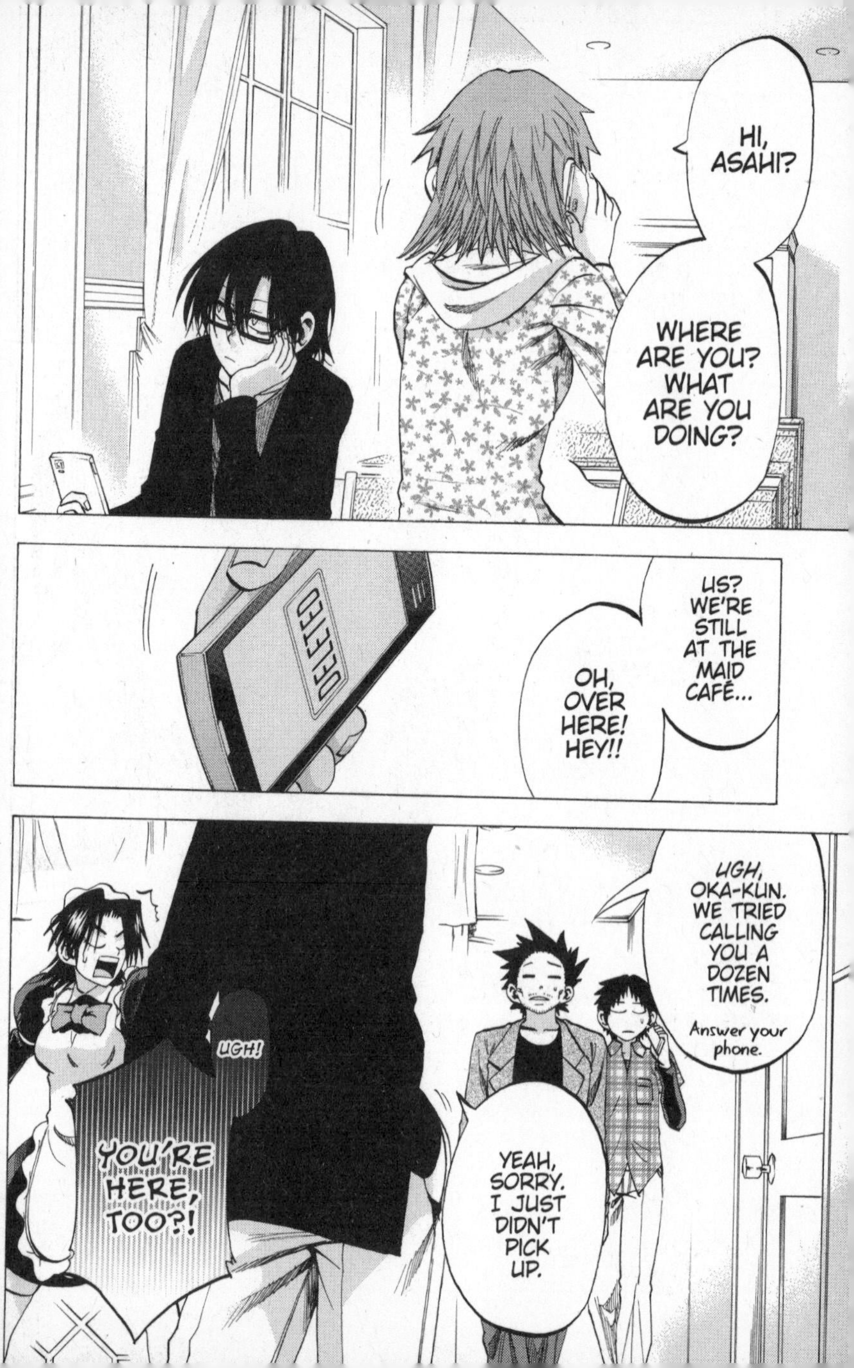
HI, ASAHI?
WHERE ARE YOU? WHAT ARE YOU DOING?
US? WE'RE STILL AT THE MAID CAFÉ...
OH, OVER HERE! HEY!!
DELETED
UGH, OKA-KUN. WE TRIED CALLING YOU A DOZEN TIMES.
Answer your phone.
YEAH, SORRY. I JUST DIDN'T PICK UP.
UGH!
YOU'RE HERE, TOO?!

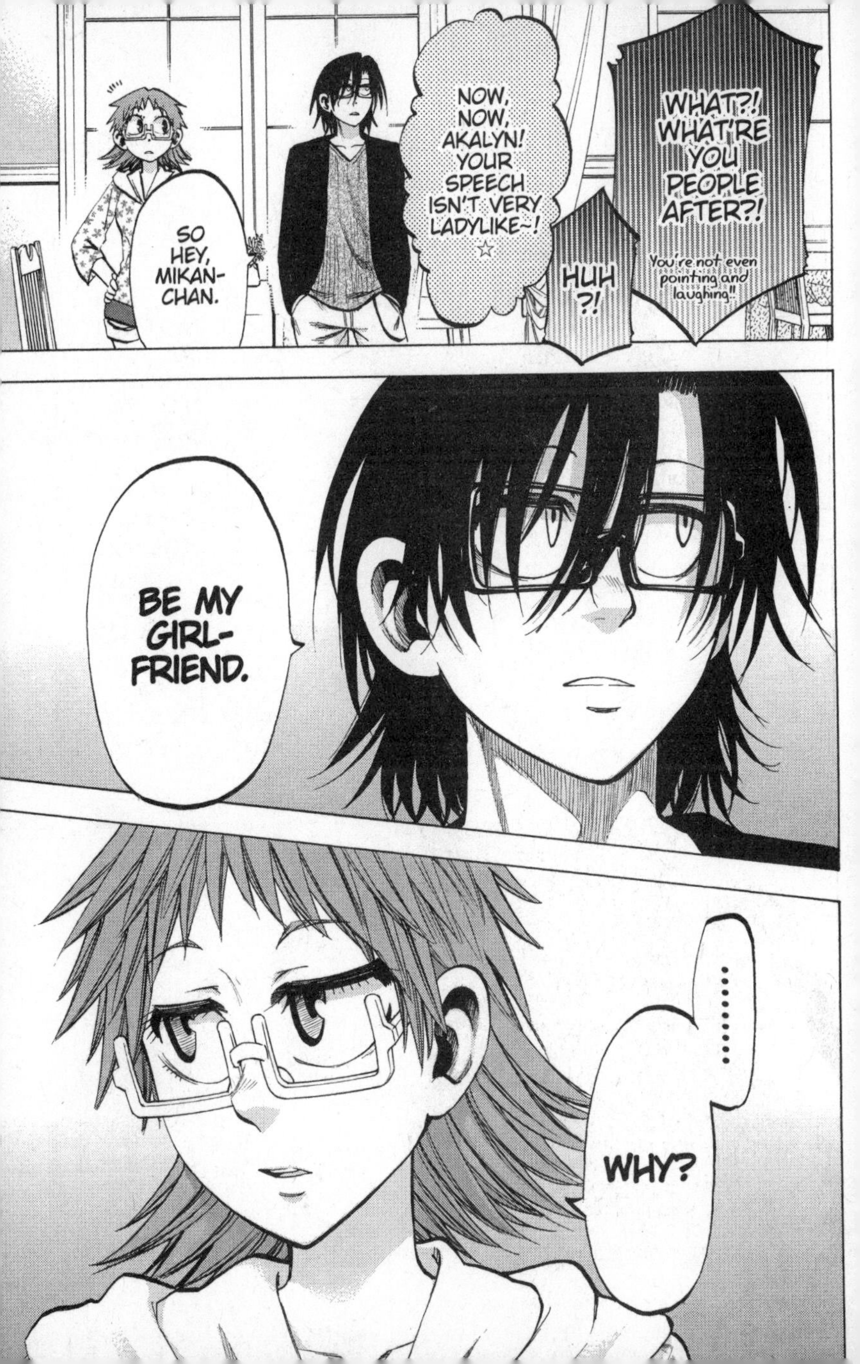
WHAT?! WHAT'RE YOU PEOPLE AFTER?!
You're not even pointing and laughing!!
HUH ?!
NOW, NOW, AKALYN! YOUR SPEECH ISN'T VERY LADYLIKE~! ☆
SO HEY, MIKAN-CHAN.
BE MY GIRL-FRIEND.
....
WHY?

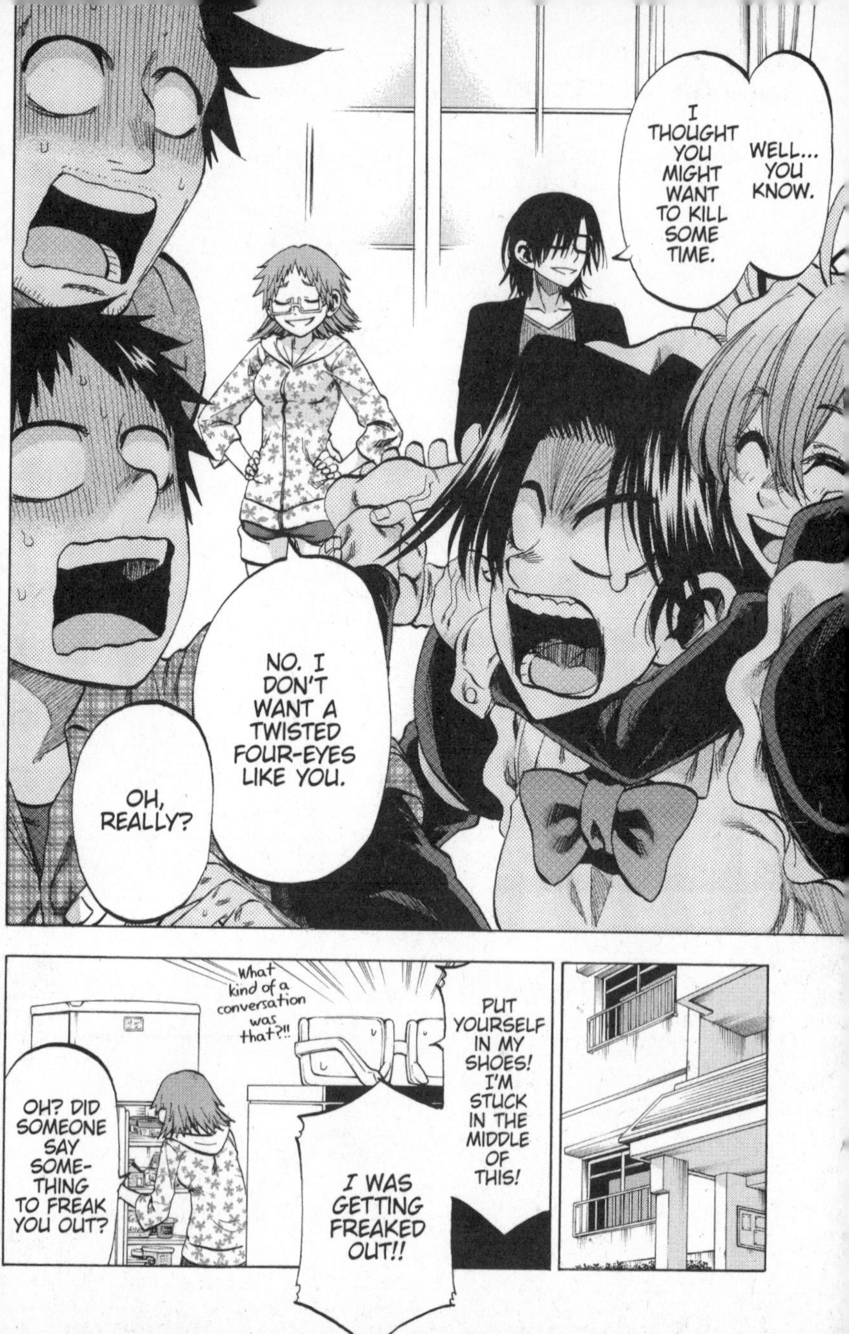
WELL... YOU KNOW.
I THOUGHT YOU MIGHT WANT TO KILL SOME TIME.
NO. I DON'T WANT A TWISTED FOUR-EYES LIKE YOU.
OH, REALLY?
PUT YOURSELF IN MY SHOES! I'M STUCK IN THE MIDDLE OF THIS!
What kind of a conversation was that?!!
I WAS GETTING FREAKED OUT!!
OH? DID SOMEONE SAY SOME-THING TO FREAK YOU OUT?

Chapter 100:
"Let's Go on a Date!"

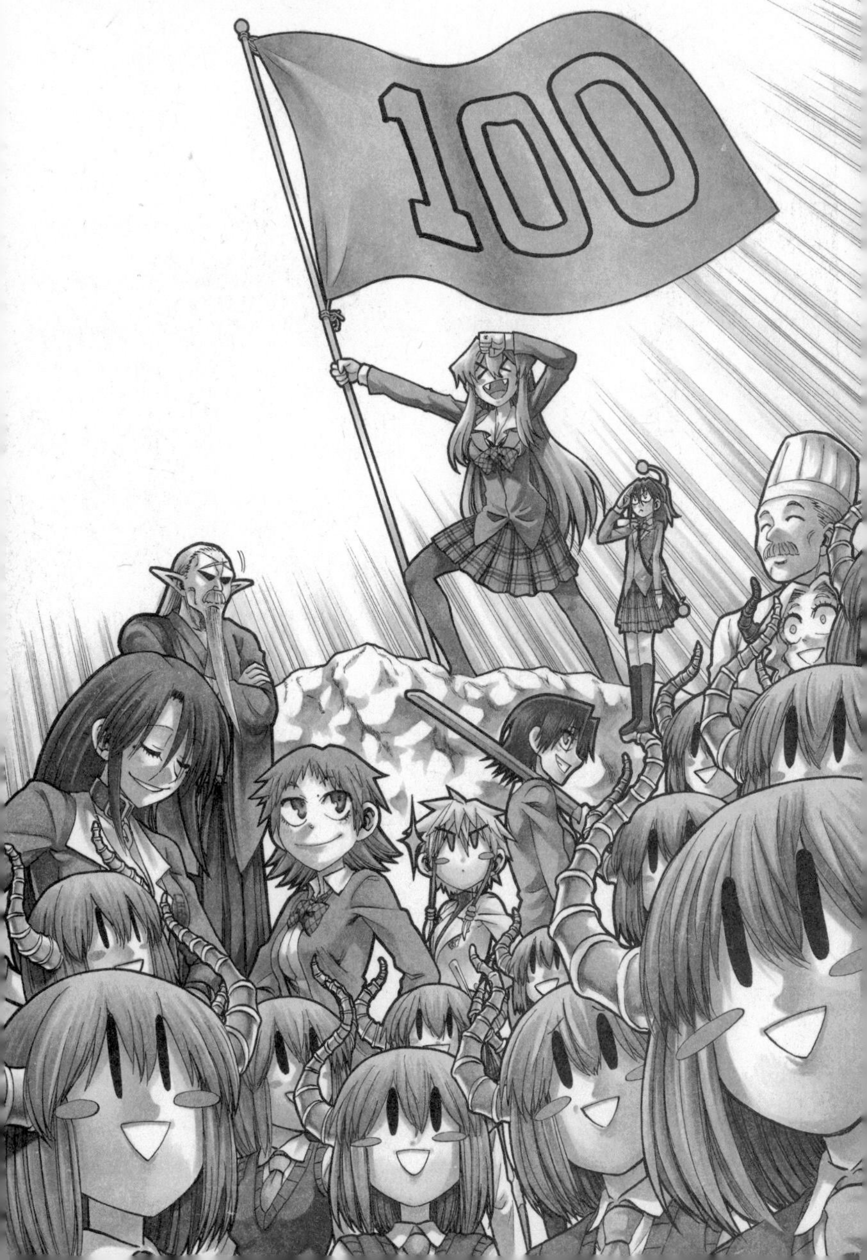
100

TOP SECRET

My Monster Secret 12

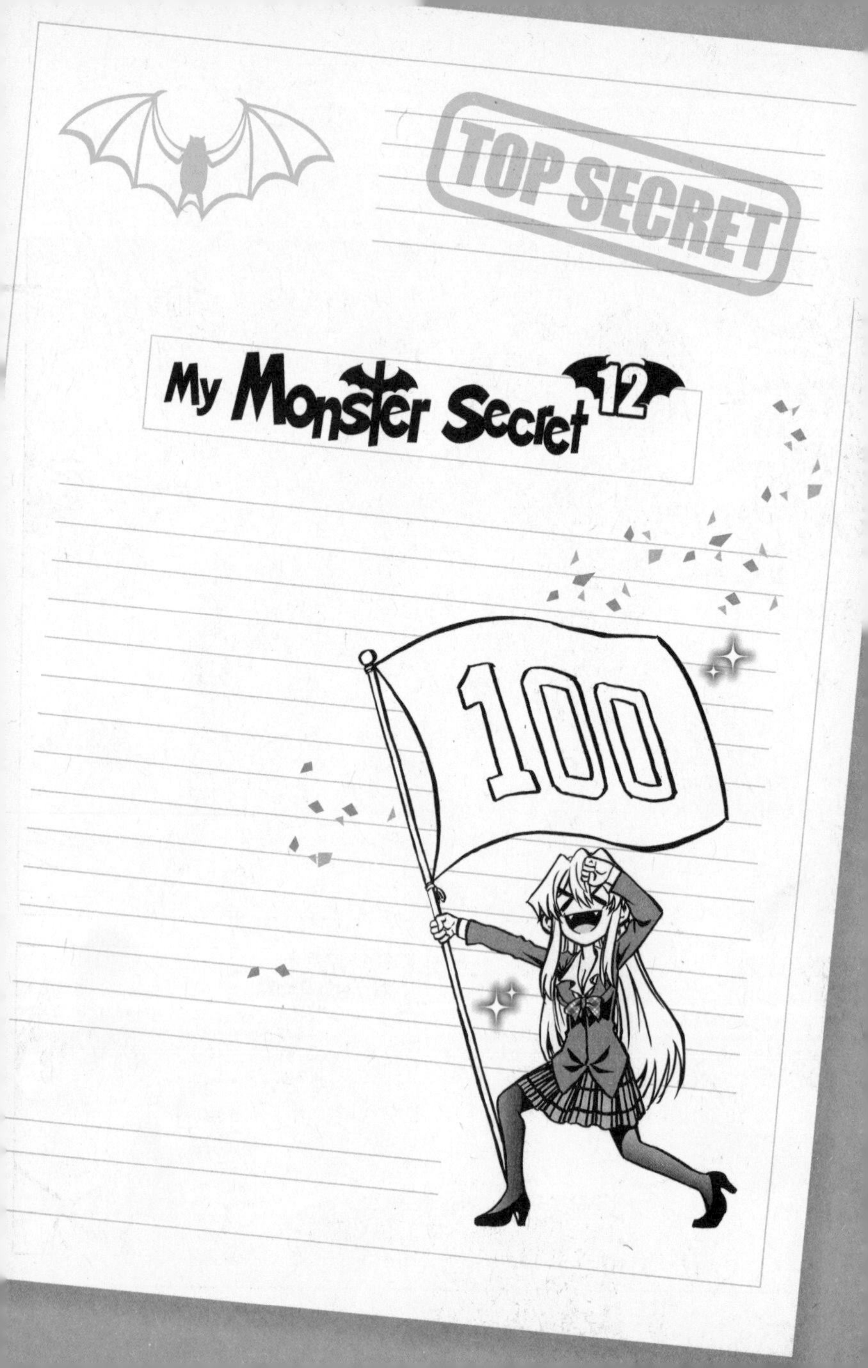
100

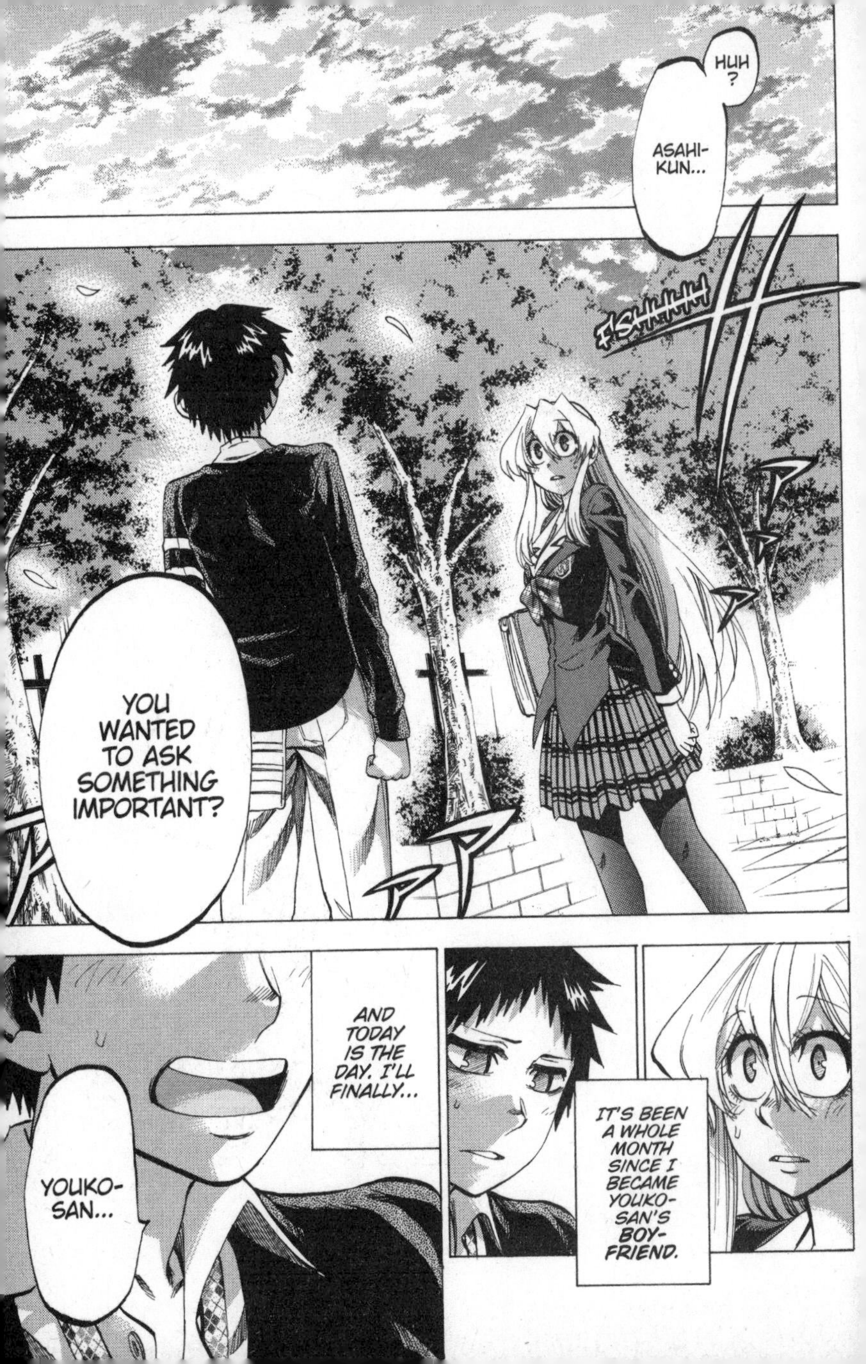
HUH?
ASAHI-KUN...
FSHHHHH
YOU WANTED TO ASK SOMETHING IMPORTANT?
IT'S BEEN A WHOLE MONTH SINCE I BECAME YOUKO-SAN'S BOYFRIEND.
AND TODAY IS THE DAY. I'LL FINALLY...
YOUKO-SAN...

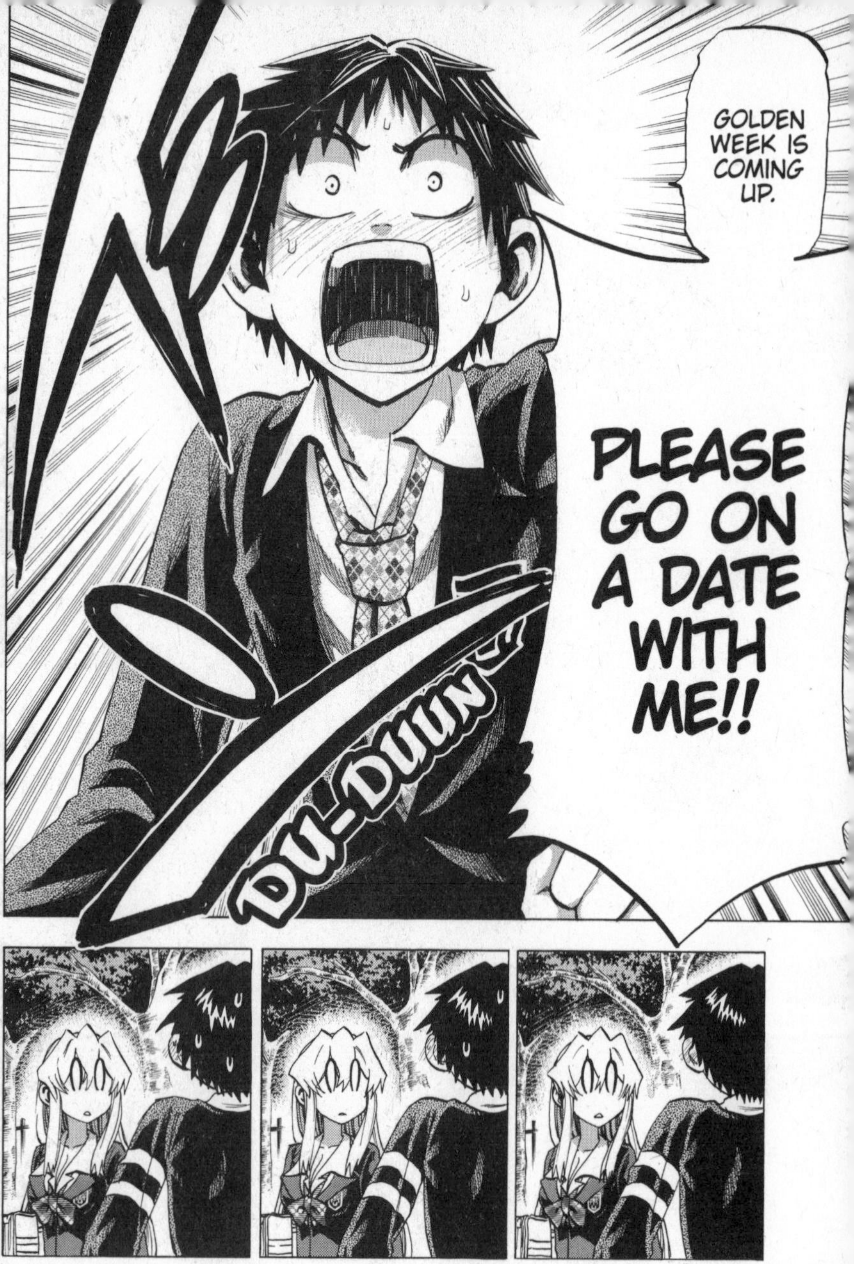
GOLDEN WEEK IS COMING UP.
PLEASE GO ON A DATE WITH ME!!
DU-DUUN

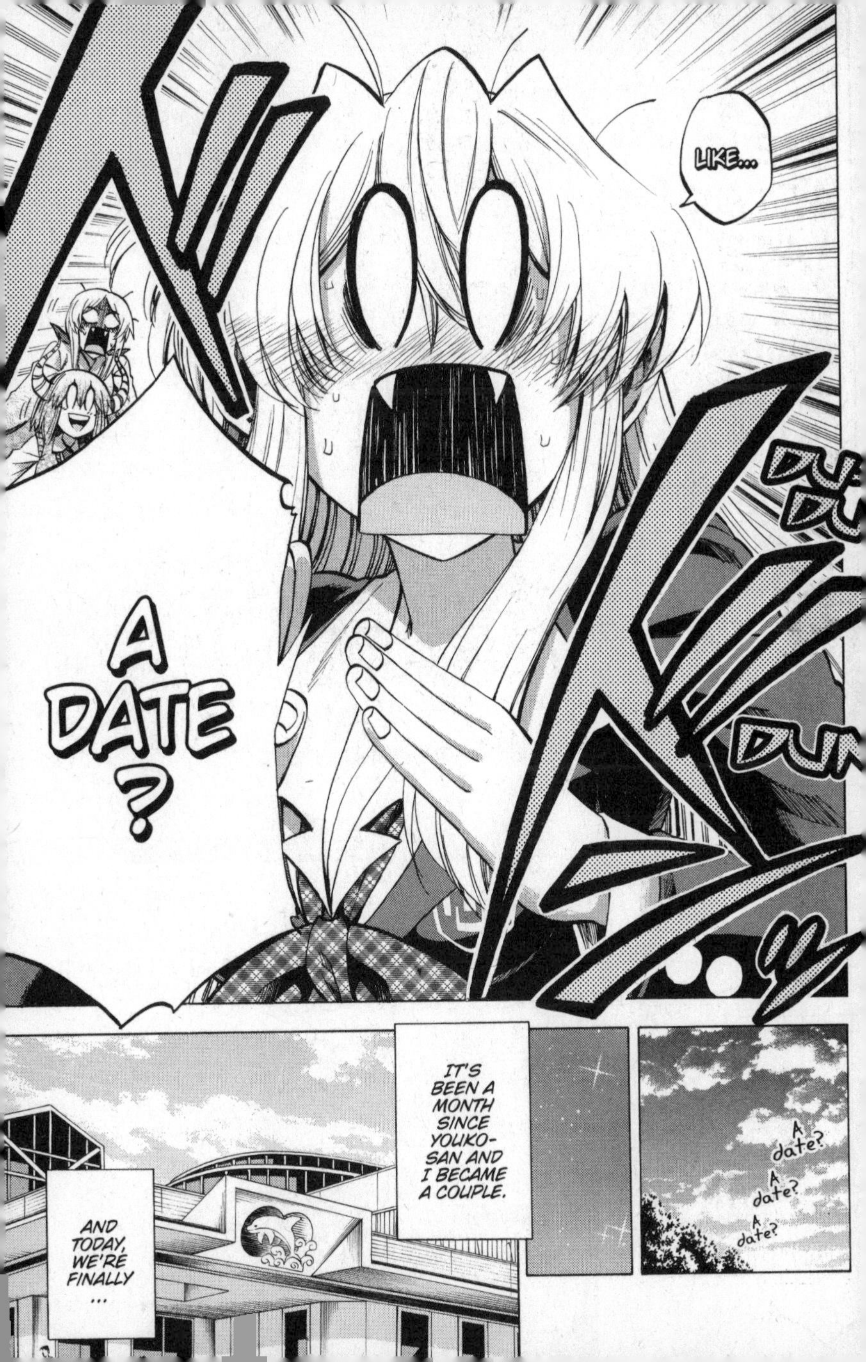
LIKE...
DUN DUN DUN
A DATE?
A date? A date? A date?
IT'S BEEN A MONTH SINCE YOUKO-SAN AND I BECAME A COUPLE.
AND TODAY, WE'RE FINALLY ...

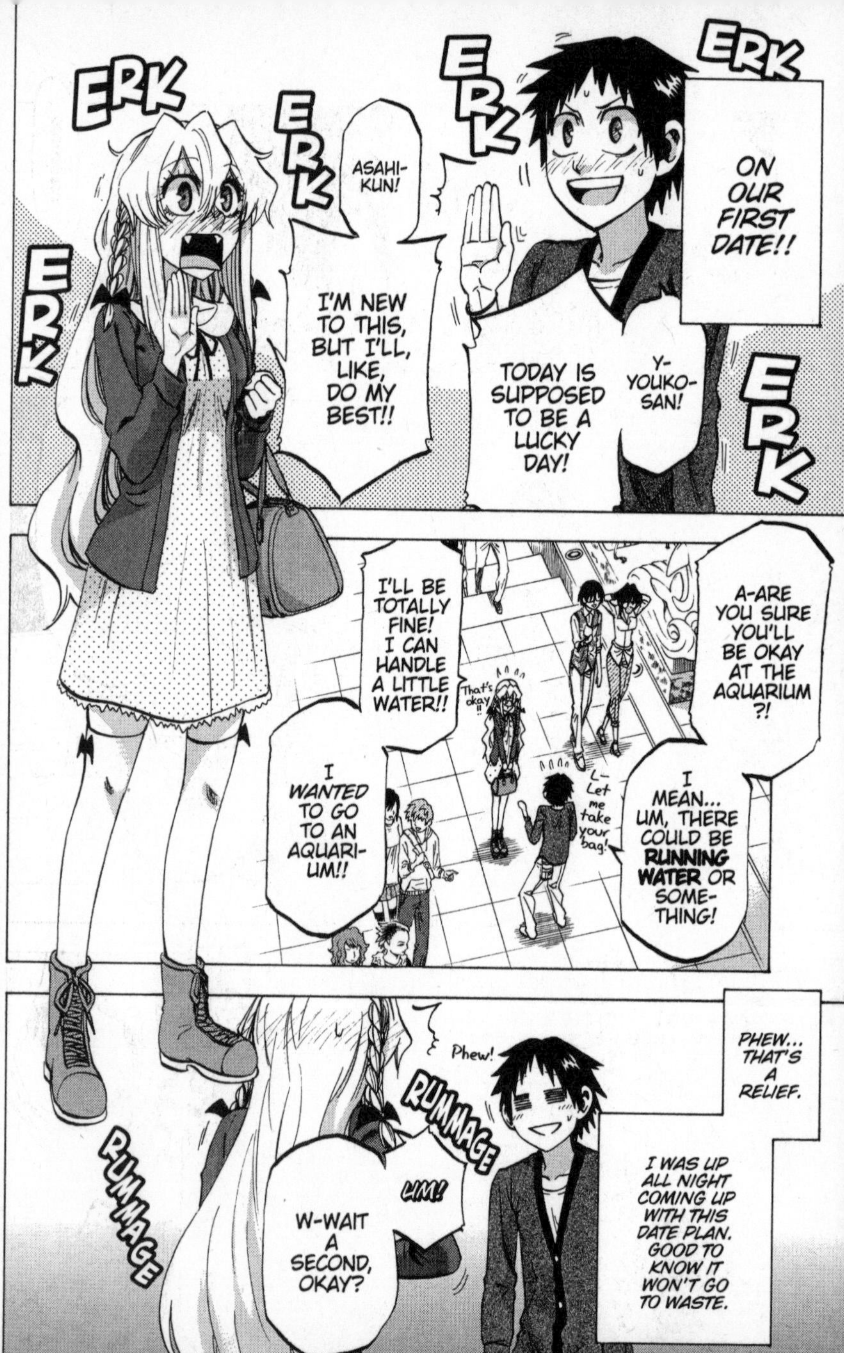
ERK
ON OUR FIRST DATE!!
ERK
Y-YOUKO-SAN!
TODAY IS SUPPOSED TO BE A LUCKY DAY!
ERK
ERK
ASAHI-KUN!
I'M NEW TO THIS, BUT I'LL, LIKE, DO MY BEST!!
ERK
ERK
A-ARE YOU SURE YOU'LL BE OKAY AT THE AQUARIUM?!
I MEAN... UM, THERE COULD BE **RUNNING WATER** OR SOME-THING!
L-Let me take your bag!
I'LL BE TOTALLY FINE! I CAN HANDLE A LITTLE WATER!!
That's okay!!
I WANTED TO GO TO AN AQUARI-UM!!
PHEW... THAT'S A RELIEF.
I WAS UP ALL NIGHT COMING UP WITH THIS DATE PLAN. GOOD TO KNOW IT WON'T GO TO WASTE.
Phew!
RUMMAGE
UM!
W-WAIT A SECOND, OKAY?
RUMMAGE

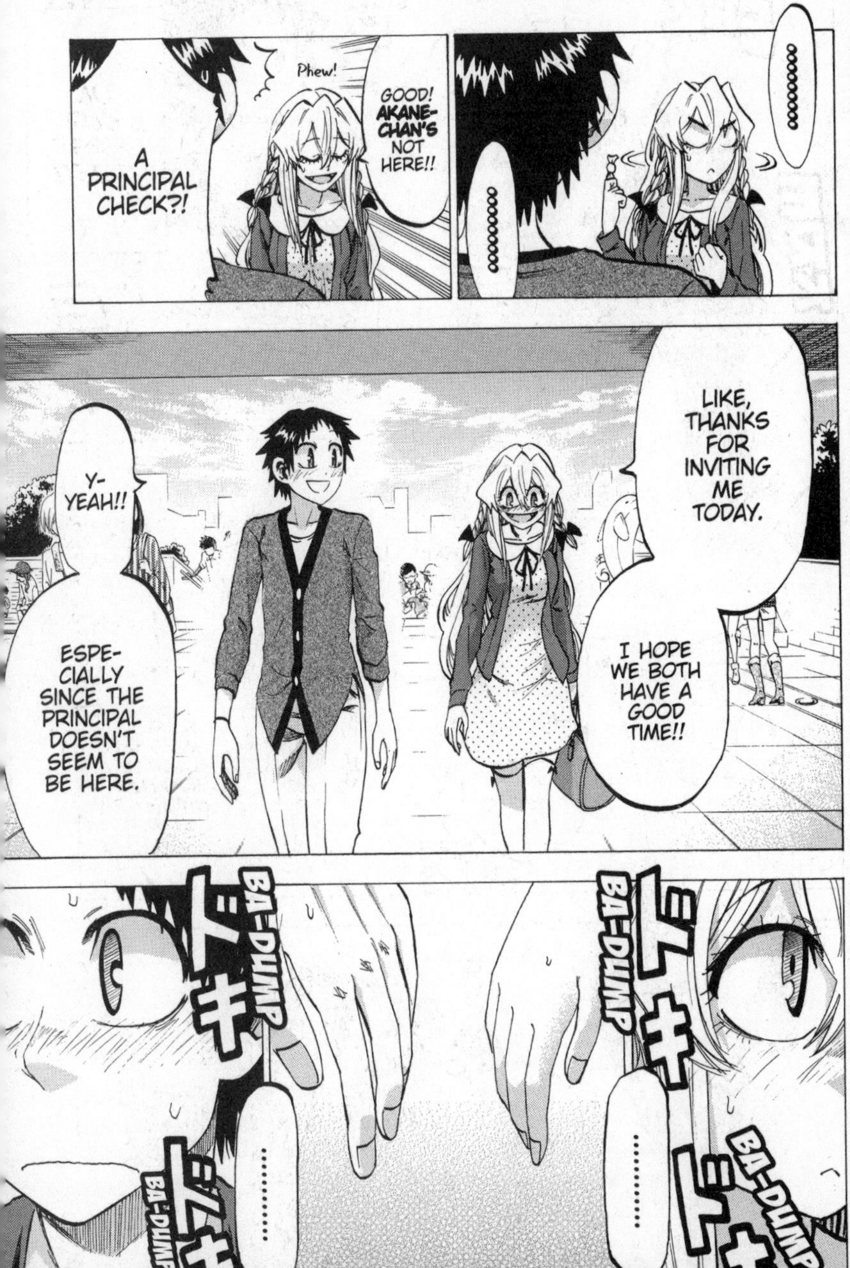
……
……
Phew!
GOOD! AKANE-CHAN'S NOT HERE!!
A PRINCIPAL CHECK?!
LIKE, THANKS FOR INVITING ME TODAY.
I HOPE WE BOTH HAVE A GOOD TIME!!
Y-YEAH!!
ESPE-CIALLY SINCE THE PRINCIPAL DOESN'T SEEM TO BE HERE.
BA-DUMP
BA-DUMP
……
BA-DUMP
BA-DUMP
……

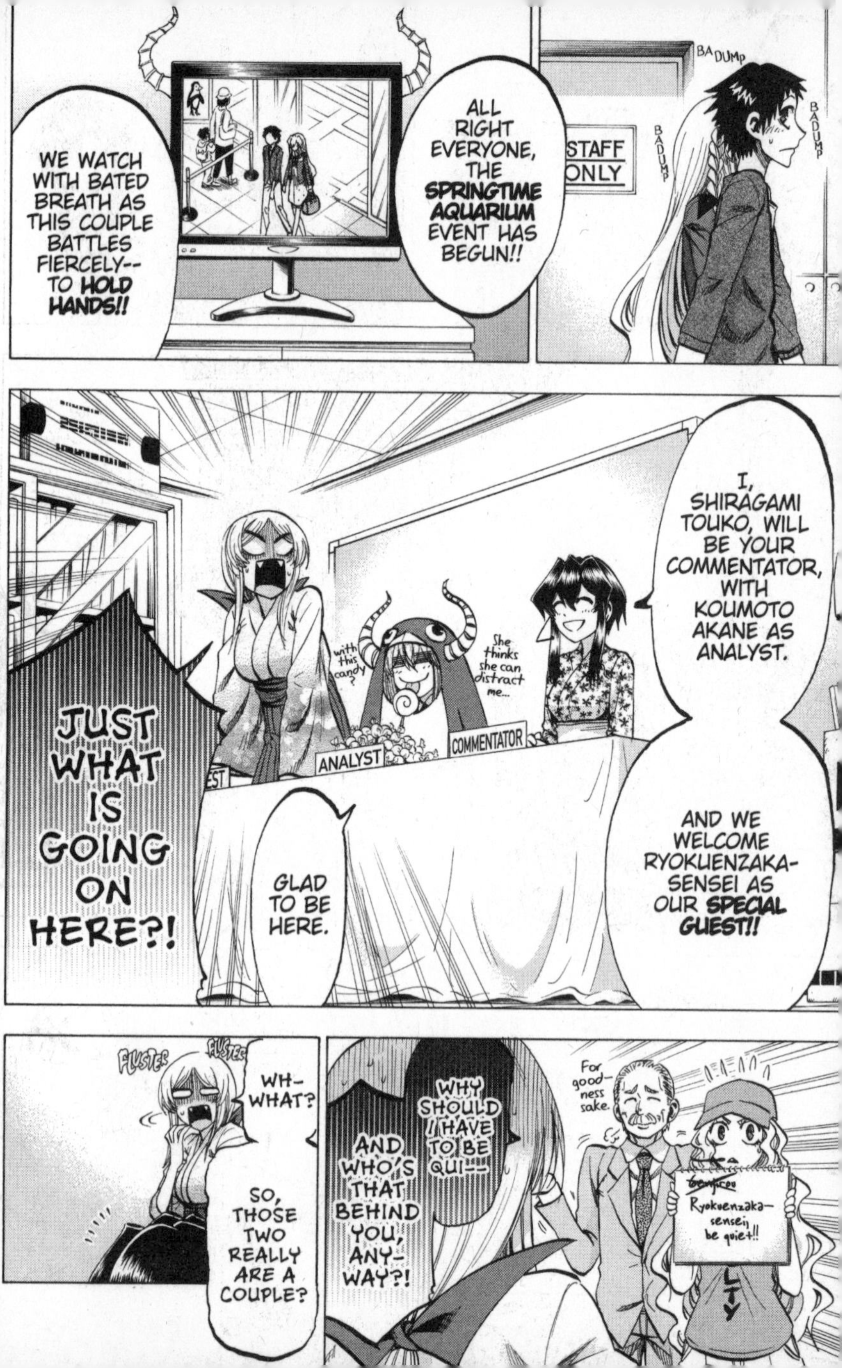
BADUMP
BADUMP
BADUMP
STAFF ONLY
ALL RIGHT EVERYONE, THE SPRINGTIME AQUARIUM EVENT HAS BEGUN!!
WE WATCH WITH BATED BREATH AS THIS COUPLE BATTLES FIERCELY-- TO HOLD HANDS!!
I, SHIRAGAMI TOUKO, WILL BE YOUR COMMENTATOR, WITH KOUMOTO AKANE AS ANALYST.
She thinks she can distract me...
with this candy?
AND WE WELCOME RYOKUENZAKA-SENSEI AS OUR SPECIAL GUEST!!
COMMENTATOR
ANALYST
GLAD TO BE HERE.
JUST WHAT IS GOING ON HERE?!
For goodness sake.
Ryokuenzaka-sensei, be quiet!!
WHY SHOULD I HAVE TO BE QUI--
AND WHO'S THAT BEHIND YOU, ANY-WAY?!
FLUSTER
FLUSTER
WH-WHAT?
SO, THOSE TWO REALLY ARE A COUPLE?

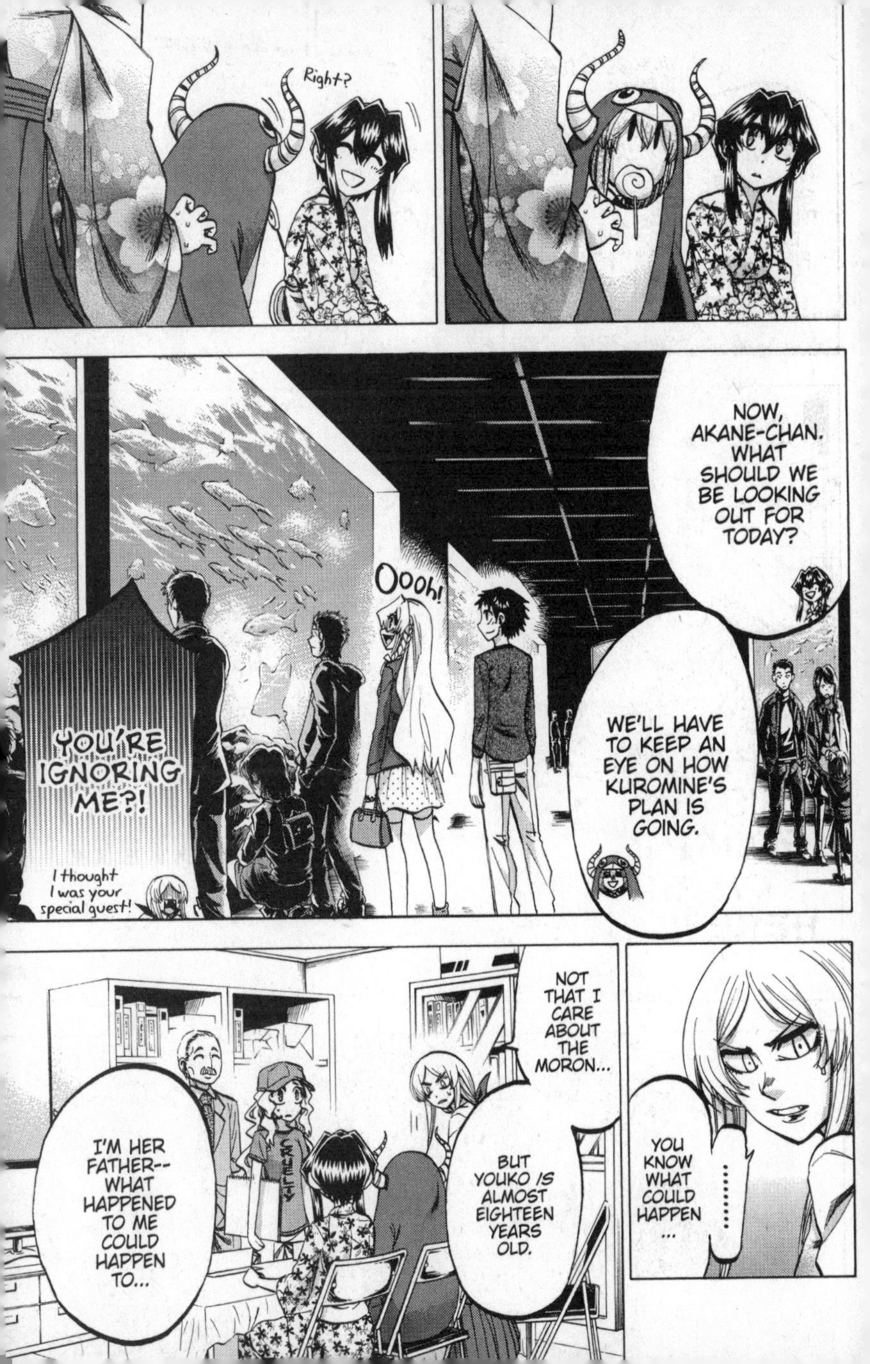
Right?
NOW, AKANE-CHAN. WHAT SHOULD WE BE LOOKING OUT FOR TODAY?
WE'LL HAVE TO KEEP AN EYE ON HOW KUROMINE'S PLAN IS GOING.
Oooh!
YOU'RE IGNORING ME?!
I thought I was your special guest!
YOU KNOW WHAT COULD HAPPEN...
......
NOT THAT I CARE ABOUT THE MORON...
BUT YOUKO IS ALMOST EIGHTEEN YEARS OLD.
I'M HER FATHER-- WHAT HAPPENED TO ME COULD HAPPEN TO...

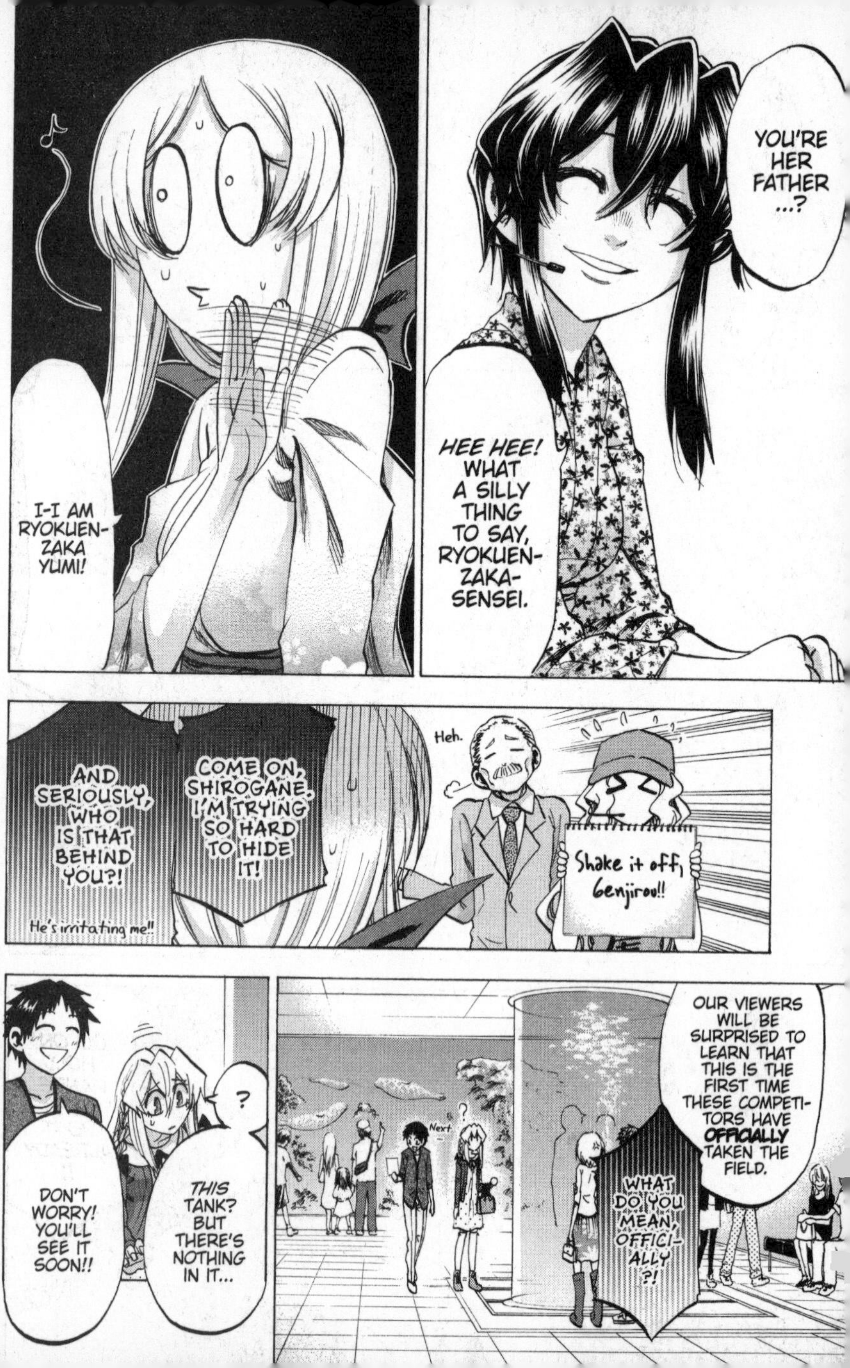
YOU'RE HER FATHER ...?
HEE HEE! WHAT A SILLY THING TO SAY, RYOKUEN-ZAKA-SENSEI.
I-I AM RYOKUEN-ZAKA YUMI!
Heh.
Shake it off, Genjirou!!
COME ON, SHIROGANE, I'M TRYING SO HARD TO HIDE IT!
AND SERIOUSLY, WHO IS THAT BEHIND YOU?!
He's irritating me!!
OUR VIEWERS WILL BE SURPRISED TO LEARN THAT THIS IS THE FIRST TIME THESE COMPETITORS HAVE OFFICIALLY TAKEN THE FIELD.
WHAT DO YOU MEAN, OFFICIALLY?!
?
Next
?
THIS TANK? BUT THERE'S NOTHING IN IT...
DON'T WORRY! YOU'LL SEE IT SOON!!

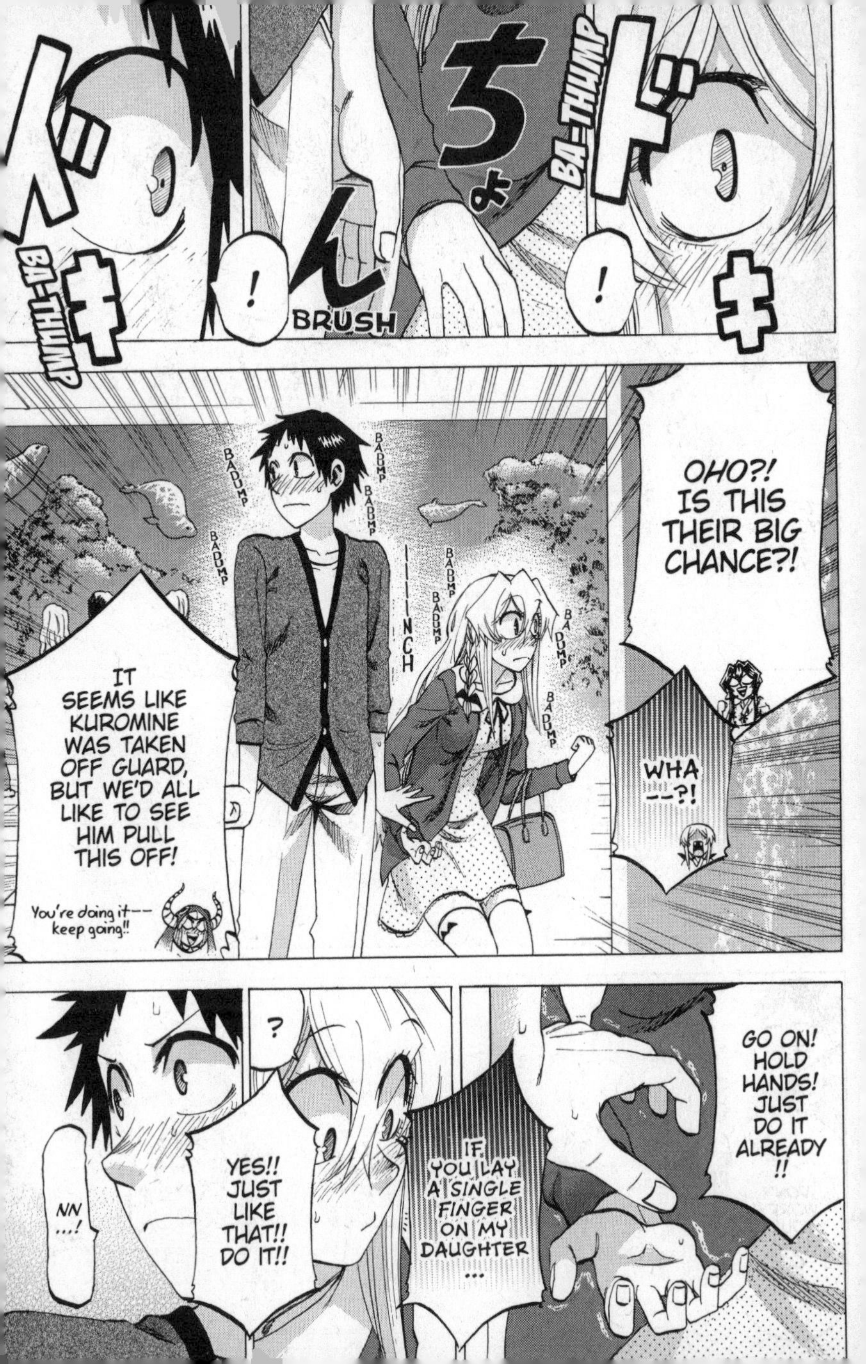

ドキ
BA-THUMP
!
ちょん
BRUSH
ドキ
BA-THUMP
!
OHO?! IS THIS THEIR BIG CHANCE?!
WHA--?!
BADUMP BADUMP BADUMP
INCH
BADUMP BADUMP BADUMP BADUMP
IT SEEMS LIKE KUROMINE WAS TAKEN OFF GUARD, BUT WE'D ALL LIKE TO SEE HIM PULL THIS OFF!
You're doing it-- keep going!!
GO ON! HOLD HANDS! JUST DO IT ALREADY!!
IF YOU LAY A SINGLE FINGER ON MY DAUGHTER...
YES!! JUST LIKE THAT!! DO IT!!
?
NN...!

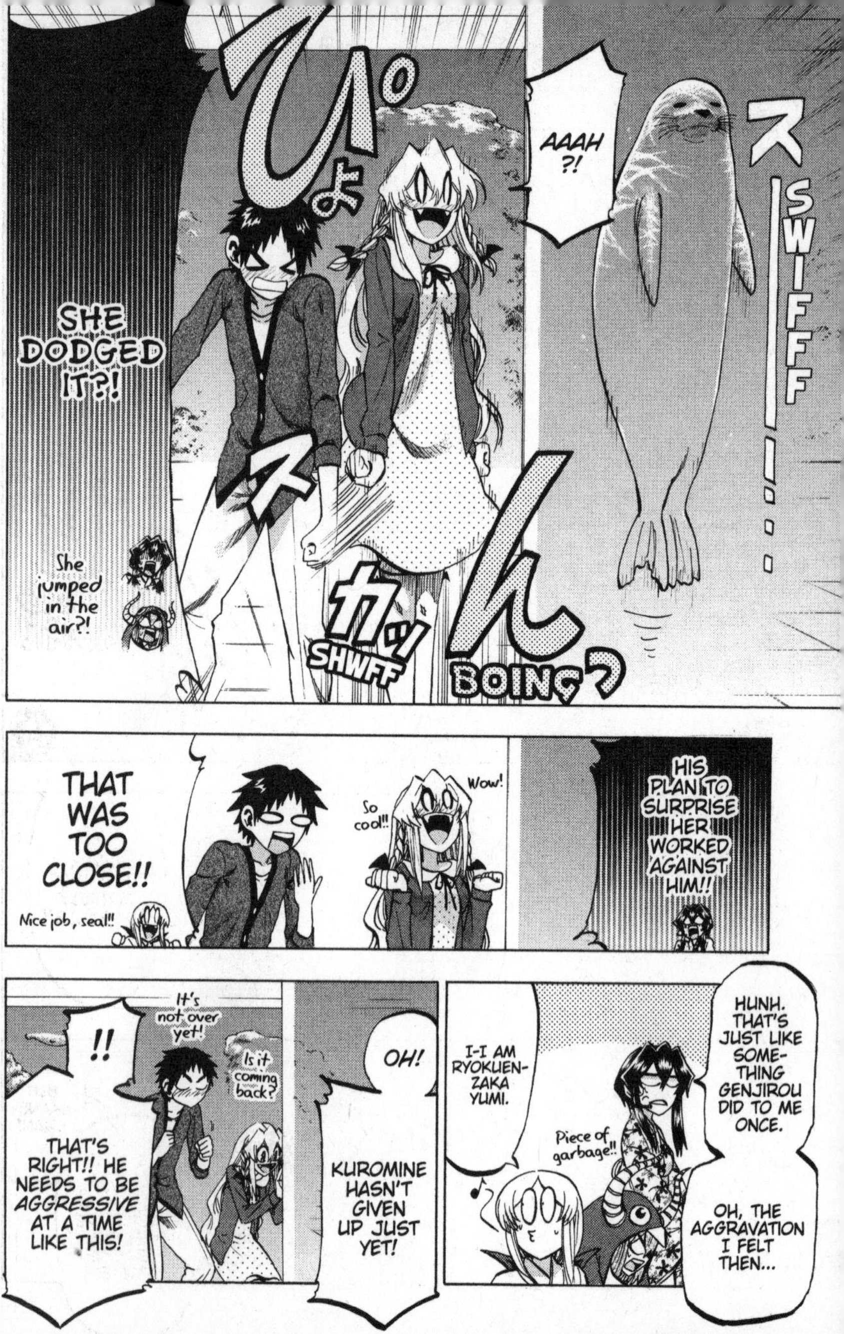

スー
SWIFFF
AAAH ?!
ぴょ
ん
BOING
カッ
SHWFF
ス
SHE DODGED IT?!
She jumped in the air?!
HIS PLAN TO SURPRISE HER WORKED AGAINST HIM!!
Wow!
So cool!!
THAT WAS TOO CLOSE!!
Nice job, seal!!
HUNH. THAT'S JUST LIKE SOMETHING GENJIROU DID TO ME ONCE.
OH, THE AGGRAVATION I FELT THEN...
I-I AM RYOKUEN-ZAKA YUMI.
Piece of garbage!!
OH!
KUROMINE HASN'T GIVEN UP JUST YET!
It's not over yet!
Is it coming back?
!!
THAT'S RIGHT!! HE NEEDS TO BE *AGGRESSIVE* AT A TIME LIKE THIS!

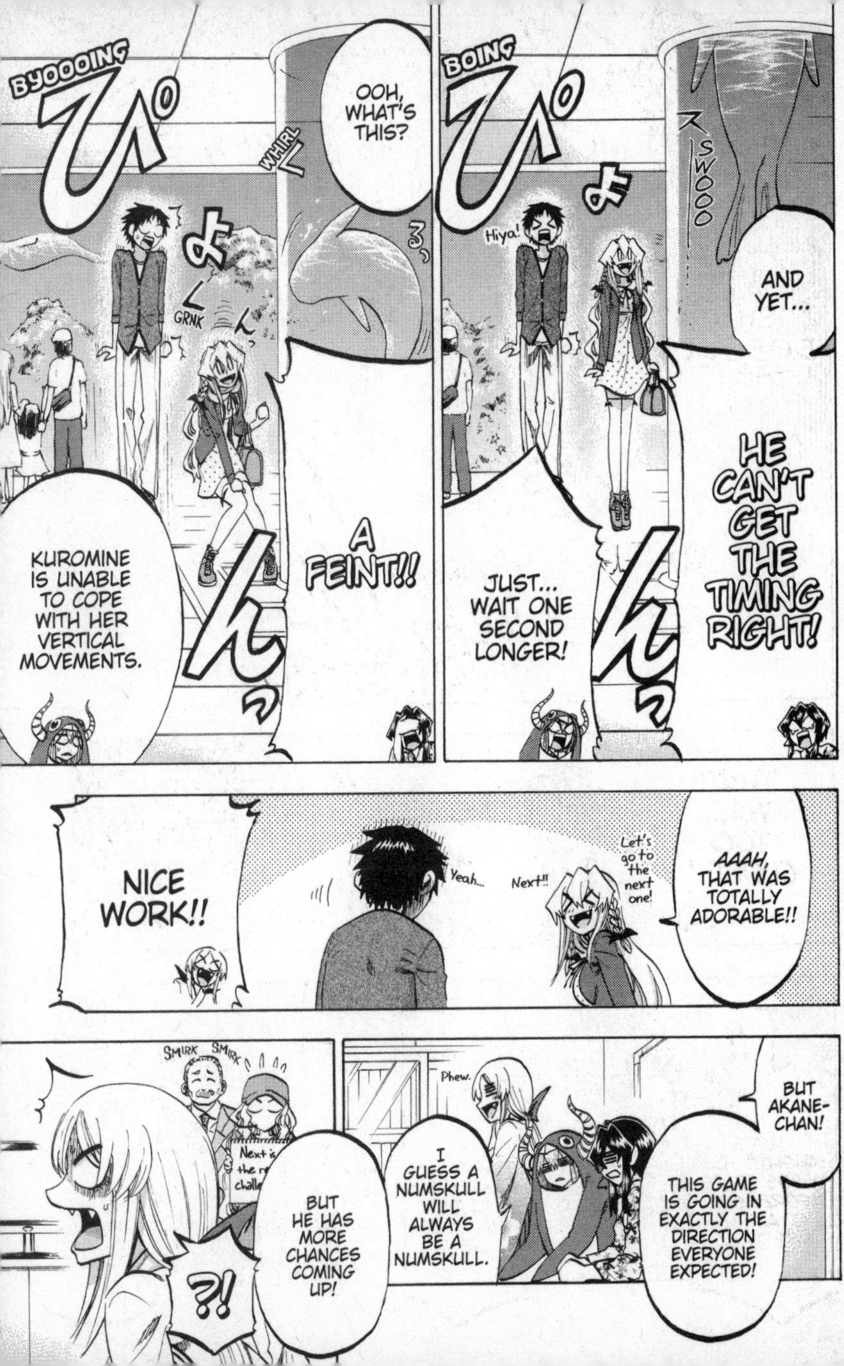
BOING
SWOOO
AND YET...
Hiya!
HE CAN'T GET THE TIMING RIGHT!
JUST... WAIT ONE SECOND LONGER!
OOH, WHAT'S THIS?
WHIRL
BYOOOING
GRNK
A FEINT!!
KUROMINE IS UNABLE TO COPE WITH HER VERTICAL MOVEMENTS.
AAAH, THAT WAS TOTALLY ADORABLE!!
Let's go to the next one!
Next!!
Yeah...
NICE WORK!!
BUT AKANE-CHAN!
THIS GAME IS GOING IN EXACTLY THE DIRECTION EVERYONE EXPECTED!
Phew.
I GUESS A NUMSKULL WILL ALWAYS BE A NUMSKULL.
BUT HE HAS MORE CHANCES COMING UP!
SMIRK SMIRK
?!

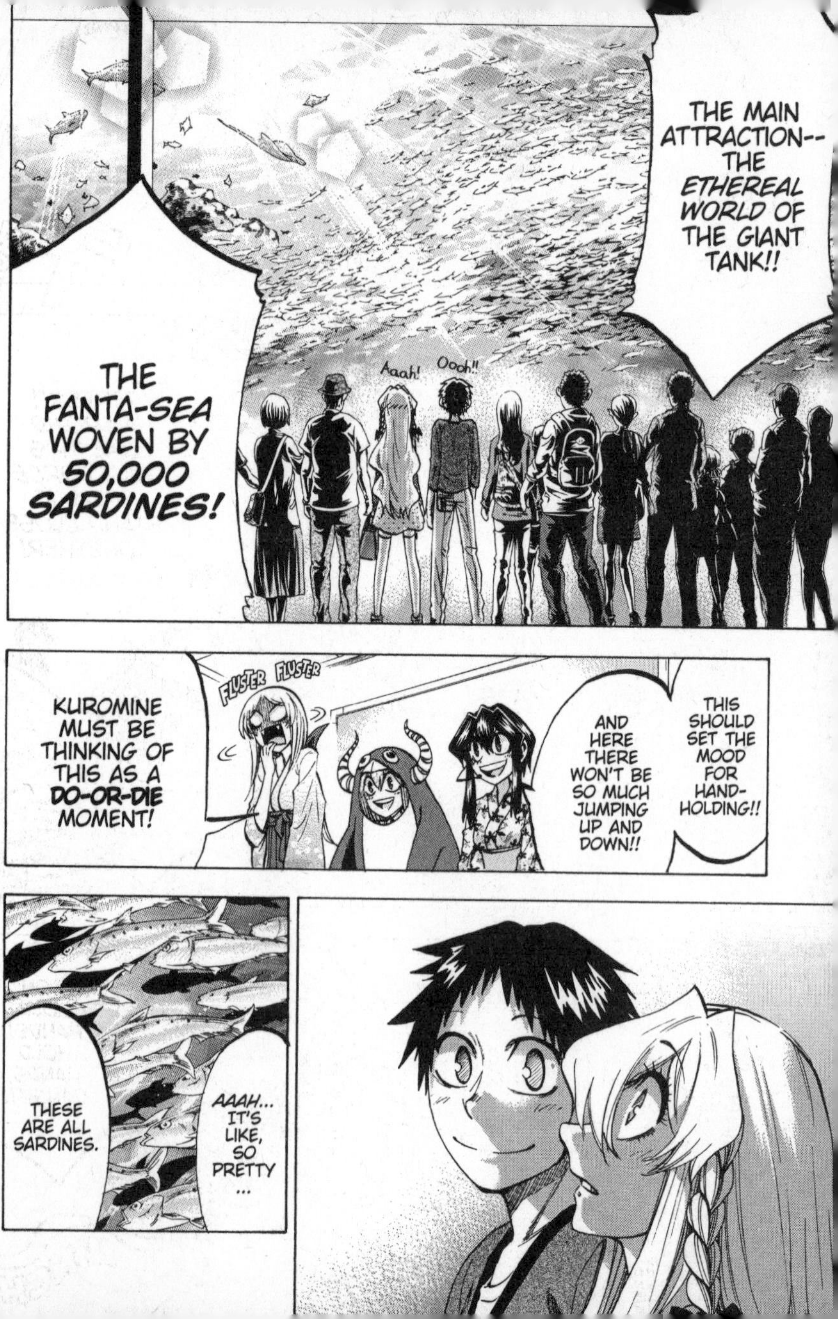
THE MAIN ATTRACTION-- THE ETHEREAL WORLD OF THE GIANT TANK!!
Oooh!!
Aaah!
THE FANTA-SEA WOVEN BY 50,000 SARDINES!
THIS SHOULD SET THE MOOD FOR HAND-HOLDING!!
AND HERE THERE WON'T BE SO MUCH JUMPING UP AND DOWN!!
FLUSTER FLUSTER
KUROMINE MUST BE THINKING OF THIS AS A DO-OR-DIE MOMENT!
AAAH... IT'S LIKE, SO PRETTY ...
THESE ARE ALL SARDINES.

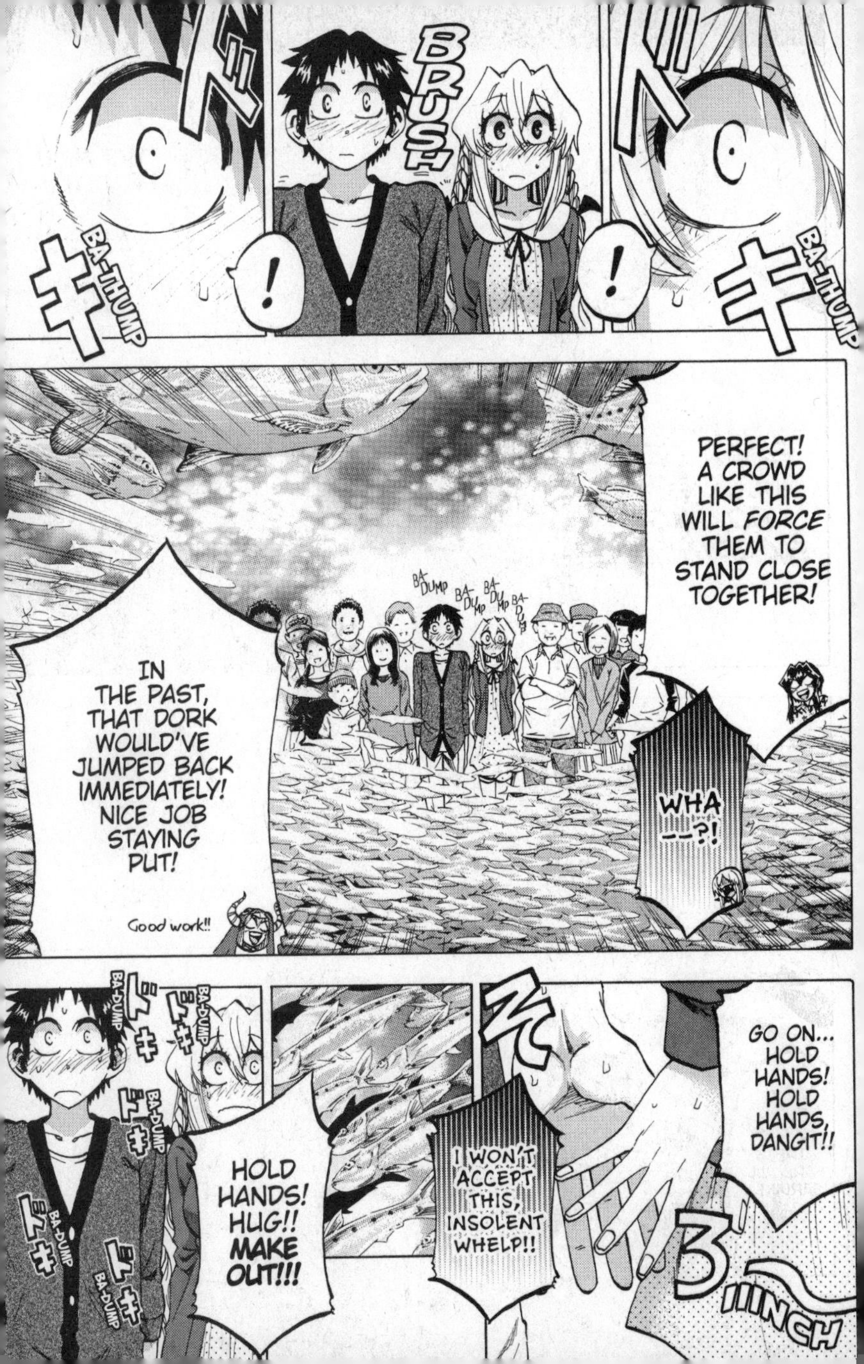
BA-THUMP
!
BRUSH
!
BA-THUMP
PERFECT! A CROWD LIKE THIS WILL *FORCE* THEM TO STAND CLOSE TOGETHER!
WHA--?!
BA-DUMP BA-DUMP BA-DUMP BA-DUMP
IN THE PAST, THAT DORK WOULD'VE JUMPED BACK IMMEDIATELY! NICE JOB STAYING PUT!
Good work!!
GO ON... HOLD HANDS! HOLD HANDS, DANGIT!!
IIINCH
I WON'T ACCEPT THIS, INSOLENT WHELP!!
HOLD HANDS! HUG!! MAKE OUT!!!
BA-DUMP
BA-DUMP
BA-DUMP
BA-DUMP

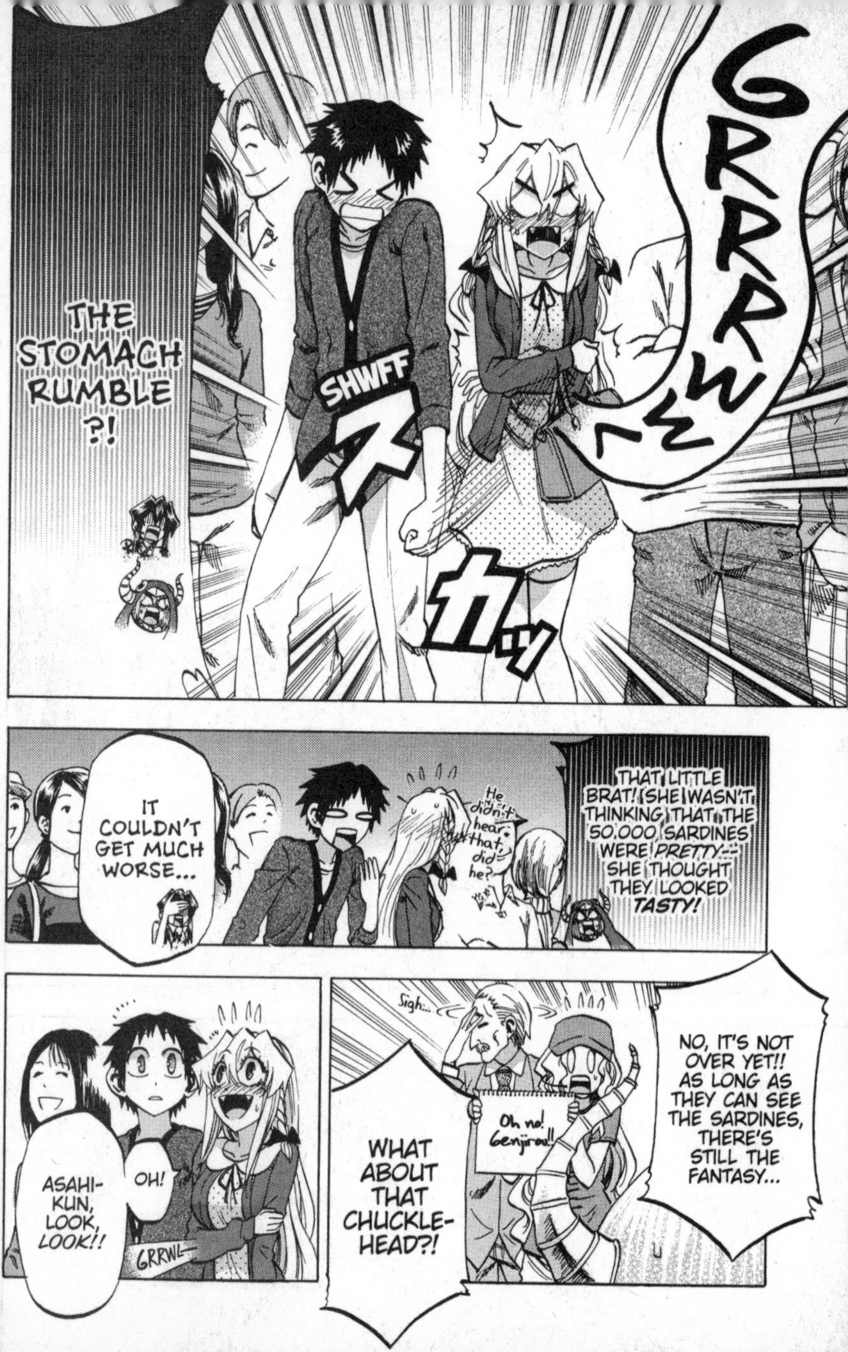
GRRRW~
SHWFF
ス
カッ
THE STOMACH RUMBLE?!
THAT LITTLE BRAT! SHE WASN'T THINKING THAT THE 50,000 SARDINES WERE *PRETTY*-- SHE THOUGHT THEY LOOKED *TASTY!*
He didn't hear that, did he?
IT COULDN'T GET MUCH WORSE...
NO, IT'S NOT OVER YET!! AS LONG AS THEY CAN SEE THE SARDINES, THERE'S STILL THE FANTASY...
Sigh...
Oh no! Genjirou!!
WHAT ABOUT THAT CHUCKLE-HEAD?!
OH!
ASAHI-KUN, LOOK, LOOK!!
GRRWL

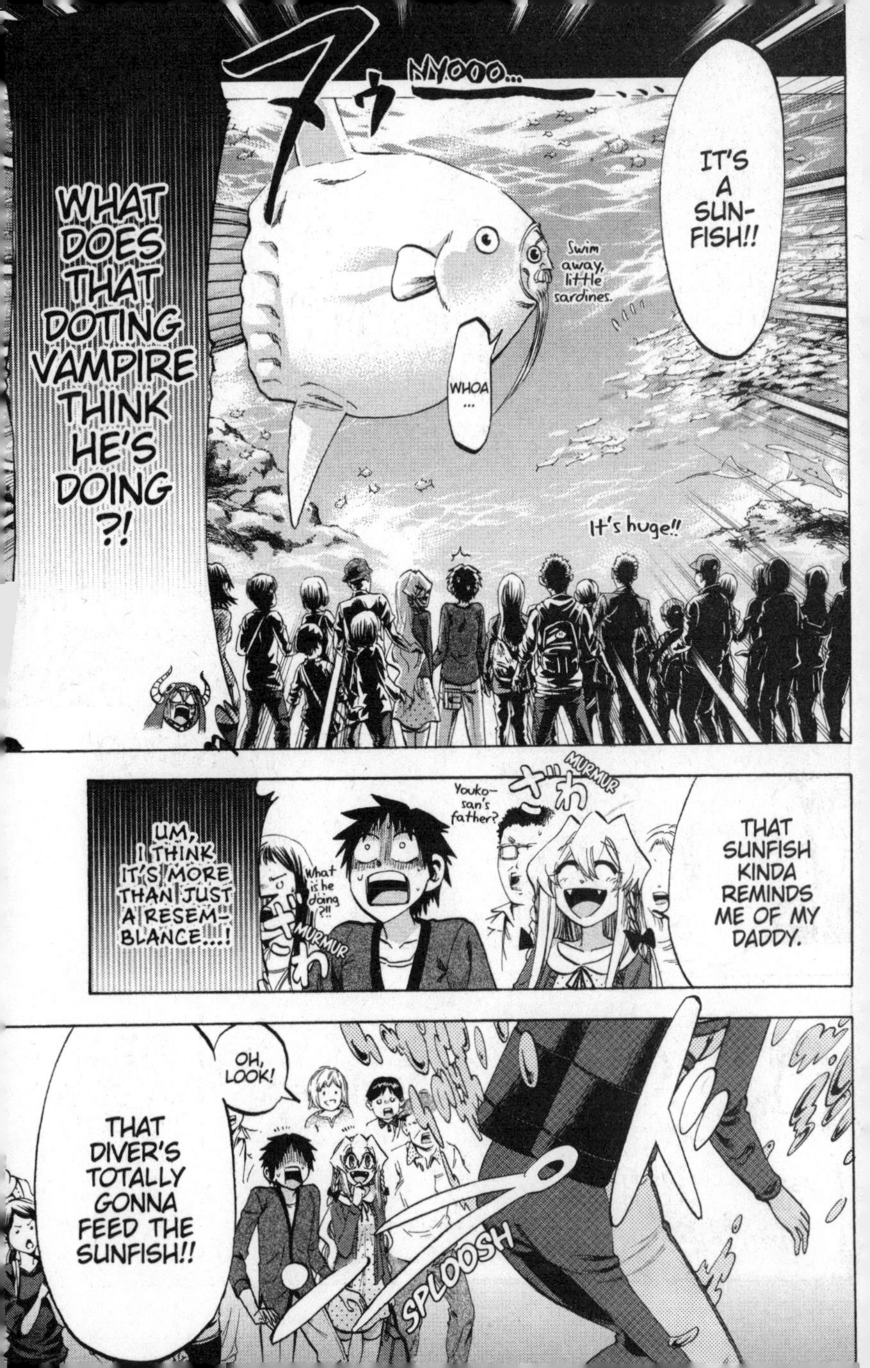
NYOOO...
IT'S A SUN-FISH!!
Swim away, little sardines.
WHOA...
It's huge!!
WHAT DOES THAT DOTING VAMPIRE THINK HE'S DOING?!
THAT SUNFISH KINDA REMINDS ME OF MY DADDY.
MURMUR
Youko-san's father?
What is he doing?!!
UM, I THINK IT'S MORE THAN JUST A RESEM-BLANCE...!
MURMUR
OH, LOOK!
THAT DIVER'S TOTALLY GONNA FEED THE SUNFISH!!
SPLOOSH

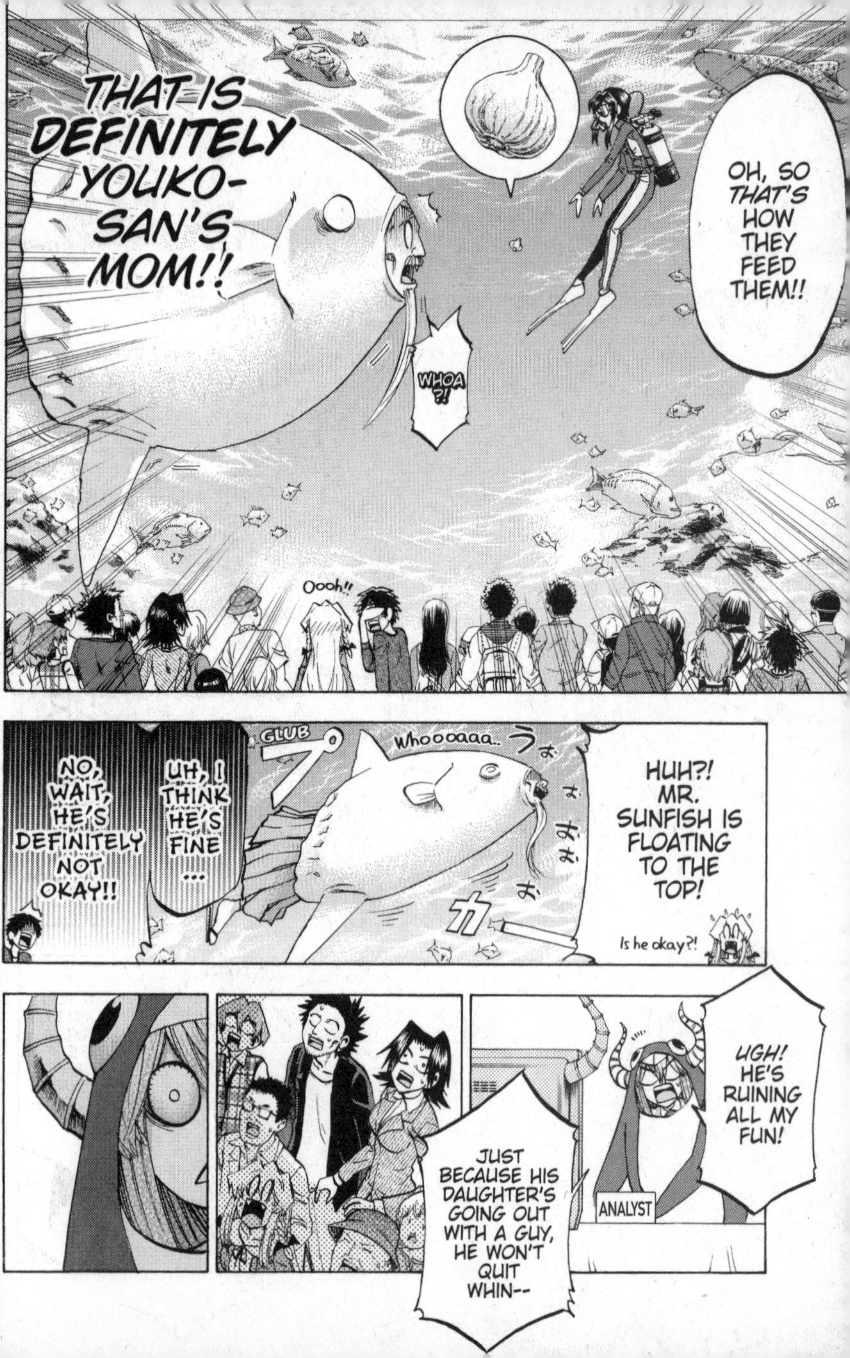
OH, SO THAT'S HOW THEY FEED THEM!!
THAT IS DEFINITELY YOUKO-SAN'S MOM!!
WHOA ?!
Oooh!!
HUH?! MR. SUNFISH IS FLOATING TO THE TOP!
Is he okay?!
Whoooaaa..
GLUB
UH, I THINK HE'S FINE ...
NO, WAIT, HE'S DEFINITELY NOT OKAY!!
UGH! HE'S RUINING ALL MY FUN!
ANALYST
JUST BECAUSE HIS DAUGHTER'S GOING OUT WITH A GUY, HE WON'T QUIT WHIN--

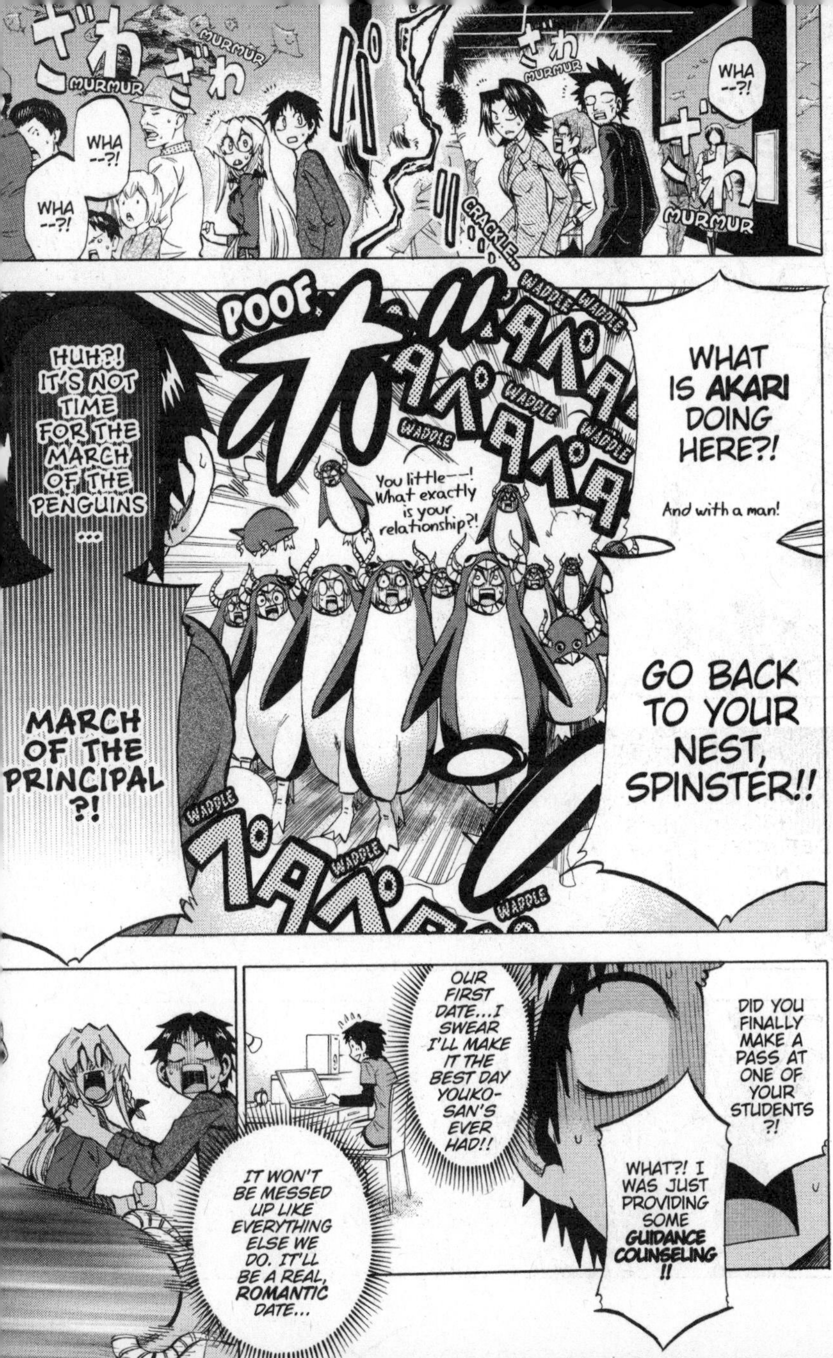
WHA --?!
MURMUR
MURMUR
CRACKLE...
MURMUR
MURMUR
WHA --?!
WHA --?!
WHAT IS AKARI DOING HERE?!
And with a man!
GO BACK TO YOUR NEST, SPINSTER!!
WADDLE WADDLE
WADDLE
WADDLE
WADDLE
POOF
You little--! What exactly is your relationship?!
HUH?! IT'S NOT TIME FOR THE MARCH OF THE PENGUINS ...
MARCH OF THE PRINCIPAL ?!
WADDLE
WADDLE
WADDLE
DID YOU FINALLY MAKE A PASS AT ONE OF YOUR STUDENTS ?!
WHAT?! I WAS JUST PROVIDING SOME GUIDANCE COUNSELING !!
OUR FIRST DATE...I SWEAR I'LL MAKE IT THE BEST DAY YOUKO-SAN'S EVER HAD!!
IT WON'T BE MESSED UP LIKE EVERYTHING ELSE WE DO. IT'LL BE A REAL, ROMANTIC DATE...

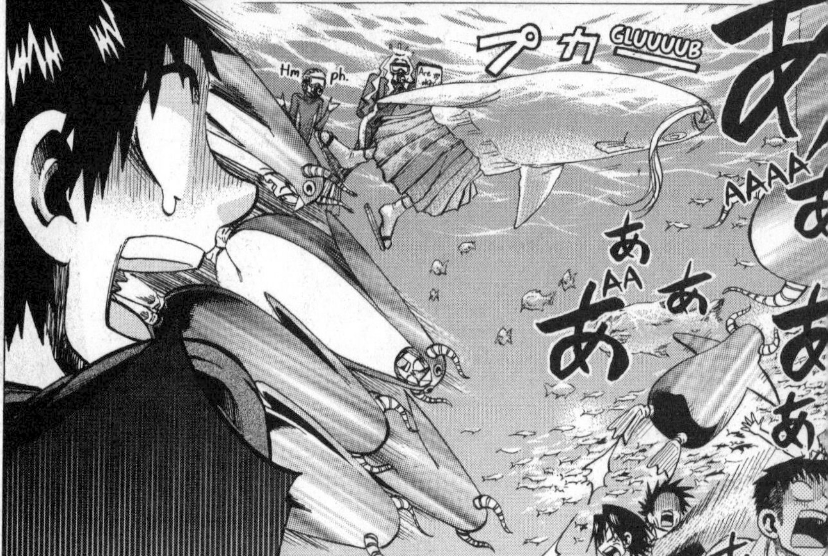
プカ
GLUUUUB
Hm ph.
あ
AAAA
あ
AA
あ
あ
IT'S ALREADY MESSED UP!!
あ
AAAA
あ
あ
AAAA
あ
あ
AH!!
My long-awaited first date!!

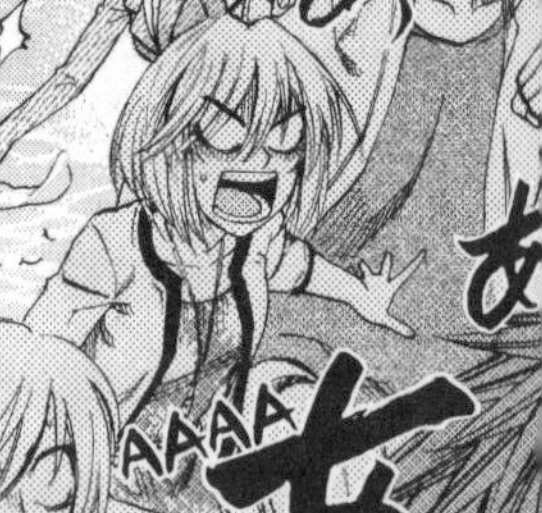
DUE TO A NECES-SARY INSPEC-TION, THE AQUARI-UM--
HUFF HUFF

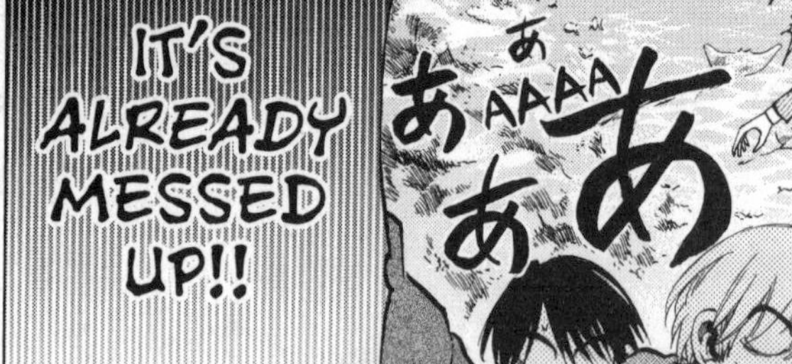
I--
I SPENT ALL NIGHT WRITING THIS DATE PLAN...
Now we're not even in the aquarium...
HUFF HUFF
HUFF HUFF
NN-NGH...!
I TOTALLY KNEW AKANE-CHAN WOULD TAG ALONG...

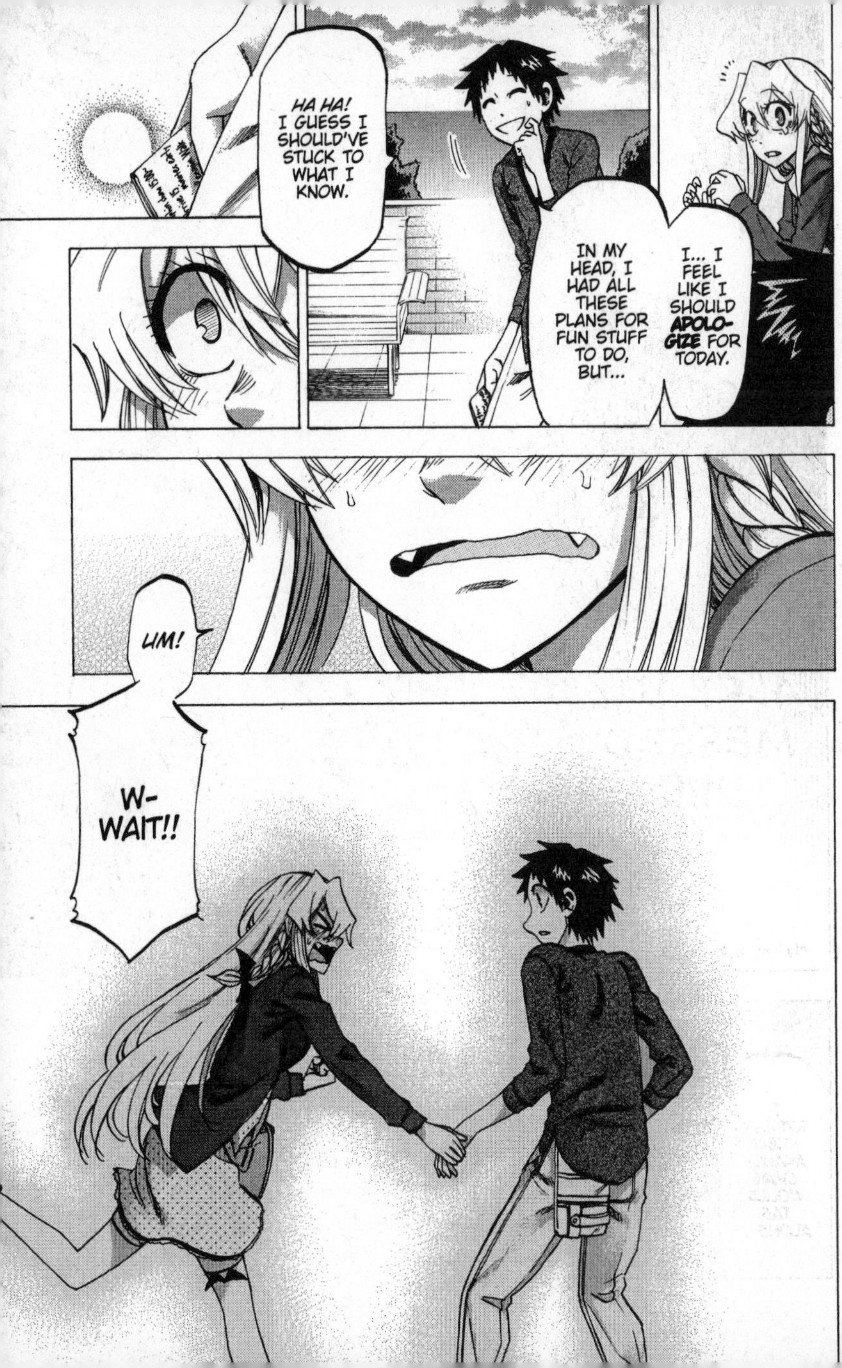
I... I FEEL LIKE I SHOULD APOLOGIZE FOR TODAY.
IN MY HEAD, I HAD ALL THESE PLANS FOR FUN STUFF TO DO, BUT...
HA HA! I GUESS I SHOULD'VE STUCK TO WHAT I KNOW.
UM!
W-WAIT!!

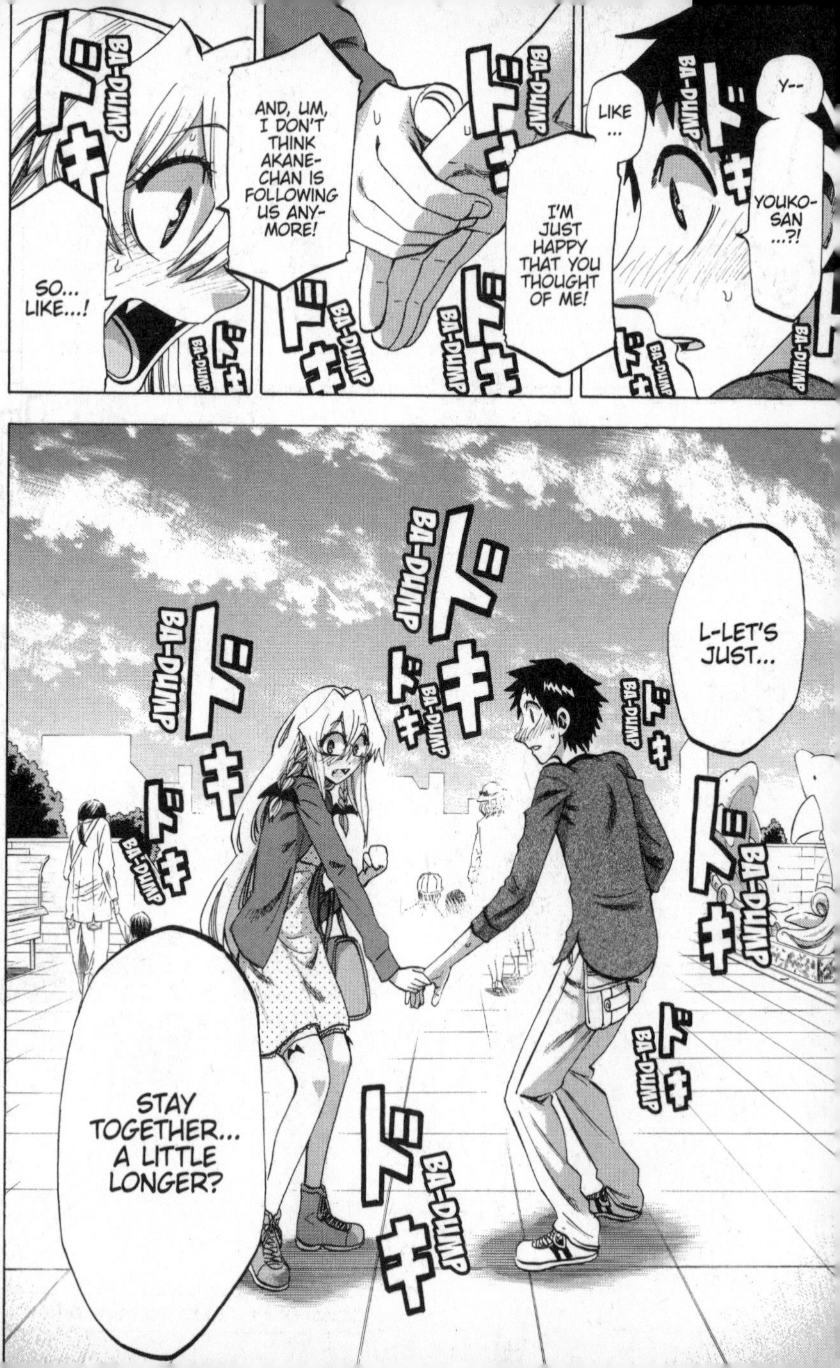
Y--
YOUKO-SAN ...?!
ドキ
BA-DUMP
LIKE ...
I'M JUST HAPPY THAT YOU THOUGHT OF ME!
ドキ
BA-DUMP
ドキ
BA-DUMP
AND, UM, I DON'T THINK AKANE-CHAN IS FOLLOWING US ANYMORE!
ドキ
BA-DUMP
ドキ
BA-DUMP
SO... LIKE...!
ドキ
BA-DUMP
L-LET'S JUST...
ドキ
BA-DUMP
ドキ
BA-DUMP
ドキ
BA-DUMP
ドキ
BA-DUMP
ドキ
BA-DUMP
ドキ
BA-DUMP
ドキ
BA-DUMP
STAY TOGETHER... A LITTLE LONGER?

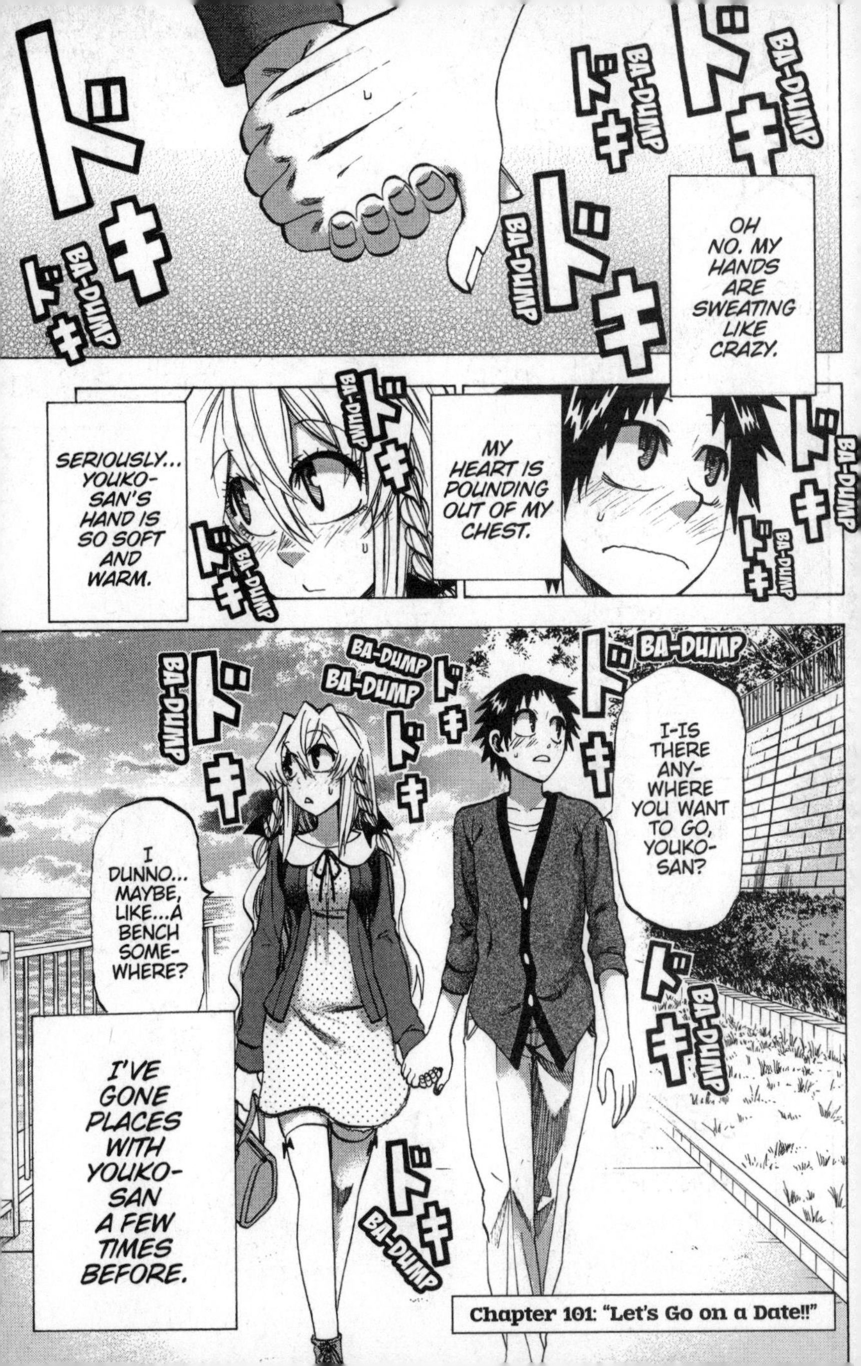

ドキ
BA-DUMP
ドキ
BA-DUMP
ドキ
BA-DUMP
ドキ
BA-DUMP
OH NO. MY HANDS ARE SWEATING LIKE CRAZY.
ドキ
BA-DUMP
ドキ
BA-DUMP
MY HEART IS POUNDING OUT OF MY CHEST.
ドキ
BA-DUMP
ドキ
BA-DUMP
SERIOUSLY... YOUKO-SAN'S HAND IS SO SOFT AND WARM.
ドキ
BA-DUMP
I-IS THERE ANY-WHERE YOU WANT TO GO, YOUKO-SAN?
ドキ
BA-DUMP
ドキ
BA-DUMP
ドキ
BA-DUMP
ドキ
BA-DUMP
I DUNNO... MAYBE, LIKE...A BENCH SOME-WHERE?
ドキ
BA-DUMP
I'VE GONE PLACES WITH YOUKO-SAN A FEW TIMES BEFORE.

Chapter 101: "Let's Go on a Date!!"

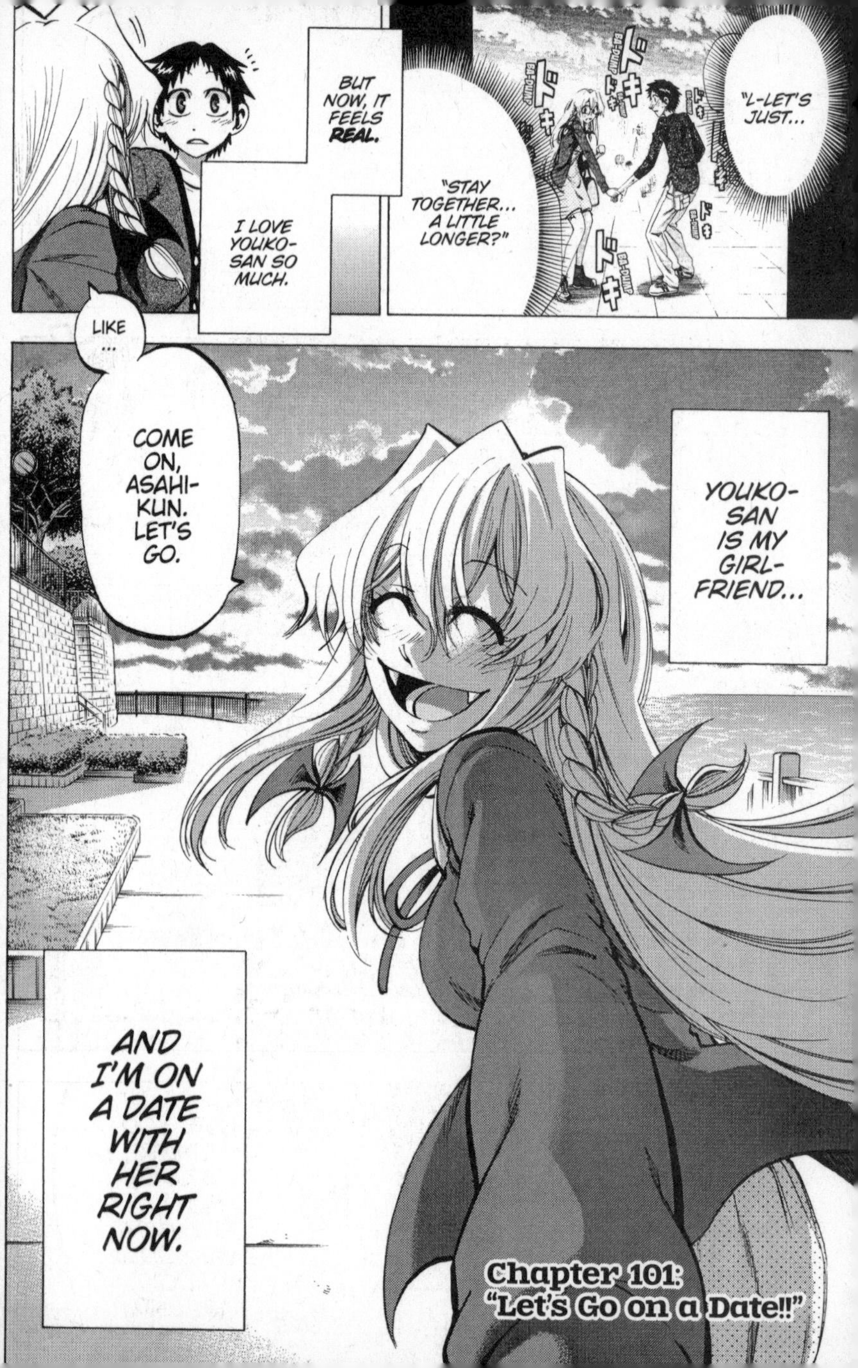
"L-LET'S JUST...
BA-DUMP ドキ
BA-DUMP ドキ
BA-DUMP ドキ
BA-DUMP ドキ
"STAY TOGETHER... A LITTLE LONGER?"
BUT NOW, IT FEELS **REAL.**
I LOVE YOUKO-SAN SO MUCH.
LIKE...
YOUKO-SAN IS MY GIRLFRIEND...
COME ON, ASAHI-KUN. LET'S GO.
AND I'M ON A DATE WITH HER RIGHT NOW.
Chapter 101: "Let's Go on a Date!!"

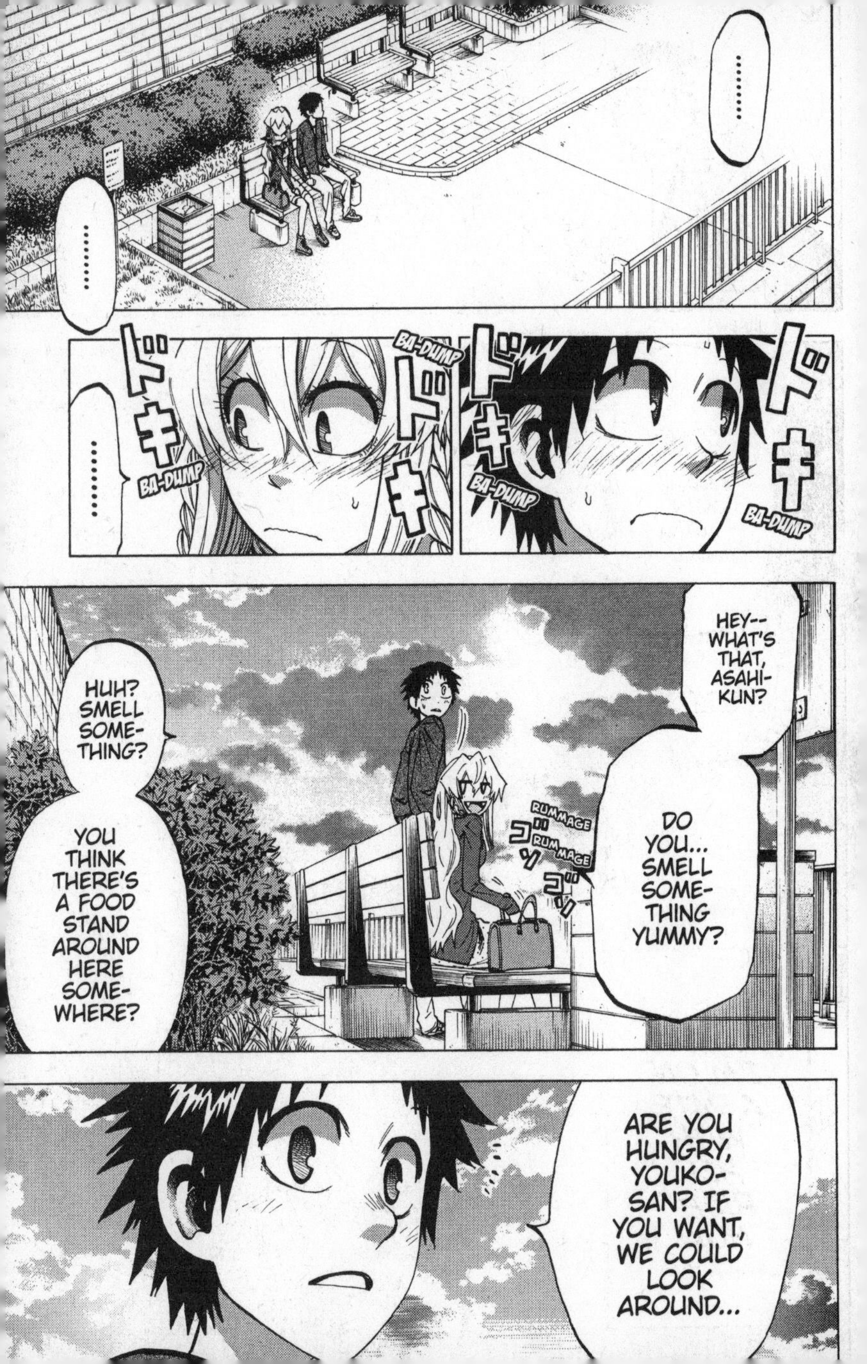
......
......
ドキ
ドキ
BA-DUMP
BA-DUMP
......
ドキ
ドキ
BA-DUMP
BA-DUMP
HEY--WHAT'S THAT, ASAHI-KUN?
DO YOU... SMELL SOMETHING YUMMY?
RUMMAGE
ゴソ
RUMMAGE
ゴソ
HUH? SMELL SOMETHING?
YOU THINK THERE'S A FOOD STAND AROUND HERE SOMEWHERE?
ARE YOU HUNGRY, YOUKO-SAN? IF YOU WANT, WE COULD LOOK AROUND...

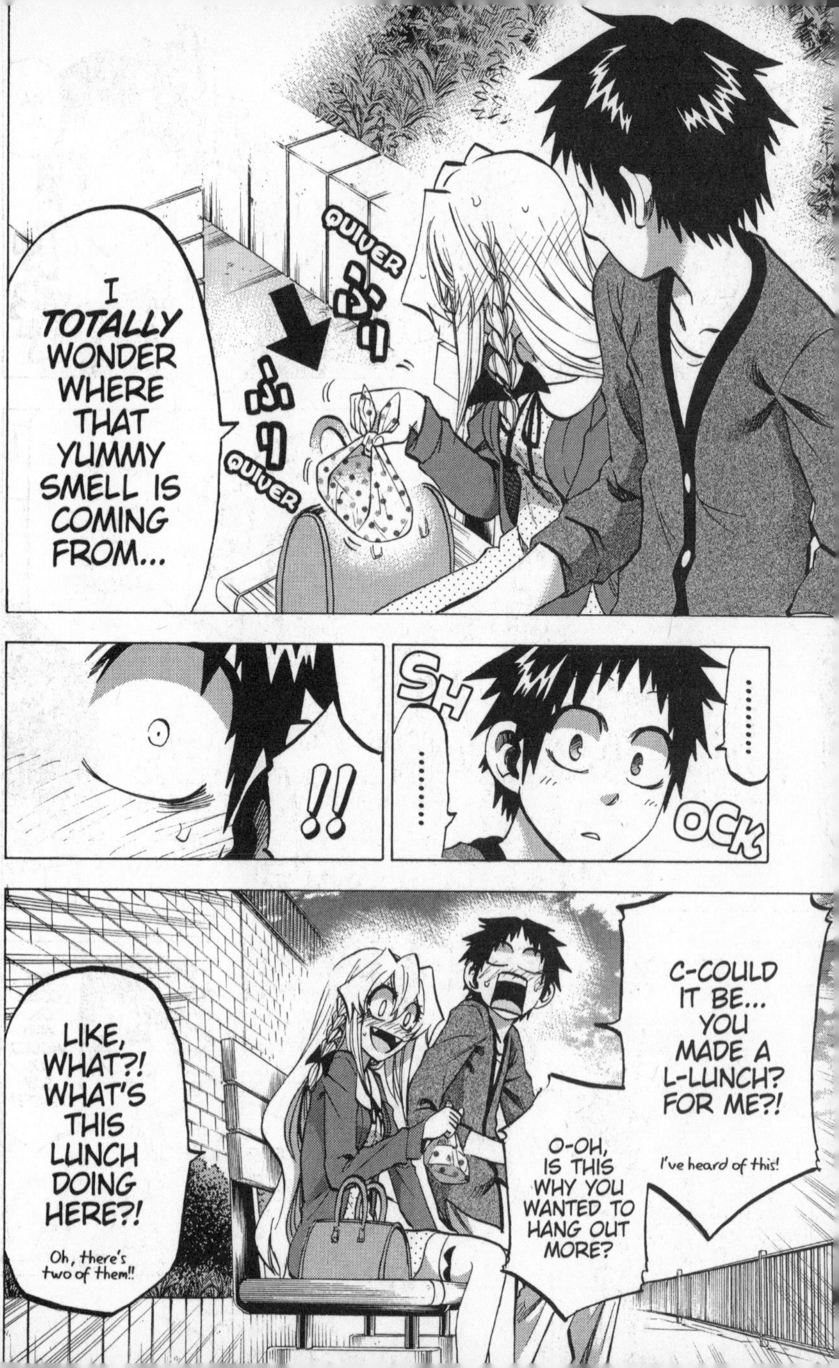
QUIVER
QUIVER
I *TOTALLY* WONDER WHERE THAT YUMMY SMELL IS COMING FROM...
SH
OCK
......
......
!!
C-COULD IT BE... YOU MADE A L-LUNCH? FOR ME?!
I've heard of this!
O-OH, IS THIS WHY YOU WANTED TO HANG OUT MORE?
LIKE, WHAT?! WHAT'S THIS LUNCH DOING HERE?!
Oh, there's two of them!!

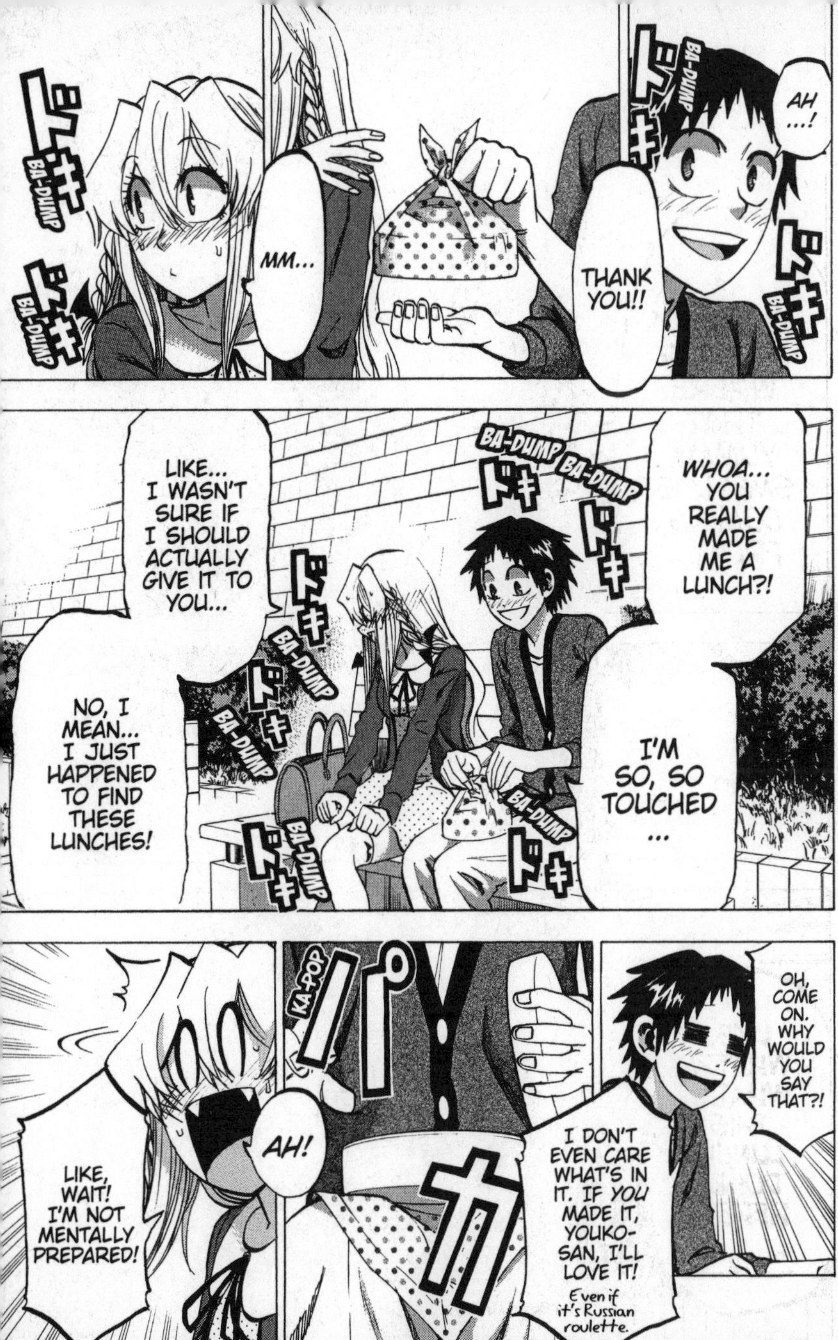
AH ...!
BA-DUMP ドキ
BA-DUMP ドキ
THANK YOU!!
MM...
BA-DUMP ドキ
BA-DUMP ドキ
WHOA... YOU REALLY MADE ME A LUNCH?!
BA-DUMP ドキ
BA-DUMP ドキ
I'M SO, SO TOUCHED ...
BA-DUMP ドキ
BA-DUMP ドキ
BA-DUMP ドキ
BA-DUMP ドキ
LIKE... I WASN'T SURE IF I SHOULD ACTUALLY GIVE IT TO YOU...
NO, I MEAN... I JUST HAPPENED TO FIND THESE LUNCHES!
OH, COME ON. WHY WOULD YOU SAY THAT?!
I DON'T EVEN CARE WHAT'S IN IT. IF YOU MADE IT, YOUKO-SAN, I'LL LOVE IT!
Even if it's Russian roulette.
KA-POP パ
カ
AH!
LIKE, WAIT! I'M NOT MENTALLY PREPARED!

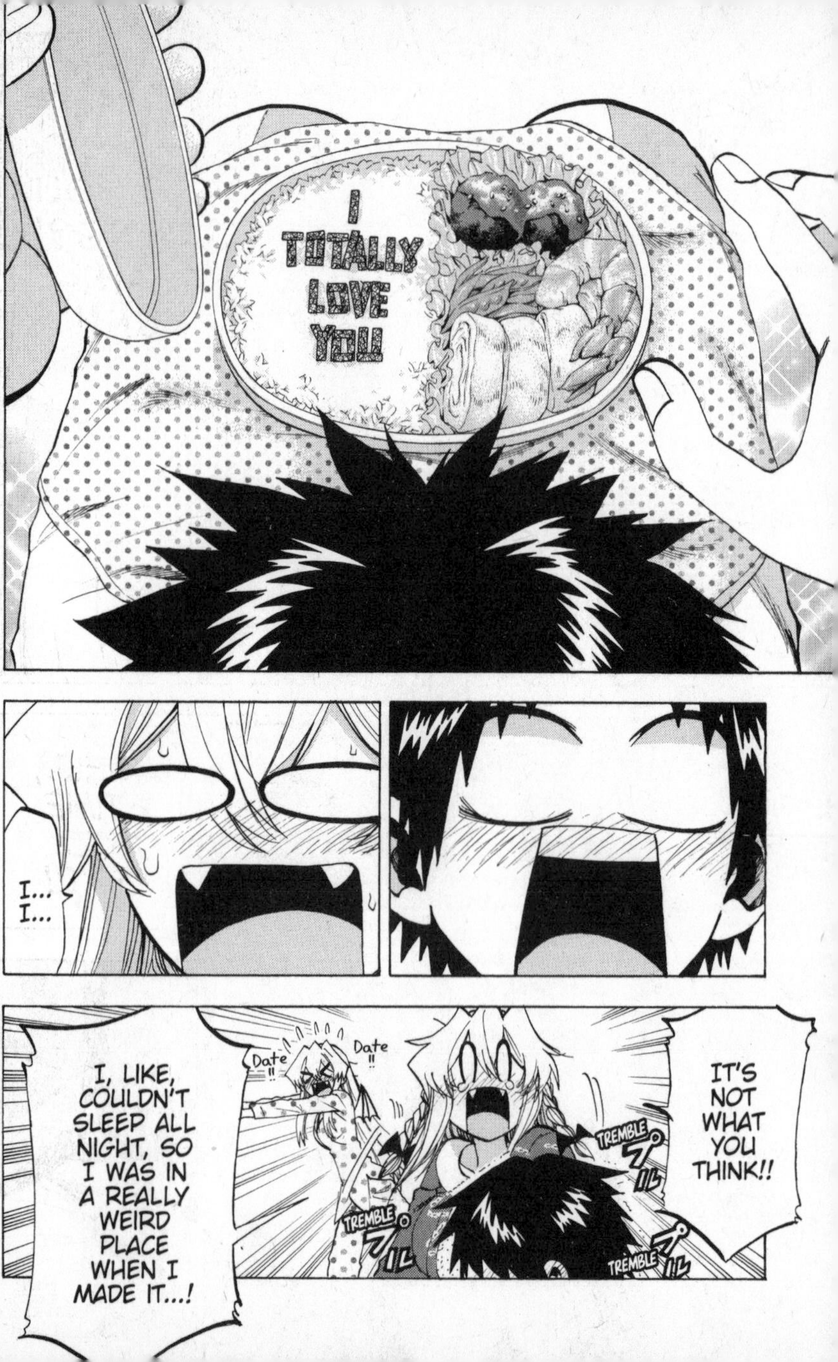

I TOTALLY LOVE YOU
I... I...
IT'S NOT WHAT YOU THINK!!
TREMBLE
TREMBLE
TREMBLE
Date !!
Date !!
I, LIKE, COULDN'T SLEEP ALL NIGHT, SO I WAS IN A REALLY WEIRD PLACE WHEN I MADE IT...!

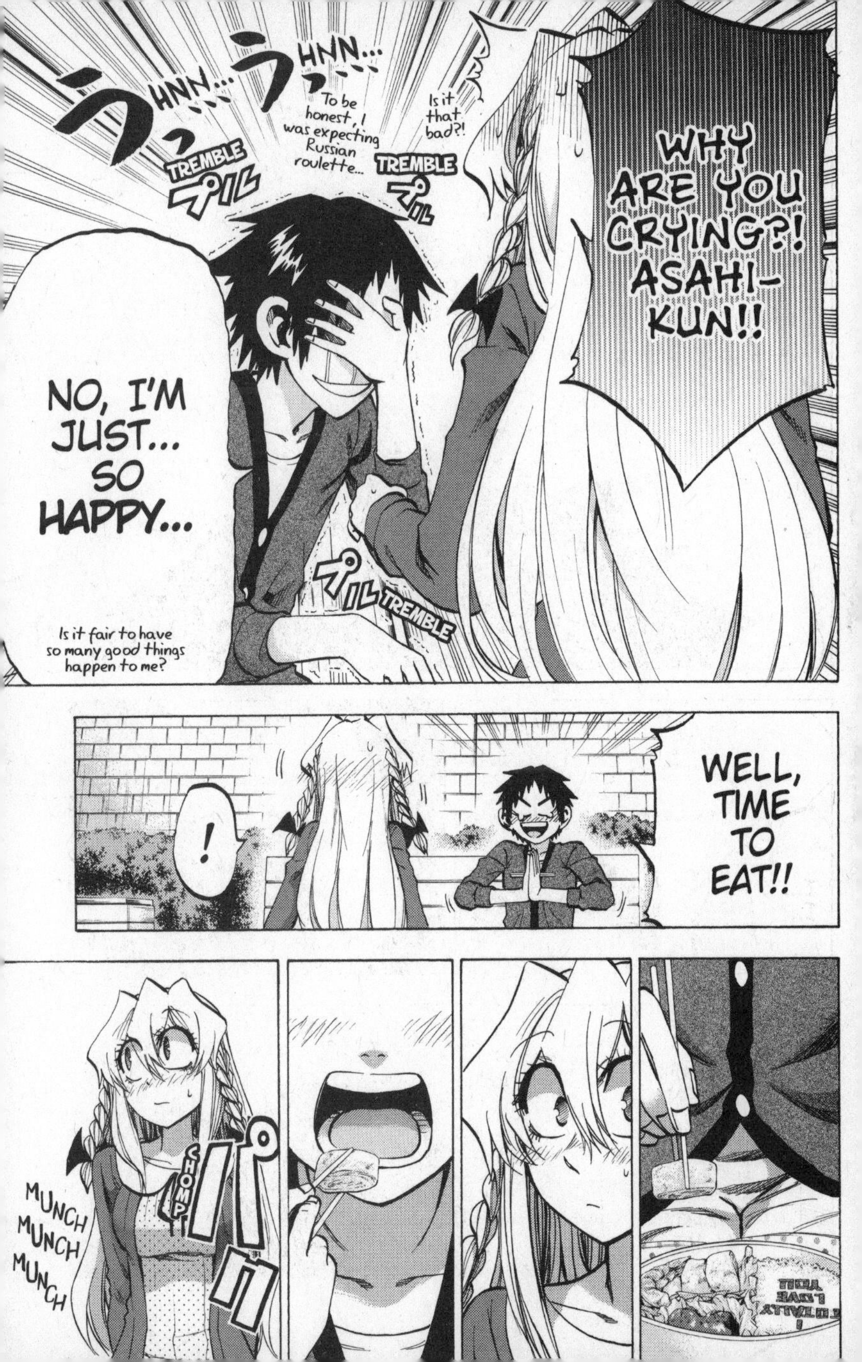WHY ARE YOU CRYING?! ASAHI-KUN!!
Is it that bad?!
TREMBLE ぷル
To be honest, I was expecting Russian roulette...
うっ HNN...
うっ HNN...
TREMBLE ぷル
NO, I'M JUST... SO HAPPY...
ぷル TREMBLE
Is it fair to have so many good things happen to me?
WELL, TIME TO EAT!!
!
CHOMP パク
MUNCH MUNCH MUNCH

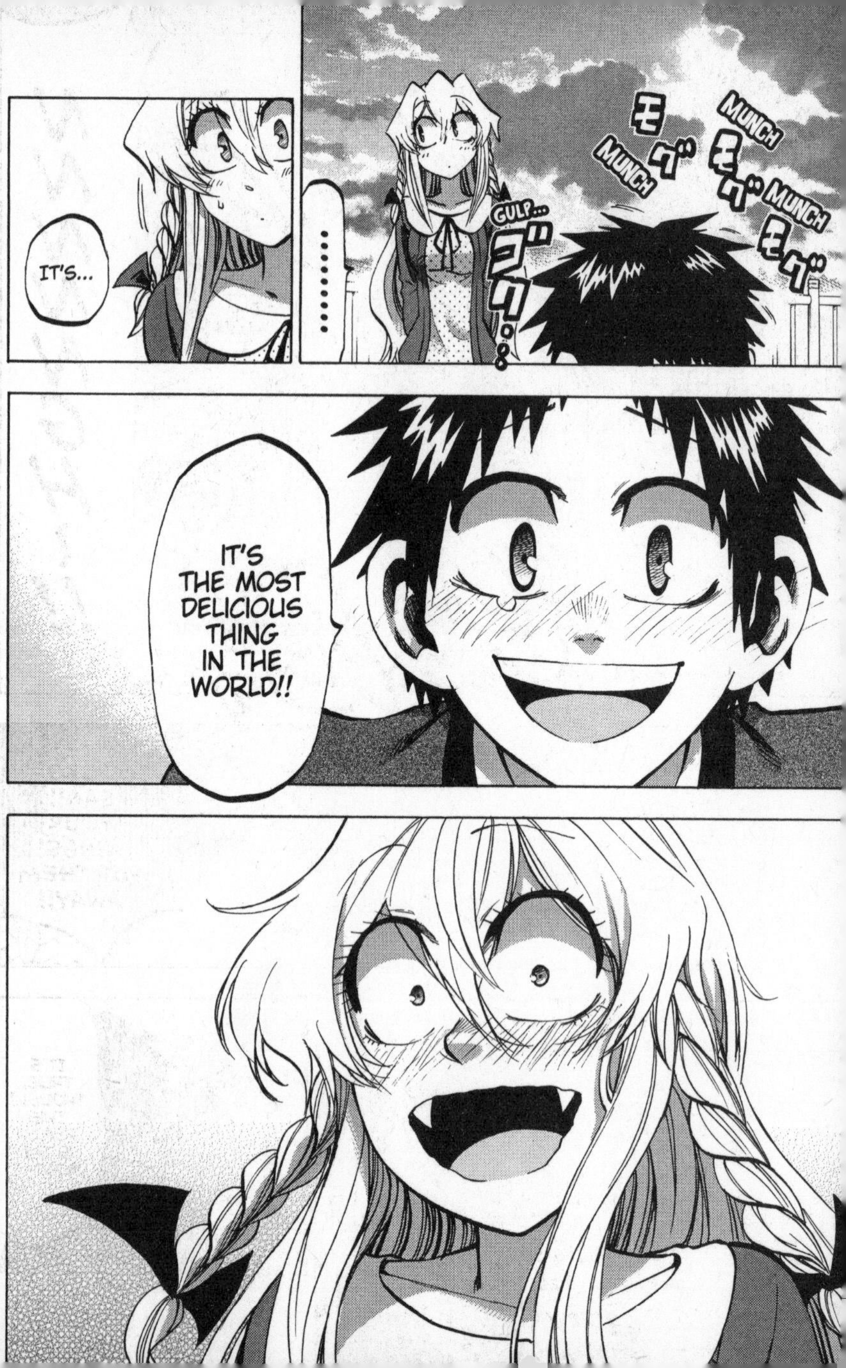

MUNCH
MUNCH
MUNCH
GULP...
......
IT'S...
IT'S THE MOST DELICIOUS THING IN THE WORLD!!

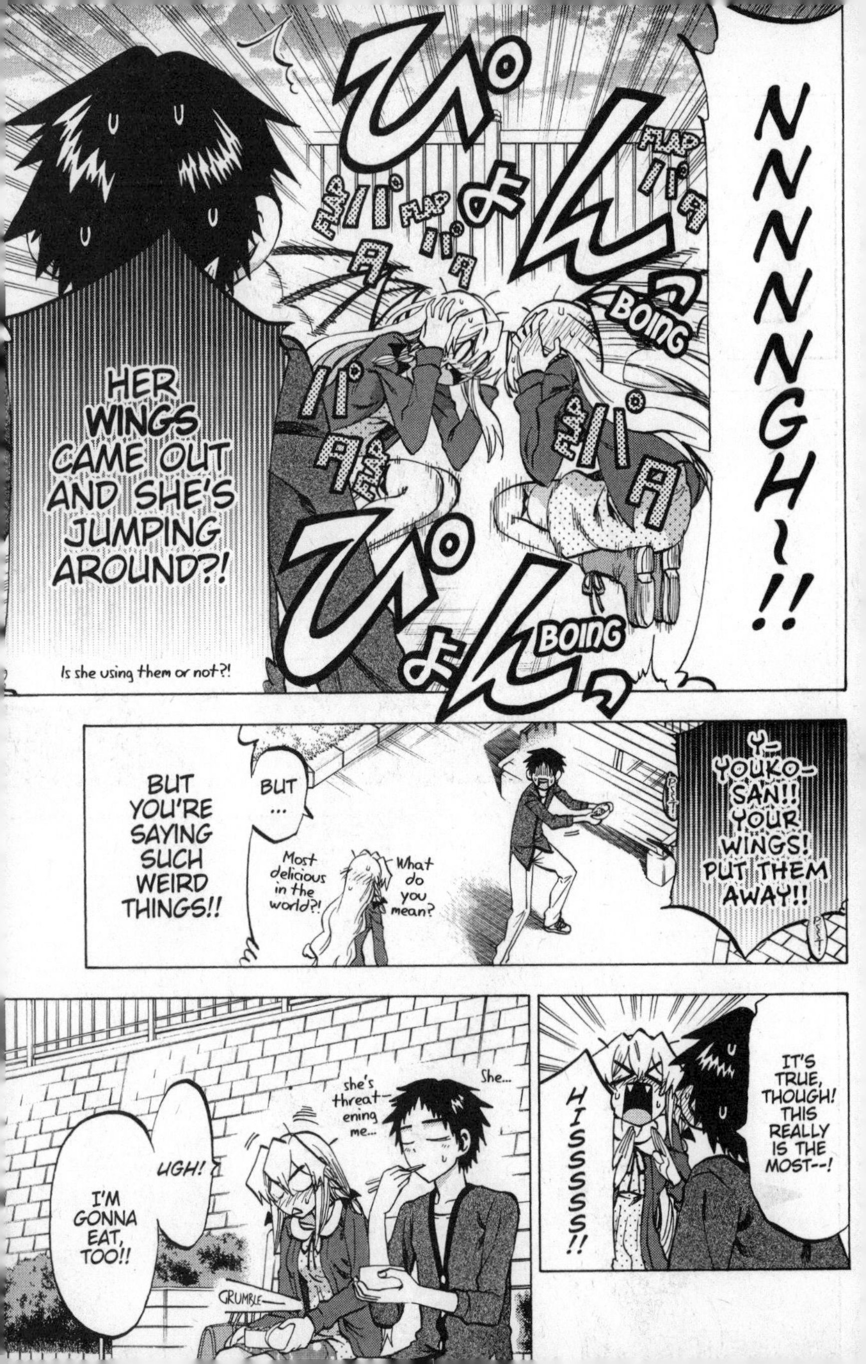
NNNNNGH~!!
BOING
FLAP
FLAP
FLAP
FLAP
HER WINGS CAME OUT AND SHE'S JUMPING AROUND?!
BOING
Is she using them or not?!
Y-YOUKO-SAN!! YOUR WINGS! PUT THEM AWAY!!
PSST
PSST
What do you mean?
Most delicious in the world?!
BUT...
BUT YOU'RE SAYING SUCH WEIRD THINGS!!
IT'S TRUE, THOUGH! THIS REALLY IS THE MOST--!
HISSSSS!!
She...
she's threatening me...
UGH!
I'M GONNA EAT, TOO!!
GRUMBLE

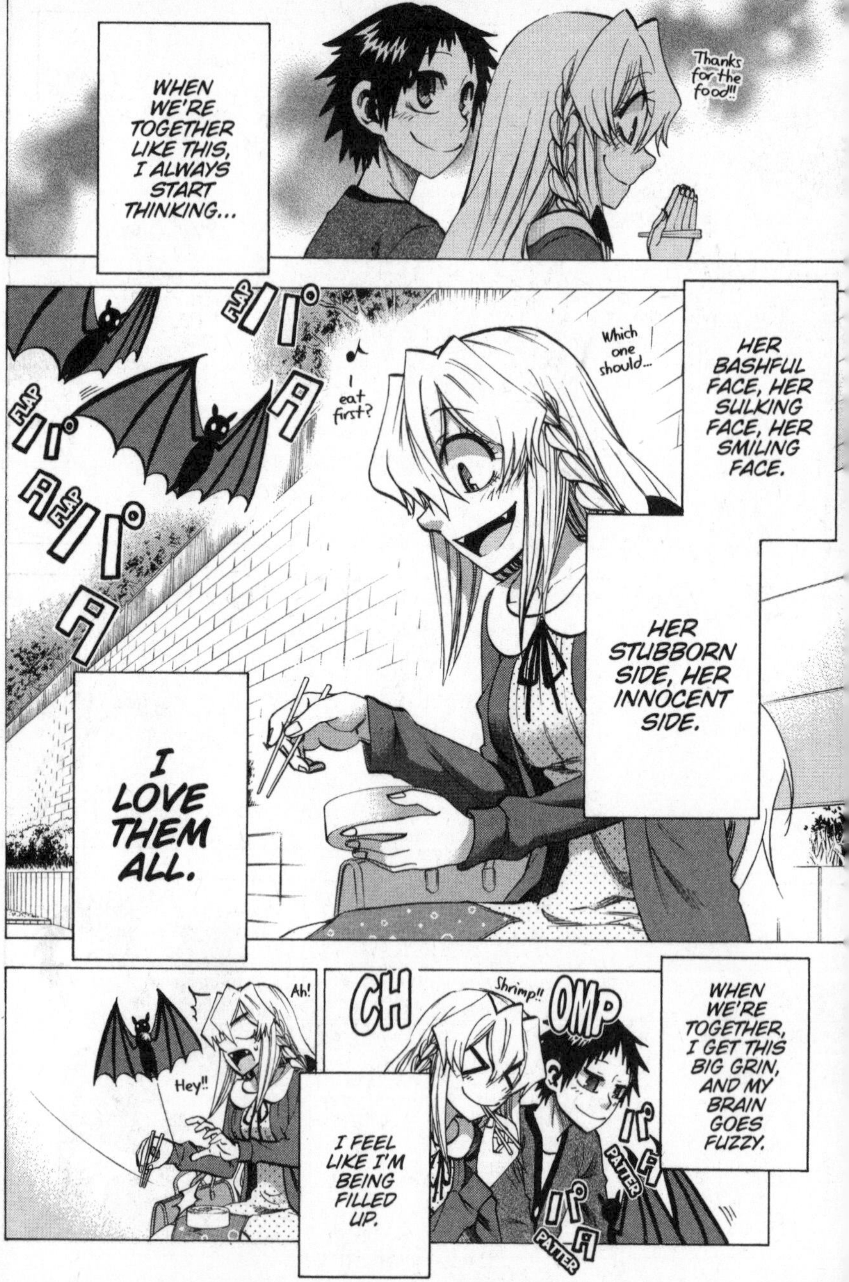
Thanks for the food!!
WHEN WE'RE TOGETHER LIKE THIS, I ALWAYS START THINKING...
HER BASHFUL FACE, HER SULKING FACE, HER SMILING FACE.
Which one should...
I eat first?
FLAP
FLAP
FLAP
HER STUBBORN SIDE, HER INNOCENT SIDE.
I LOVE THEM ALL.
WHEN WE'RE TOGETHER, I GET THIS BIG GRIN, AND MY BRAIN GOES FUZZY.
CH
Shrimp!!
OMP
PATTER
PATTER
I FEEL LIKE I'M BEING FILLED UP.
Ah!
Hey!!

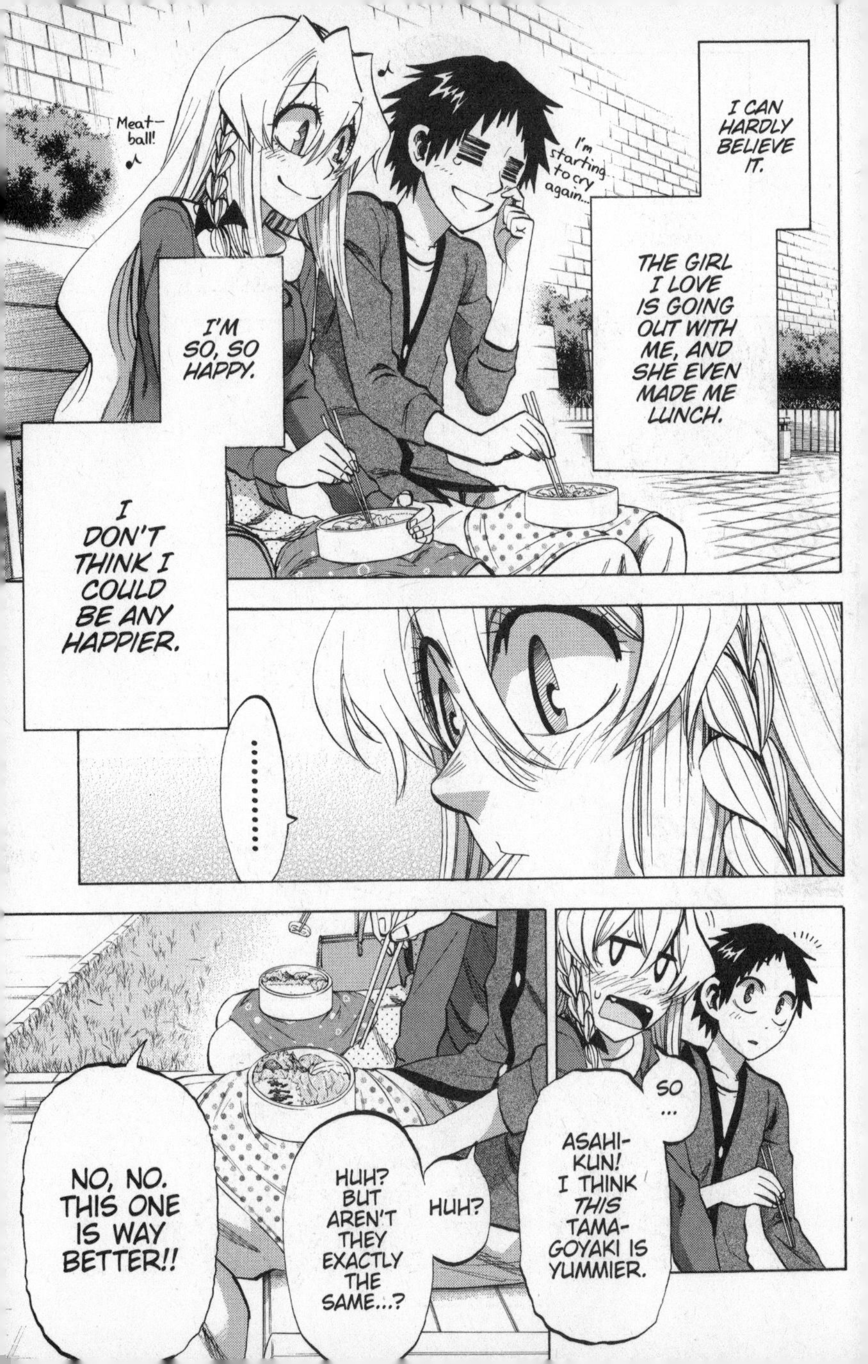

I CAN HARDLY BELIEVE IT.
THE GIRL I LOVE IS GOING OUT WITH ME, AND SHE EVEN MADE ME LUNCH.
I'm starting to cry again...
Meat-ball!
I'M SO, SO HAPPY.
I DON'T THINK I COULD BE ANY HAPPIER.
......
SO ...
ASAHI-KUN! I THINK *THIS* TAMAGOYAKI IS YUMMIER.
HUH?
HUH? BUT AREN'T THEY EXACTLY THE SAME...?
NO, NO. THIS ONE IS WAY BETTER!!

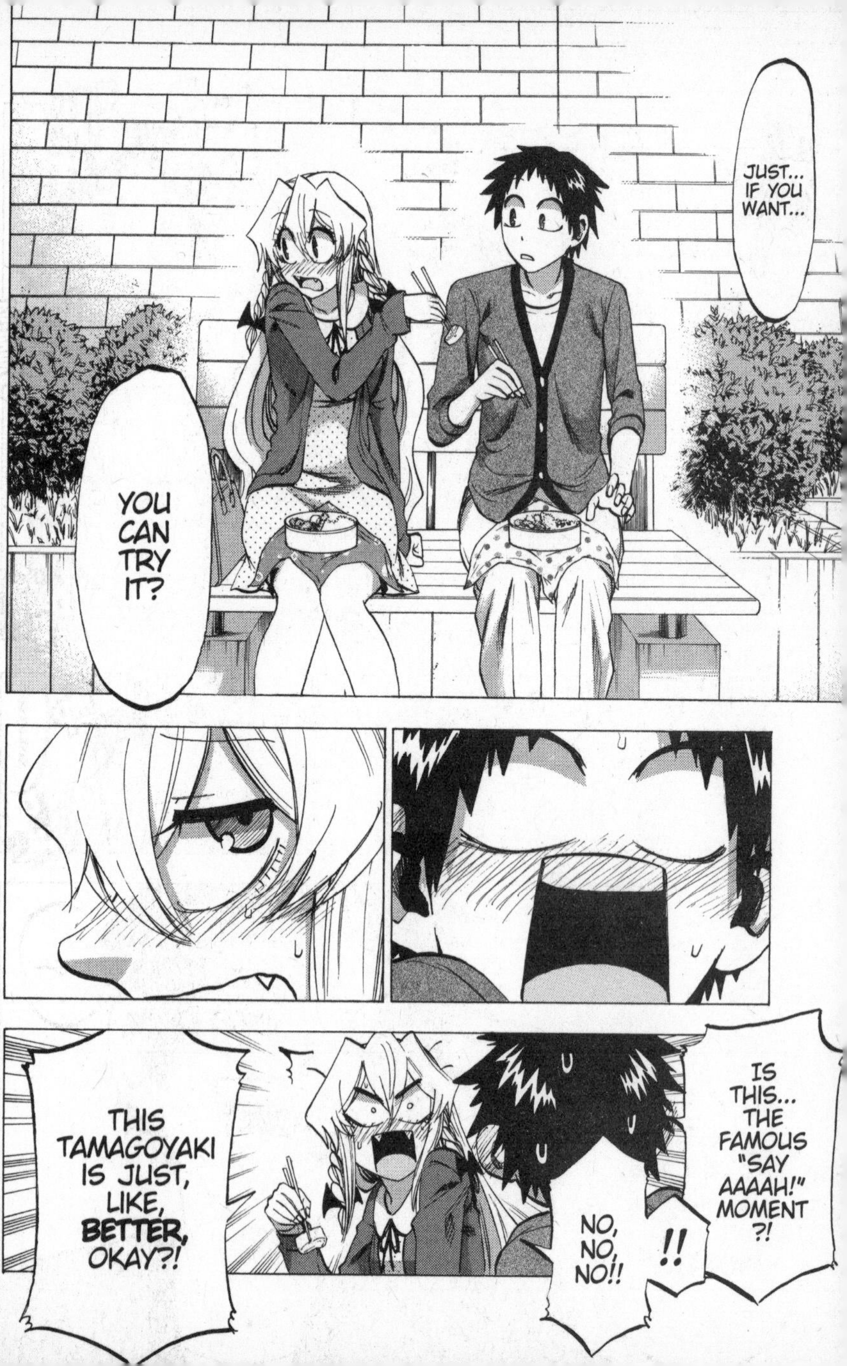
JUST... IF YOU WANT...
YOU CAN TRY IT?
IS THIS... THE FAMOUS "SAY AAAAH!" MOMENT ?!
!!
NO, NO, NO!!
THIS TAMAGOYAKI IS JUST, LIKE, BETTER, OKAY?!

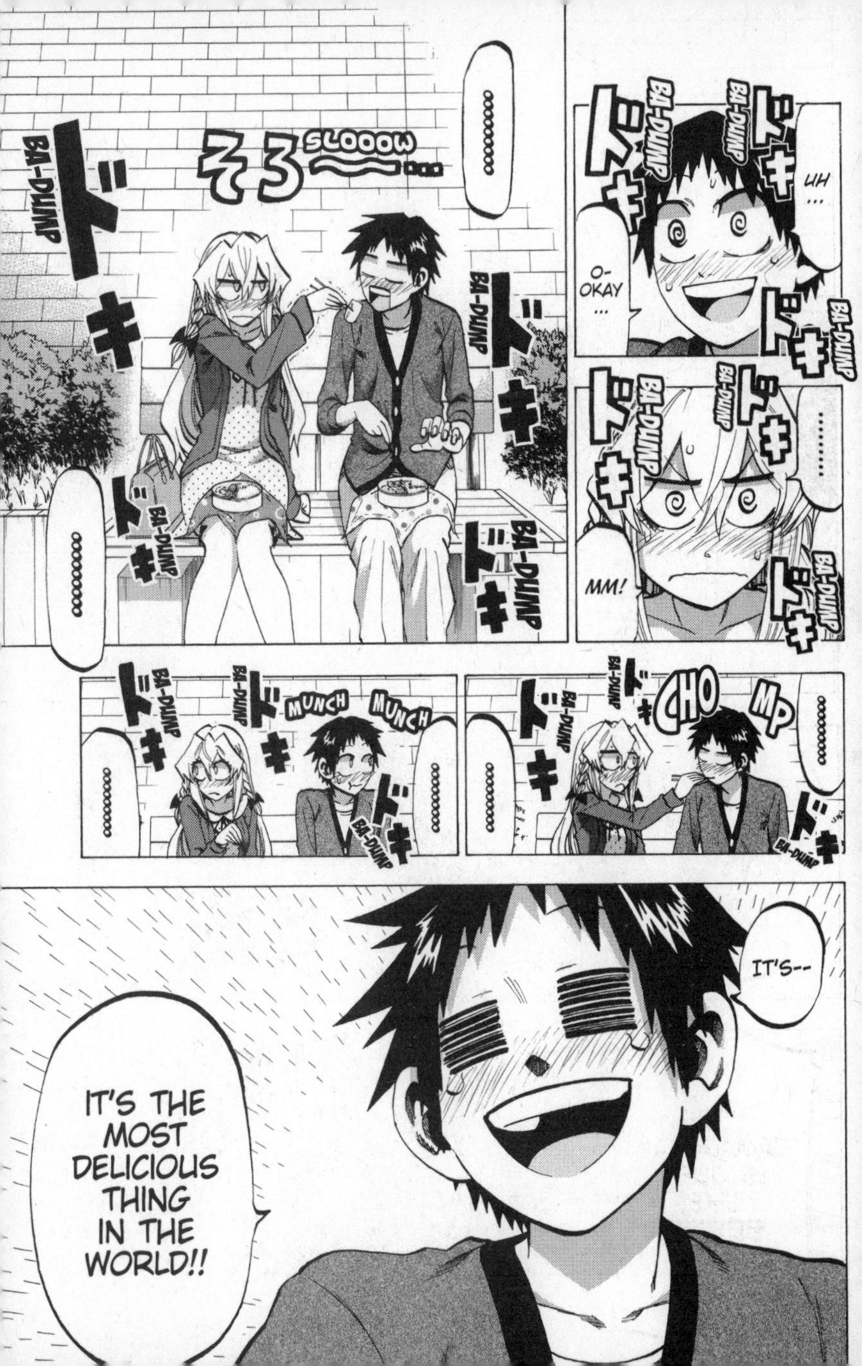

BA-DUMP ドキ
BA-DUMP ドキ
UH ...
O-OKAY ...
BA-DUMP ドキ
BA-DUMP ドキ
BA-DUMP ドキ
......
MM!
BA-DUMP ドキ
......
そろ〜〜... SLOOOW
BA-DUMP ドキ
BA-DUMP ドキ
BA-DUMP ドキ
BA-DUMP ドキ
......
......
CHOMP
BA-DUMP ドキ
BA-DUMP ドキ
BA-DUMP ドキ
......
MUNCH MUNCH
BA-DUMP ドキ
BA-DUMP ドキ
BA-DUMP ドキ
......
IT'S--
IT'S THE MOST DELICIOUS THING IN THE WORLD!!

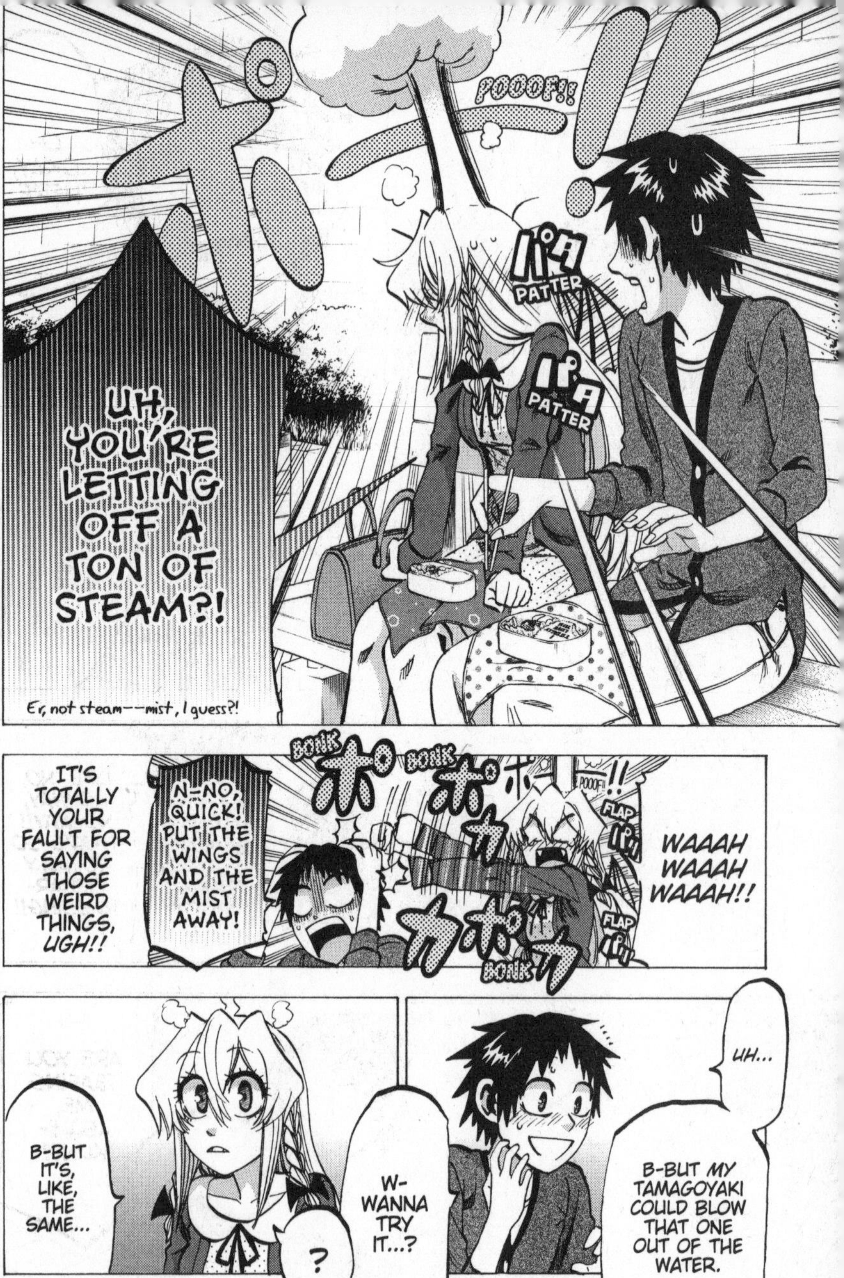
POOOF!!
PATTER
PATTER
UH, YOU'RE LETTING OFF A TON OF STEAM?!
Er, not steam--mist, I guess?!
WAAAH WAAAH WAAAH!!
FLAP
FLAP
POOOF!!
BONK
BONK
BONK
N-NO, QUICK! PUT THE WINGS AND THE MIST AWAY!
IT'S TOTALLY YOUR FAULT FOR SAYING THOSE WEIRD THINGS, UGH!!
UH...
B-BUT MY TAMAGOYAKI COULD BLOW THAT ONE OUT OF THE WATER.
W-WANNA TRY IT...?
?
B-BUT IT'S, LIKE, THE SAME...

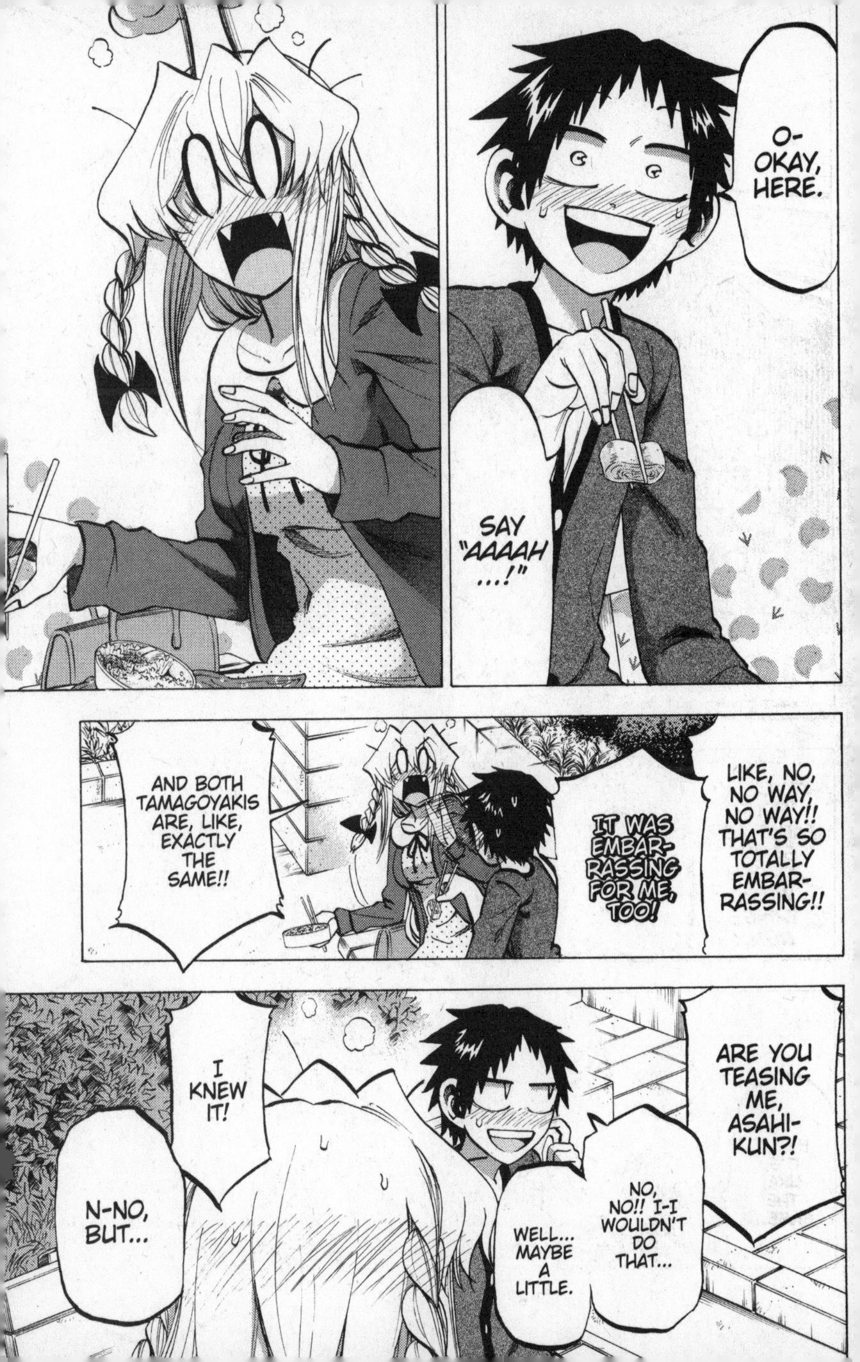
O-OKAY, HERE.
SAY "AAAAH...!"
LIKE, NO, NO WAY, NO WAY!! THAT'S SO TOTALLY EMBARRASSING!!
IT WAS EMBARRASSING FOR ME, TOO!
AND BOTH TAMAGOYAKIS ARE, LIKE, EXACTLY THE SAME!!
ARE YOU TEASING ME, ASAHI-KUN?!
NO, NO!! I-I WOULDN'T DO THAT...
WELL... MAYBE A LITTLE.
I KNEW IT!
N-NO, BUT...

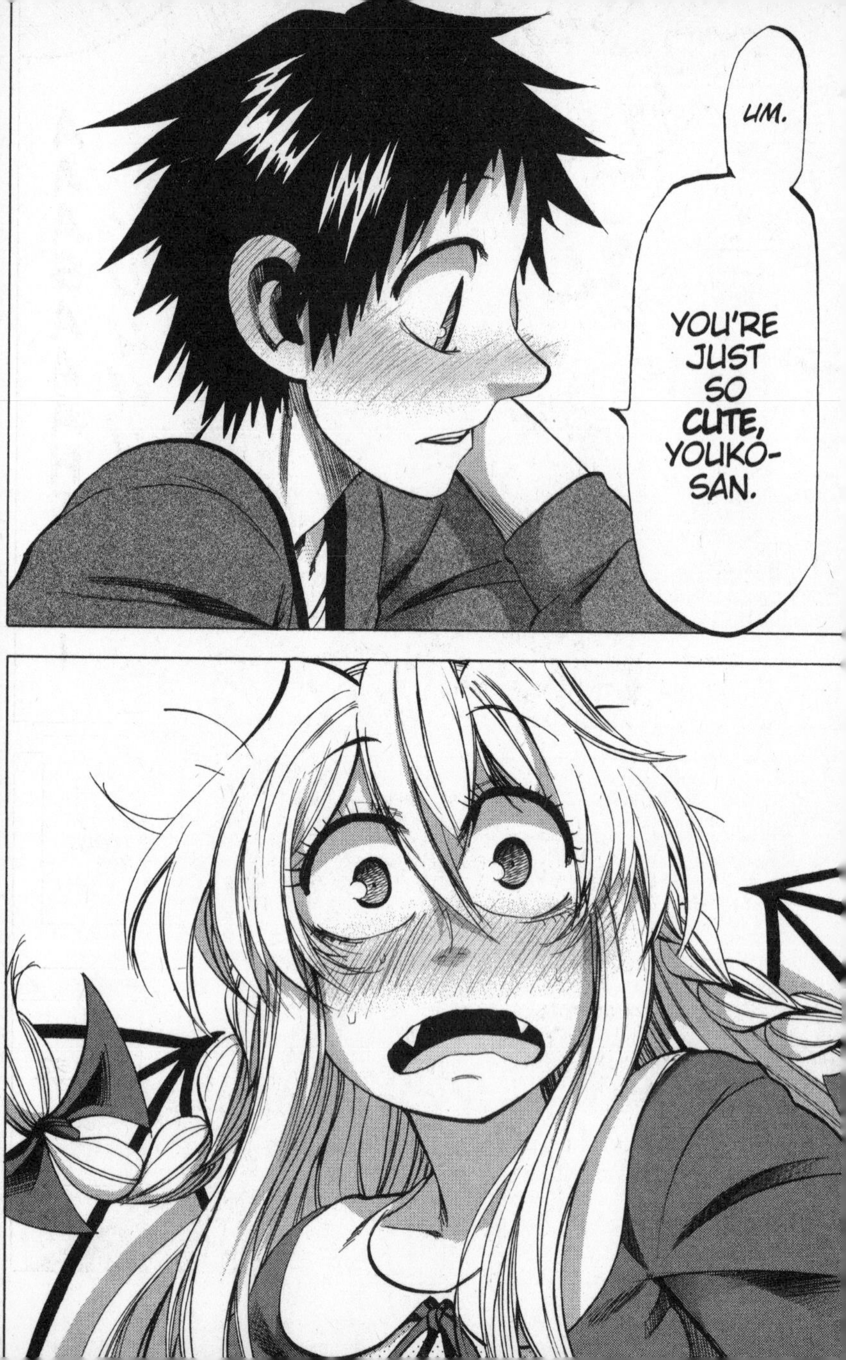
UM.
YOU'RE JUST SO CUTE, YOUKO-SAN.

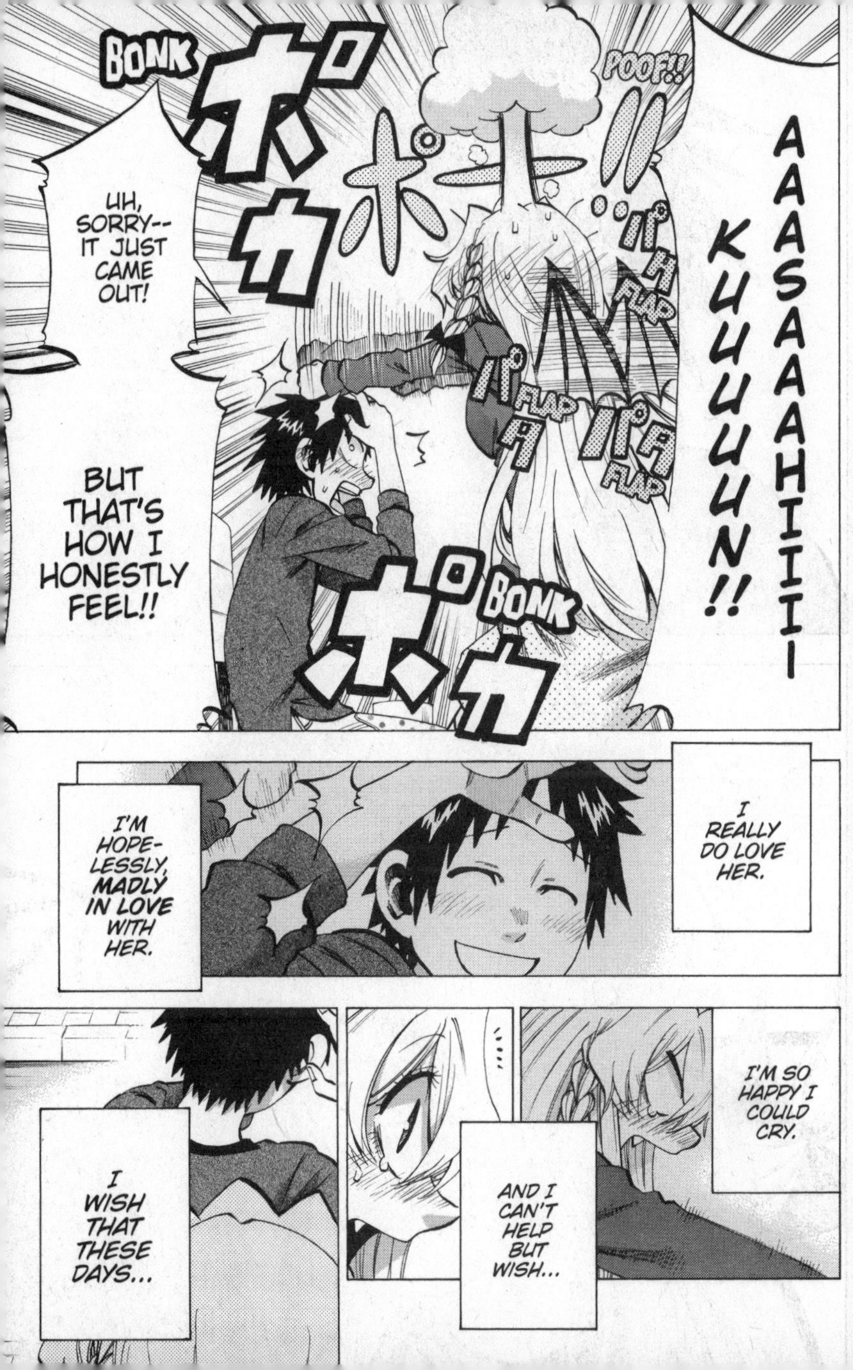
AAASAAAHIIII
KUUUUUN!!
POOF!!
パタ
FLAP
パタ
FLAP
パタ
FLAP
ポカ
BONK
UH, SORRY-- IT JUST CAME OUT!
ポカ
BONK
BUT THAT'S HOW I HONESTLY FEEL!!
I REALLY DO LOVE HER.
I'M HOPE-LESSLY, MADLY IN LOVE WITH HER.
I'M SO HAPPY I COULD CRY.
...!
AND I CAN'T HELP BUT WISH...
I WISH THAT THESE DAYS...

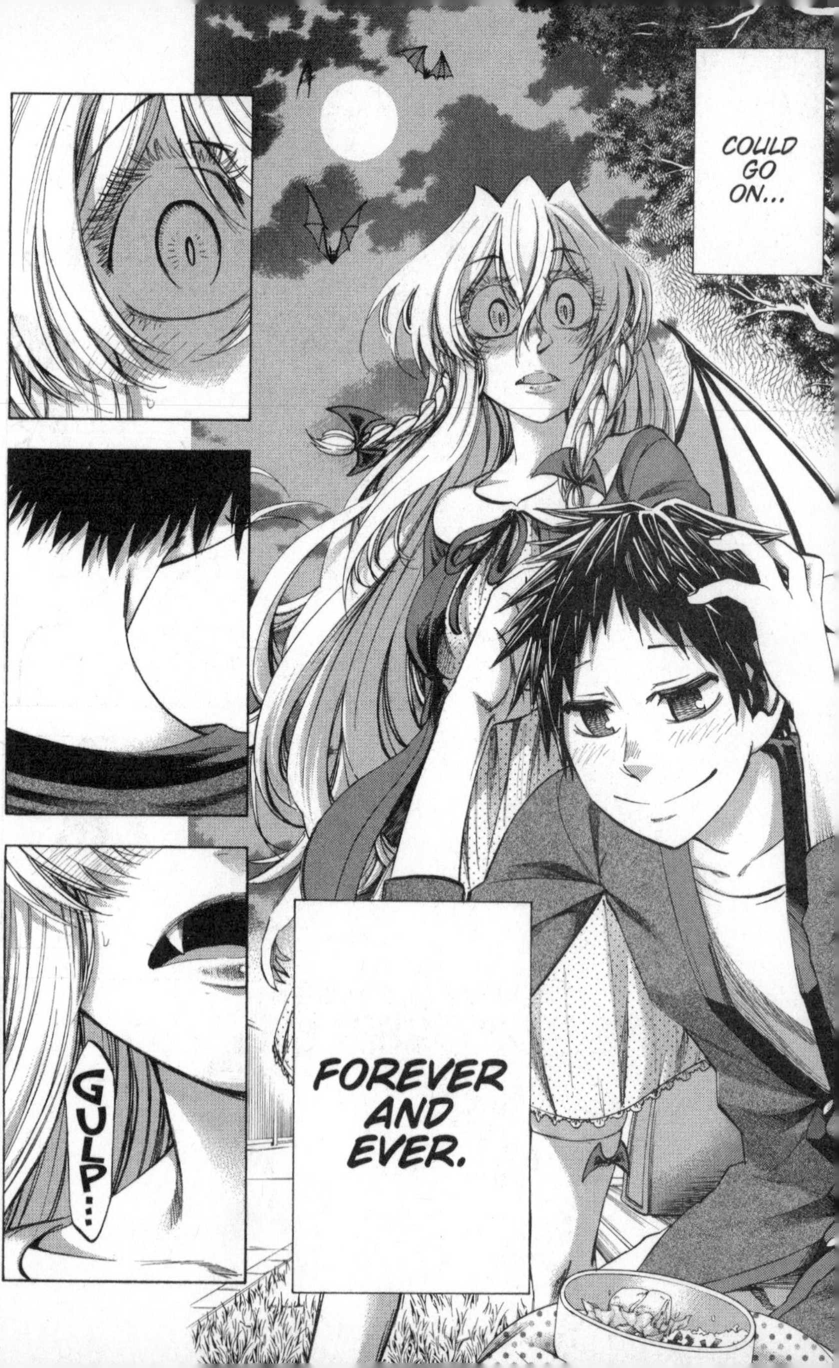
COULD GO ON...
FOREVER AND EVER.
GULP...

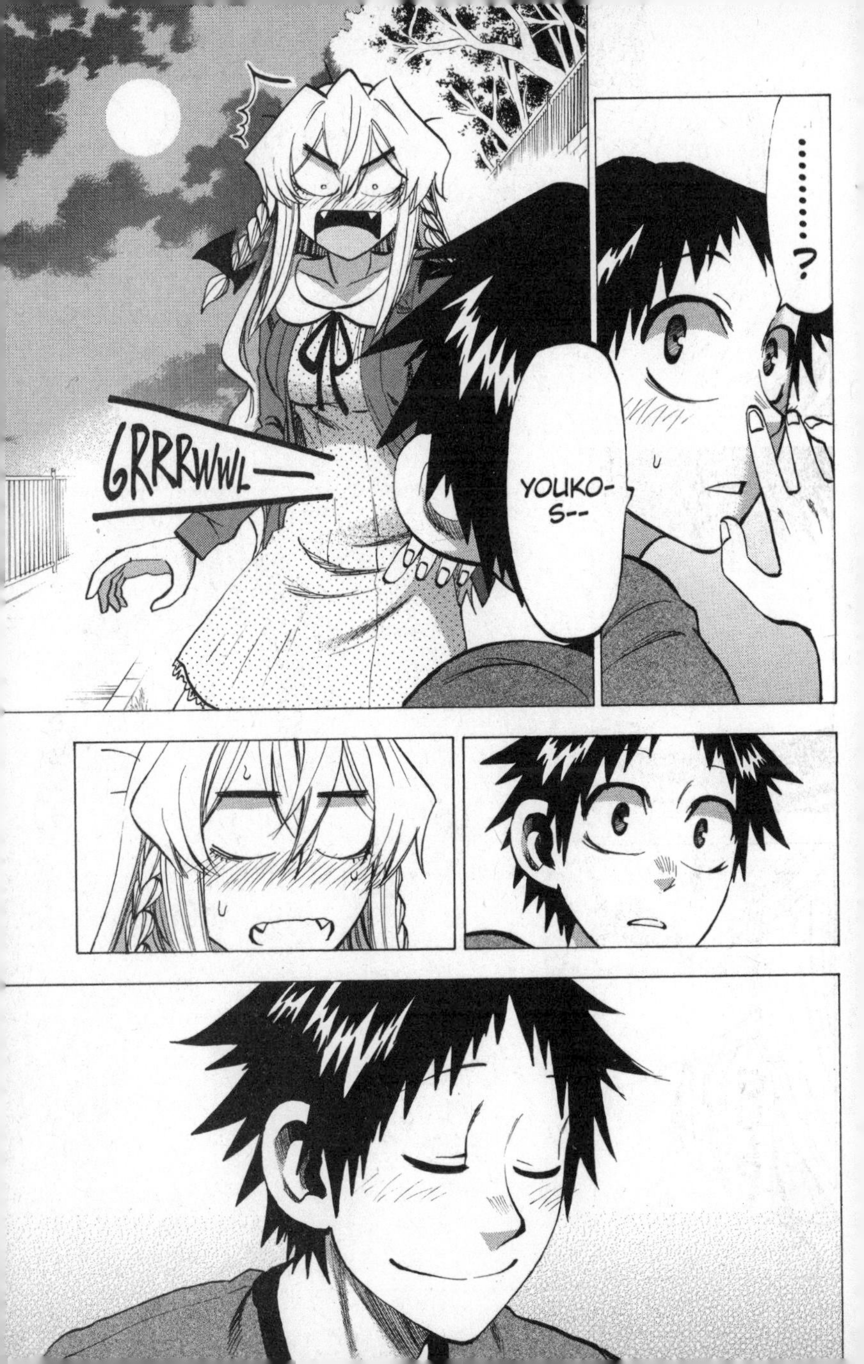
......?
YOUKO-S--
GRRRWWL

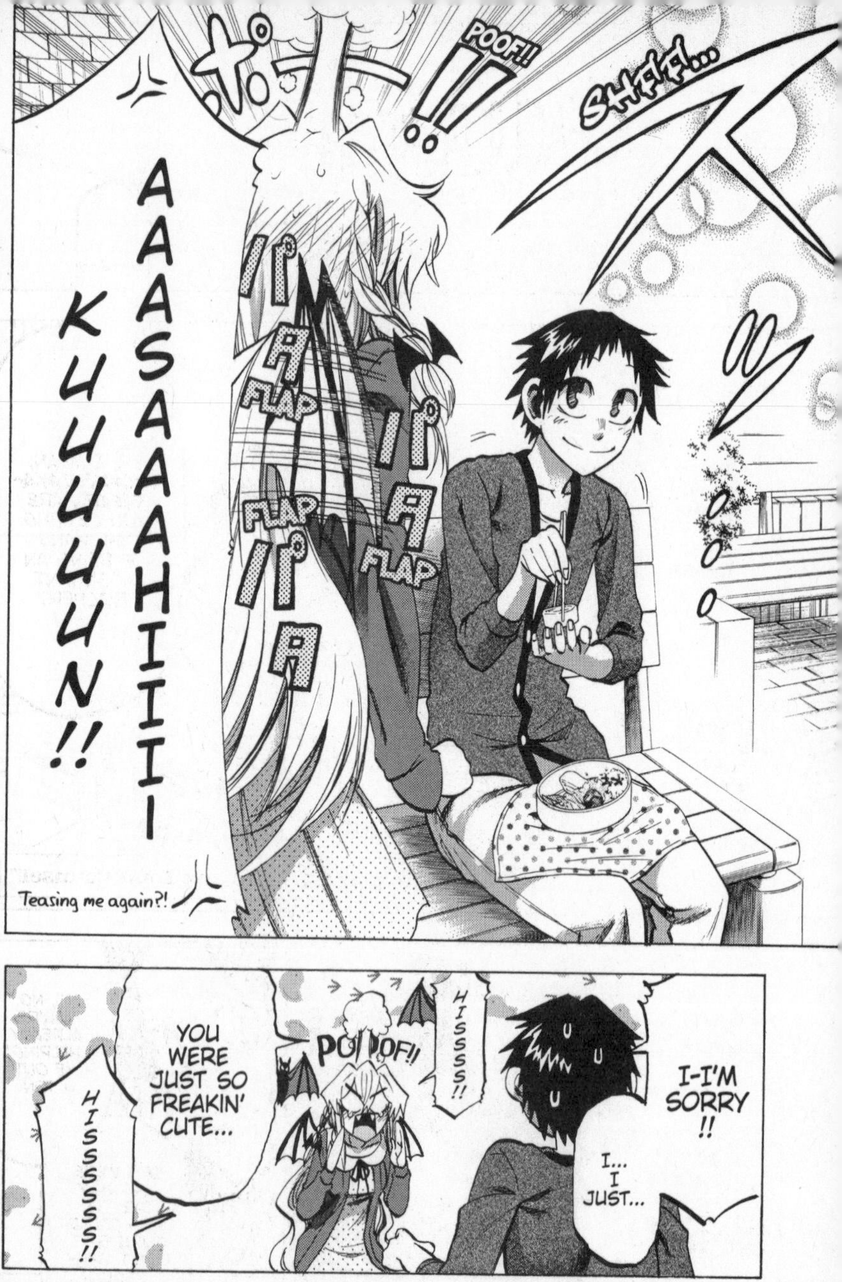
POOF!!
SHFFT...
AAAASAAAHIIII
KUUUUUN!!
FLAP
FLAP
FLAP
Teasing me again?!
I-I'M SORRY!!
I... I JUST...
HISSSS!!
POOF!!
YOU WERE JUST SO FREAKIN' CUTE...
HISSSSSS!!

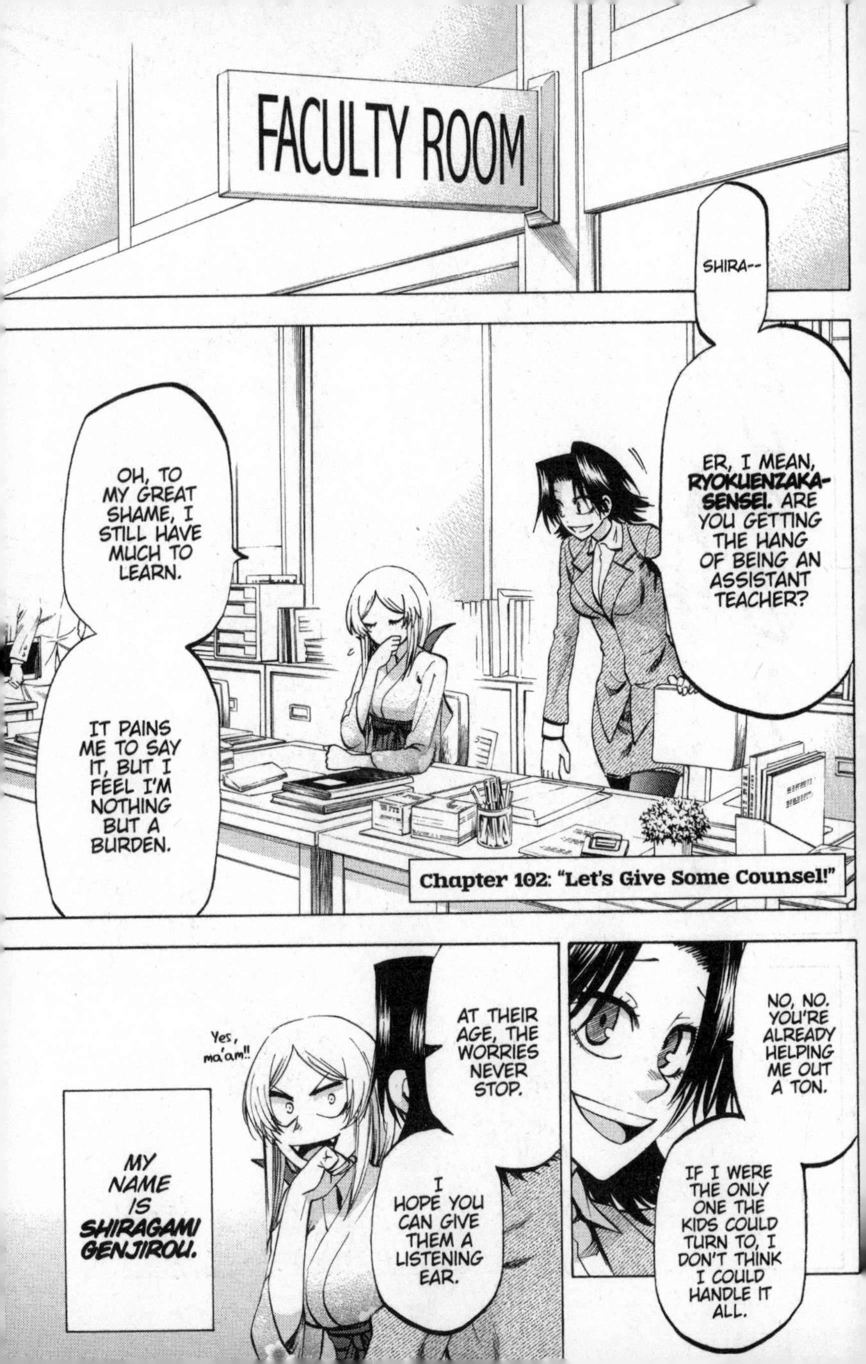

FACULTY ROOM
SHIRA--
ER, I MEAN, RYOKUENZAKA-SENSEI. ARE YOU GETTING THE HANG OF BEING AN ASSISTANT TEACHER?
OH, TO MY GREAT SHAME, I STILL HAVE MUCH TO LEARN.
IT PAINS ME TO SAY IT, BUT I FEEL I'M NOTHING BUT A BURDEN.
Chapter 102: "Let's Give Some Counsel!"
NO, NO. YOU'RE ALREADY HELPING ME OUT A TON.
IF I WERE THE ONLY ONE THE KIDS COULD TURN TO, I DON'T THINK I COULD HANDLE IT ALL.
AT THEIR AGE, THE WORRIES NEVER STOP.
I HOPE YOU CAN GIVE THEM A LISTENING EAR.
Yes, ma'am!!
MY NAME IS SHIRAGAMI GENJIROU.

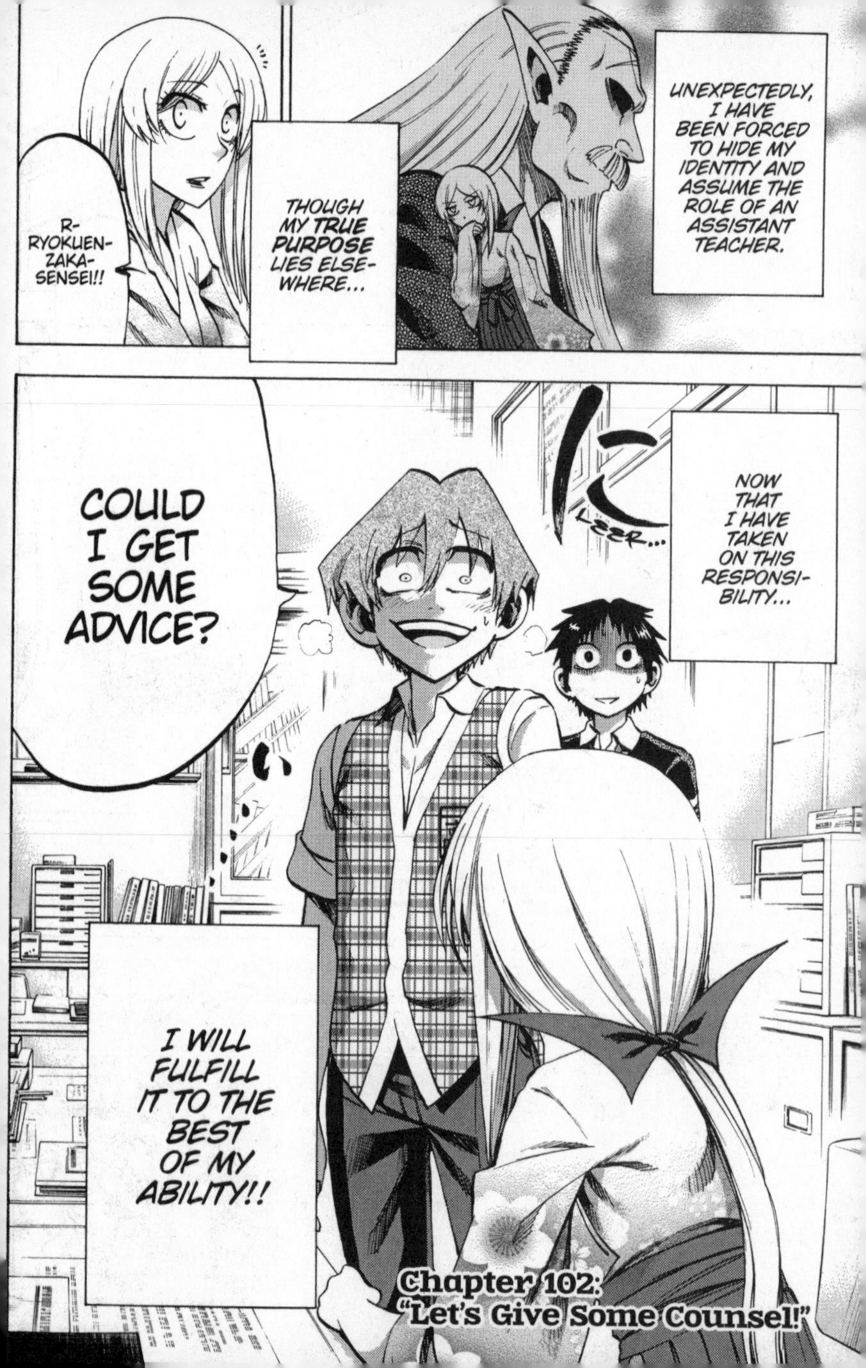
UNEXPECTEDLY, I HAVE BEEN FORCED TO HIDE MY IDENTITY AND ASSUME THE ROLE OF AN ASSISTANT TEACHER.
THOUGH MY TRUE PURPOSE LIES ELSEWHERE...
R-RYOKUEN-ZAKA-SENSEI!!
NOW THAT I HAVE TAKEN ON THIS RESPONSIBILITY...
LEER...
COULD I GET SOME ADVICE?
I WILL FULFILL IT TO THE BEST OF MY ABILITY!!
Chapter 102: "Let's Give Some Counsel!"

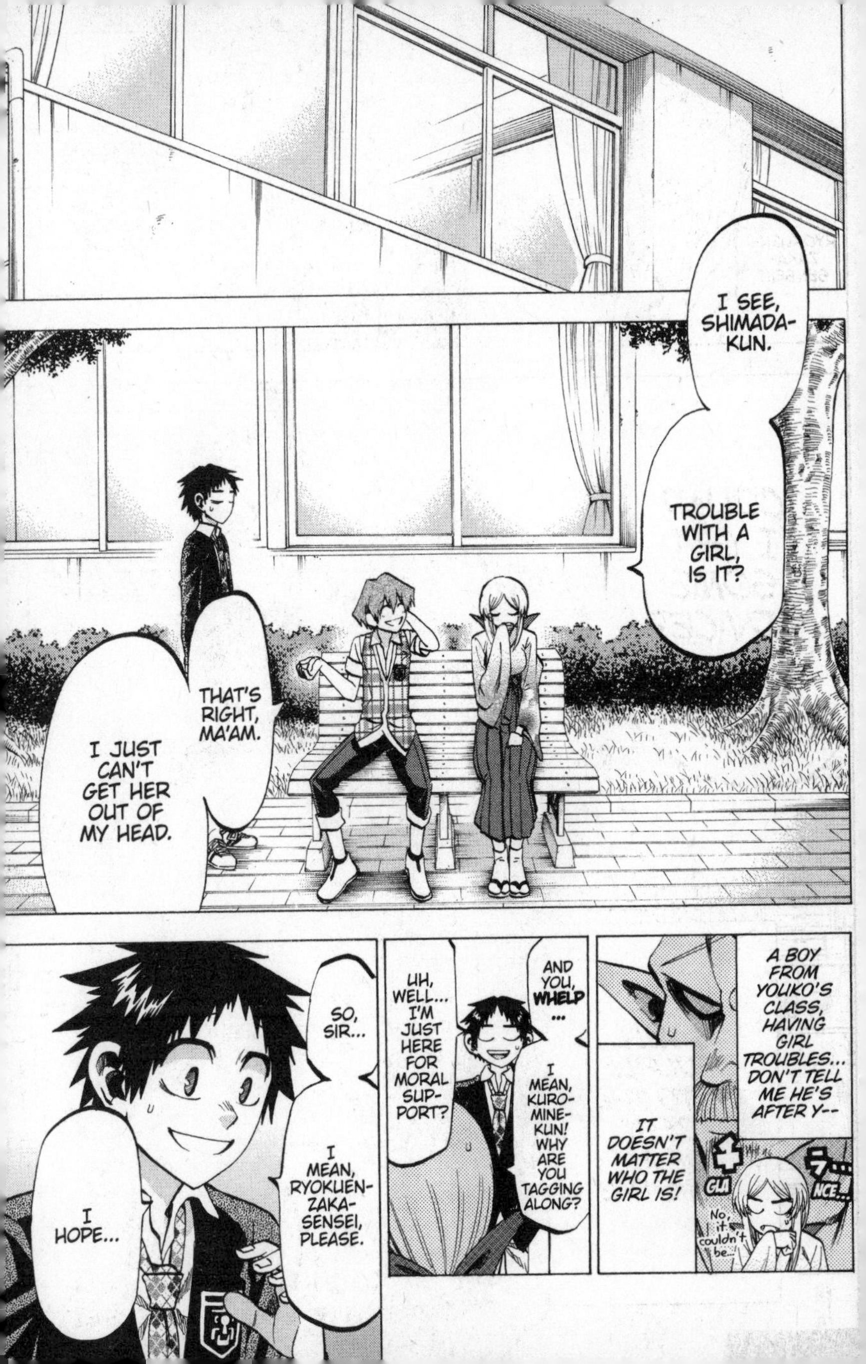
I SEE, SHIMADA-KUN.
TROUBLE WITH A GIRL, IS IT?
THAT'S RIGHT, MA'AM.
I JUST CAN'T GET HER OUT OF MY HEAD.
A BOY FROM YOUKO'S CLASS, HAVING GIRL TROUBLES... DON'T TELL ME HE'S AFTER Y--
GLA
NCE...
No, it couldn't be...
IT DOESN'T MATTER WHO THE GIRL IS!
AND YOU, **WHELP**...
I MEAN, KURO-MINE-KUN! WHY ARE YOU TAGGING ALONG?
UH, WELL... I'M JUST HERE FOR MORAL SUP-PORT?
SO, SIR...
I MEAN, RYOKUEN-ZAKA-SENSEI, PLEASE.
I HOPE...

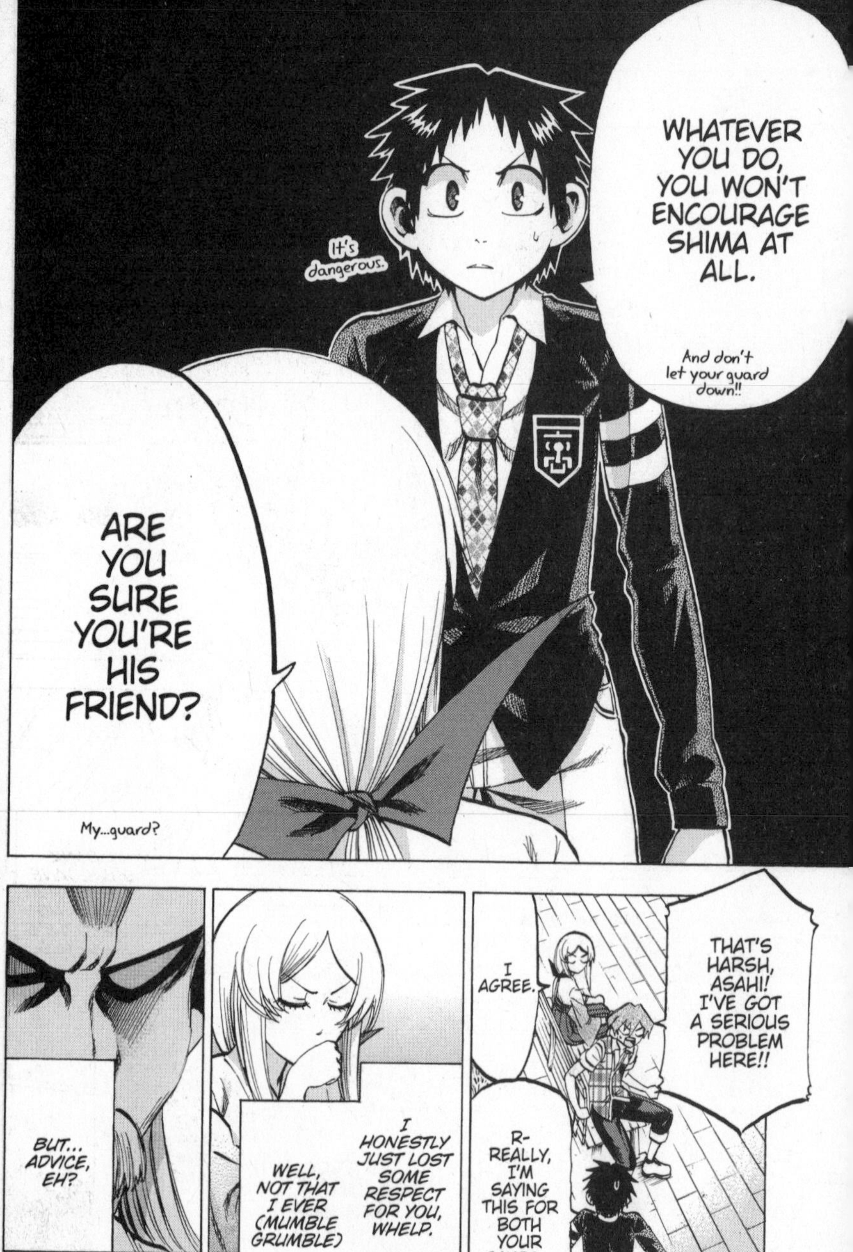
WHATEVER YOU DO, YOU WON'T ENCOURAGE SHIMA AT ALL.
It's dangerous.
And don't let your guard down!!
ARE YOU SURE YOU'RE HIS FRIEND?
My...guard?
THAT'S HARSH, ASAHI! I'VE GOT A SERIOUS PROBLEM HERE!!
I AGREE.
R-REALLY, I'M SAYING THIS FOR BOTH YOUR SAKES...
I HONESTLY JUST LOST SOME RESPECT FOR YOU, WHELP.
WELL, NOT THAT I EVER (MUMBLE GRUMBLE) ...
BUT... ADVICE, EH?

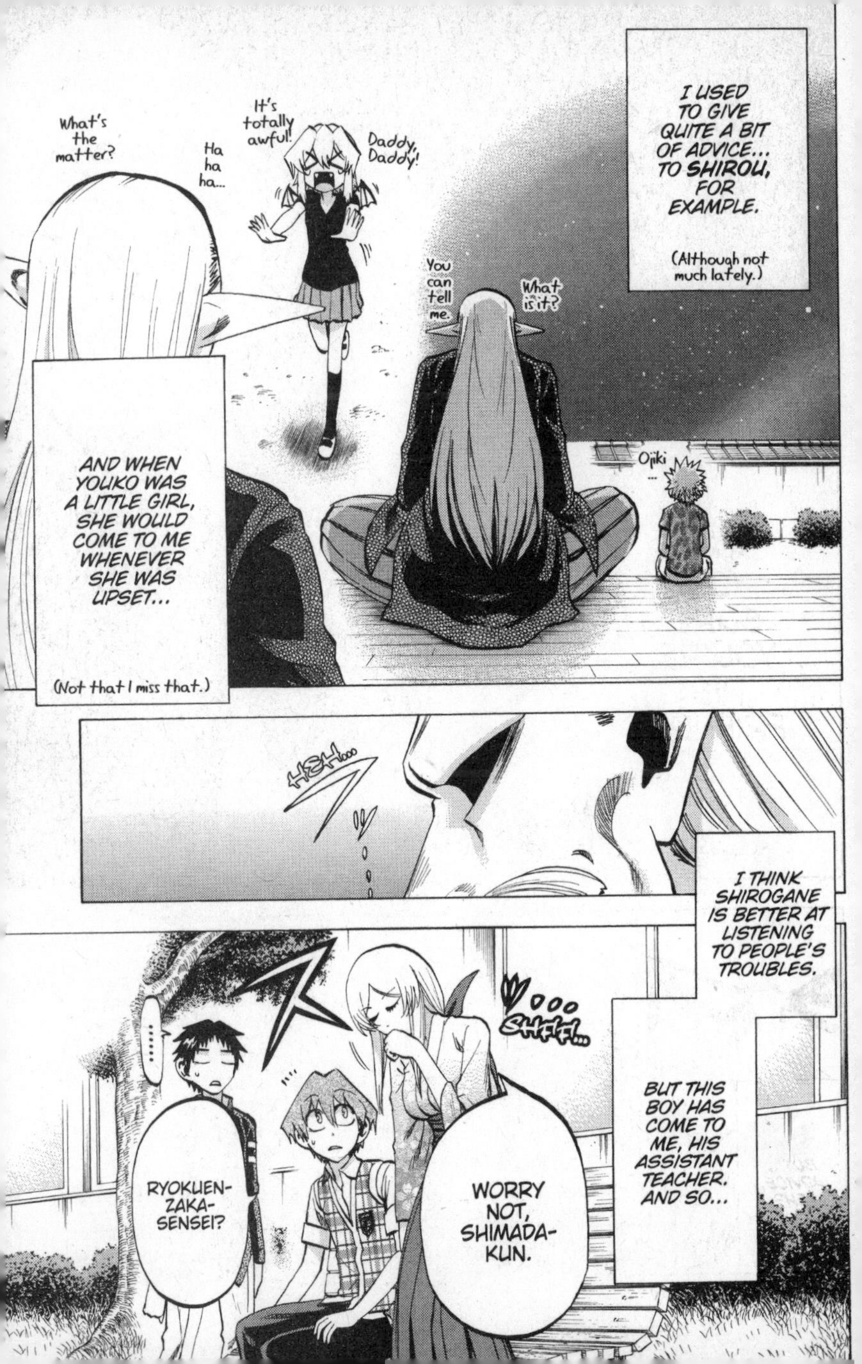

I USED TO GIVE QUITE A BIT OF ADVICE... TO SHIROU, FOR EXAMPLE.
(Although not much lately.)
Ojiki...
What is it?
You can tell me.
Daddy, Daddy!
It's totally awful!
Ha ha ha...
What's the matter?
AND WHEN YOUKO WAS A LITTLE GIRL, SHE WOULD COME TO ME WHENEVER SHE WAS UPSET...
(Not that I miss that.)
HEH...
I THINK SHIROGANE IS BETTER AT LISTENING TO PEOPLE'S TROUBLES.
BUT THIS BOY HAS COME TO ME, HIS ASSISTANT TEACHER. AND SO...
...SHFF!...
WORRY NOT, SHIMADA-KUN.
RYOKUEN-ZAKA-SENSEI?
......

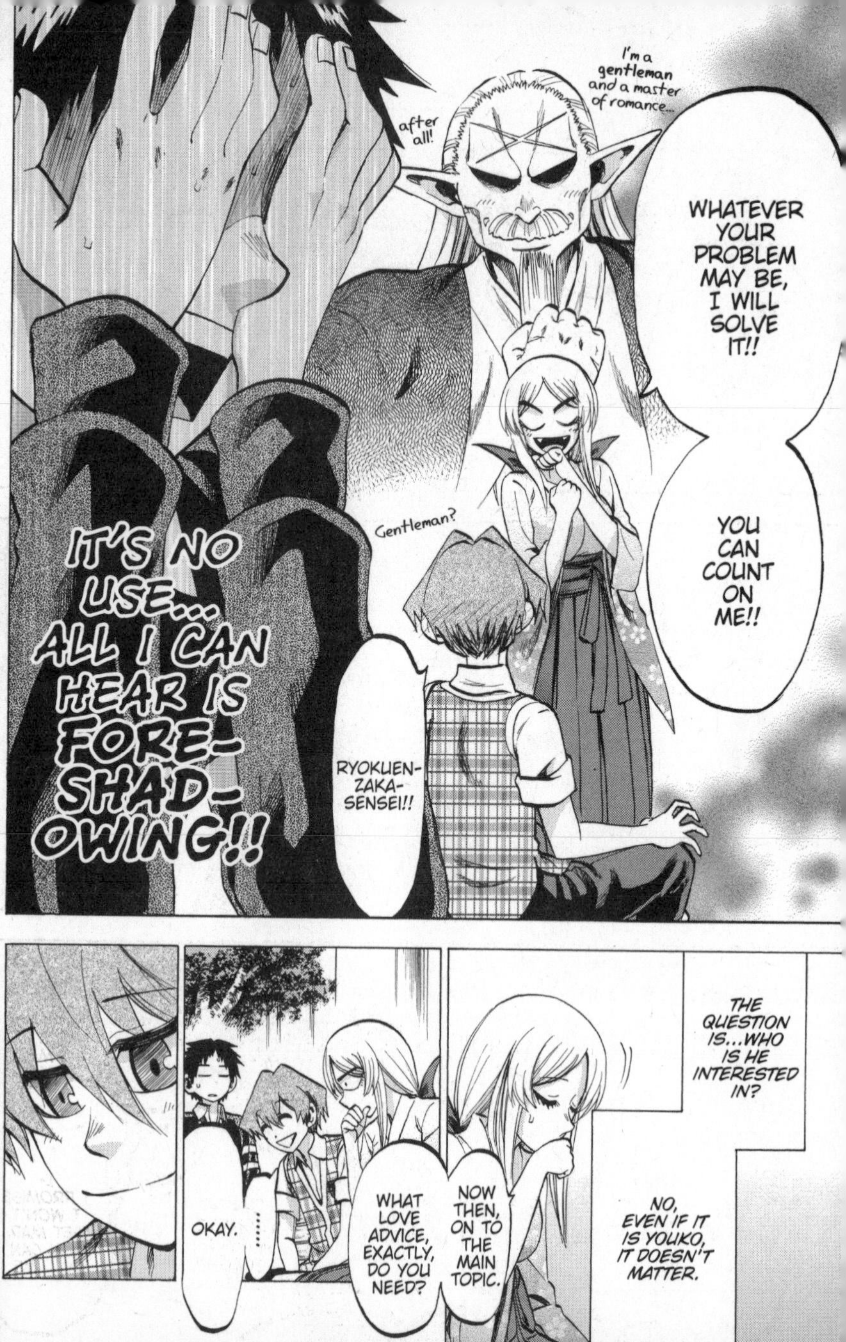
WHATEVER YOUR PROBLEM MAY BE, I WILL SOLVE IT!!
YOU CAN COUNT ON ME!!
I'm a gentleman and a master of romance...
after all!
Gentleman?
RYOKUEN-ZAKA-SENSEI!!
IT'S NO USE... ALL I CAN HEAR IS FORE-SHAD-OWING!!
THE QUESTION IS...WHO IS HE INTERESTED IN?
NO, EVEN IF IT IS YOUKO, IT DOESN'T MATTER.
NOW THEN, ON TO THE MAIN TOPIC.
WHAT LOVE ADVICE, EXACTLY, DO YOU NEED?
......
OKAY.

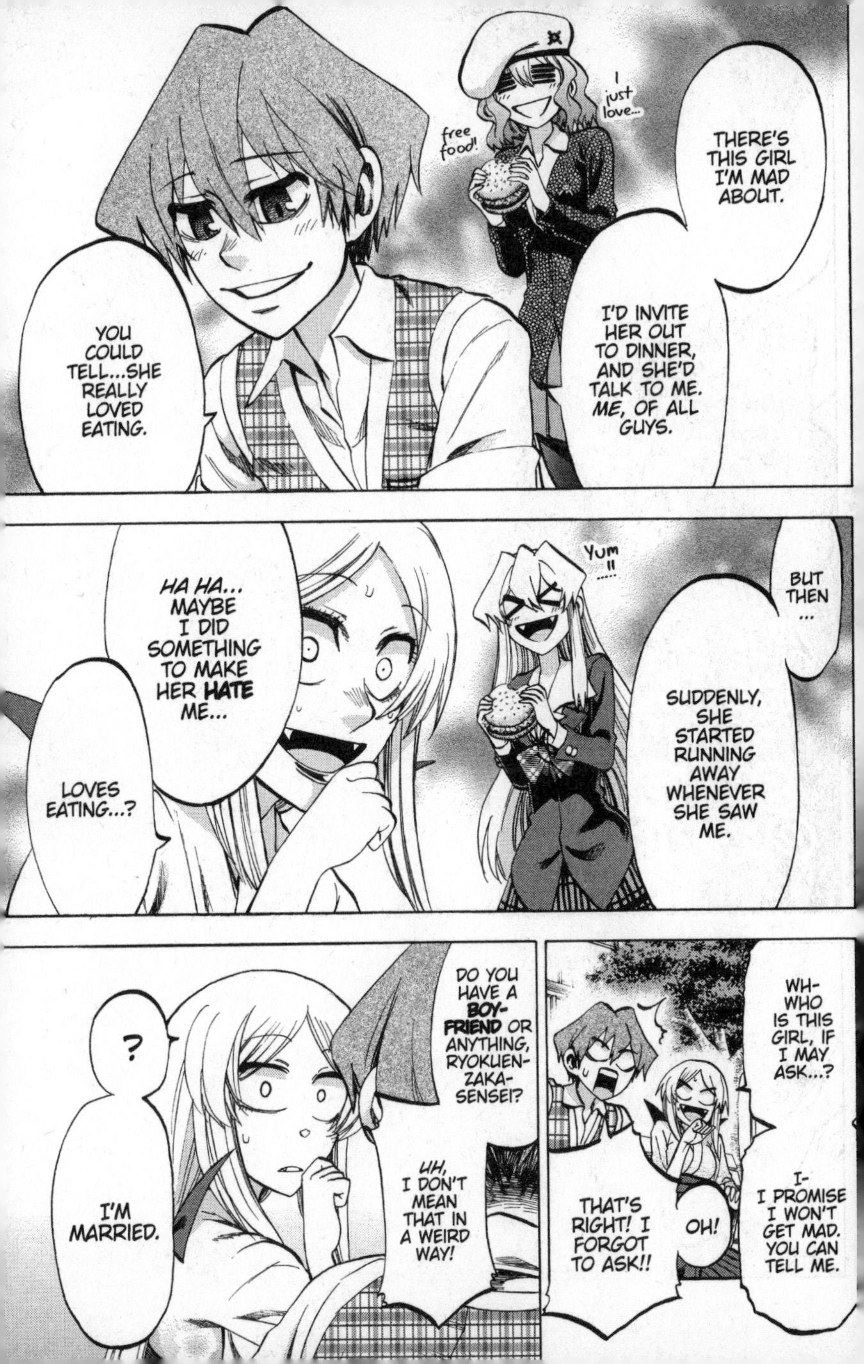
THERE'S THIS GIRL I'M MAD ABOUT.
I just love...
free food!
I'D INVITE HER OUT TO DINNER, AND SHE'D TALK TO ME. ME, OF ALL GUYS.
YOU COULD TELL...SHE REALLY LOVED EATING.
BUT THEN...
SUDDENLY, SHE STARTED RUNNING AWAY WHENEVER SHE SAW ME.
Yum!!......
HA HA... MAYBE I DID SOMETHING TO MAKE HER HATE ME...
LOVES EATING...?
WH-WHO IS THIS GIRL, IF I MAY ASK...?
I- I PROMISE I WON'T GET MAD. YOU CAN TELL ME.
OH!
THAT'S RIGHT! I FORGOT TO ASK!!
DO YOU HAVE A BOYFRIEND OR ANYTHING, RYOKUEN-ZAKA-SENSEI?
UH, I DON'T MEAN THAT IN A WEIRD WAY!
?
I'M MARRIED.

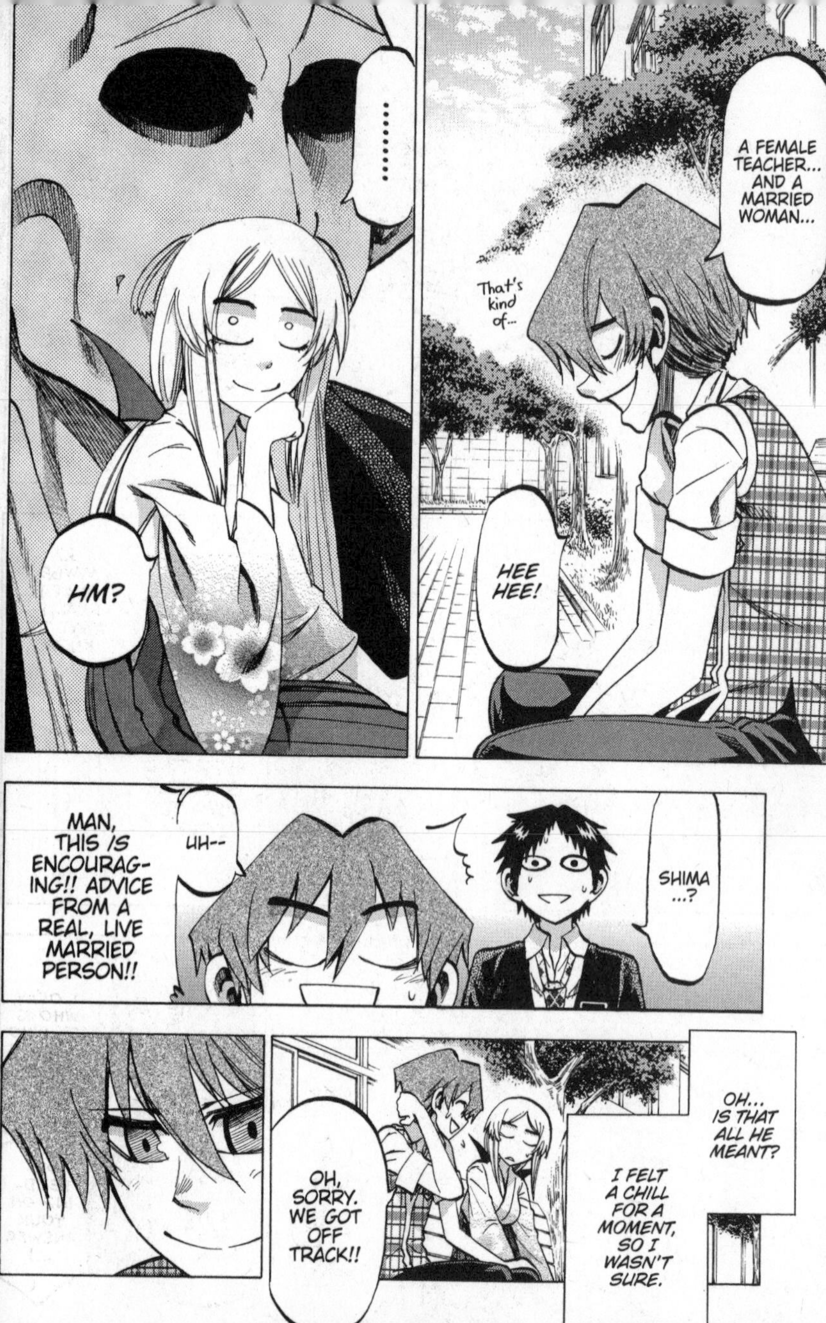
A FEMALE TEACHER... AND A MARRIED WOMAN...
That's kind of...
HEE HEE!
....
HM?
SHIMA ...?
UH--
MAN, THIS *IS* ENCOURAGING!! ADVICE FROM A REAL, LIVE MARRIED PERSON!!
OH... IS THAT ALL HE MEANT?
I FELT A CHILL FOR A MOMENT, SO I WASN'T SURE.
OH, SORRY. WE GOT OFF TRACK!!

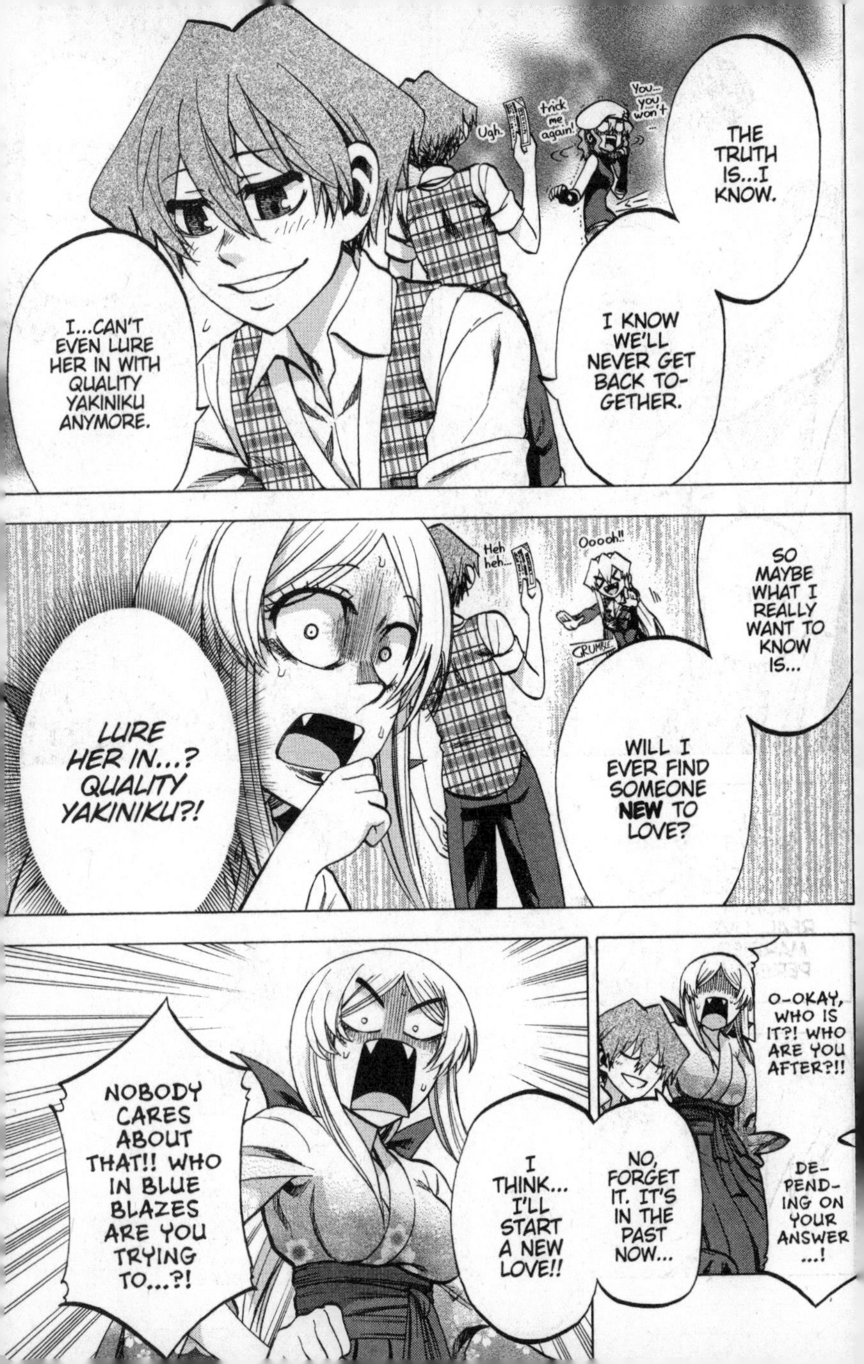
THE TRUTH IS...I KNOW.
You... you won't ...
trick me again!
Ugh.
I KNOW WE'LL NEVER GET BACK TO-GETHER.
I...CAN'T EVEN LURE HER IN WITH QUALITY YAKINIKU ANYMORE.
SO MAYBE WHAT I REALLY WANT TO KNOW IS...
Ooooh!!
Heh heh...
GRUMBLE
WILL I EVER FIND SOMEONE NEW TO LOVE?
LURE HER IN...? QUALITY YAKINIKU?!
O-OKAY, WHO IS IT?! WHO ARE YOU AFTER?!!
DE-PEND-ING ON YOUR ANSWER...!
NO, FORGET IT. IT'S IN THE PAST NOW...
I THINK... I'LL START A NEW LOVE!!
NOBODY CARES ABOUT THAT!! WHO IN BLUE BLAZES ARE YOU TRYING TO...?!

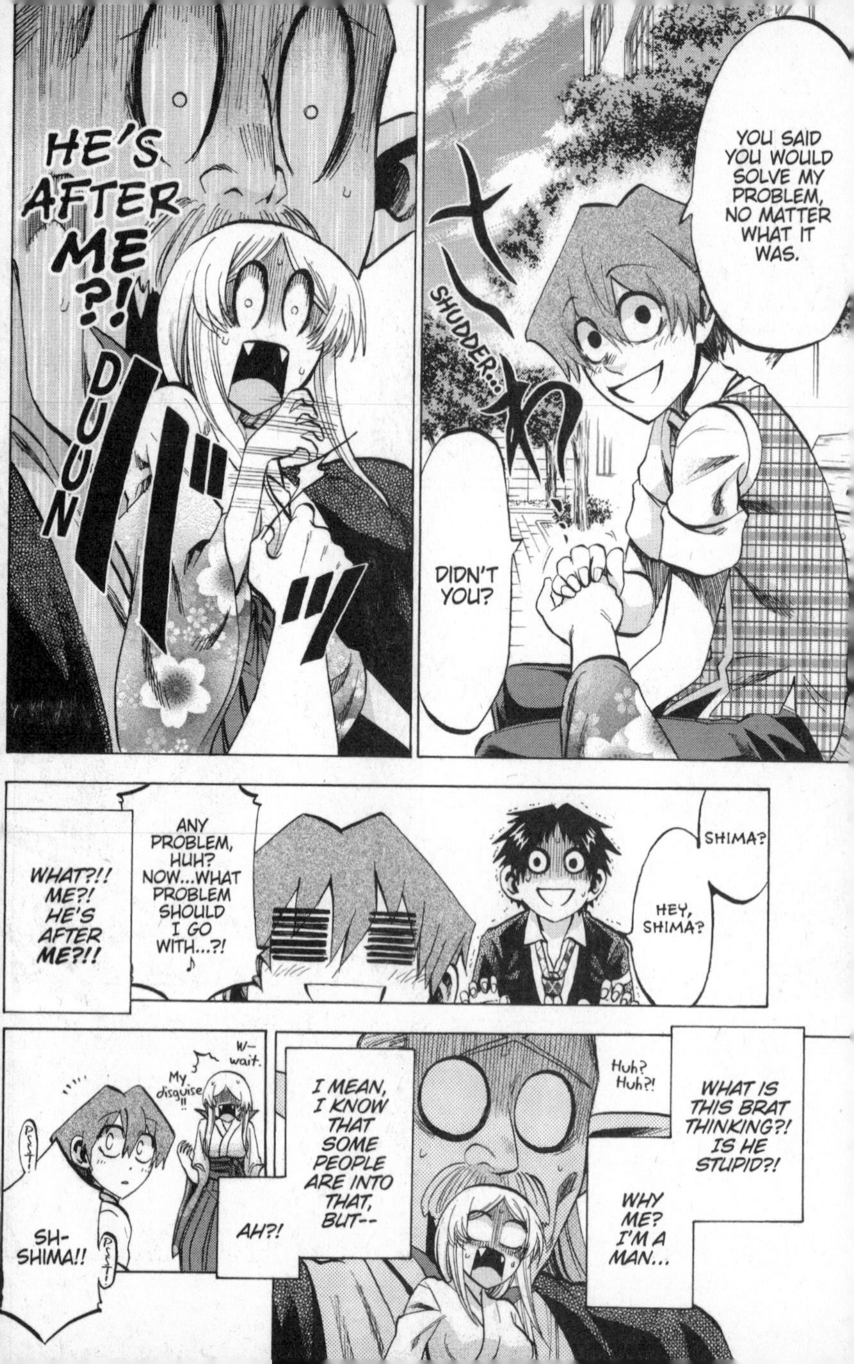
YOU SAID YOU WOULD SOLVE MY PROBLEM, NO MATTER WHAT IT WAS.
SHUDDER...
DIDN'T YOU?
HE'S AFTER ME?!
DUUUN
SHIMA?
HEY, SHIMA?
ANY PROBLEM, HUH? NOW...WHAT PROBLEM SHOULD I GO WITH...?! ♪
WHAT?!! ME?! HE'S AFTER ME?!!
WHAT IS THIS BRAT THINKING?! IS HE STUPID?!
Huh? Huh?!
WHY ME? I'M A MAN...
I MEAN, I KNOW THAT SOME PEOPLE ARE INTO THAT, BUT--
AH?!
W-wait.
My disguise!!
SH-SHIMA!!

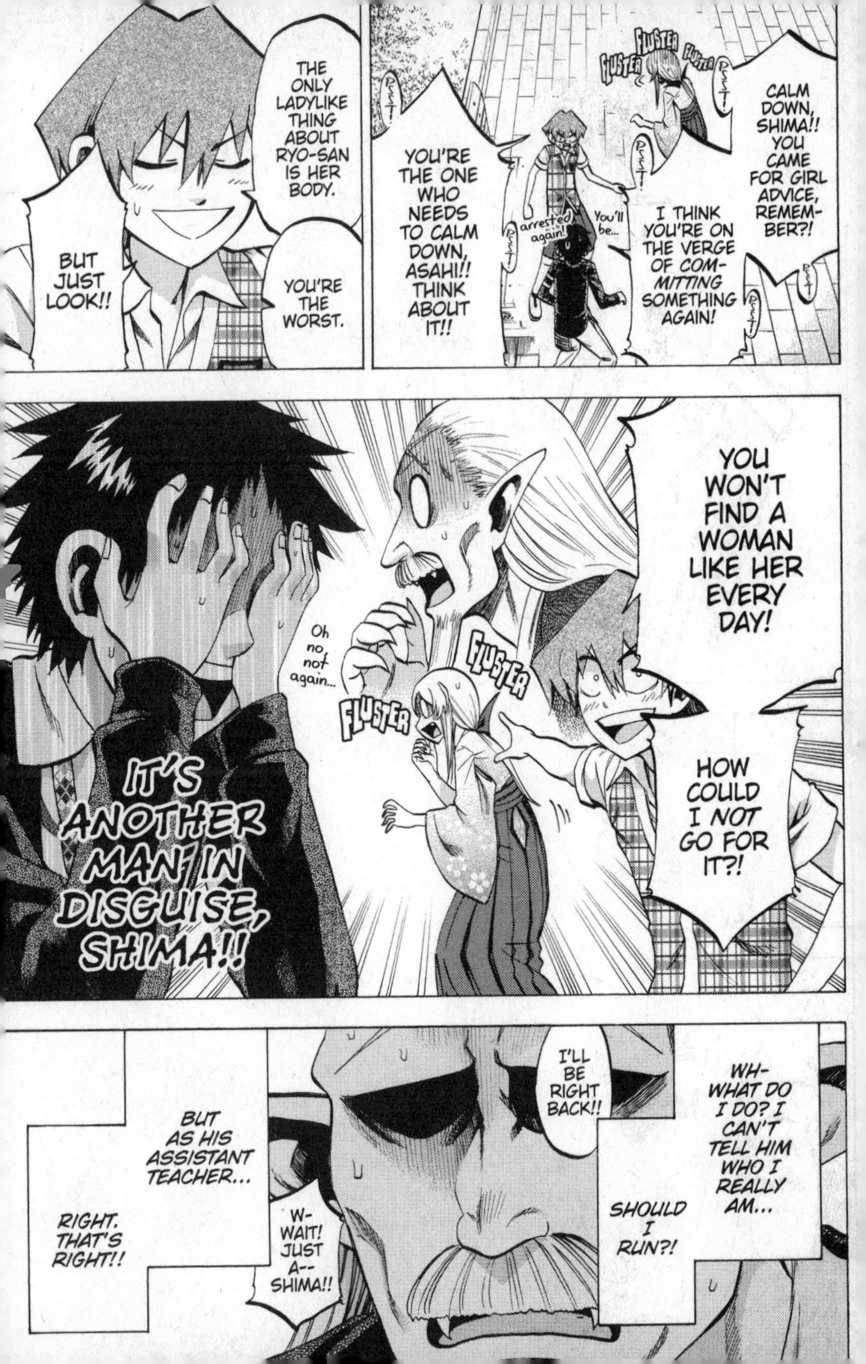
FLUSTER
FLUSTER
FLUSTER
PSST!
CALM DOWN, SHIMA!! YOU CAME FOR GIRL ADVICE, REMEMBER?!
PSST!
PSST!
I THINK YOU'RE ON THE VERGE OF COMMITTING SOMETHING AGAIN!
You'll be...
arrested again!
PSST!
PSST!
YOU'RE THE ONE WHO NEEDS TO CALM DOWN, ASAHI!! THINK ABOUT IT!!
PSST!
PSST!
THE ONLY LADYLIKE THING ABOUT RYO-SAN IS HER BODY.
YOU'RE THE WORST.
BUT JUST LOOK!!
YOU WON'T FIND A WOMAN LIKE HER EVERY DAY!
HOW COULD I NOT GO FOR IT?!
FLUSTER
FLUSTER
Oh no not again...
IT'S ANOTHER MAN IN DISGUISE, SHIMA!!
WH- WHAT DO I DO? I CAN'T TELL HIM WHO I REALLY AM...
SHOULD I RUN?!
I'LL BE RIGHT BACK!!
W-WAIT! JUST A-- SHIMA!!
BUT AS HIS ASSISTANT TEACHER...
RIGHT. THAT'S RIGHT!!

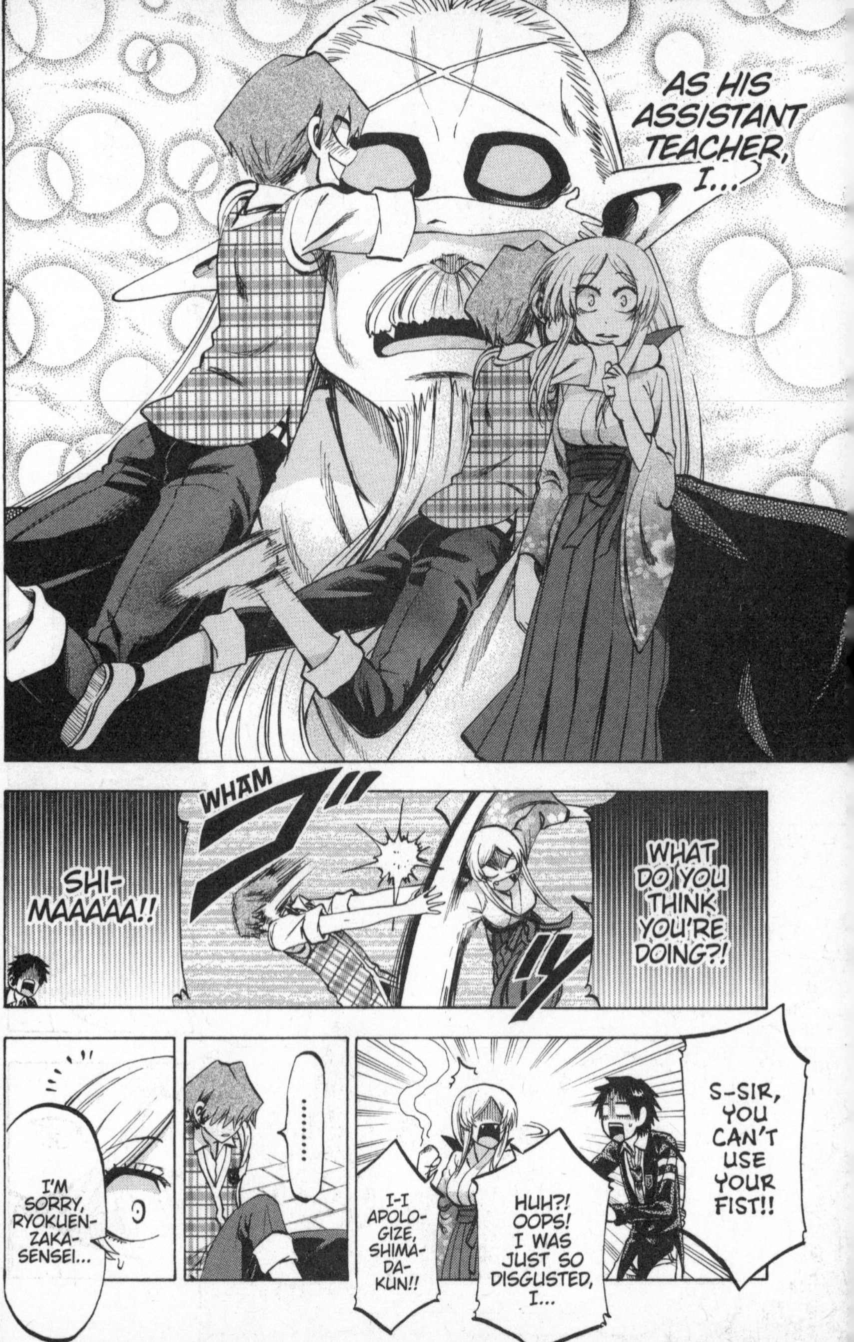
AS HIS ASSISTANT TEACHER, I...
WHAT DO YOU THINK YOU'RE DOING?!
WHAM
SHI-MAAAAAA!!
S-SIR, YOU CAN'T USE YOUR FIST!!
HUH?! OOPS! I WAS JUST SO DISGUSTED, I...
I-I APOLOGIZE, SHIMA-DA-KUN!!
......
I'M SORRY, RYOKUEN-ZAKA-SENSEI...

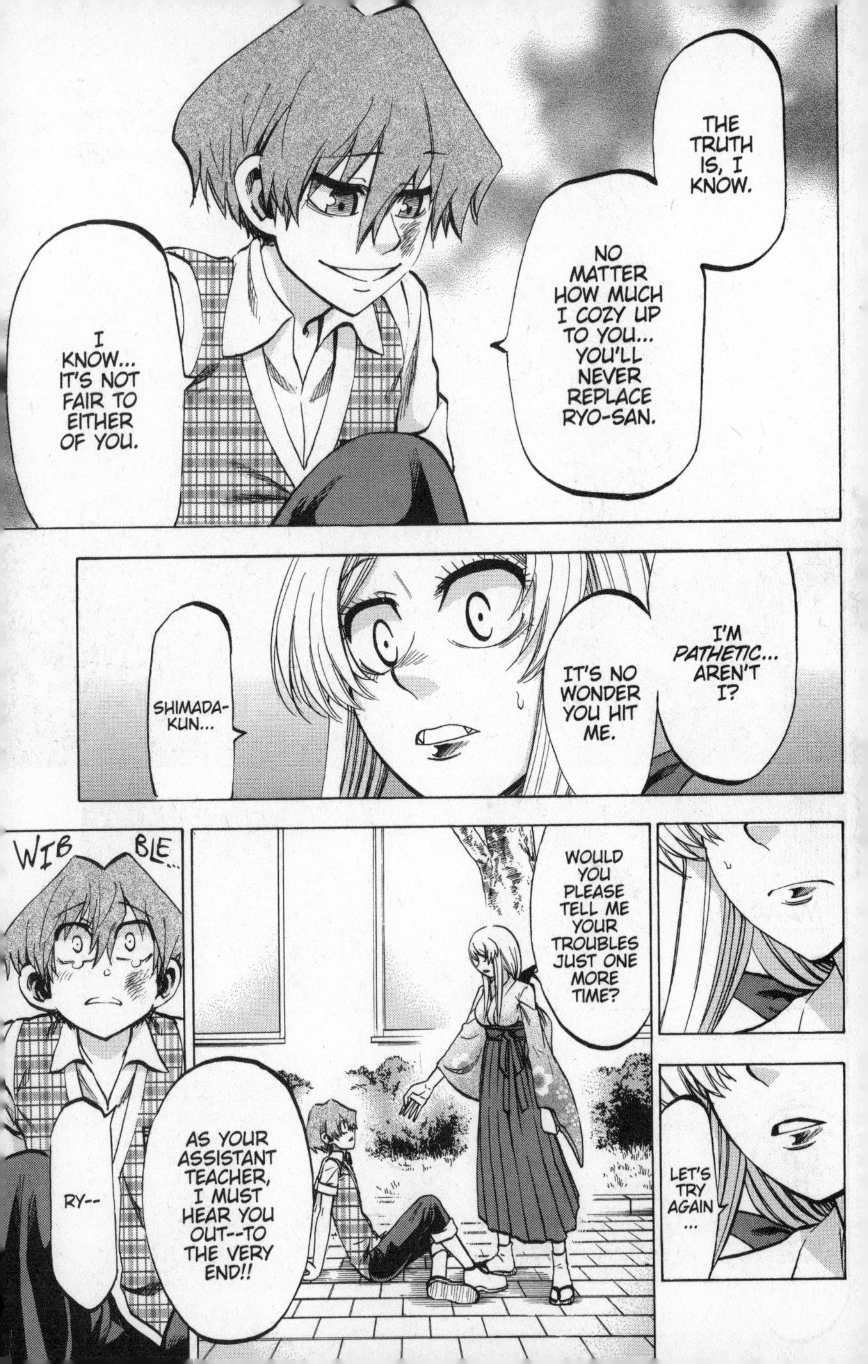
THE TRUTH IS, I KNOW.
NO MATTER HOW MUCH I COZY UP TO YOU... YOU'LL NEVER REPLACE RYO-SAN.
I KNOW... IT'S NOT FAIR TO EITHER OF YOU.
I'M *PATHETIC*... AREN'T I?
IT'S NO WONDER YOU HIT ME.
SHIMADA-KUN...
LET'S TRY AGAIN...
WOULD YOU PLEASE TELL ME YOUR TROUBLES JUST ONE MORE TIME?
AS YOUR ASSISTANT TEACHER, I MUST HEAR YOU OUT--TO THE VERY END!!
WIB BLE...
RY--

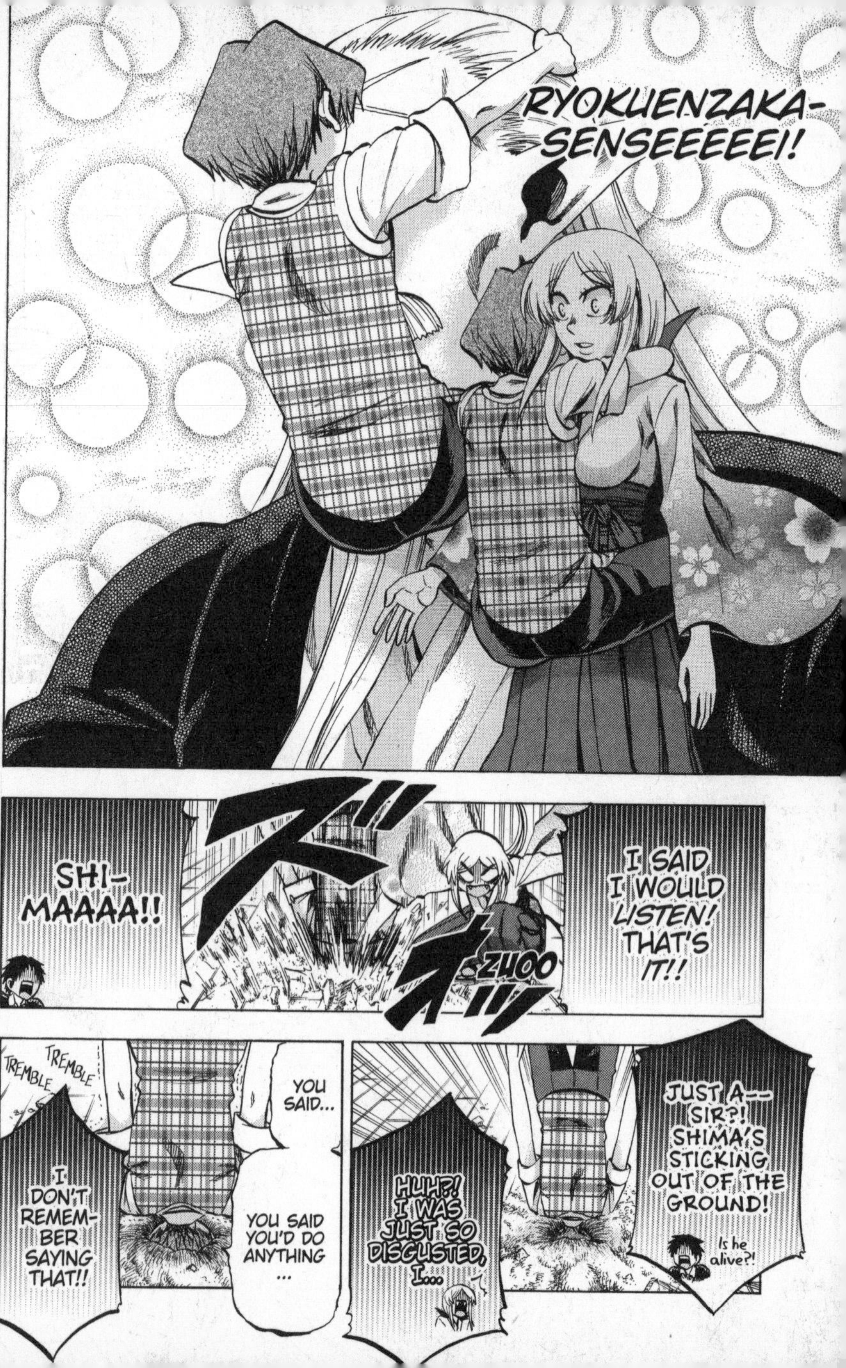
RYOKUENZAKA-SENSEEEEEI!
I SAID I WOULD LISTEN! THAT'S IT!!
ZUOO
SHI-MAAAA!!
JUST A-- SIR?! SHIMA'S STICKING OUT OF THE GROUND!
Is he alive?!
HUH?! I WAS JUST SO DISGUSTED, I...
YOU SAID...
TREMBLE TREMBLE
YOU SAID YOU'D DO ANYTHING ...
I DON'T REMEM-BER SAYING THAT!!

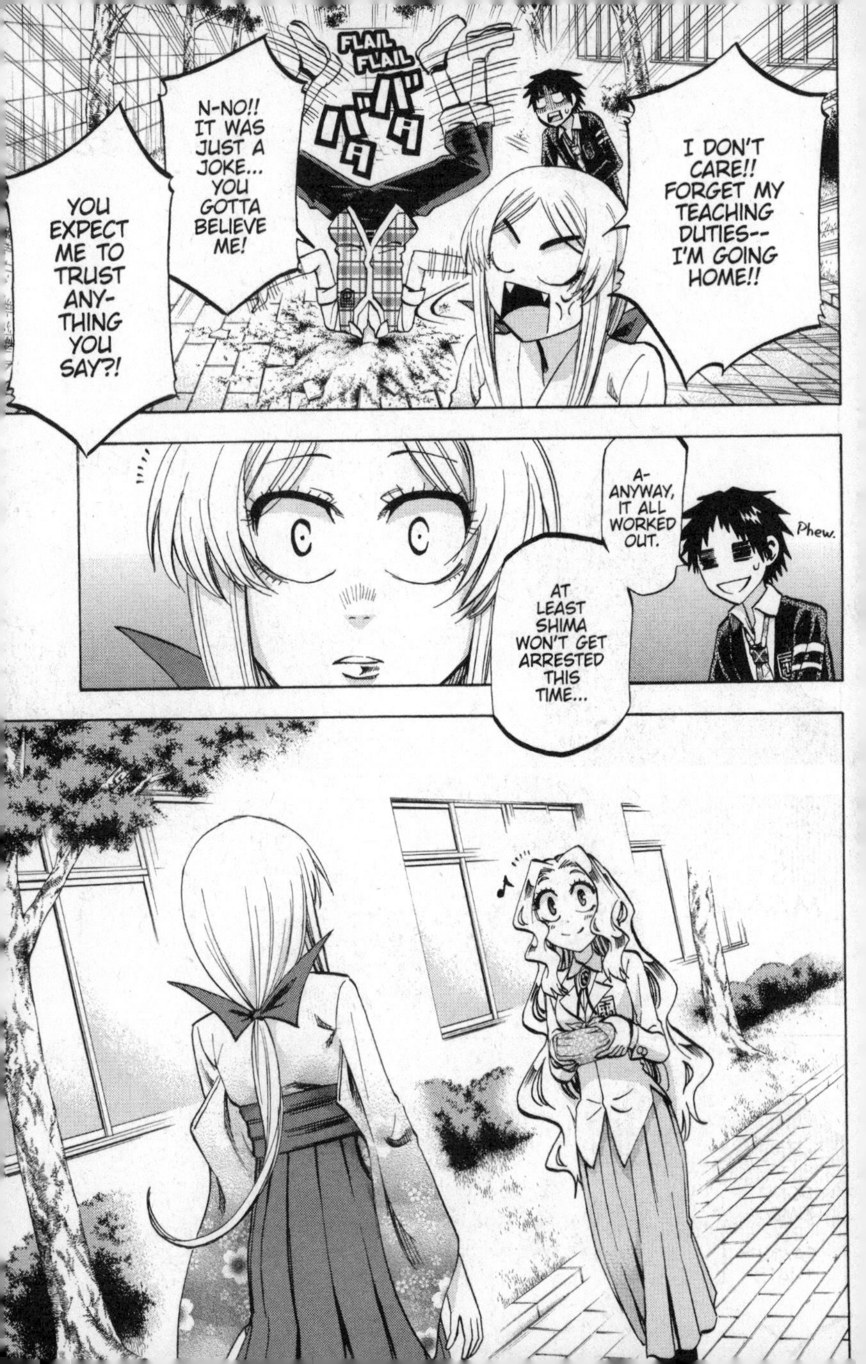
I DON'T CARE!! FORGET MY TEACHING DUTIES-- I'M GOING HOME!!
FLAIL FLAIL
バタバタ
N-NO!! IT WAS JUST A JOKE... YOU GOTTA BELIEVE ME!
YOU EXPECT ME TO TRUST ANY-THING YOU SAY?!
A- ANYWAY, IT ALL WORKED OUT.
Phew.
AT LEAST SHIMA WON'T GET ARRESTED THIS TIME...

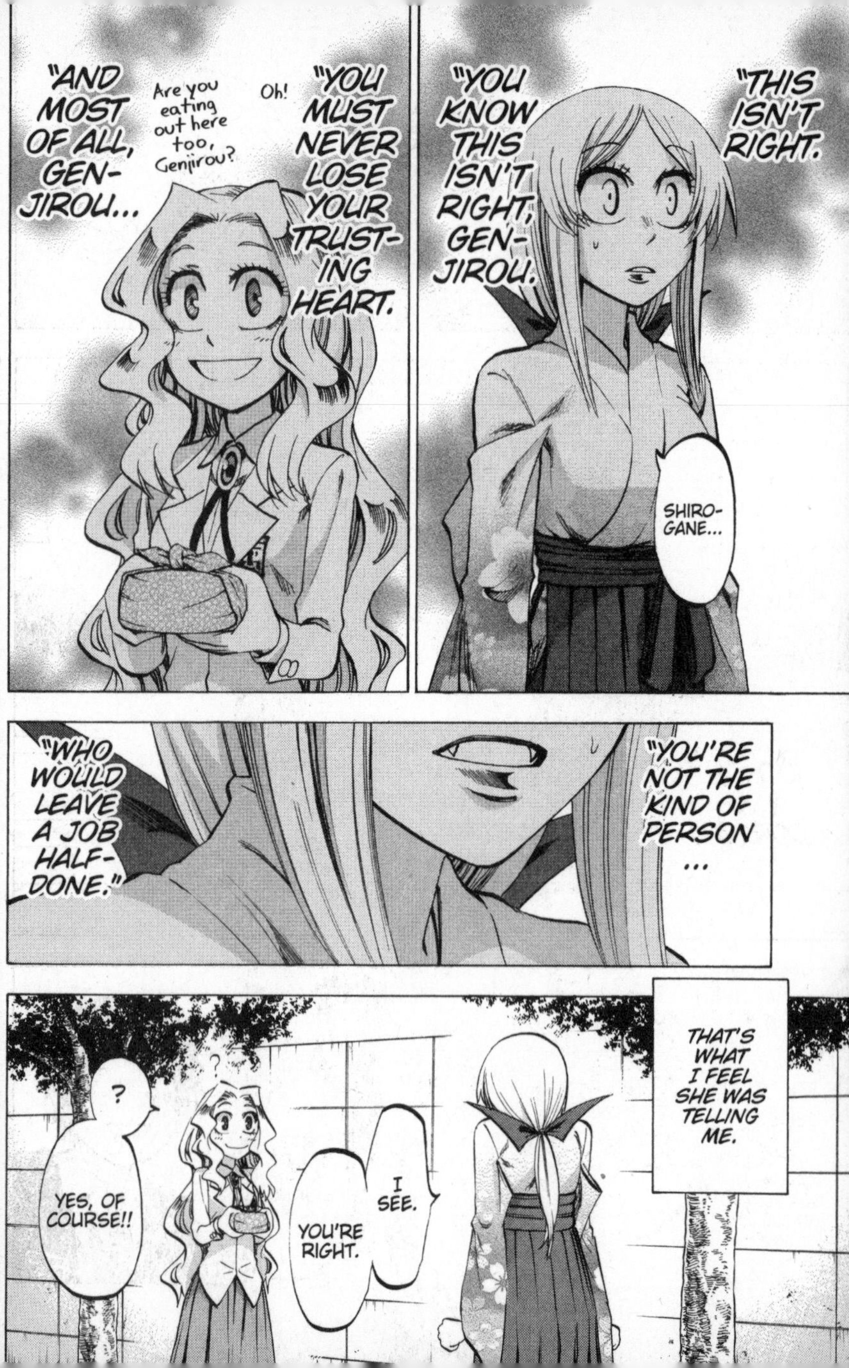
"THIS ISN'T RIGHT.
"YOU KNOW THIS ISN'T RIGHT, GEN-JIROU.
SHIRO-GANE...
"YOU MUST NEVER LOSE YOUR TRUST-ING HEART.
Oh!
Are you eating out here too, Genjirou?
"AND MOST OF ALL, GEN-JIROU...
"YOU'RE NOT THE KIND OF PERSON...
"WHO WOULD LEAVE A JOB HALF-DONE."
THAT'S WHAT I FEEL SHE WAS TELLING ME.
I SEE.
YOU'RE RIGHT.
?
?
YES, OF COURSE!!

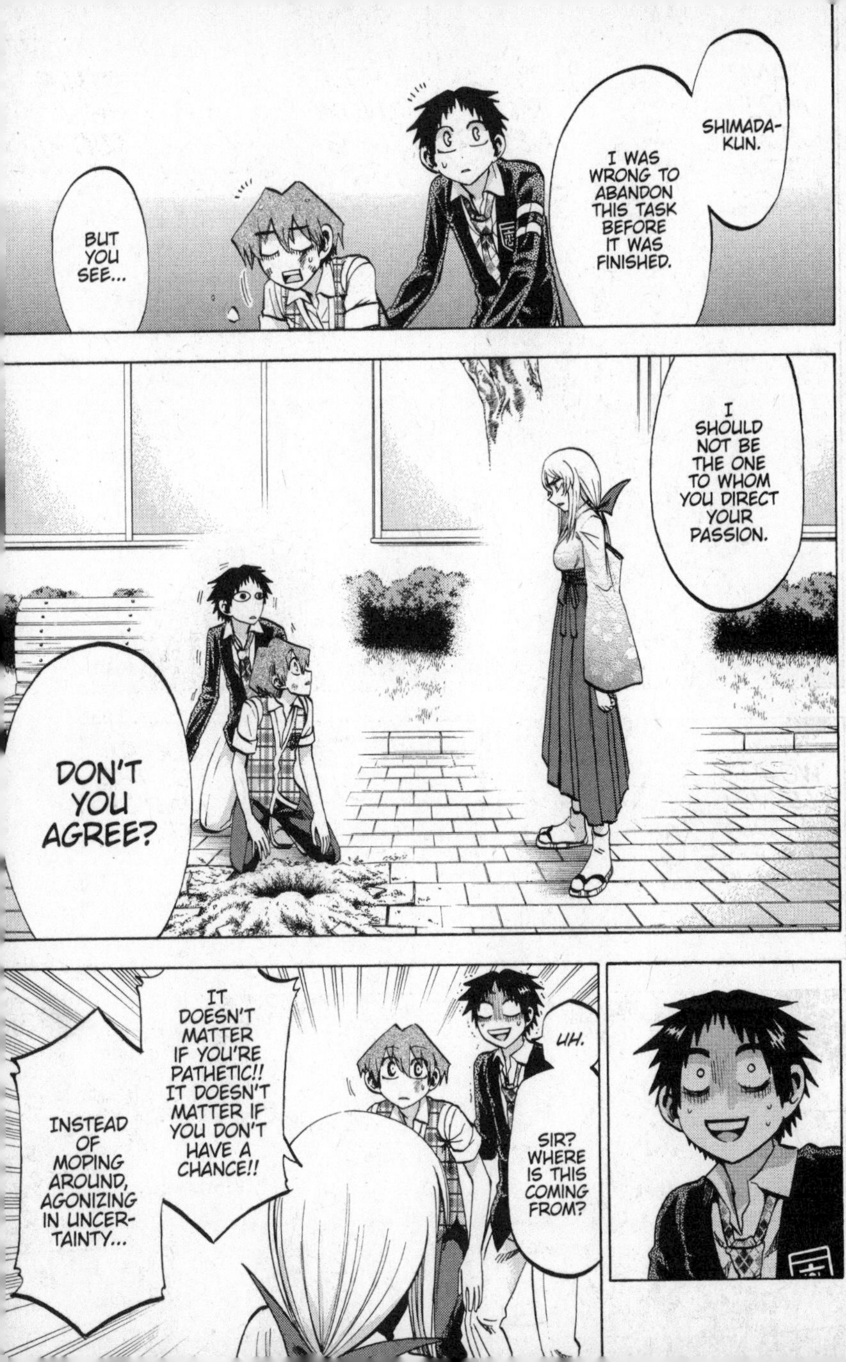
SHIMADA-KUN.
I WAS WRONG TO ABANDON THIS TASK BEFORE IT WAS FINISHED.
BUT YOU SEE...
I SHOULD NOT BE THE ONE TO WHOM YOU DIRECT YOUR PASSION.
DON'T YOU AGREE?
UH.
SIR? WHERE IS THIS COMING FROM?
IT DOESN'T MATTER IF YOU'RE PATHETIC!! IT DOESN'T MATTER IF YOU DON'T HAVE A CHANCE!!
INSTEAD OF MOPING AROUND, AGONIZING IN UNCERTAINTY...

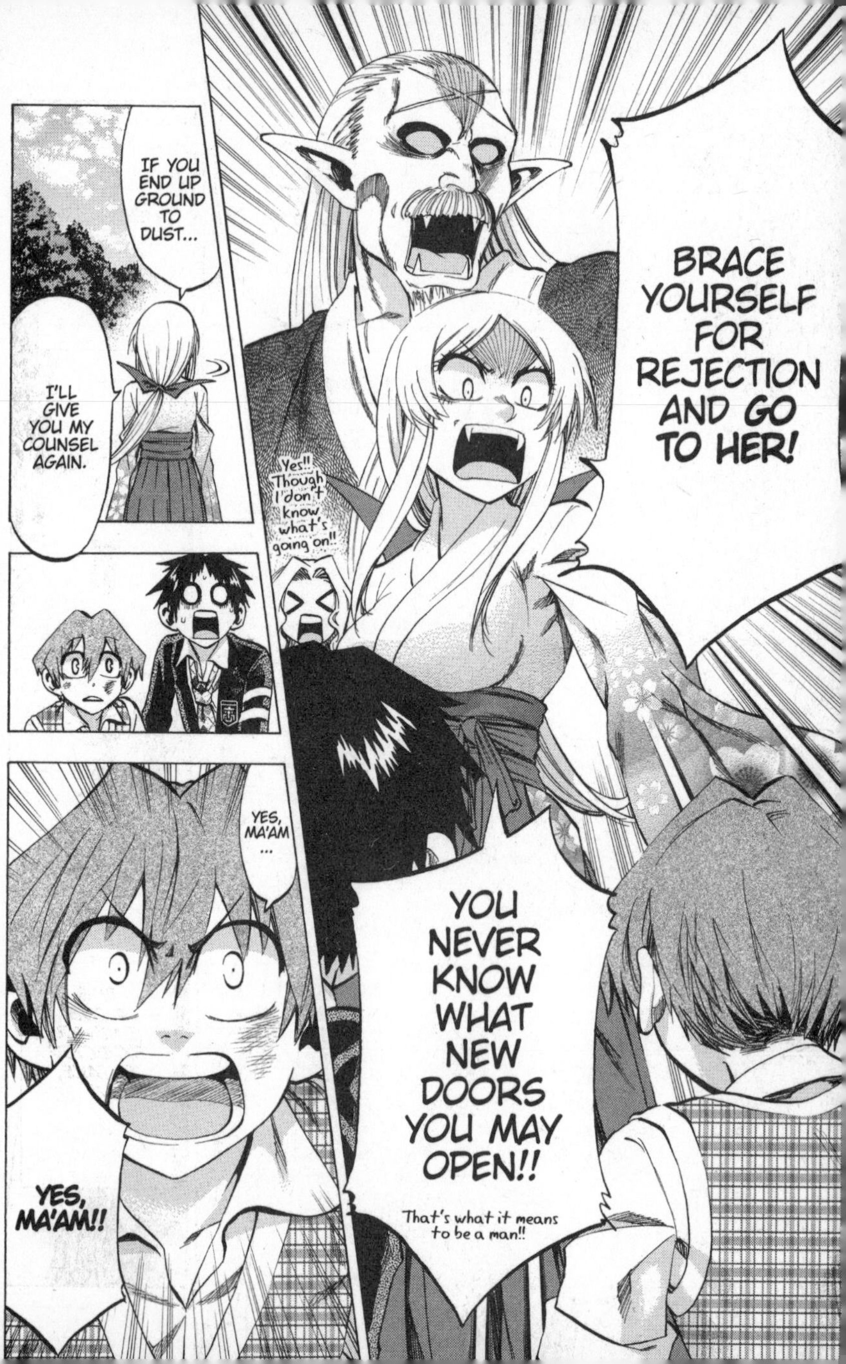
BRACE YOURSELF FOR REJECTION AND GO TO HER!
Yes!! Though I don't know what's going on!!
YOU NEVER KNOW WHAT NEW DOORS YOU MAY OPEN!!
That's what it means to be a man!!
IF YOU END UP GROUND TO DUST...
I'LL GIVE YOU MY COUNSEL AGAIN.
YES, MA'AM ...
YES, MA'AM!!

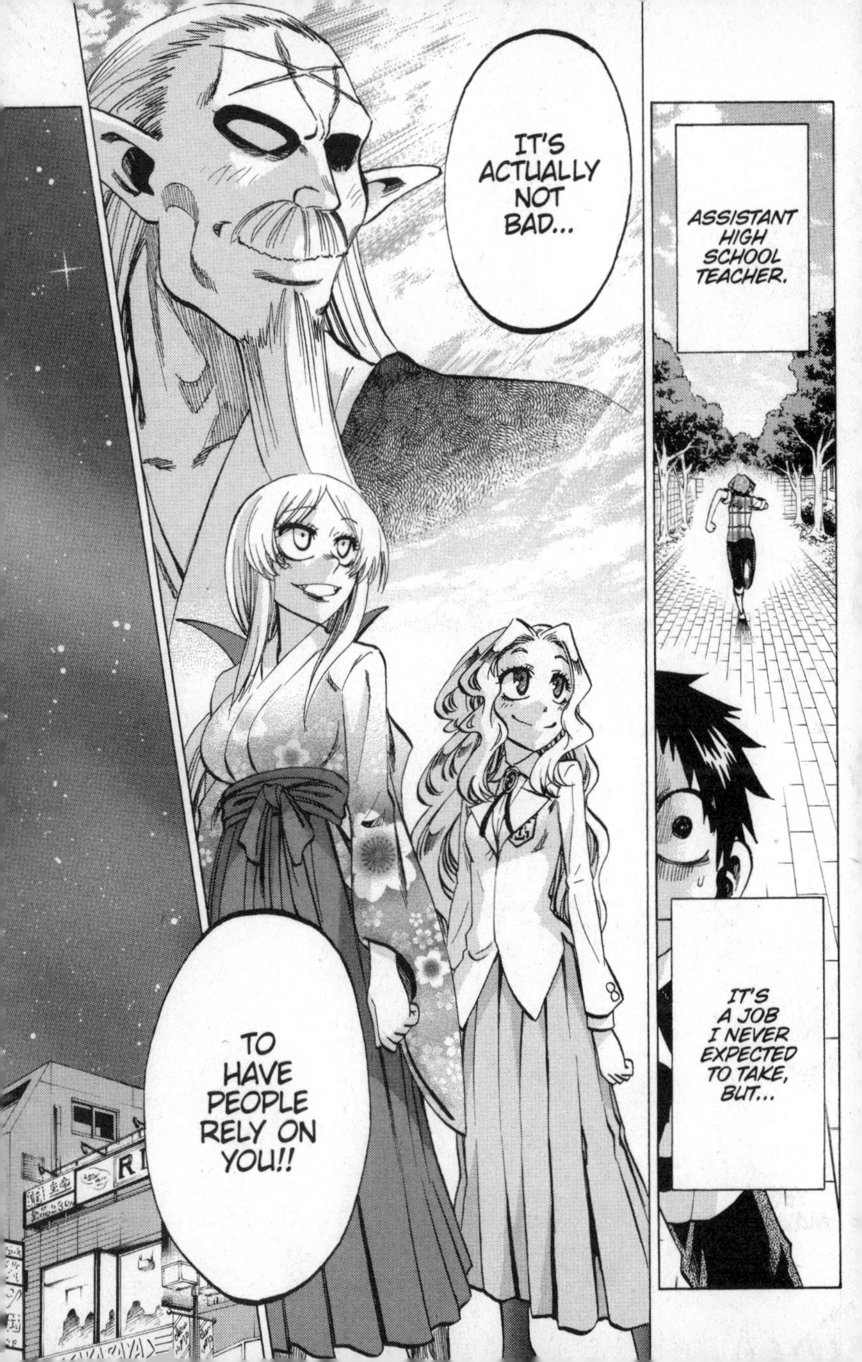
ASSISTANT HIGH SCHOOL TEACHER.
IT'S A JOB I NEVER EXPECTED TO TAKE, BUT...
IT'S ACTUALLY NOT BAD...
TO HAVE PEOPLE RELY ON YOU!!

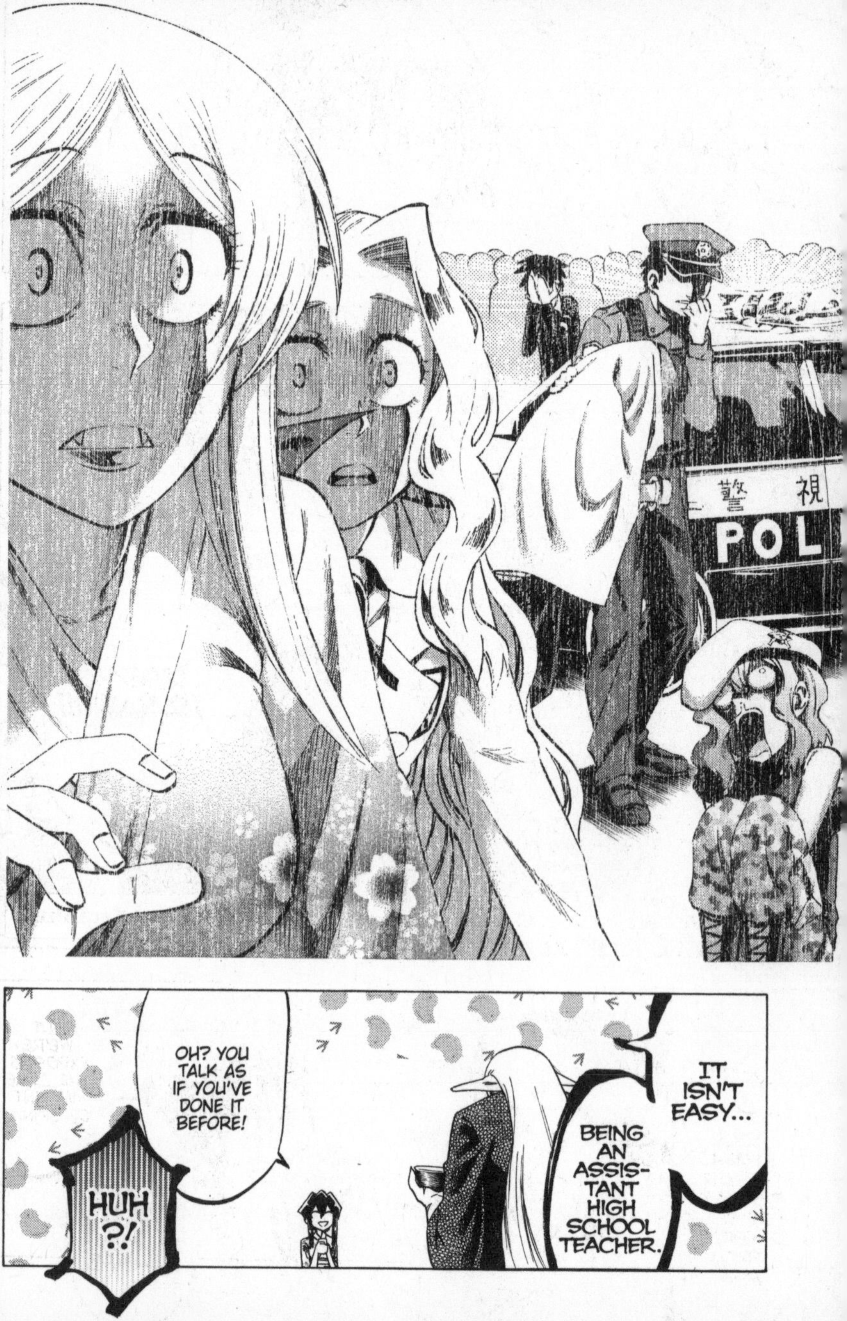

警視
POL
IT ISN'T EASY...
BEING AN ASSISTANT HIGH SCHOOL TEACHER.
OH? YOU TALK AS IF YOU'VE DONE IT BEFORE!
HUH?!

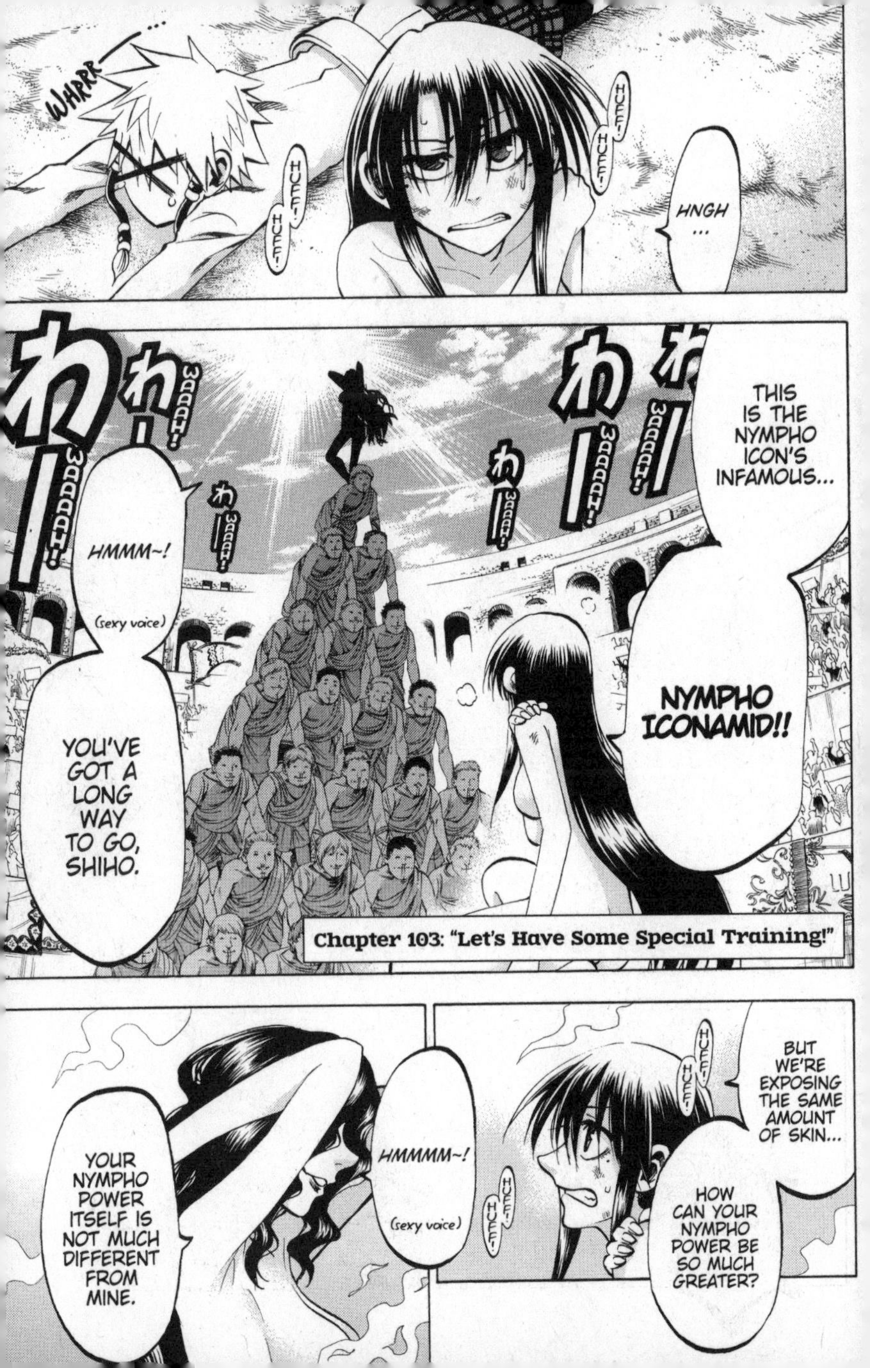
HUFF! HUFF!
HNGH ...
WHRRR—...
HUFF! HUFF!
わー
WAAAAH!
わー
WAAAAH!
わー
WAAAH!
THIS IS THE NYMPHO ICON'S INFAMOUS...
NYMPHO ICONAMID!!
わー
WAAAH!
わー
WAAAH!
わー
WAAAAAH!
HMMM~!
(sexy voice)
YOU'VE GOT A LONG WAY TO GO, SHIHO.
Chapter 103: "Let's Have Some Special Training!"
HUFF! HUFF!
BUT WE'RE EXPOSING THE SAME AMOUNT OF SKIN...
HOW CAN YOUR NYMPHO POWER BE SO MUCH GREATER?
HUFF! HUFF!
HMMMM~!
(sexy voice)
YOUR NYMPHO POWER ITSELF IS NOT MUCH DIFFERENT FROM MINE.

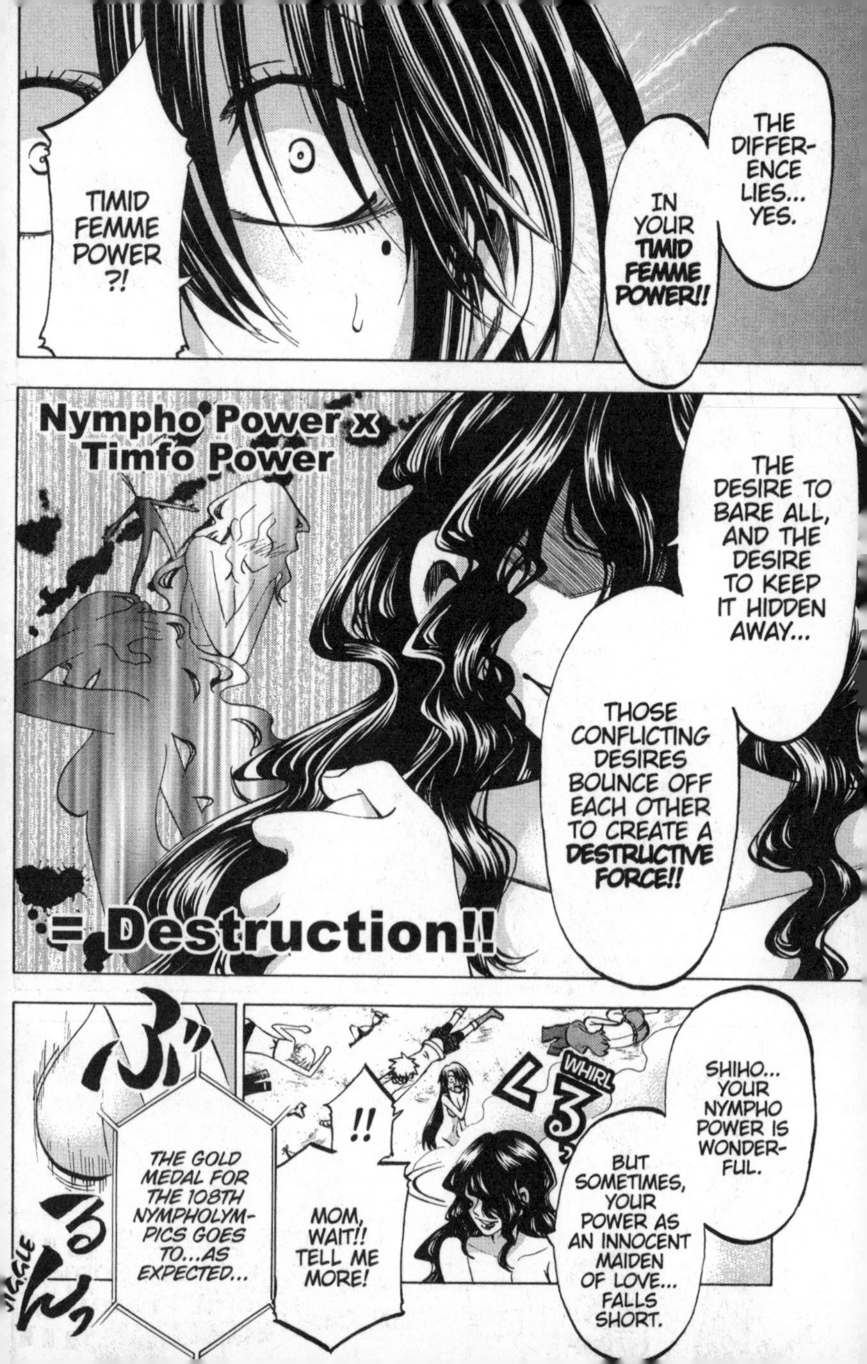
THE DIFFERENCE LIES... YES.
IN YOUR **TIMID FEMME POWER!!**
TIMID FEMME POWER?!
THE DESIRE TO BARE ALL, AND THE DESIRE TO KEEP IT HIDDEN AWAY...
THOSE CONFLICTING DESIRES BOUNCE OFF EACH OTHER TO CREATE A **DESTRUCTIVE FORCE!!**
Nympho Power x Timfo Power
= Destruction!!
SHIHO... YOUR NYMPHO POWER IS WONDERFUL.
BUT SOMETIMES, YOUR POWER AS AN INNOCENT MAIDEN OF LOVE... FALLS SHORT.
WHIRL
!!
MOM, WAIT!! TELL ME MORE!
THE GOLD MEDAL FOR THE 108TH NYMPHOLYMPICS GOES TO...AS EXPECTED...
JIGGLE

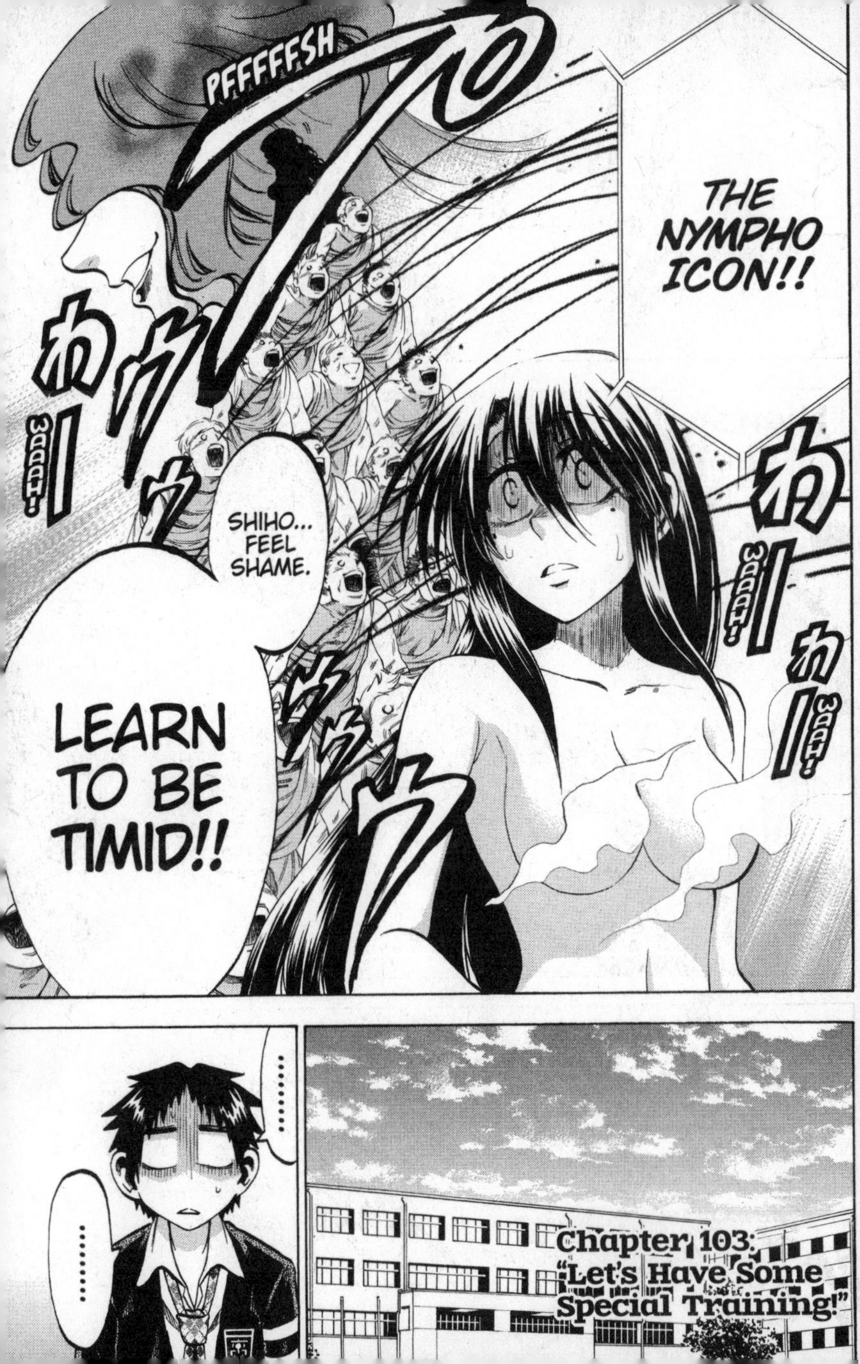
THE NYMPHO ICON!!
WAAAH!
WAAAH!
SHIHO... FEEL SHAME.
LEARN TO BE TIMID!!
PFFFFFSH
WAAAH!
Chapter 103: "Let's Have Some Special Training!"
......
......

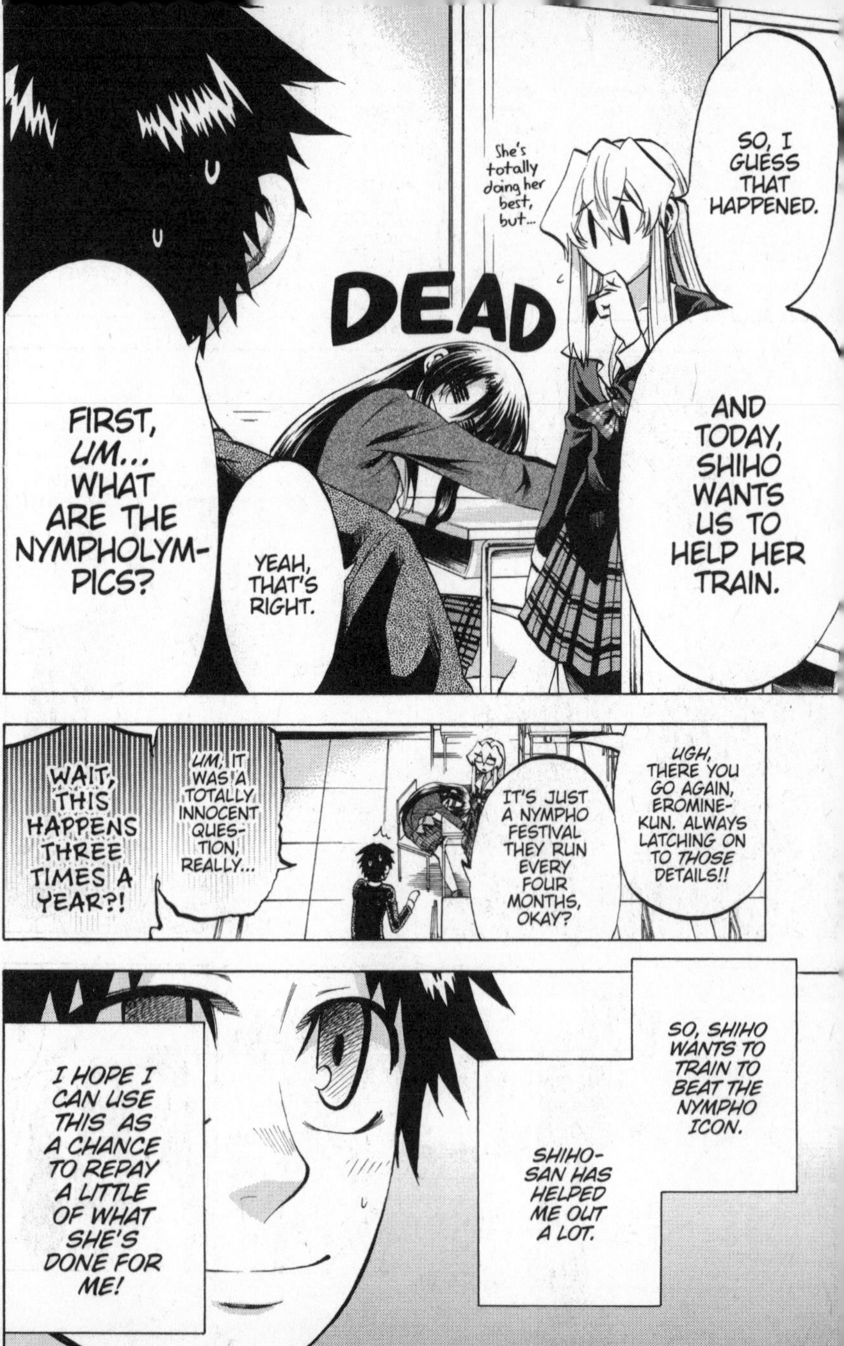
SO, I GUESS THAT HAPPENED.
AND TODAY, SHIHO WANTS US TO HELP HER TRAIN.
She's totally doing her best, but...
DEAD
YEAH, THAT'S RIGHT.
FIRST, UM... WHAT ARE THE NYMPHOLYMPICS?
UGH, THERE YOU GO AGAIN, EROMINE-KUN. ALWAYS LATCHING ON TO THOSE DETAILS!!
IT'S JUST A NYMPHO FESTIVAL THEY RUN EVERY FOUR MONTHS, OKAY?
UM, IT WAS A TOTALLY INNOCENT QUESTION, REALLY...
WAIT, THIS HAPPENS THREE TIMES A YEAR?!
SO, SHIHO WANTS TO TRAIN TO BEAT THE NYMPHO ICON.
SHIHO-SAN HAS HELPED ME OUT A LOT.
I HOPE I CAN USE THIS AS A CHANCE TO REPAY A LITTLE OF WHAT SHE'S DONE FOR ME!

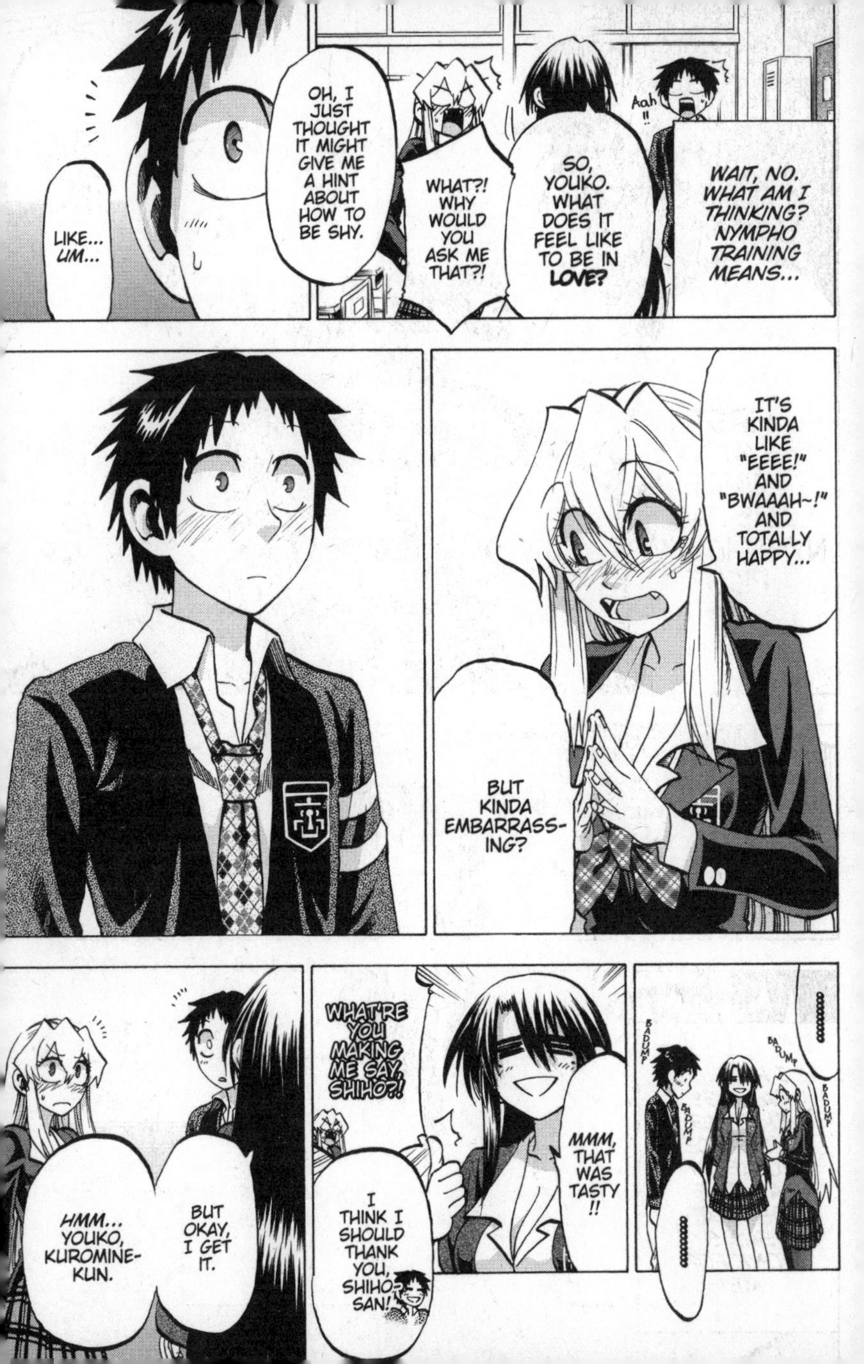
Aah!!
WAIT, NO. WHAT AM I THINKING? NYMPHO TRAINING MEANS...
SO, YOUKO. WHAT DOES IT FEEL LIKE TO BE IN **LOVE?**
WHAT?! WHY WOULD YOU ASK ME THAT?!
OH, I JUST THOUGHT IT MIGHT GIVE ME A HINT ABOUT HOW TO BE SHY.
LIKE... UM...
IT'S KINDA LIKE "EEEE!" AND "BWAAAH~!" AND TOTALLY HAPPY...
BUT KINDA EMBARRASSING?
....
BADUMP
BADUMP
BADUMP
BADUMP
....
WHAT'RE YOU MAKING ME SAY, SHIHO?!
MMM, THAT WAS TASTY!!
I THINK I SHOULD THANK YOU, SHIHO-SAN!
BUT OKAY, I GET IT.
HMM... YOUKO, KUROMINE-KUN.

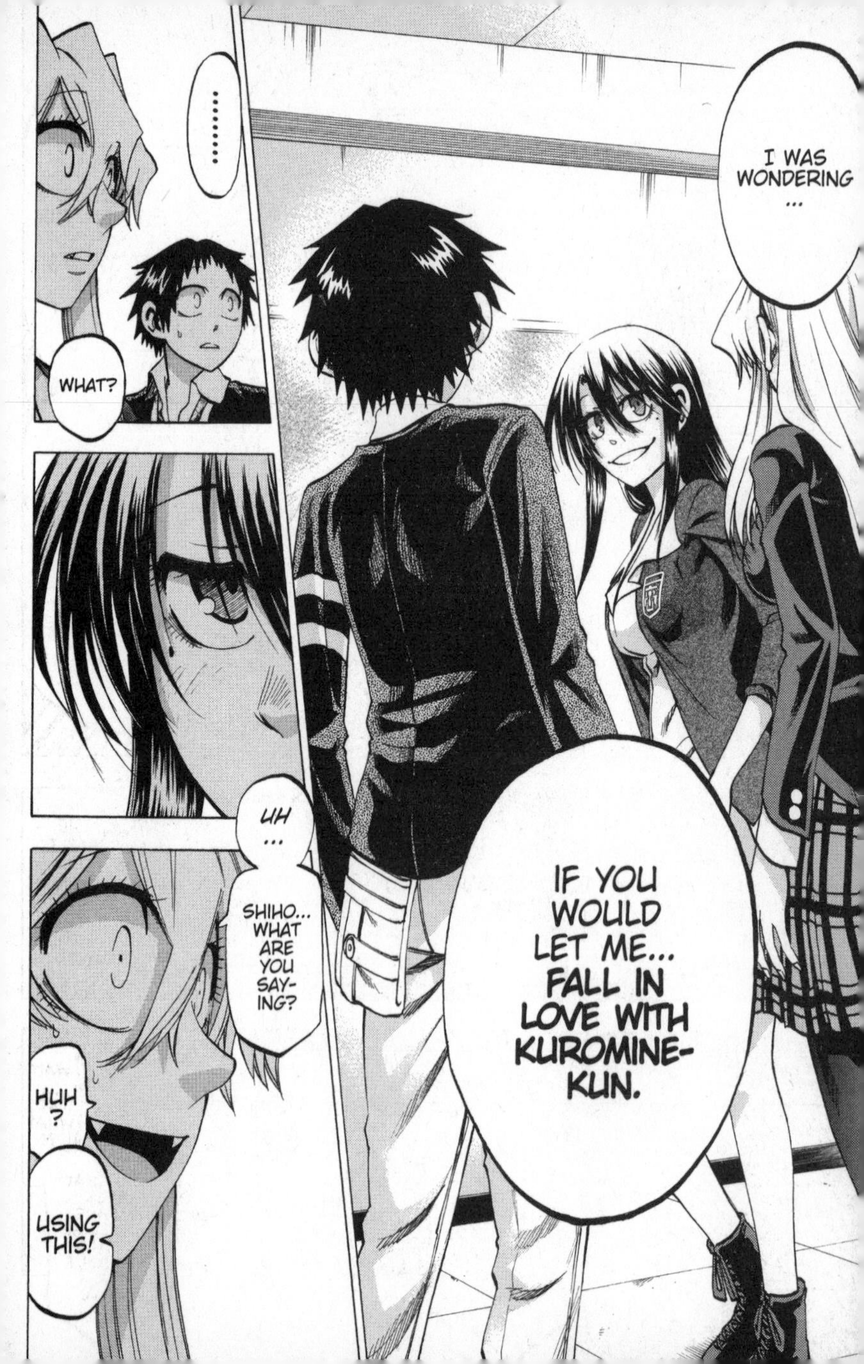
I WAS WONDERING ...
IF YOU WOULD LET ME... FALL IN LOVE WITH KUROMINE-KUN.
......
WHAT?
UH ...
SHIHO... WHAT ARE YOU SAY-ING?
HUH ?
USING THIS!

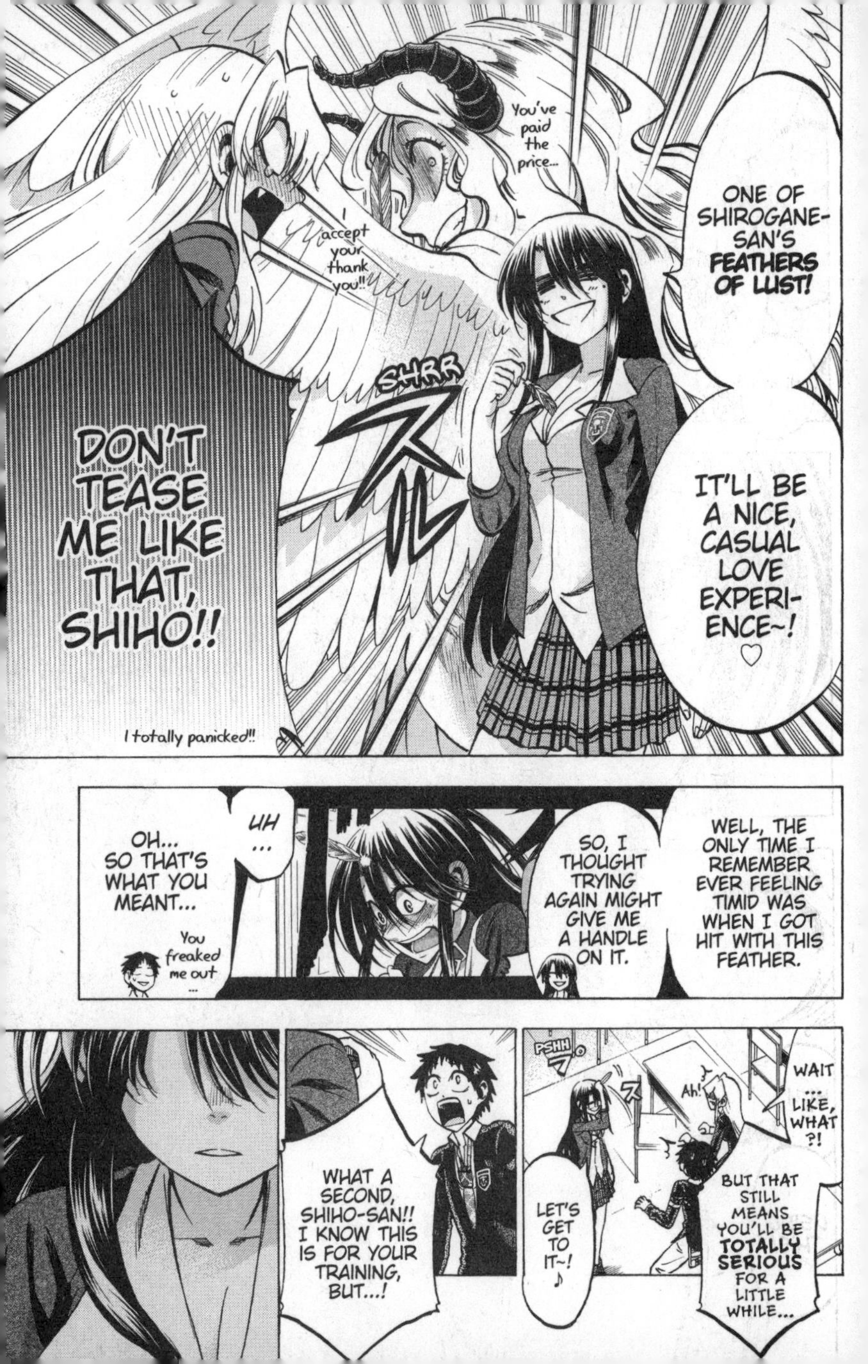
ONE OF SHIROGANE-SAN'S FEATHERS OF LUST!
IT'LL BE A NICE, CASUAL LOVE EXPERIENCE~! ♡
You've paid the price...
I accept your thank you!!
SHRR
DON'T TEASE ME LIKE THAT, SHIHO!!
I totally panicked!!
WELL, THE ONLY TIME I REMEMBER EVER FEELING TIMID WAS WHEN I GOT HIT WITH THIS FEATHER.
SO, I THOUGHT TRYING AGAIN MIGHT GIVE ME A HANDLE ON IT.
UH ...
OH... SO THAT'S WHAT YOU MEANT...
You freaked me out ...
WAIT ... LIKE, WHAT ?!
Ah!
PSHH
BUT THAT STILL MEANS YOU'LL BE TOTALLY SERIOUS FOR A LITTLE WHILE...
LET'S GET TO IT~! ♪
WHAT A SECOND, SHIHO-SAN!! I KNOW THIS IS FOR YOUR TRAINING, BUT...!

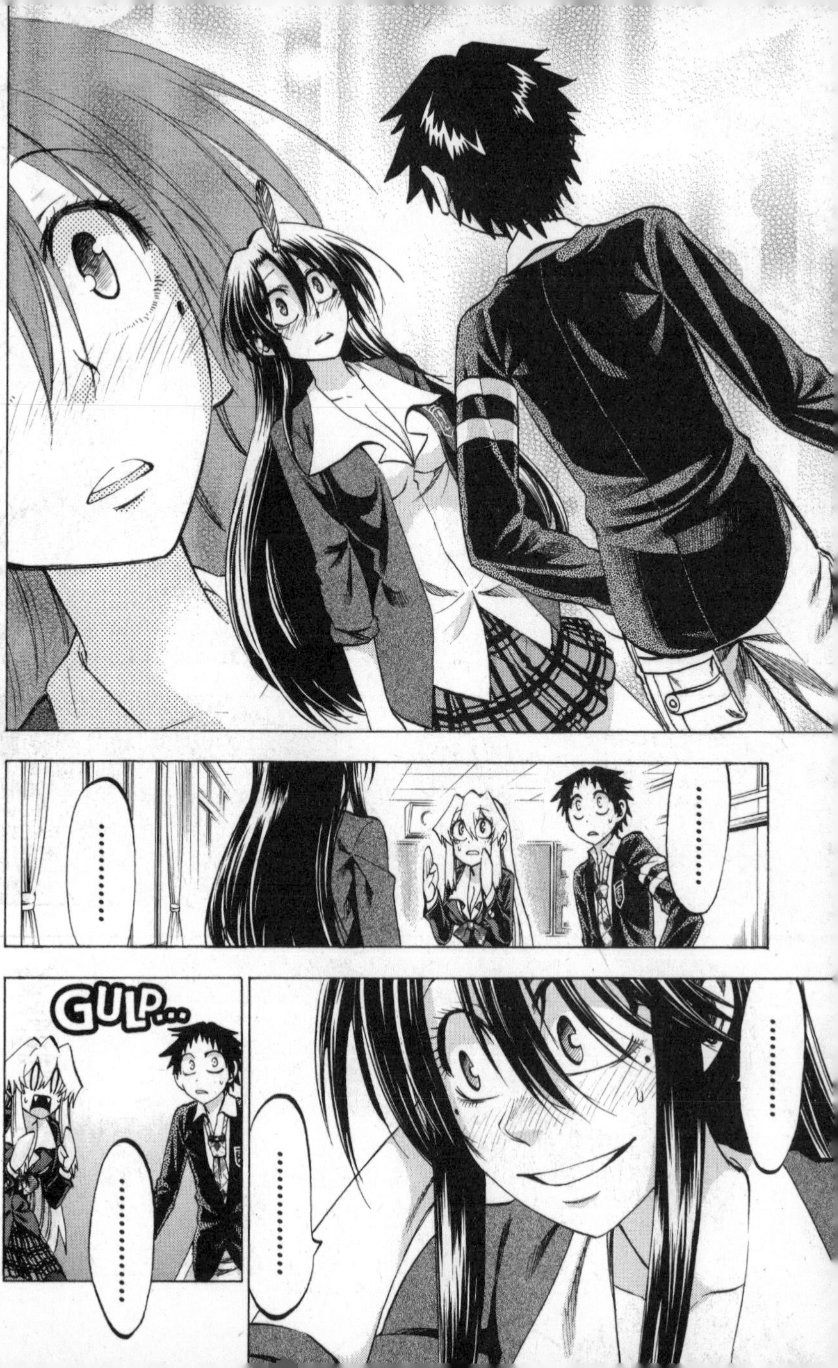........
....
....
....
GULP...
....

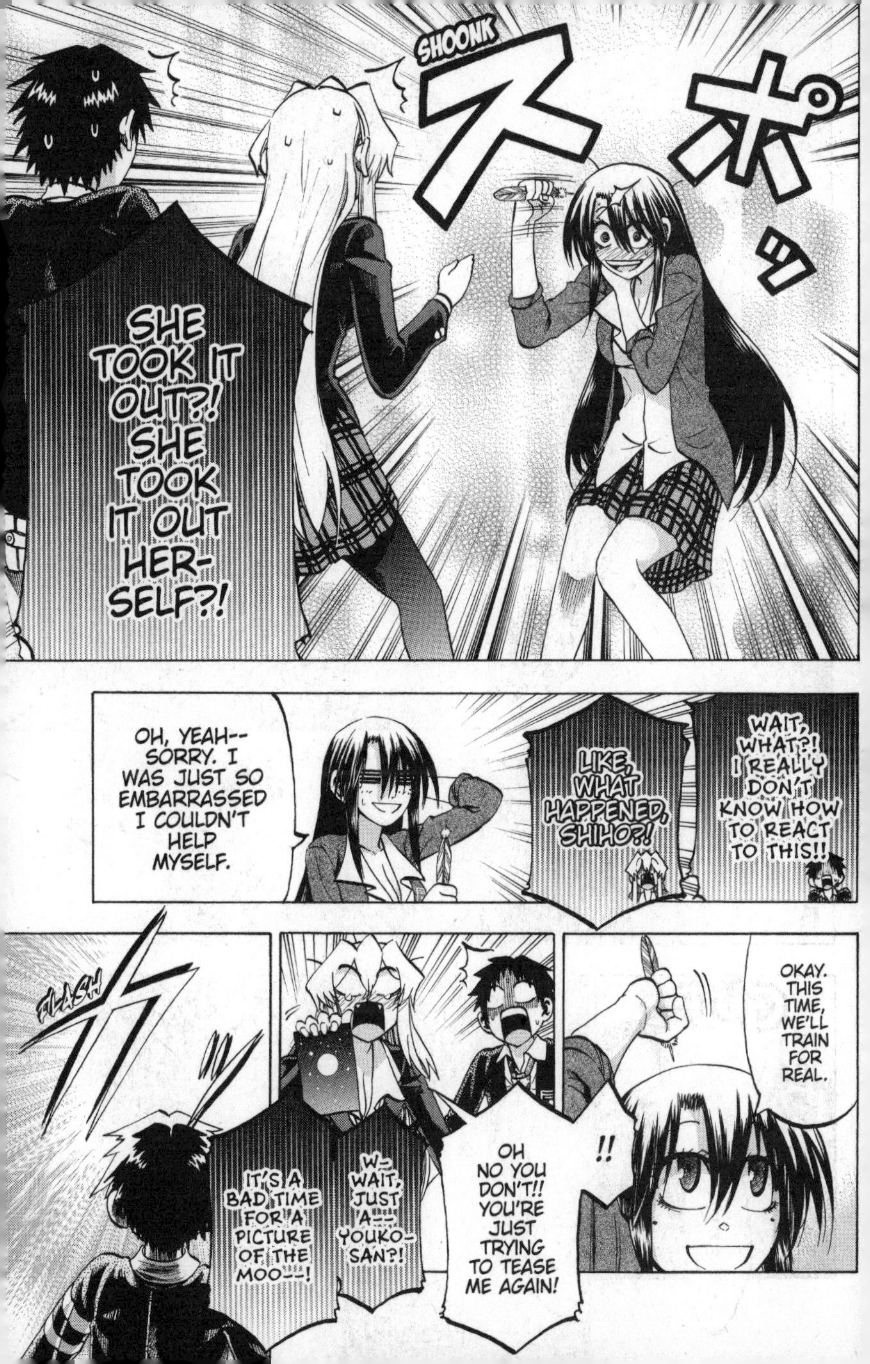
SHOONK
SHE TOOK IT OUT?! SHE TOOK IT OUT HER-SELF?!
WAIT, WHAT?! I REALLY DON'T KNOW HOW TO REACT TO THIS!!
LIKE, WHAT HAPPENED, SHIHO?!
OH, YEAH-- SORRY. I WAS JUST SO EMBARRASSED I COULDN'T HELP MYSELF.
OKAY. THIS TIME, WE'LL TRAIN FOR REAL.
!!
OH NO YOU DON'T!! YOU'RE JUST TRYING TO TEASE ME AGAIN!
W-WAIT, JUST A-- YOUKO-SAN?!
IT'S A BAD TIME FOR A PICTURE OF THE MOO--!
FLASH

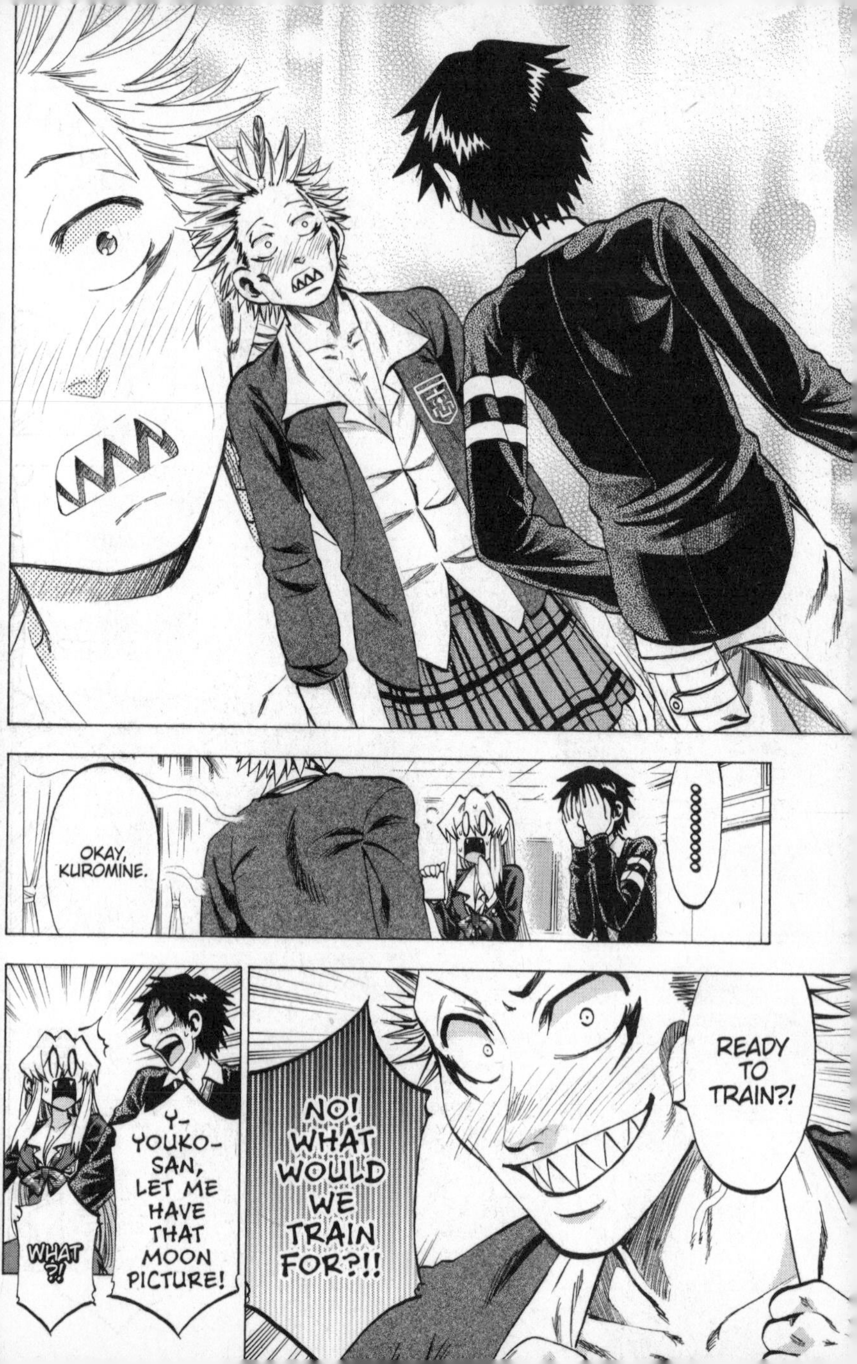
....
OKAY, KUROMINE.
READY TO TRAIN?!
NO! WHAT WOULD WE TRAIN FOR?!!
Y-YOUKO-SAN, LET ME HAVE THAT MOON PICTURE!
WHAT?!

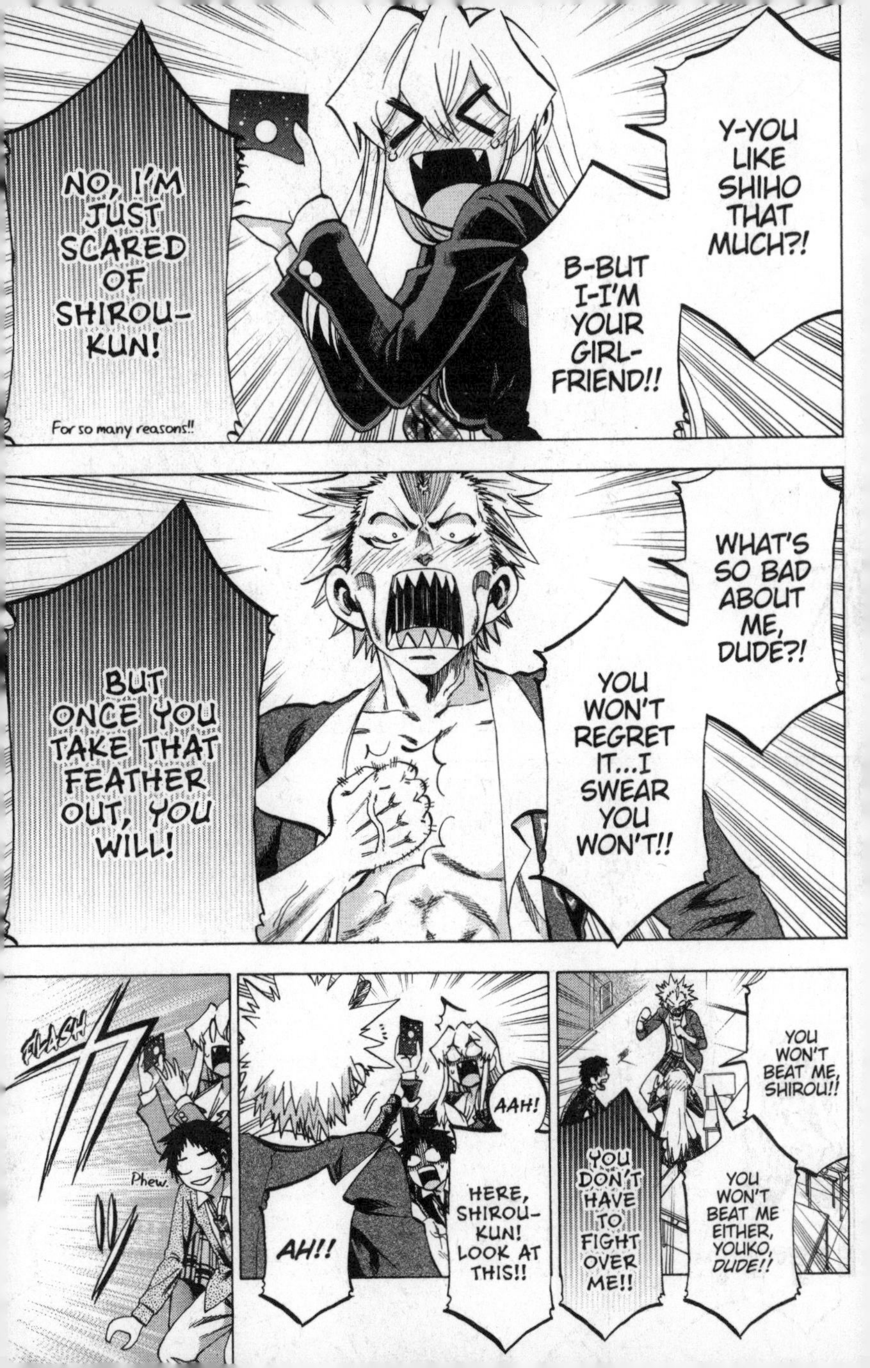
Y-YOU LIKE SHIHO THAT MUCH?!
B-BUT I-I'M YOUR GIRL-FRIEND!!
NO, I'M JUST SCARED OF SHIROU-KUN!
For so many reasons!!
WHAT'S SO BAD ABOUT ME, DUDE?!
YOU WON'T REGRET IT...I SWEAR YOU WON'T!!
BUT ONCE YOU TAKE THAT FEATHER OUT, YOU WILL!
YOU WON'T BEAT ME, SHIROU!!
YOU WON'T BEAT ME EITHER, YOUKO, DUDE!!
YOU DON'T HAVE TO FIGHT OVER ME!!
AAH!
HERE, SHIROU-KUN! LOOK AT THIS!!
AH!!
FLASH
Phew.

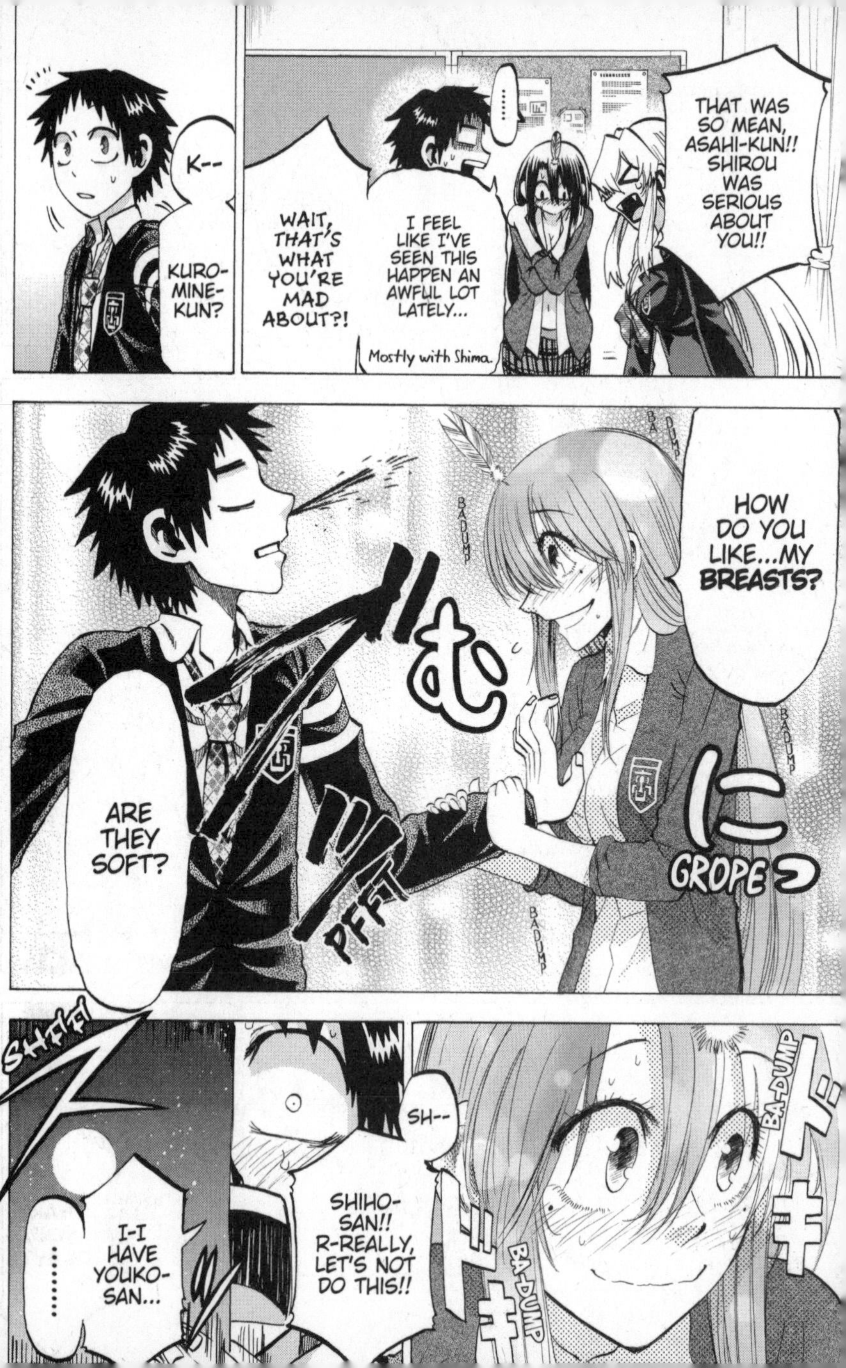
THAT WAS SO MEAN, ASAHI-KUN!! SHIROU WAS SERIOUS ABOUT YOU!!
......
I FEEL LIKE I'VE SEEN THIS HAPPEN AN AWFUL LOT LATELY...
Mostly with Shima.
WAIT, THAT'S WHAT YOU'RE MAD ABOUT?!
K--
KURO-MINE-KUN?
BA DUMP
HOW DO YOU LIKE...MY BREASTS?
BA DUMP
むに
GROPE
BA DUMP
BA DUMP
PFFT
ARE THEY SOFT?
BA-DUMP
BA-DUMP
SH--
SHIHO-SAN!! R-REALLY, LET'S NOT DO THIS!!
SHFF
I-I HAVE YOUKO-SAN...
......

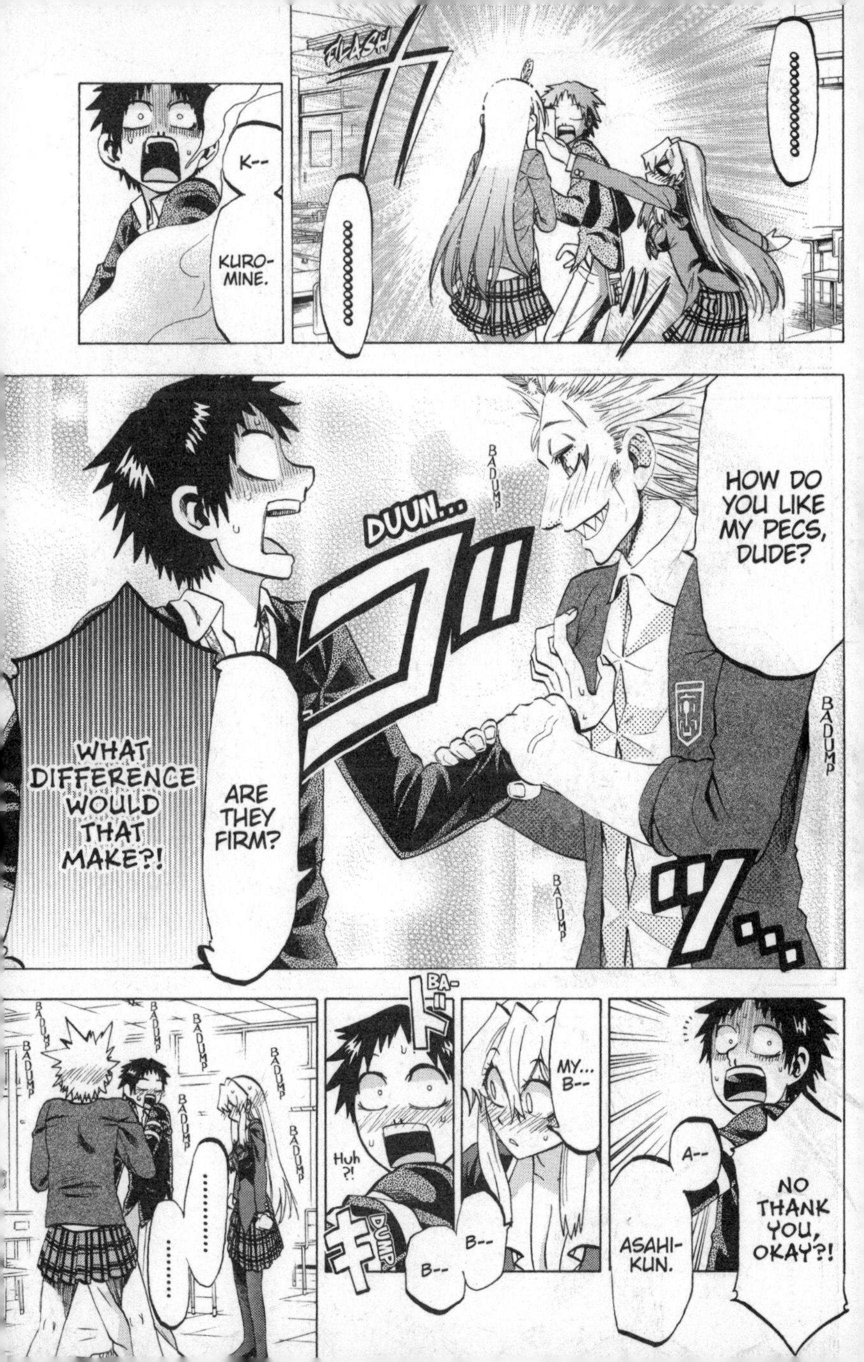
FLASH
……
……
K--
KURO-MINE.
HOW DO YOU LIKE MY PECS, DUDE?
BADUMP
BADUMP
BADUMP
DUUN...
ARE THEY FIRM?
WHAT DIFFERENCE WOULD THAT MAKE?!
A--
ASAHI-KUN.
NO THANK YOU, OKAY?!
MY... B--
B--
B--
BA--
DUMP
Huh ?!
BADUMP
BADUMP
BADUMP
BADUMP
BADUMP
BADUMP
BADUMP
……
……

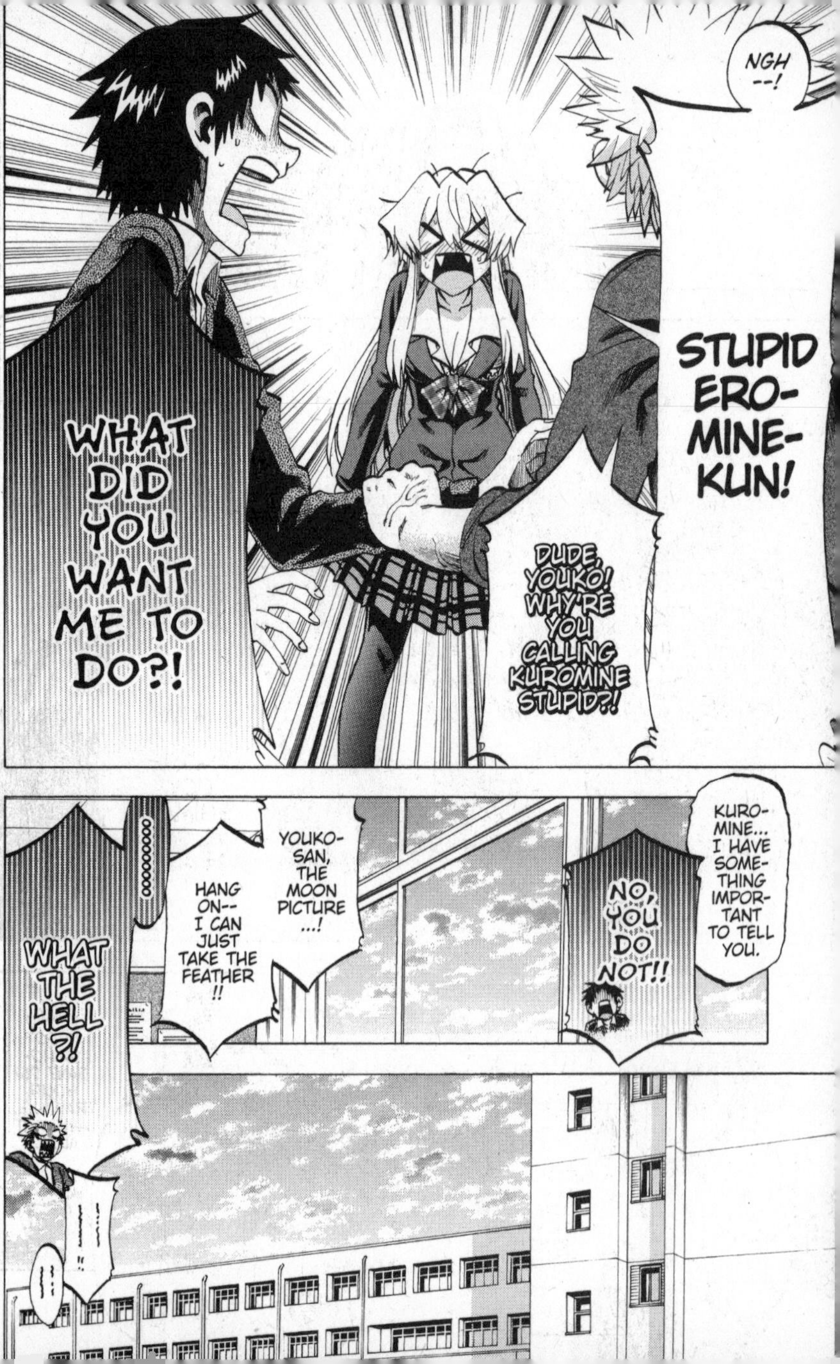
NGH --!
STUPID ERO-MINE-KUN!
DUDE, YOUKO! WHY'RE YOU CALLING KUROMINE STUPID?!
WHAT DID YOU WANT ME TO DO?!
KURO-MINE... I HAVE SOME-THING IMPOR-TANT TO TELL YOU.
NO, YOU DO NOT!!
YOUKO-SAN, THE MOON PICTURE ...!
HANG ON-- I CAN JUST TAKE THE FEATHER !!
OOOOOOOOO
WHAT THE HELL ?!

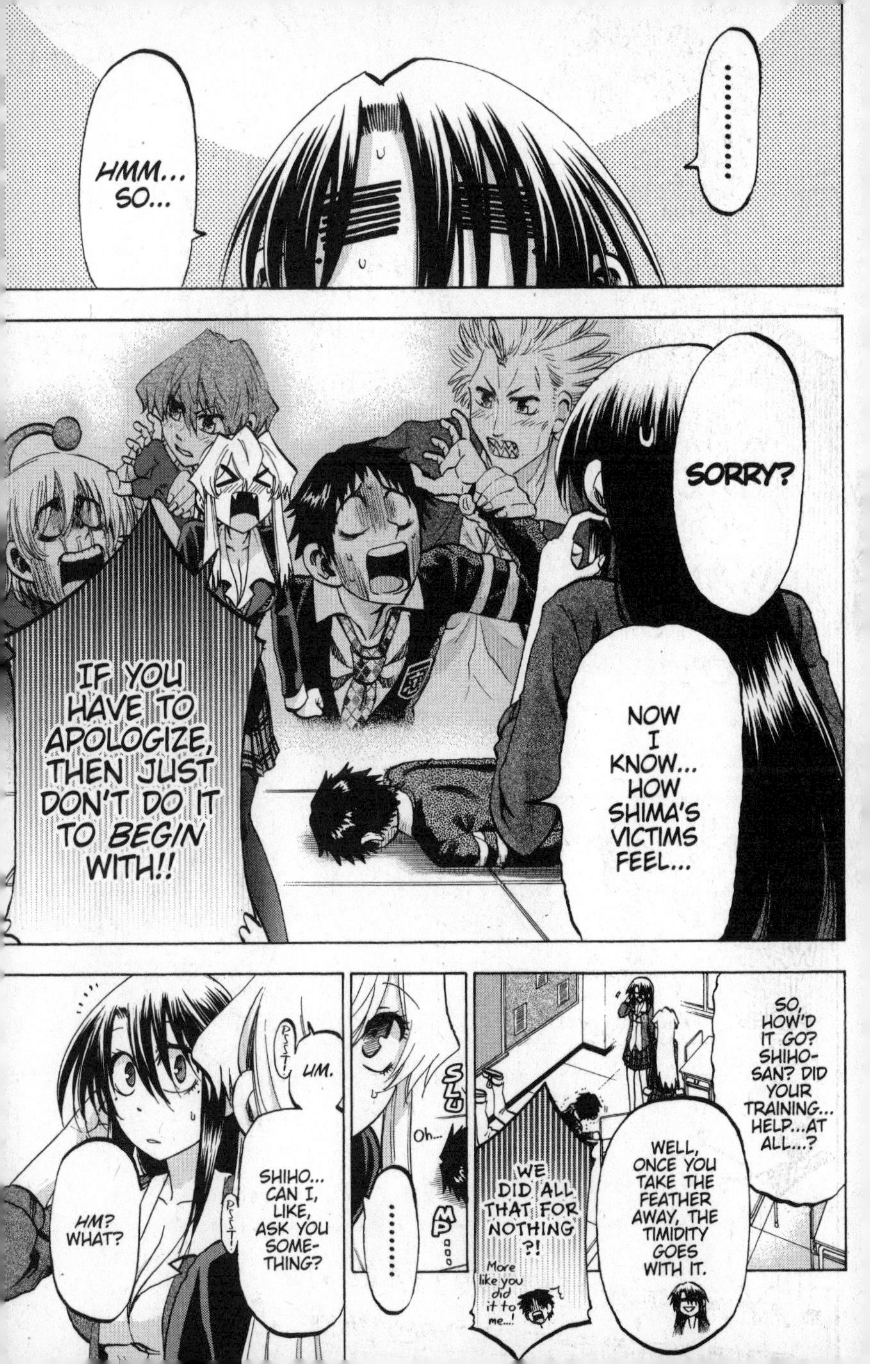
......
HMM... SO...
SORRY?
NOW I KNOW... HOW SHIMA'S VICTIMS FEEL...
IF YOU HAVE TO APOLOGIZE, THEN JUST DON'T DO IT TO BEGIN WITH!!
SO, HOW'D IT GO? SHIHO-SAN? DID YOUR TRAINING... HELP...AT ALL...?
WELL, ONCE YOU TAKE THE FEATHER AWAY, THE TIMIDITY GOES WITH IT.
WE DID ALL THAT FOR NOTHING?!
More like you did it to me...!
SLUMP...
Oh...
......
PSST
UM.
SHIHO... CAN I, LIKE, ASK YOU SOMETHING?
PSST
HM? WHAT?

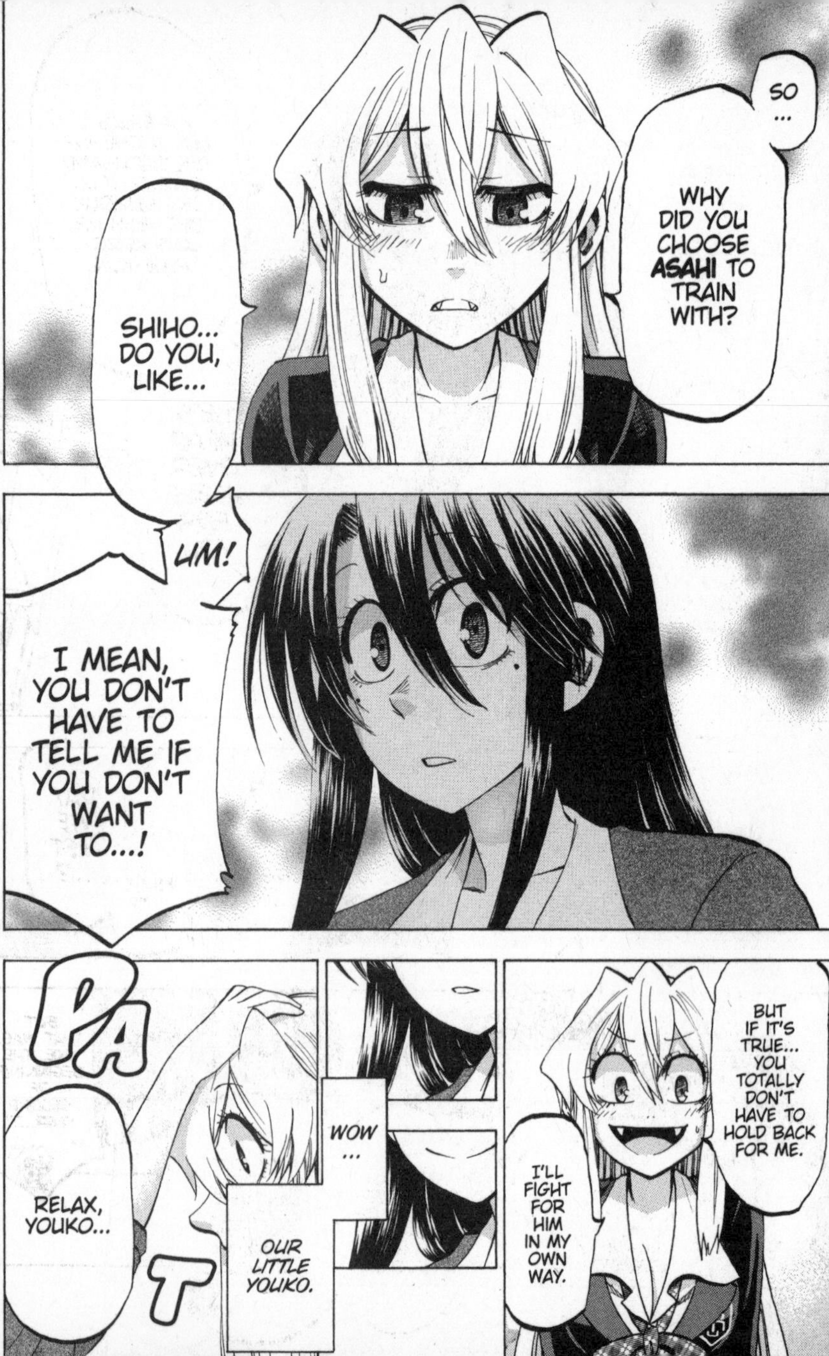
SO ...
WHY DID YOU CHOOSE ASAHI TO TRAIN WITH?
SHIHO... DO YOU, LIKE...
UM!
I MEAN, YOU DON'T HAVE TO TELL ME IF YOU DON'T WANT TO...!
BUT IF IT'S TRUE... YOU TOTALLY DON'T HAVE TO HOLD BACK FOR ME.
I'LL FIGHT FOR HIM IN MY OWN WAY.
WOW ...
OUR LITTLE YOUKO.
PAT
RELAX, YOUKO...

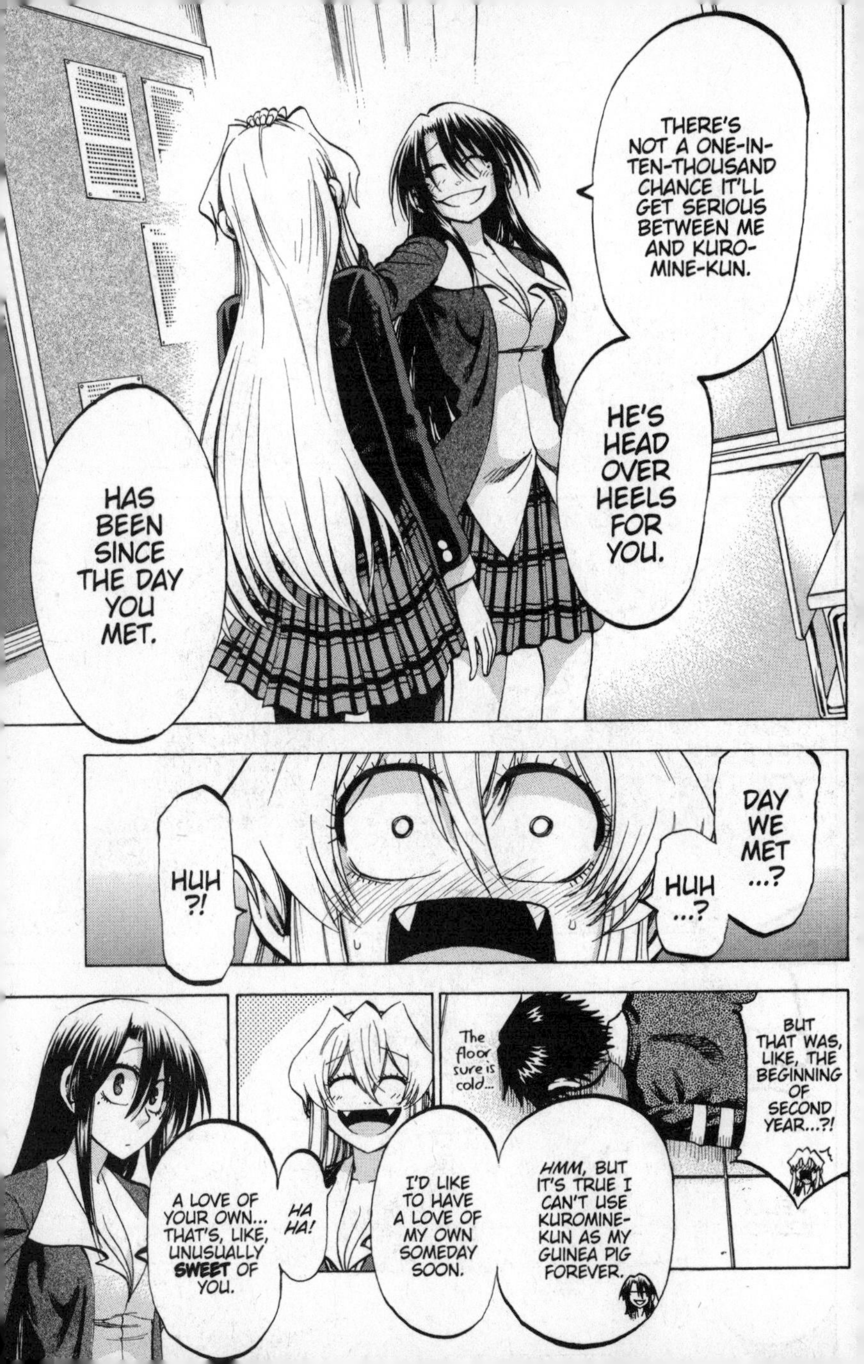
THERE'S NOT A ONE-IN-TEN-THOUSAND CHANCE IT'LL GET SERIOUS BETWEEN ME AND KURO-MINE-KUN.
HE'S HEAD OVER HEELS FOR YOU.
HAS BEEN SINCE THE DAY YOU MET.
DAY WE MET ...?
HUH ...?
HUH ?!
BUT THAT WAS, LIKE, THE BEGINNING OF SECOND YEAR...?!
The floor sure is cold...
HMM, BUT IT'S TRUE I CAN'T USE KUROMINE-KUN AS MY GUINEA PIG FOREVER.
I'D LIKE TO HAVE A LOVE OF MY OWN SOMEDAY SOON.
HA HA!
A LOVE OF YOUR OWN... THAT'S, LIKE, UNUSUALLY **SWEET** OF YOU.

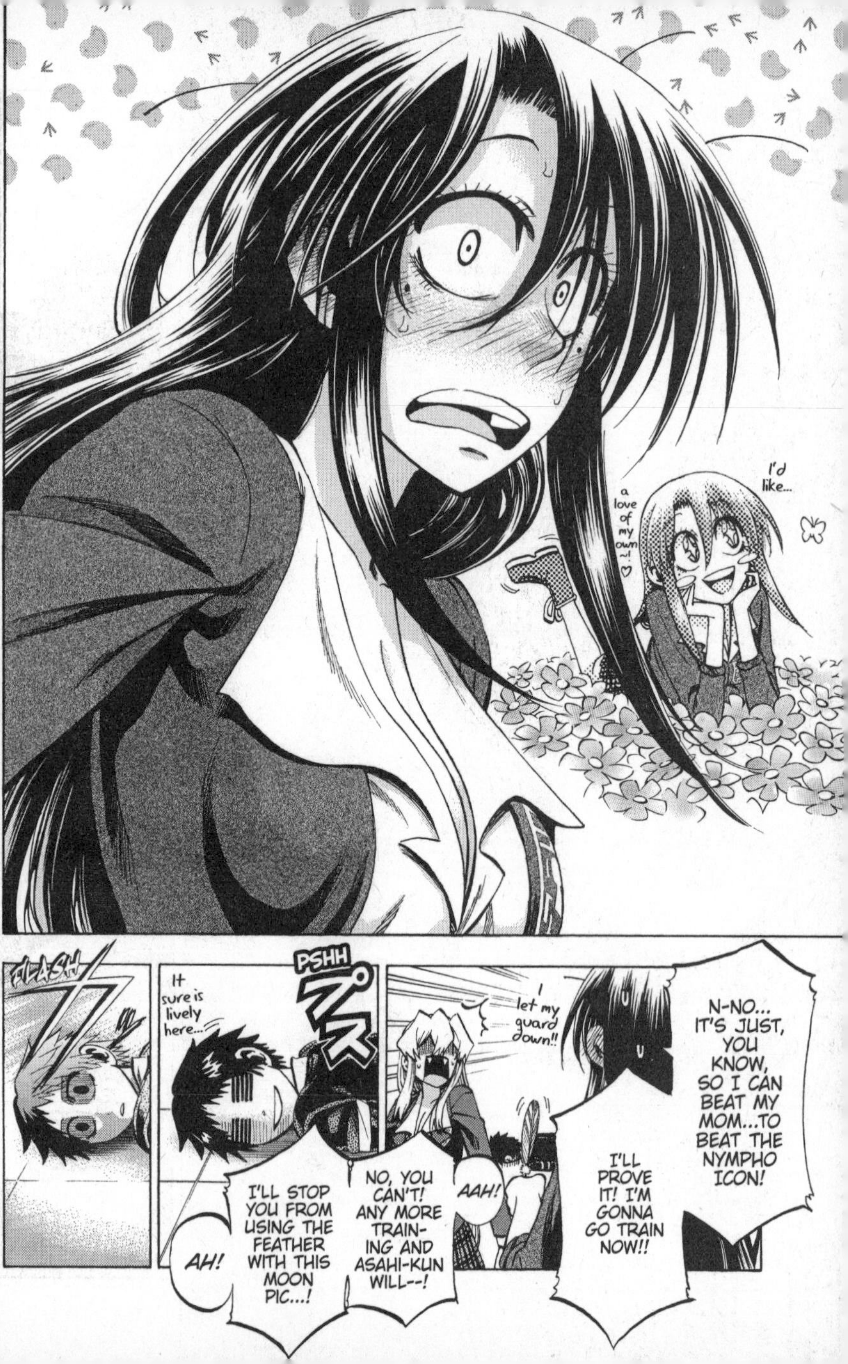
I'd like...
a love of my own~!♡
N-NO... IT'S JUST, YOU KNOW, SO I CAN BEAT MY MOM...TO BEAT THE NYMPHO ICON!
I'LL PROVE IT! I'M GONNA GO TRAIN NOW!!
I let my guard down!!
AAH!
NO, YOU CAN'T! ANY MORE TRAIN-ING AND ASAHI-KUN WILL--!
PSHH
It sure is lively here...
I'LL STOP YOU FROM USING THE FEATHER WITH THIS MOON PIC...!
FLASH
AH!

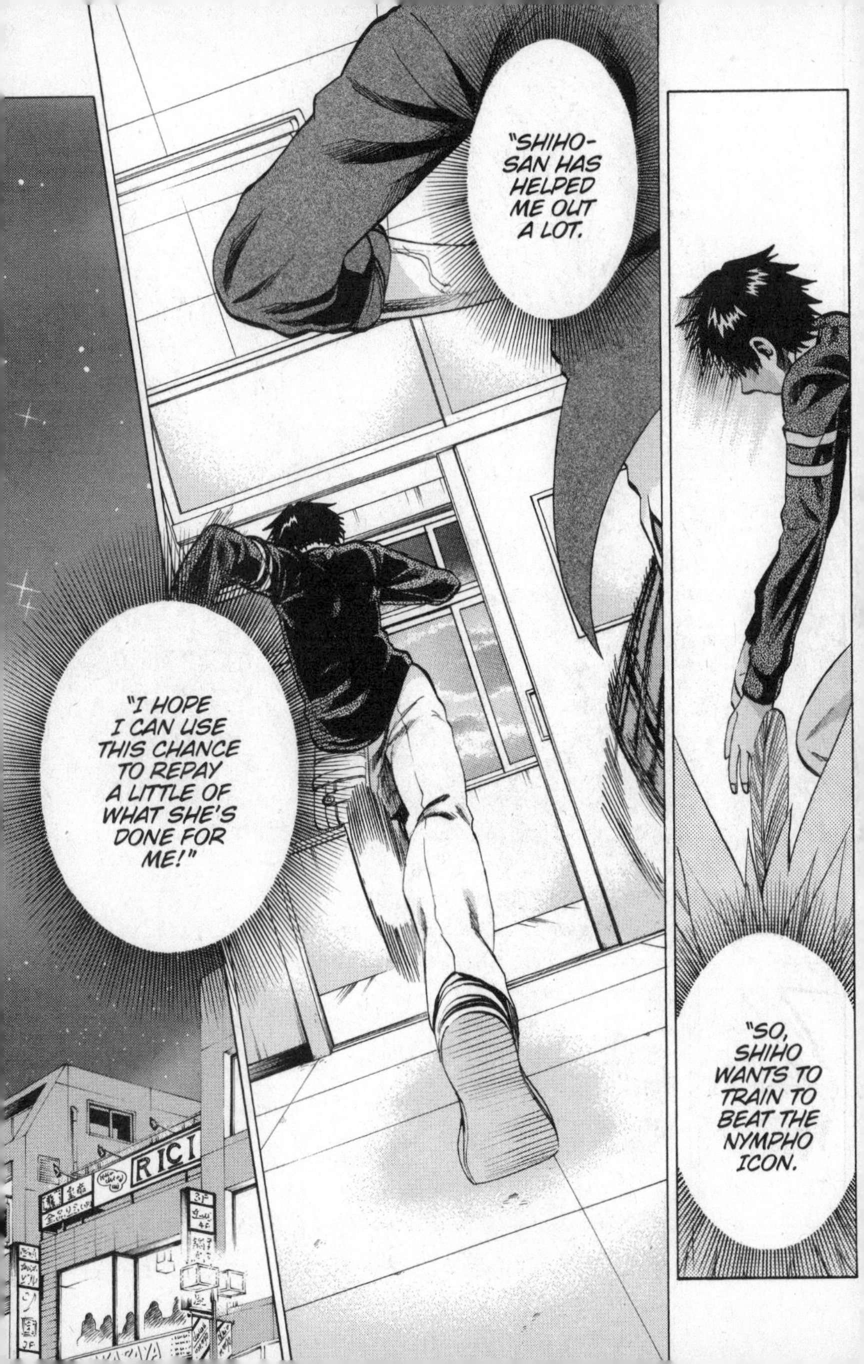
"SO, SHIHO WANTS TO TRAIN TO BEAT THE NYMPHO ICON.
"SHIHO-SAN HAS HELPED ME OUT A LOT.
"I HOPE I CAN USE THIS CHANCE TO REPAY A LITTLE OF WHAT SHE'S DONE FOR ME!"

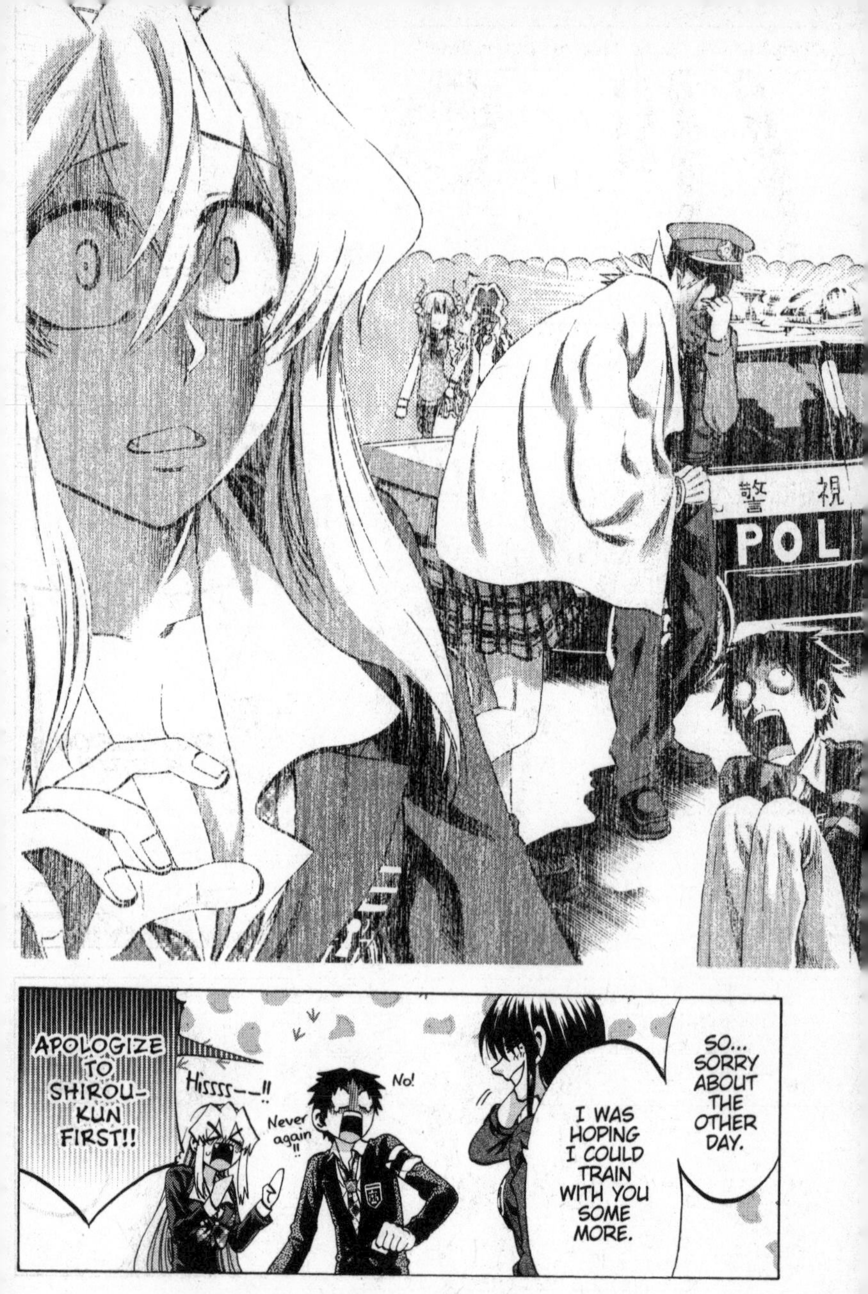
警 視
POL
SO... SORRY ABOUT THE OTHER DAY.
I WAS HOPING I COULD TRAIN WITH YOU SOME MORE.
No!
Hissss--!!
Never again!!
APOLOGIZE TO SHIROU-KUN FIRST!!

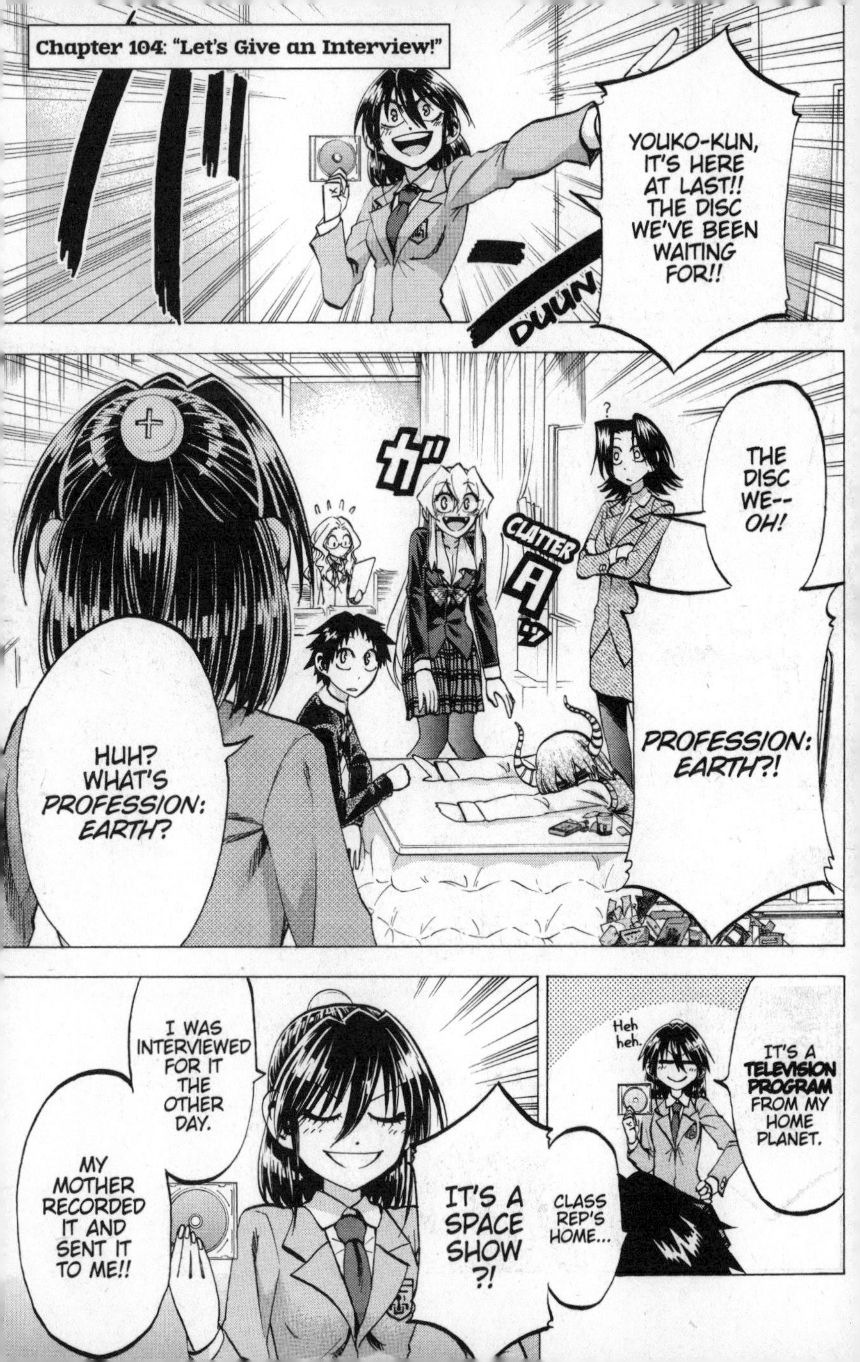
Chapter 104: "Let's Give an Interview!"
YOUKO-KUN, IT'S HERE AT LAST!! THE DISC WE'VE BEEN WAITING FOR!!
DUUN
THE DISC WE--OH!
ガ
CLATTER
ガッ
PROFESSION: EARTH?!
HUH? WHAT'S PROFESSION: EARTH?
IT'S A TELEVISION PROGRAM FROM MY HOME PLANET.
Heh heh.
CLASS REP'S HOME...
IT'S A SPACE SHOW?!
I WAS INTERVIEWED FOR IT THE OTHER DAY.
MY MOTHER RECORDED IT AND SENT IT TO ME!!

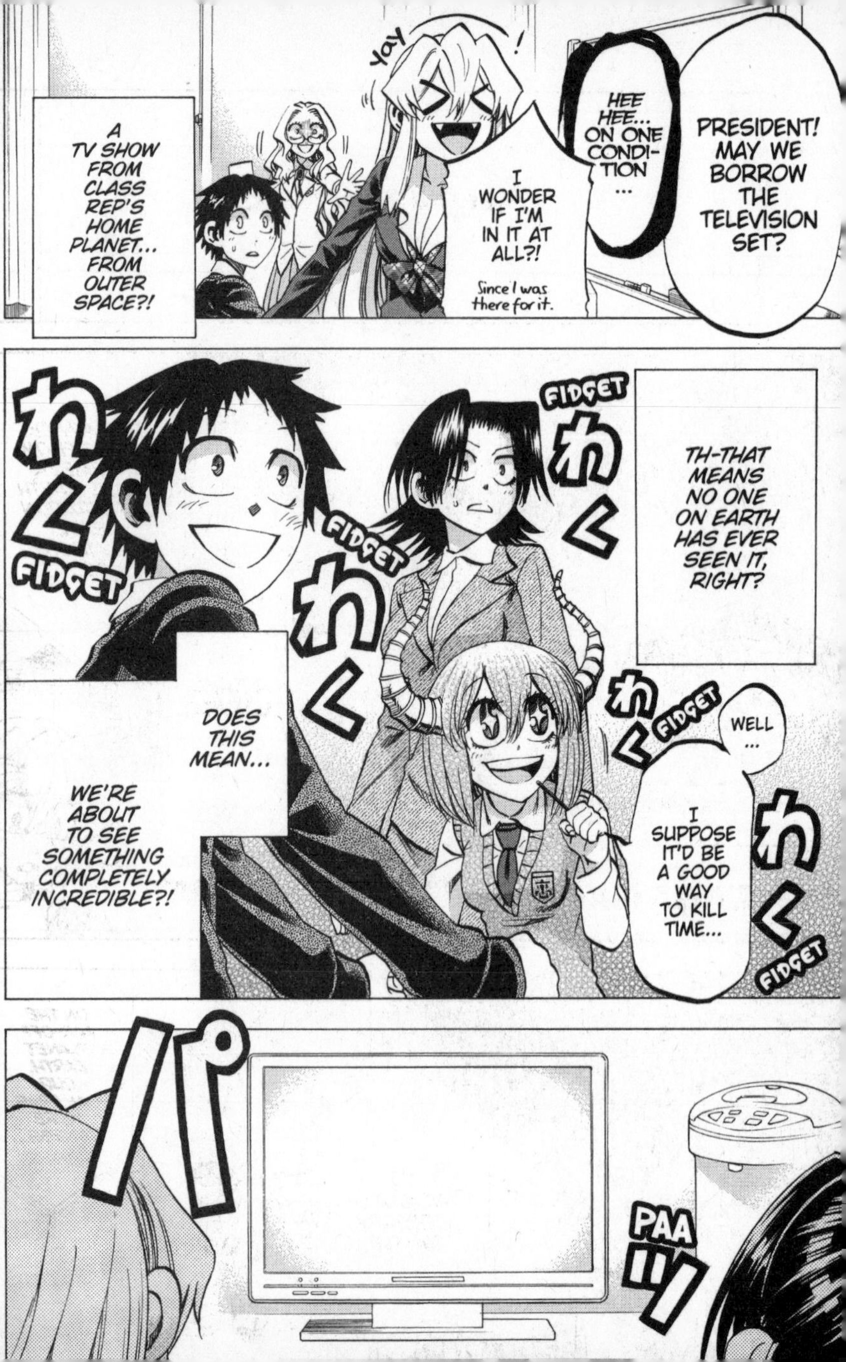
PRESIDENT! MAY WE BORROW THE TELEVISION SET?
HEE HEE... ON ONE CONDITION...
Yay !
I WONDER IF I'M IN IT AT ALL?!
Since I was there for it.
A TV SHOW FROM CLASS REP'S HOME PLANET... FROM OUTER SPACE?!
TH-THAT MEANS NO ONE ON EARTH HAS EVER SEEN IT, RIGHT?
わく FIDGET
わく FIDGET
わく FIDGET
WELL ...
I SUPPOSE IT'D BE A GOOD WAY TO KILL TIME...
わく FIDGET
わく FIDGET
DOES THIS MEAN...
WE'RE ABOUT TO SEE SOMETHING COMPLETELY INCREDIBLE?!
わく FIDGET
PAA !!
パ

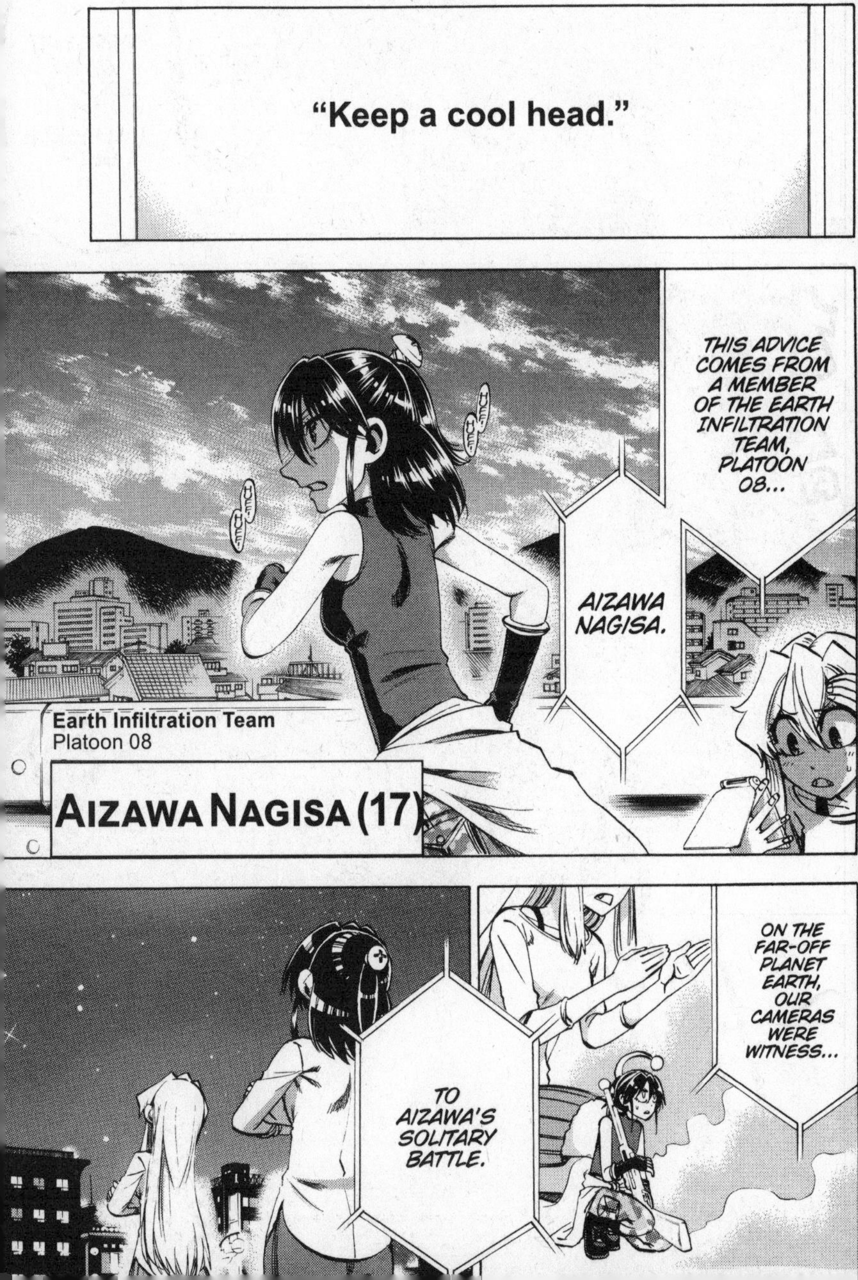
"Keep a cool head."
THIS ADVICE COMES FROM A MEMBER OF THE EARTH INFILTRATION TEAM, PLATOON 08...
AIZAWA NAGISA.
HUFF HUFF
HUFF HUFF
Earth Infiltration Team
Platoon 08
AIZAWA NAGISA (17)
ON THE FAR-OFF PLANET EARTH, OUR CAMERAS WERE WITNESS...
TO AIZAWA'S SOLITARY BATTLE.

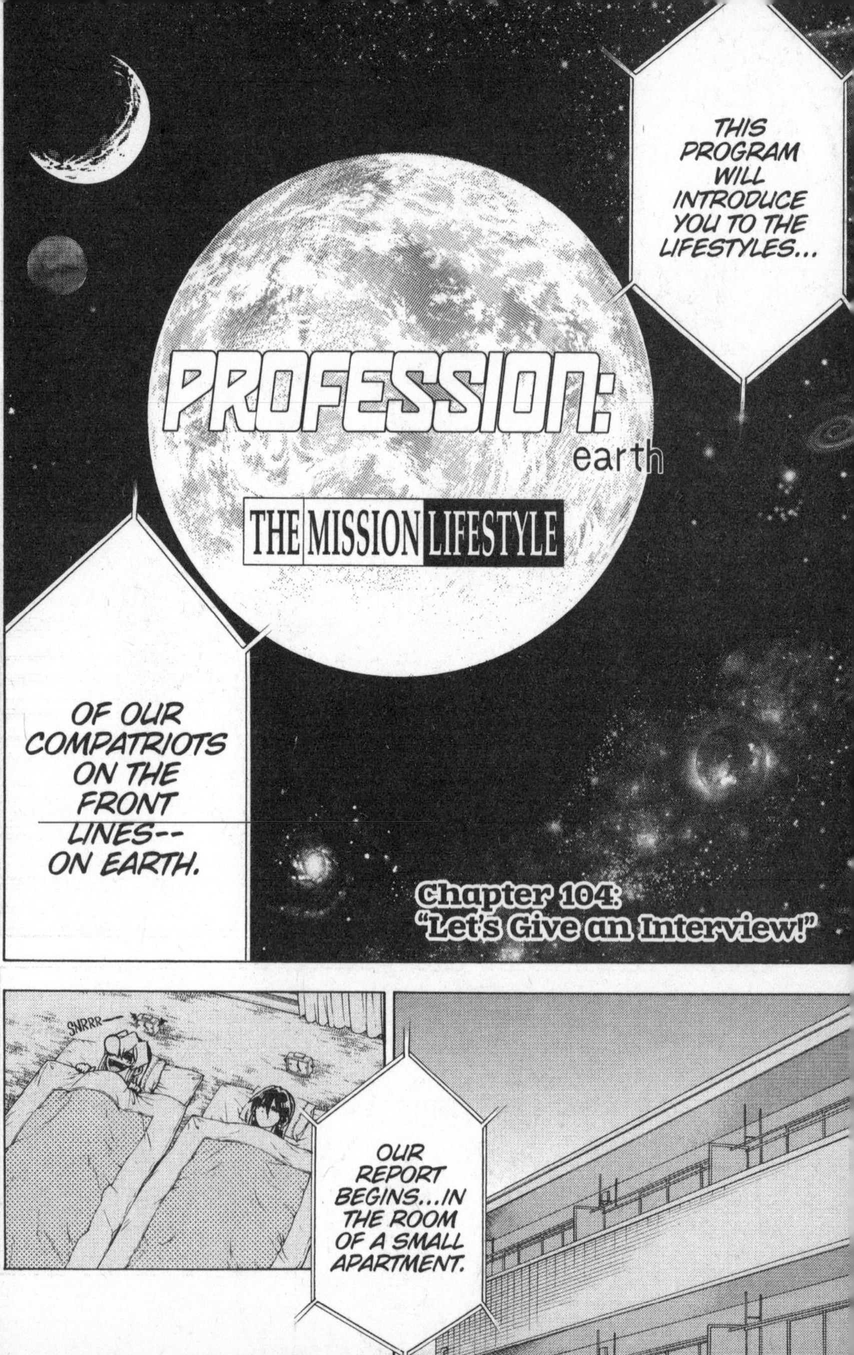
THIS PROGRAM WILL INTRODUCE YOU TO THE LIFESTYLES...
PROFESSION: earth
THE MISSION LIFESTYLE
OF OUR COMPATRIOTS ON THE FRONT LINES-- ON EARTH.
Chapter 104: "Let's Give an Interview!"
OUR REPORT BEGINS...IN THE ROOM OF A SMALL APARTMENT.
SNRRR

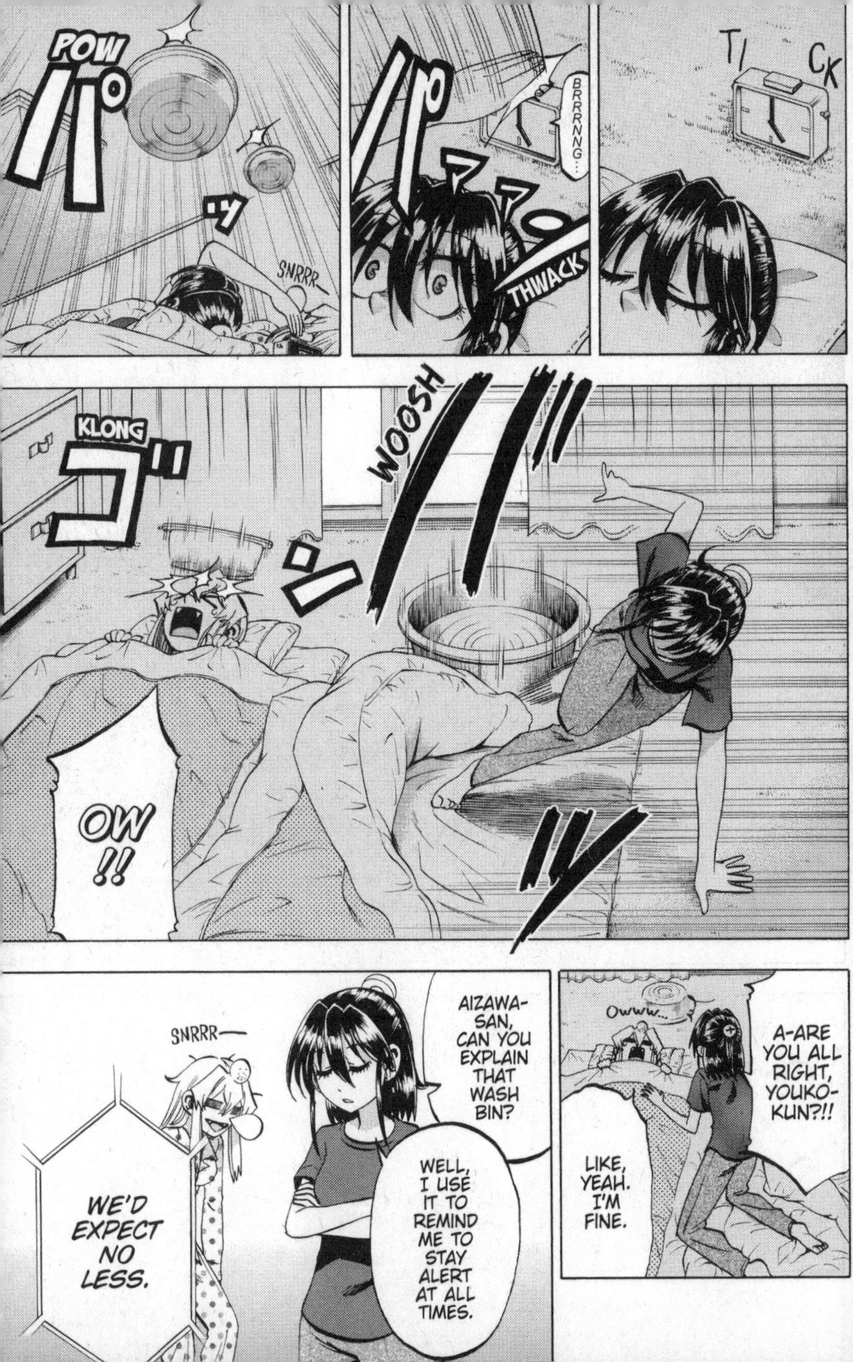
TI CK
BRRRRNNG...
THWACK
POW
SNRRR
WOOSH
KLONG
OW!!
A-ARE YOU ALL RIGHT, YOUKO-KUN?!!
Owww...
LIKE, YEAH. I'M FINE.
AIZAWA-SAN, CAN YOU EXPLAIN THAT WASH BIN?
SNRRR—
WELL, I USE IT TO REMIND ME TO STAY ALERT AT ALL TIMES.
WE'D EXPECT NO LESS.

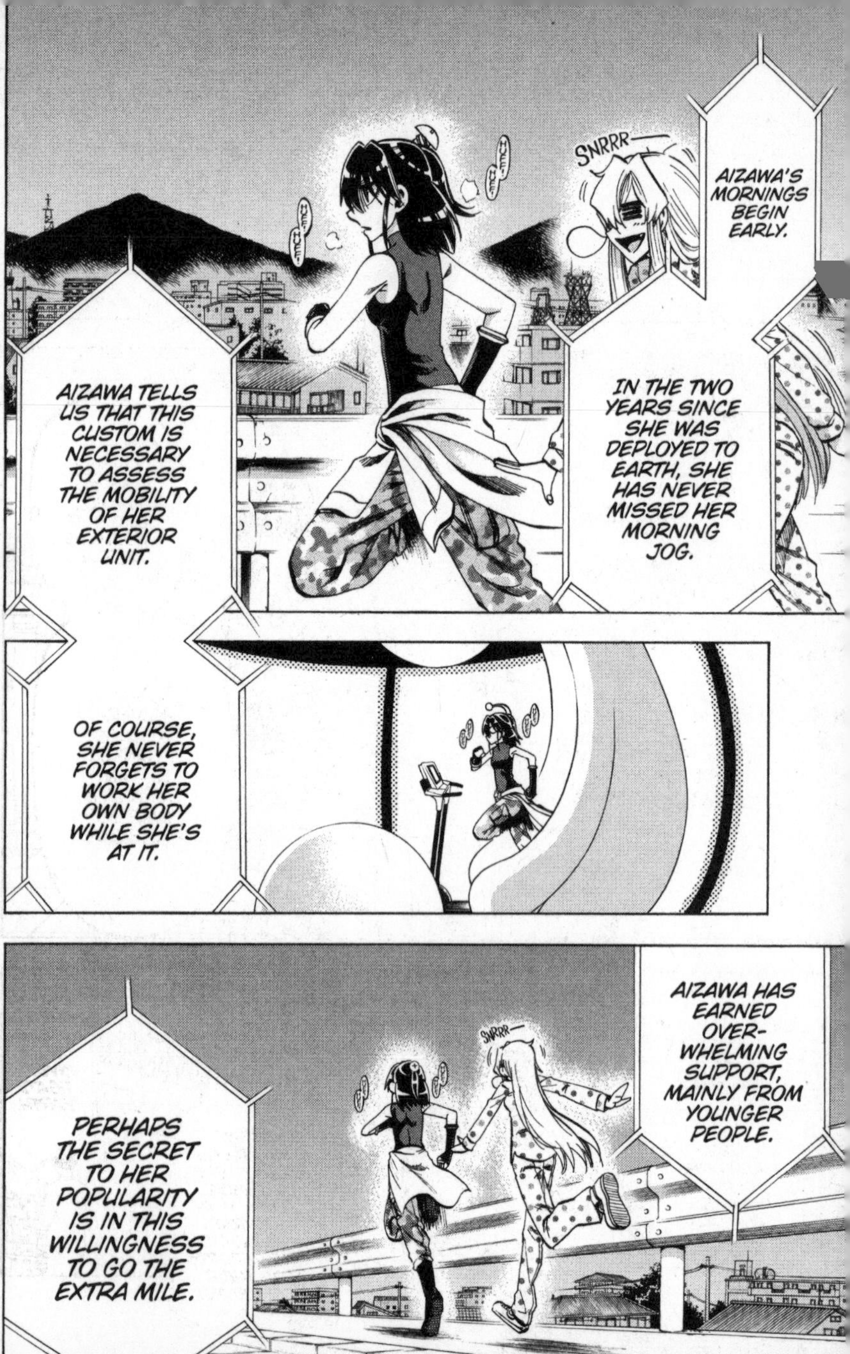
AIZAWA'S MORNINGS BEGIN EARLY.
SNRRR—
IN THE TWO YEARS SINCE SHE WAS DEPLOYED TO EARTH, SHE HAS NEVER MISSED HER MORNING JOG.
AIZAWA TELLS US THAT THIS CUSTOM IS NECESSARY TO ASSESS THE MOBILITY OF HER EXTERIOR UNIT.
OF COURSE, SHE NEVER FORGETS TO WORK HER OWN BODY WHILE SHE'S AT IT.
AIZAWA HAS EARNED OVER-WHELMING SUPPORT, MAINLY FROM YOUNGER PEOPLE.
SNRRR—
PERHAPS THE SECRET TO HER POPULARITY IS IN THIS WILLINGNESS TO GO THE EXTRA MILE.

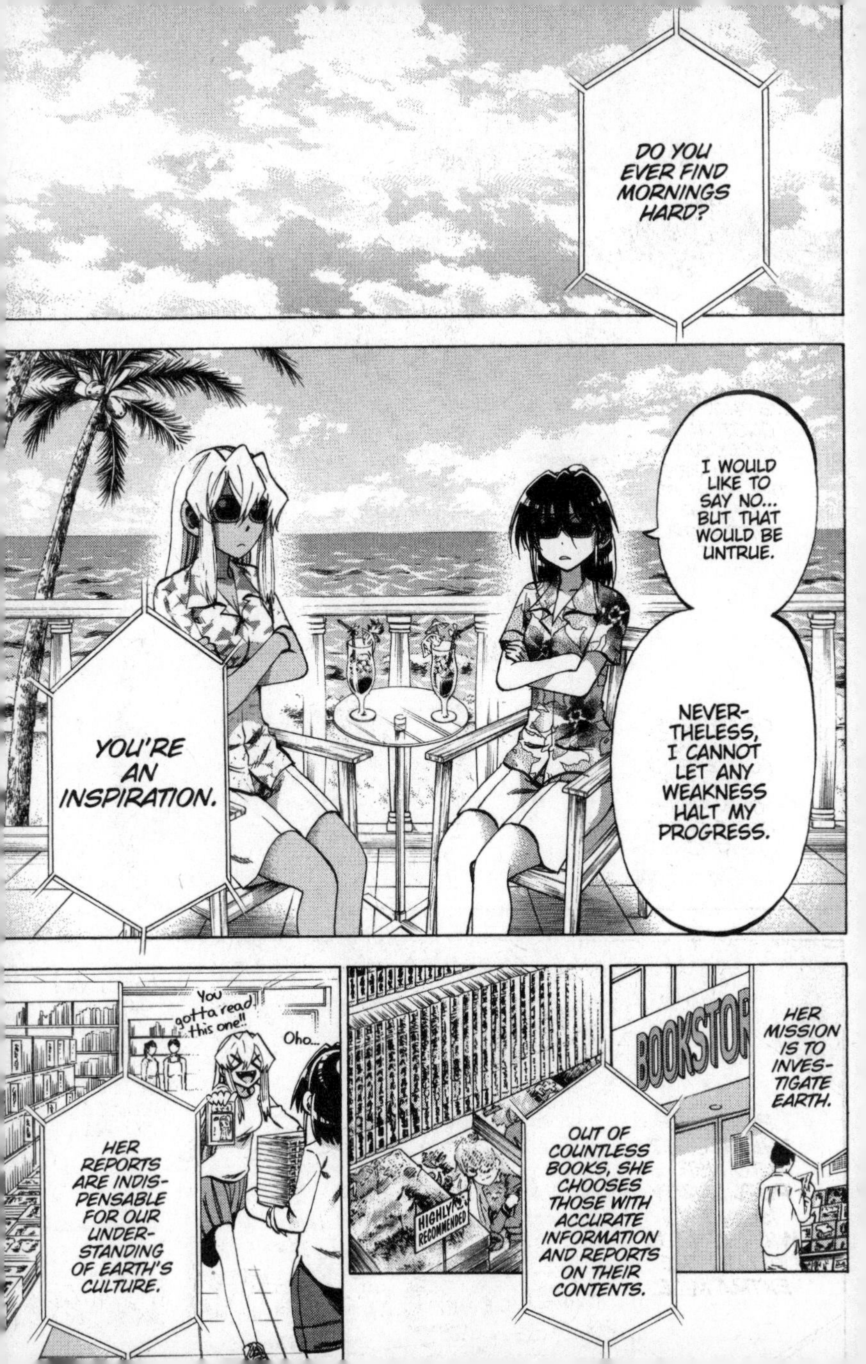
DO YOU EVER FIND MORNINGS HARD?
I WOULD LIKE TO SAY NO... BUT THAT WOULD BE UNTRUE.
NEVER-THELESS, I CANNOT LET ANY WEAKNESS HALT MY PROGRESS.
YOU'RE AN INSPIRATION.
HER MISSION IS TO INVES-TIGATE EARTH.
BOOKSTOR
OUT OF COUNTLESS BOOKS, SHE CHOOSES THOSE WITH ACCURATE INFORMATION AND REPORTS ON THEIR CONTENTS.
HIGHLY RECOMMENDED
You gotta read this one!!
Oho...
HER REPORTS ARE INDIS-PENSABLE FOR OUR UNDER-STANDING OF EARTH'S CULTURE.

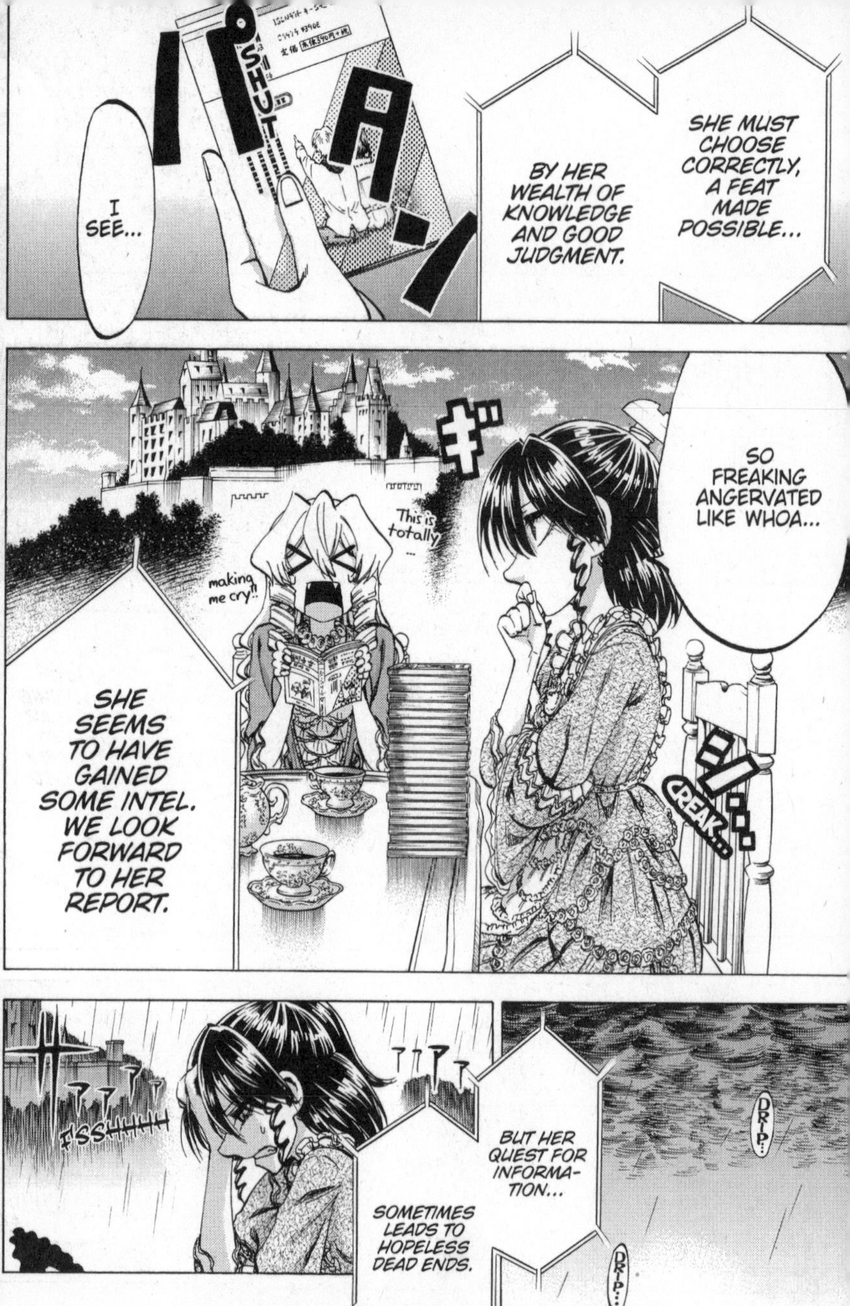
SHE MUST CHOOSE CORRECTLY, A FEAT MADE POSSIBLE...
BY HER WEALTH OF KNOWLEDGE AND GOOD JUDGMENT.
SHUT
I SEE...
SO FREAKING ANGERVATED LIKE WHOA...
This is totally ...
making me cry!!
CREAK...
SHE SEEMS TO HAVE GAINED SOME INTEL. WE LOOK FORWARD TO HER REPORT.
DRIP...
DRIP...
BUT HER QUEST FOR INFORMATION...
SOMETIMES LEADS TO HOPELESS DEAD ENDS.
FSSHHHH

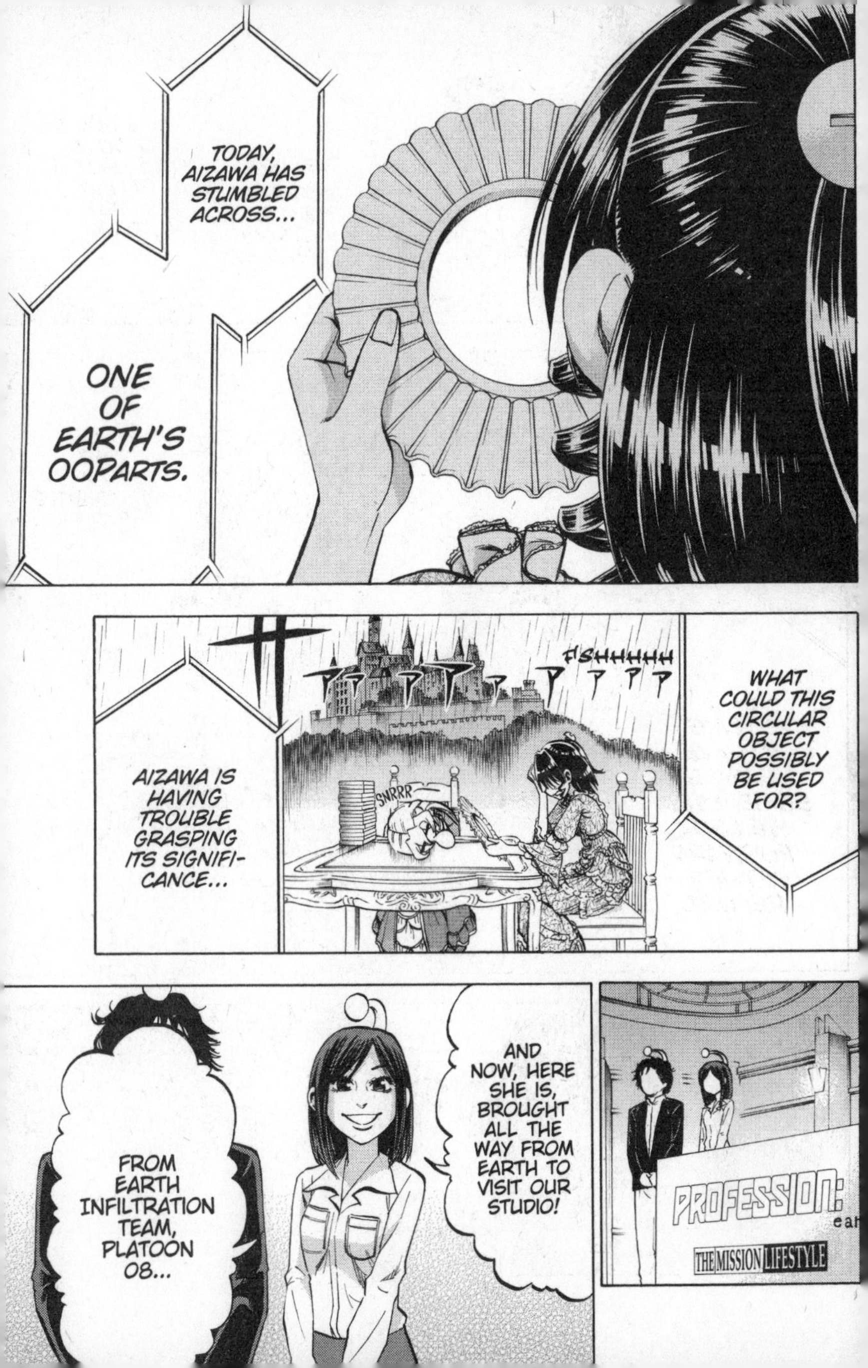
TODAY, AIZAWA HAS STUMBLED ACROSS...
ONE OF EARTH'S OOPARTS.
WHAT COULD THIS CIRCULAR OBJECT POSSIBLY BE USED FOR?
FSHHHHH
AIZAWA IS HAVING TROUBLE GRASPING ITS SIGNIFI-CANCE...
SNRRR
PROFESSION:
THE MISSION LIFESTYLE
AND NOW, HERE SHE IS, BROUGHT ALL THE WAY FROM EARTH TO VISIT OUR STUDIO!
FROM EARTH INFILTRATION TEAM, PLATOON 08...

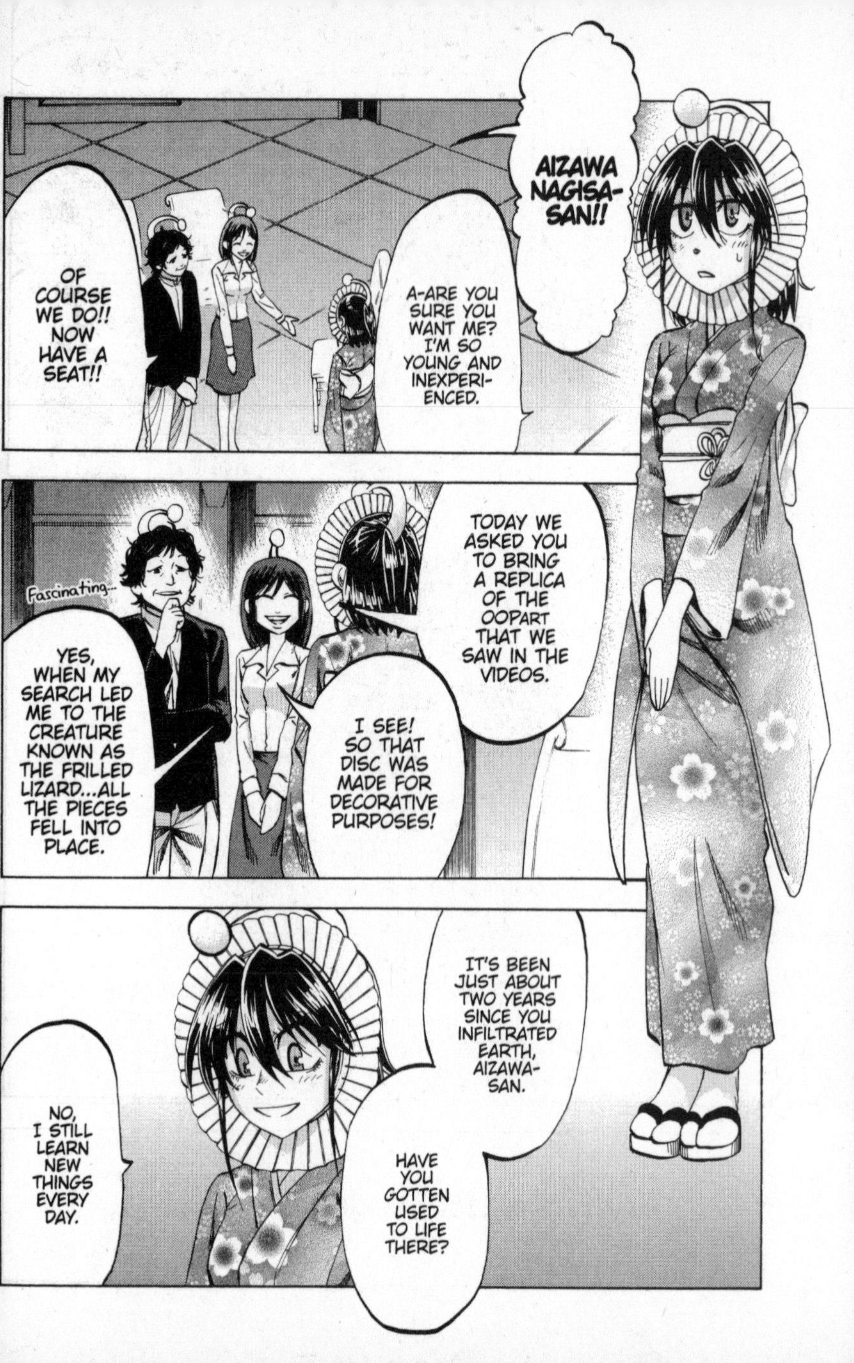
AIZAWA NAGISA-SAN!!
A-ARE YOU SURE YOU WANT ME? I'M SO YOUNG AND INEXPERIENCED.
OF COURSE WE DO!! NOW HAVE A SEAT!!
TODAY WE ASKED YOU TO BRING A REPLICA OF THE OOPART THAT WE SAW IN THE VIDEOS.
I SEE! SO THAT DISC WAS MADE FOR DECORATIVE PURPOSES!
Fascinating...
YES, WHEN MY SEARCH LED ME TO THE CREATURE KNOWN AS THE FRILLED LIZARD...ALL THE PIECES FELL INTO PLACE.
IT'S BEEN JUST ABOUT TWO YEARS SINCE YOU INFILTRATED EARTH, AIZAWA-SAN.
HAVE YOU GOTTEN USED TO LIFE THERE?
NO, I STILL LEARN NEW THINGS EVERY DAY.

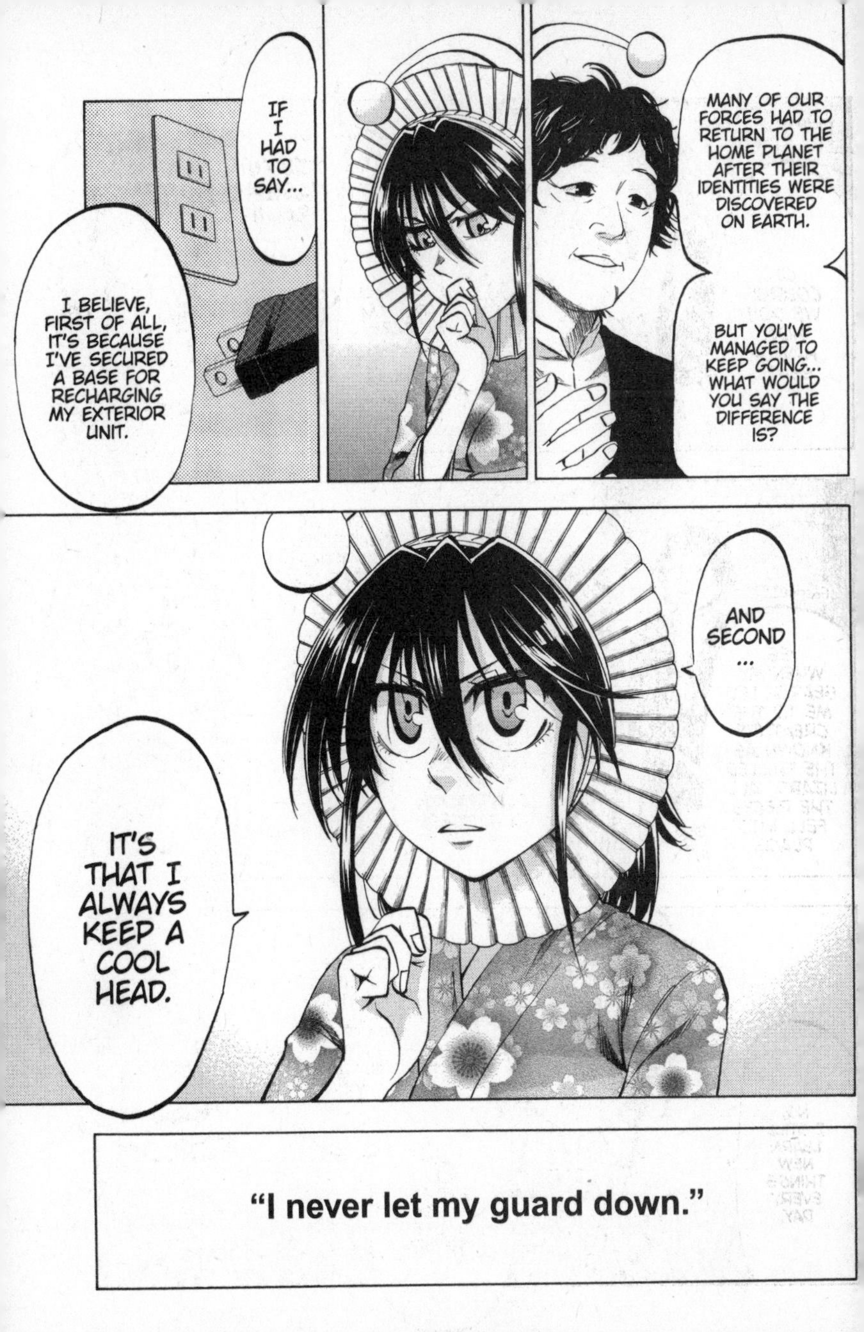
MANY OF OUR FORCES HAD TO RETURN TO THE HOME PLANET AFTER THEIR IDENTITIES WERE DISCOVERED ON EARTH.
BUT YOU'VE MANAGED TO KEEP GOING... WHAT WOULD YOU SAY THE DIFFERENCE IS?
IF I HAD TO SAY...
I BELIEVE, FIRST OF ALL, IT'S BECAUSE I'VE SECURED A BASE FOR RECHARGING MY EXTERIOR UNIT.
AND SECOND ...
IT'S THAT I ALWAYS KEEP A COOL HEAD.
"I never let my guard down."

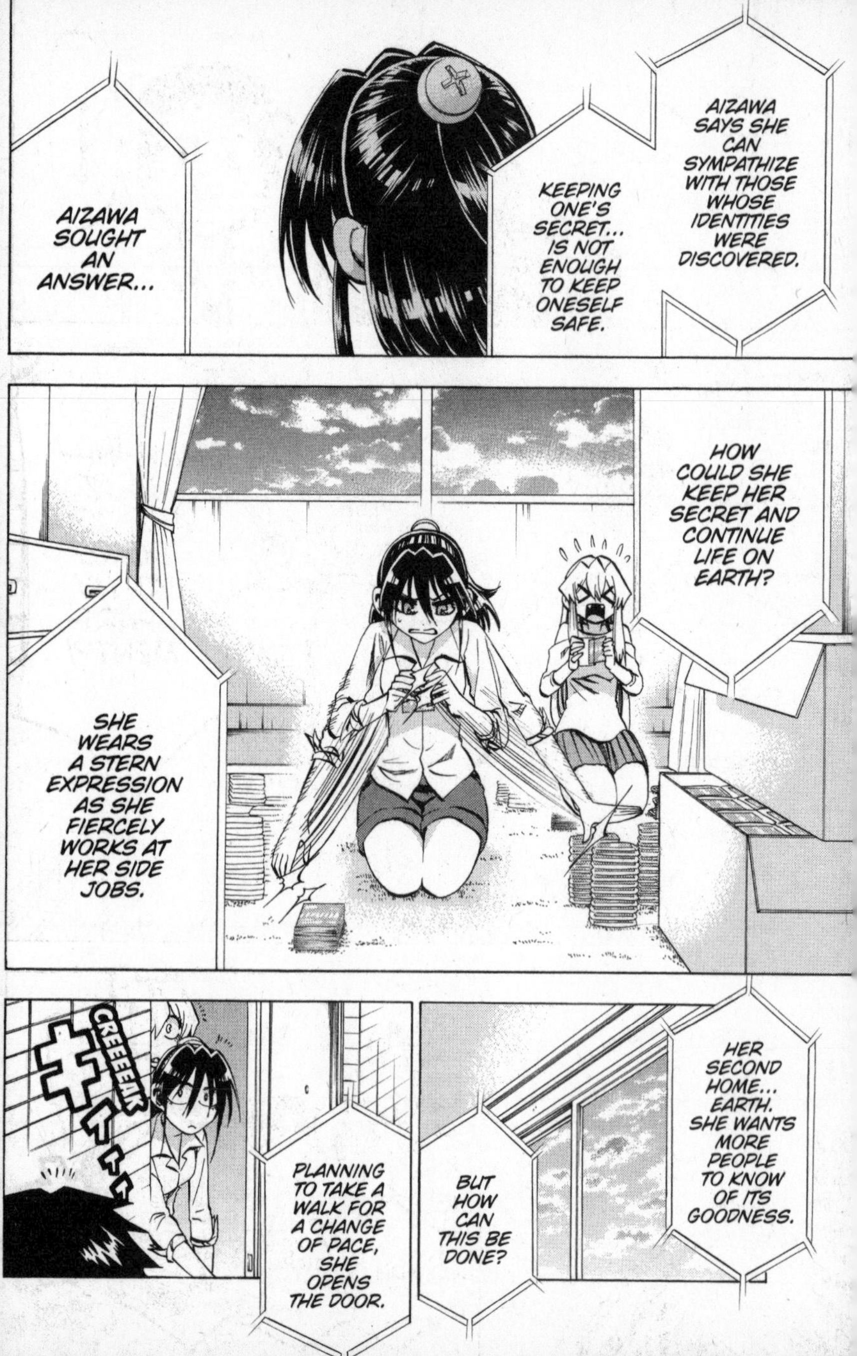
AIZAWA SAYS SHE CAN SYMPATHIZE WITH THOSE WHOSE IDENTITIES WERE DISCOVERED.
KEEPING ONE'S SECRET... IS NOT ENOUGH TO KEEP ONESELF SAFE.
AIZAWA SOUGHT AN ANSWER...
HOW COULD SHE KEEP HER SECRET AND CONTINUE LIFE ON EARTH?
SHE WEARS A STERN EXPRESSION AS SHE FIERCELY WORKS AT HER SIDE JOBS.
HER SECOND HOME... EARTH. SHE WANTS MORE PEOPLE TO KNOW OF ITS GOODNESS.
BUT HOW CAN THIS BE DONE?
PLANNING TO TAKE A WALK FOR A CHANGE OF PACE, SHE OPENS THE DOOR.
CREEEEAK

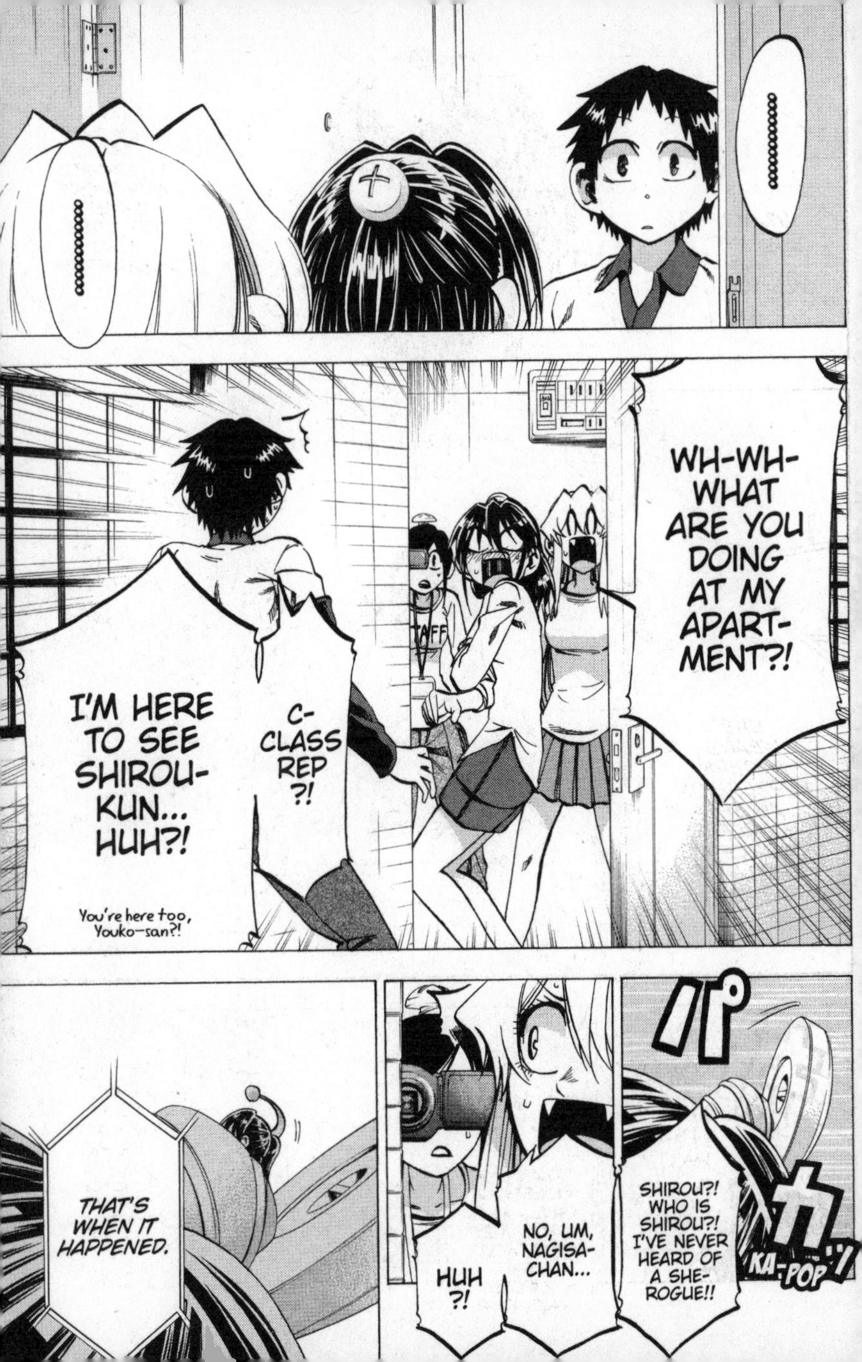
......
......
WH-WH-WHAT ARE YOU DOING AT MY APARTMENT?!
C-CLASS REP?!
I'M HERE TO SEE SHIROU-KUN... HUH?!
You're here too, Youko-san?!
パ
SHIROU?! WHO IS SHIROU?! I'VE NEVER HEARD OF A SHE-ROGUE!!
カッ
KA-POP
NO, UM, NAGISA-CHAN...
HUH?!
THAT'S WHEN IT HAPPENED.

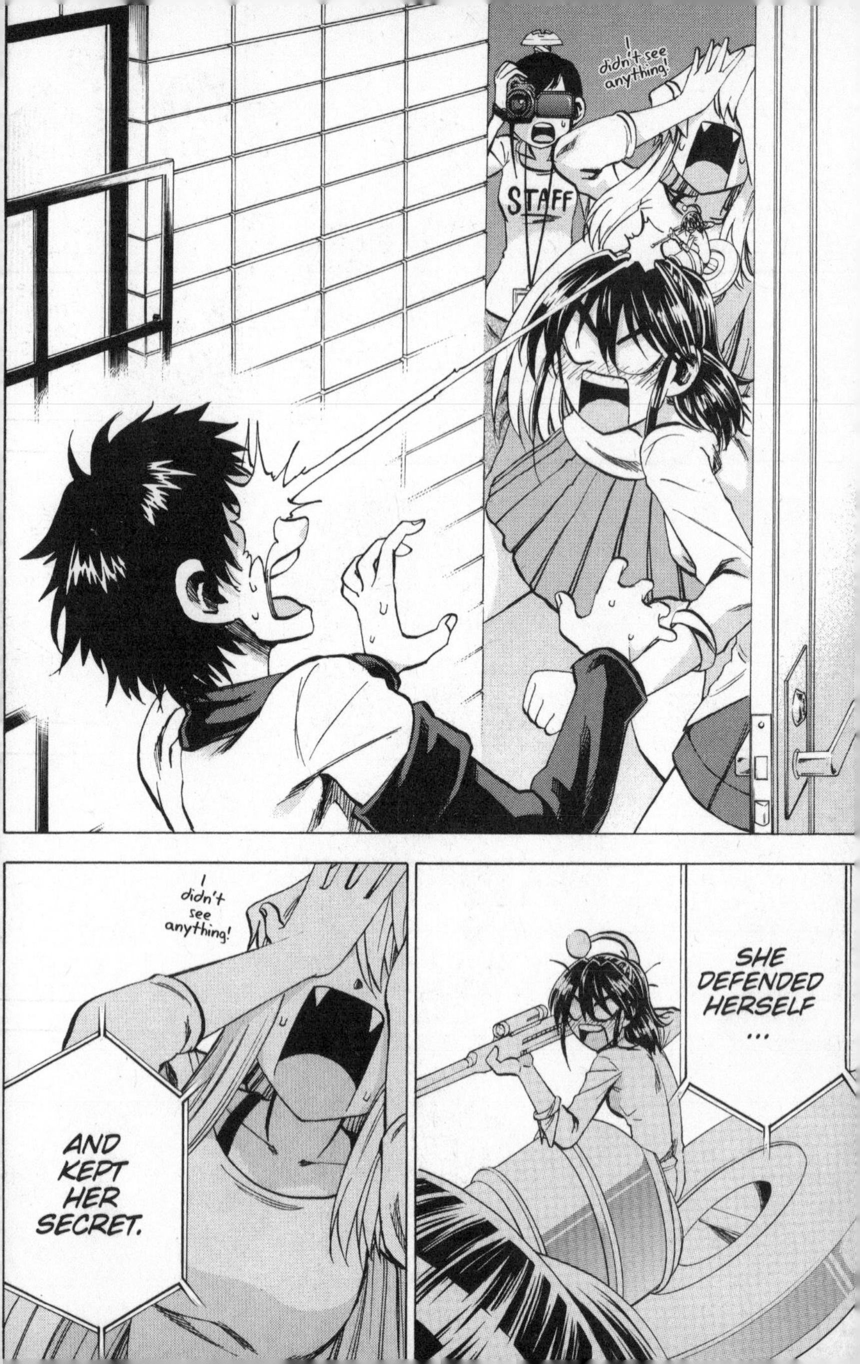
I didn't see anything!
SHE DEFENDED HERSELF...
I didn't see anything!
AND KEPT HER SECRET.

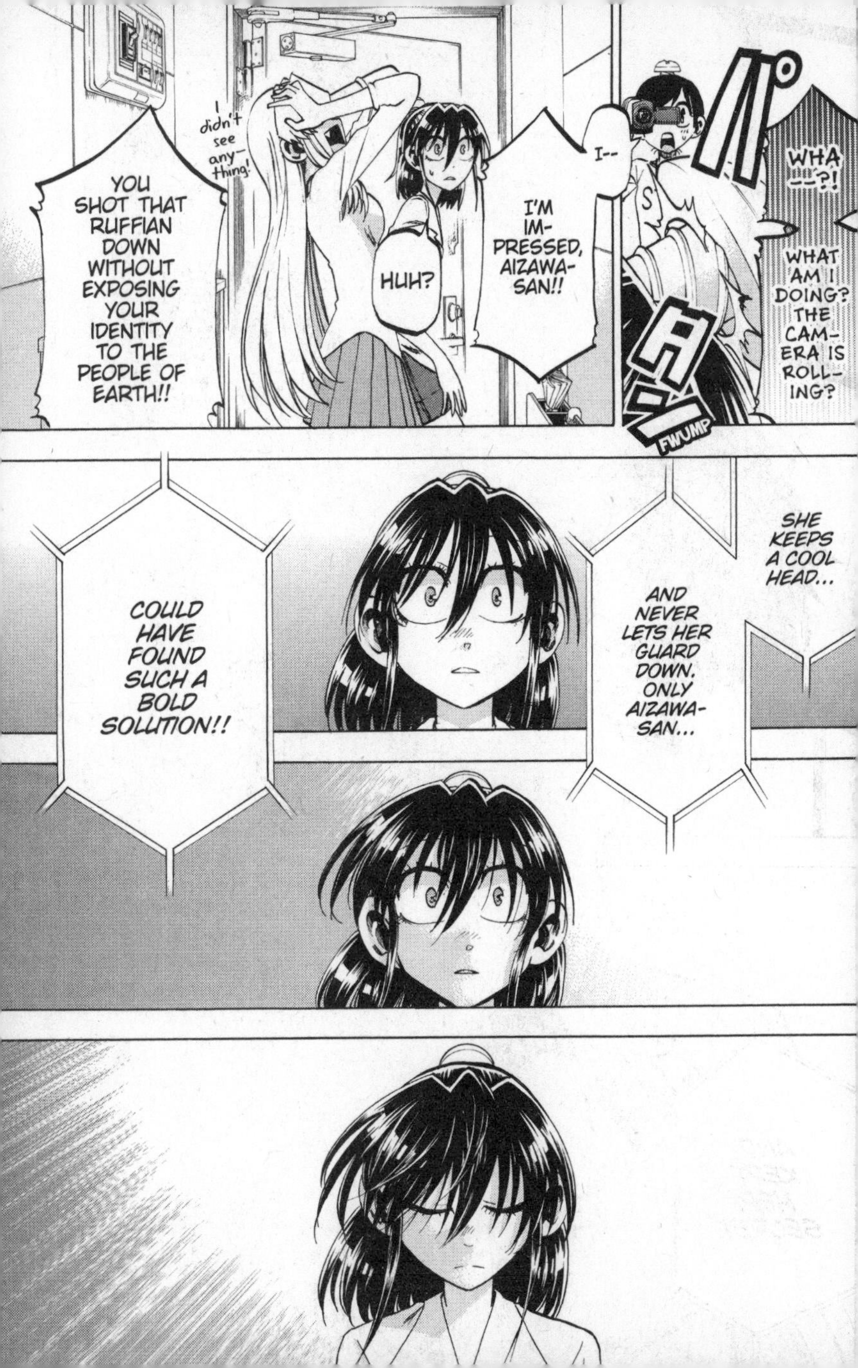
パ
WHA--?!
WHAT AM I DOING? THE CAM-ERA IS ROLL-ING?
FWUMP
I--
I'M IM-PRESSED, AIZAWA-SAN!!
HUH?
I didn't see any-thing!
YOU SHOT THAT RUFFIAN DOWN WITHOUT EXPOSING YOUR IDENTITY TO THE PEOPLE OF EARTH!!
SHE KEEPS A COOL HEAD...
AND NEVER LETS HER GUARD DOWN. ONLY AIZAWA-SAN...
COULD HAVE FOUND SUCH A BOLD SOLUTION!!

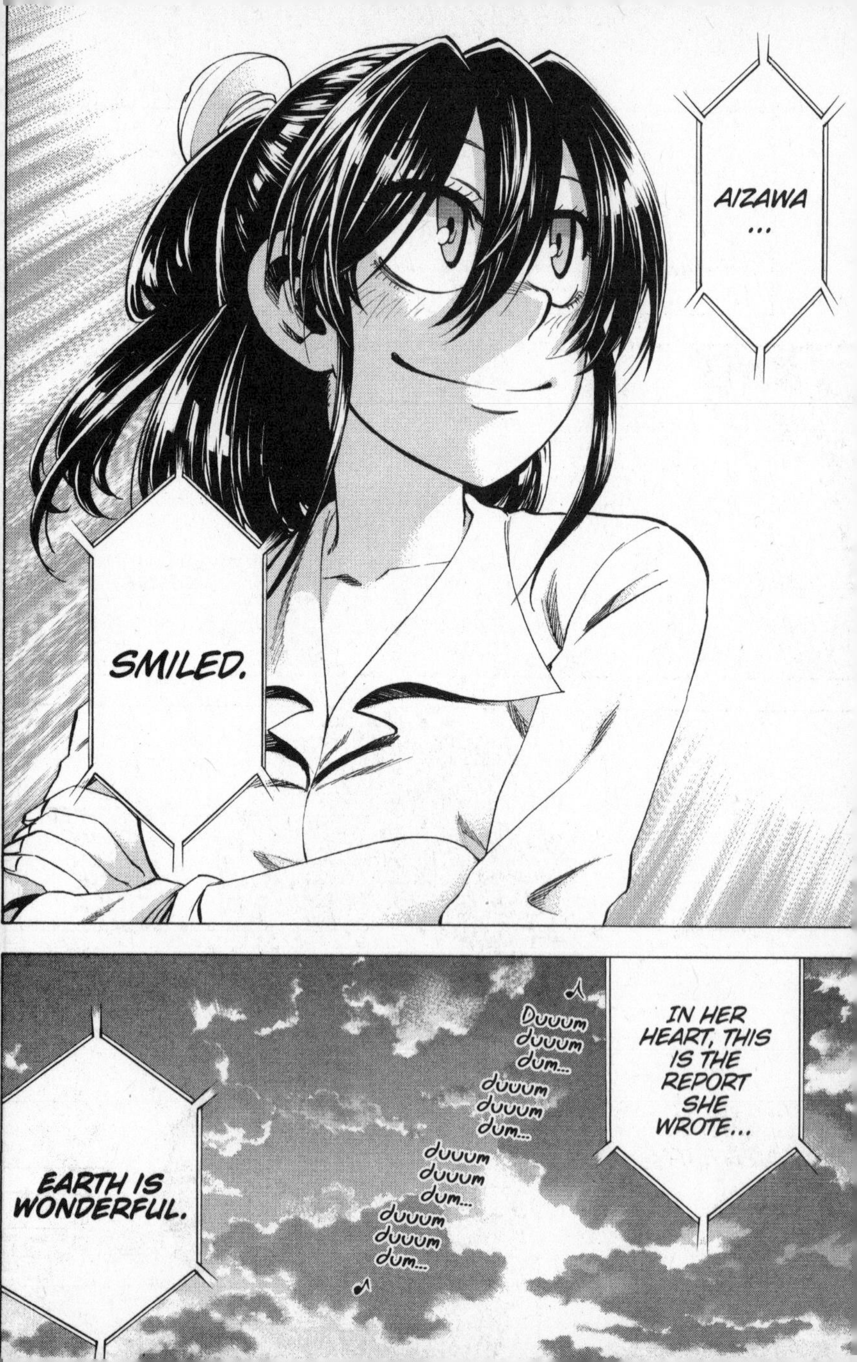
AIZAWA ...
SMILED.
IN HER HEART, THIS IS THE REPORT SHE WROTE...
♪ Duuum duuum dum... duuum duuum dum... duuum duuum dum... duuum duuum dum... ♪
EARTH IS WONDERFUL.

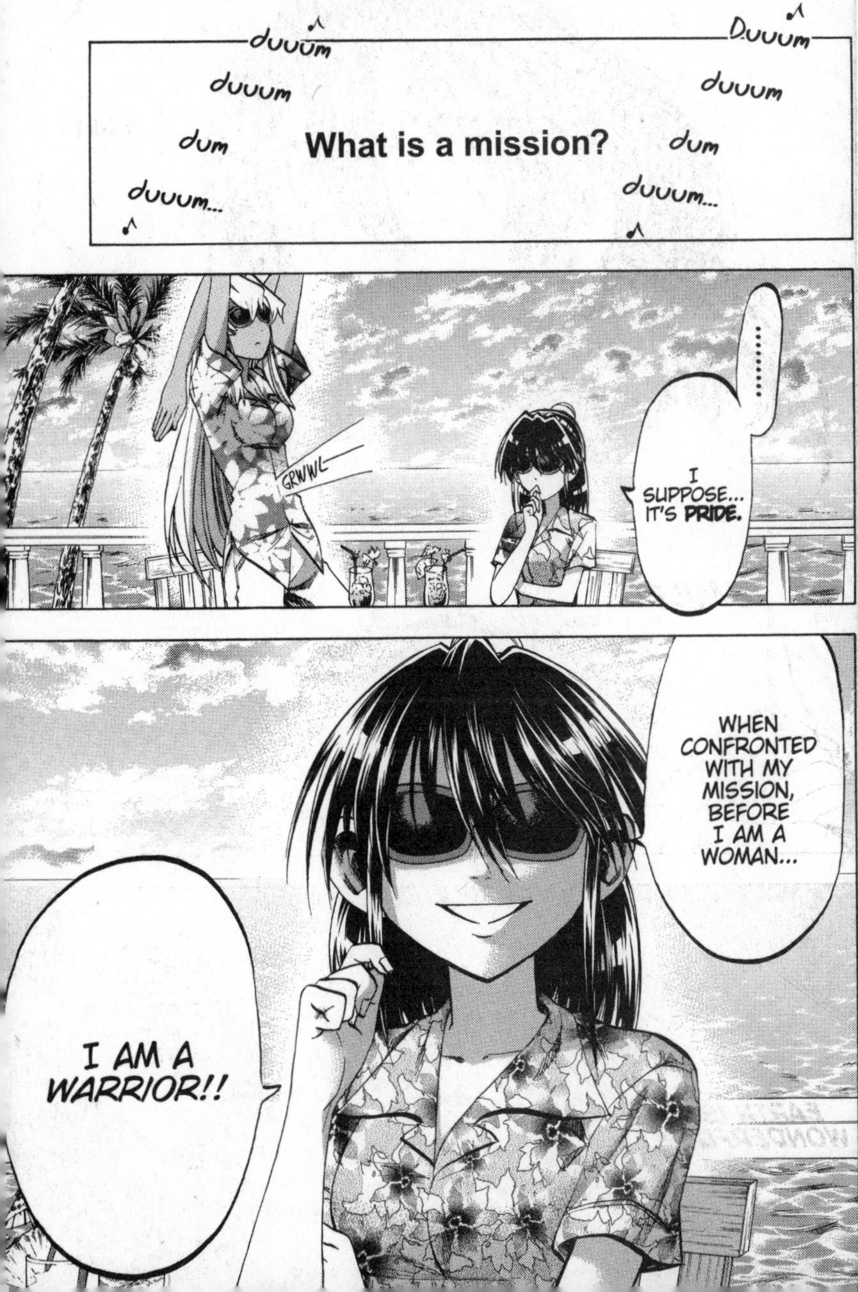
Duuum
duuum
dum
duuum...
What is a mission?
duuum
duuum
dum
duuum...
......
I SUPPOSE... IT'S PRIDE.
GRWWL
WHEN CONFRONTED WITH MY MISSION, BEFORE I AM A WOMAN...
I AM A WARRIOR!!

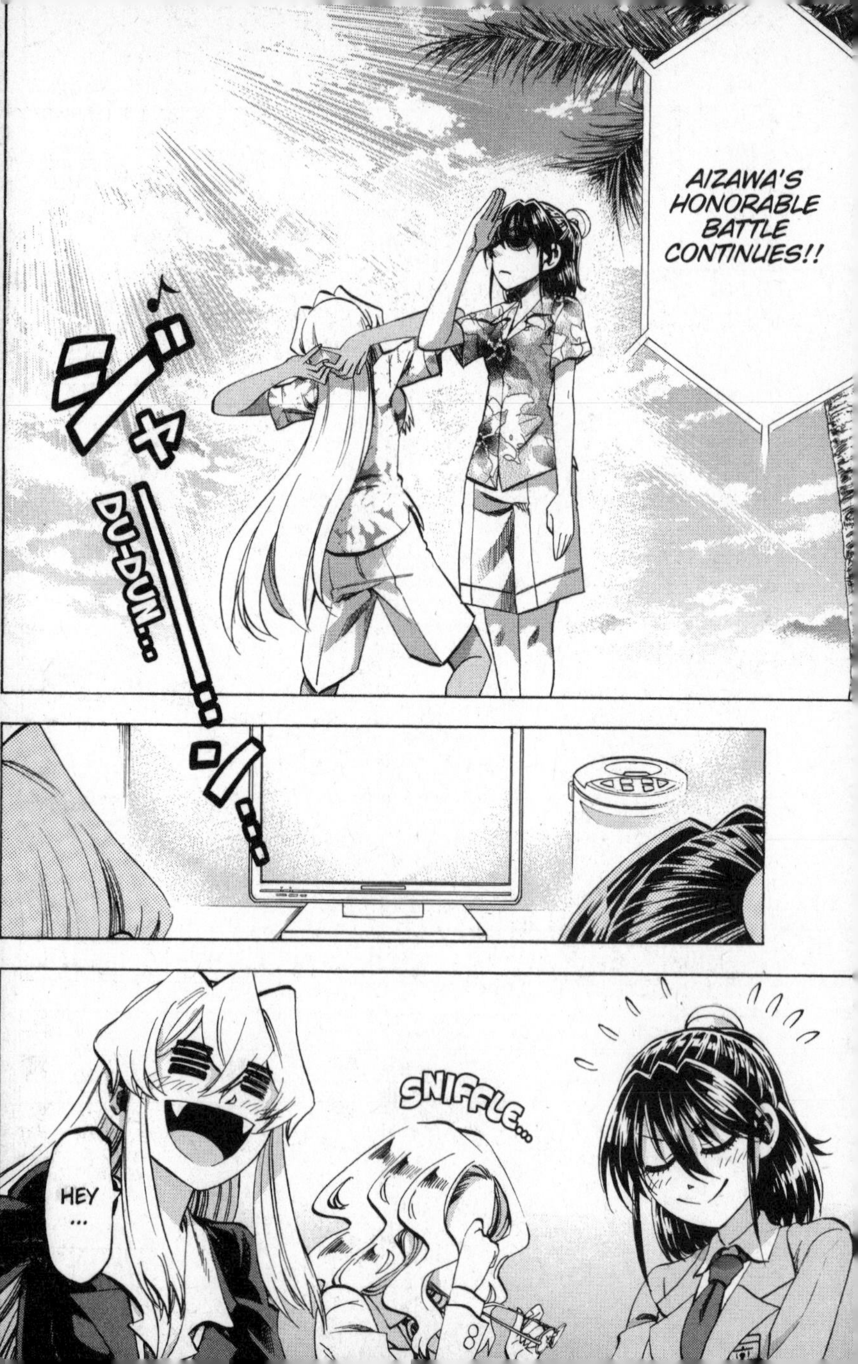
AIZAWA'S HONORABLE BATTLE CONTINUES!!
ジャーン…
DU-DUN...
SNIFFLE...
HEY ...

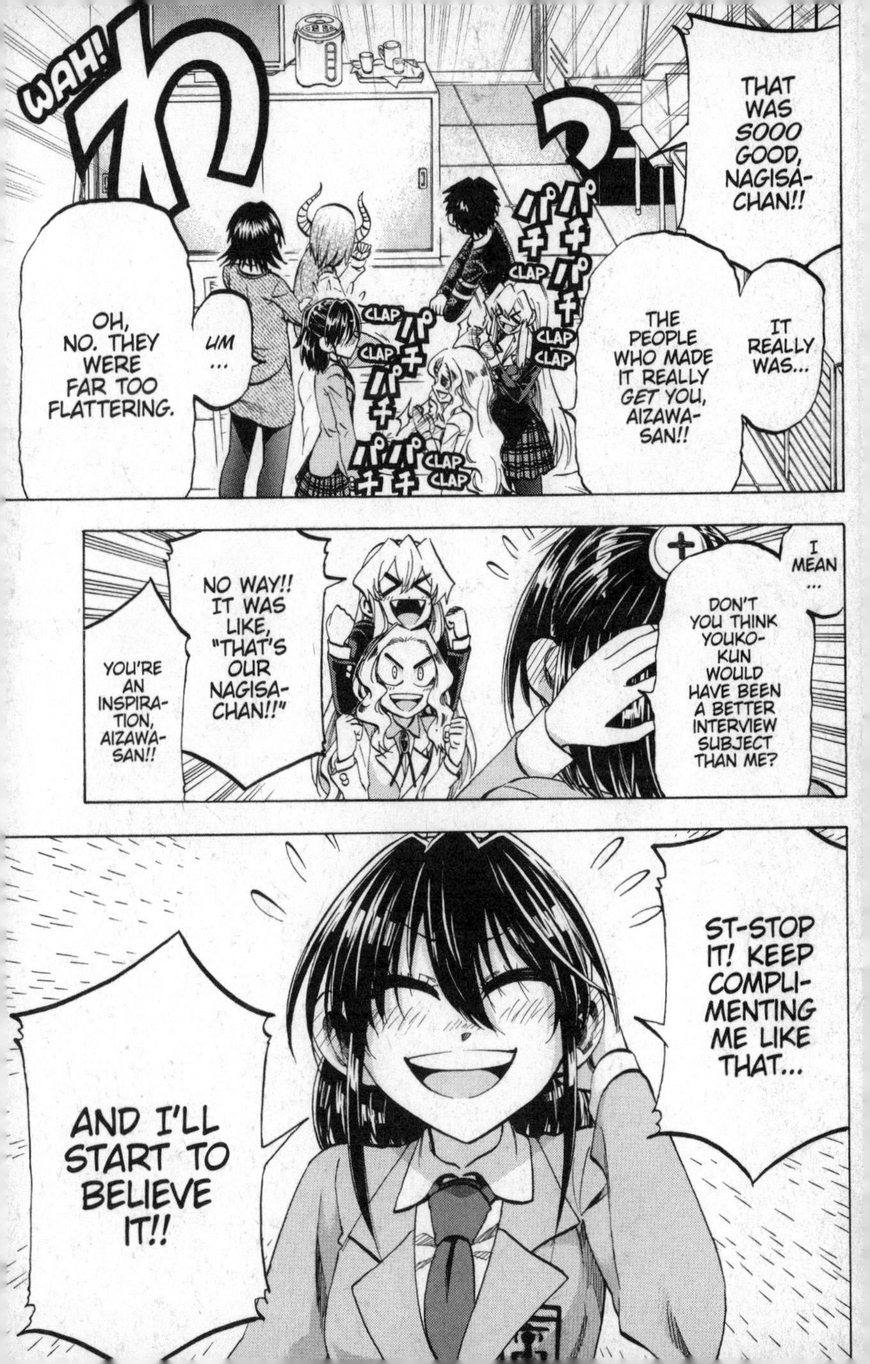
THAT WAS SOOO GOOD, NAGISA-CHAN!!
IT REALLY WAS...
THE PEOPLE WHO MADE IT REALLY GET YOU, AIZAWA-SAN!!
WAH!
CLAP CLAP
CLAP
CLAP
CLAP
CLAP CLAP
UM ...
OH, NO. THEY WERE FAR TOO FLATTERING.
I MEAN ...
DON'T YOU THINK YOUKO-KUN WOULD HAVE BEEN A BETTER INTERVIEW SUBJECT THAN ME?
NO WAY!! IT WAS LIKE, "THAT'S OUR NAGISA-CHAN!!"
YOU'RE AN INSPIRATION, AIZAWA-SAN!!
ST-STOP IT! KEEP COMPLIMENTING ME LIKE THAT...
AND I'LL START TO BELIEVE IT!!

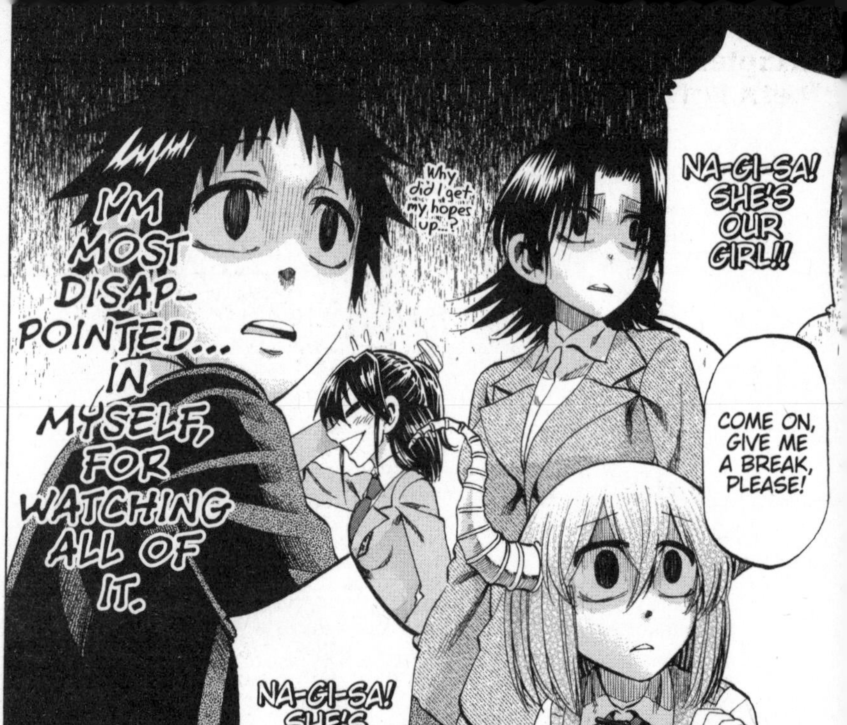
NA-GI-SA! SHE'S OUR GIRL!!
COME ON, GIVE ME A BREAK, PLEASE!
Why did I get my hopes up...?
I'M MOST DISAP-POINTED... IN MYSELF, FOR WATCHING ALL OF IT.
NA-GI-SA! SHE'S OUR GIRL!!
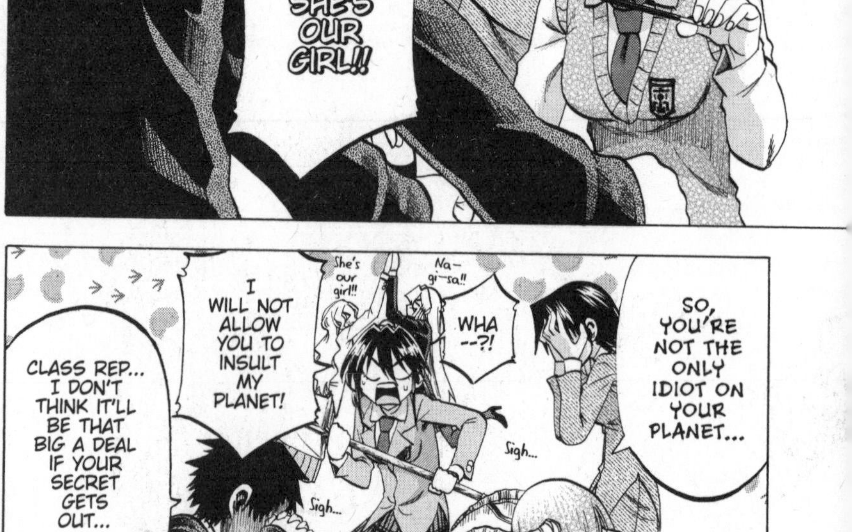
SO, YOU'RE NOT THE ONLY IDIOT ON YOUR PLANET...
Sigh...
WHA--?!
Na-gi-sa!!
She's our girl!!
I WILL NOT ALLOW YOU TO INSULT MY PLANET!
Sigh...
CLASS REP... I DON'T THINK IT'LL BE THAT BIG A DEAL IF YOUR SECRET GETS OUT...

Chapter 105:
"Let's Fall in Love!"

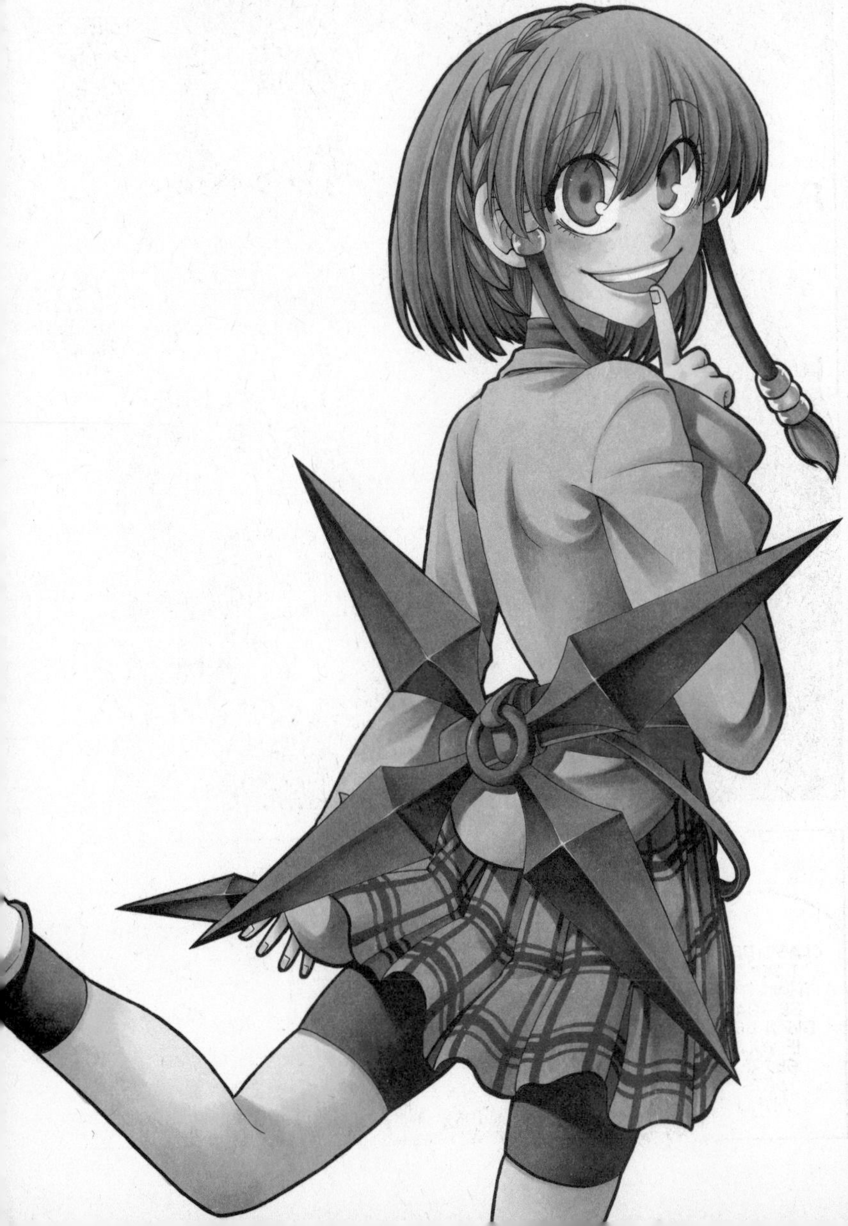

TOP SECRET

My Monster Secret 12

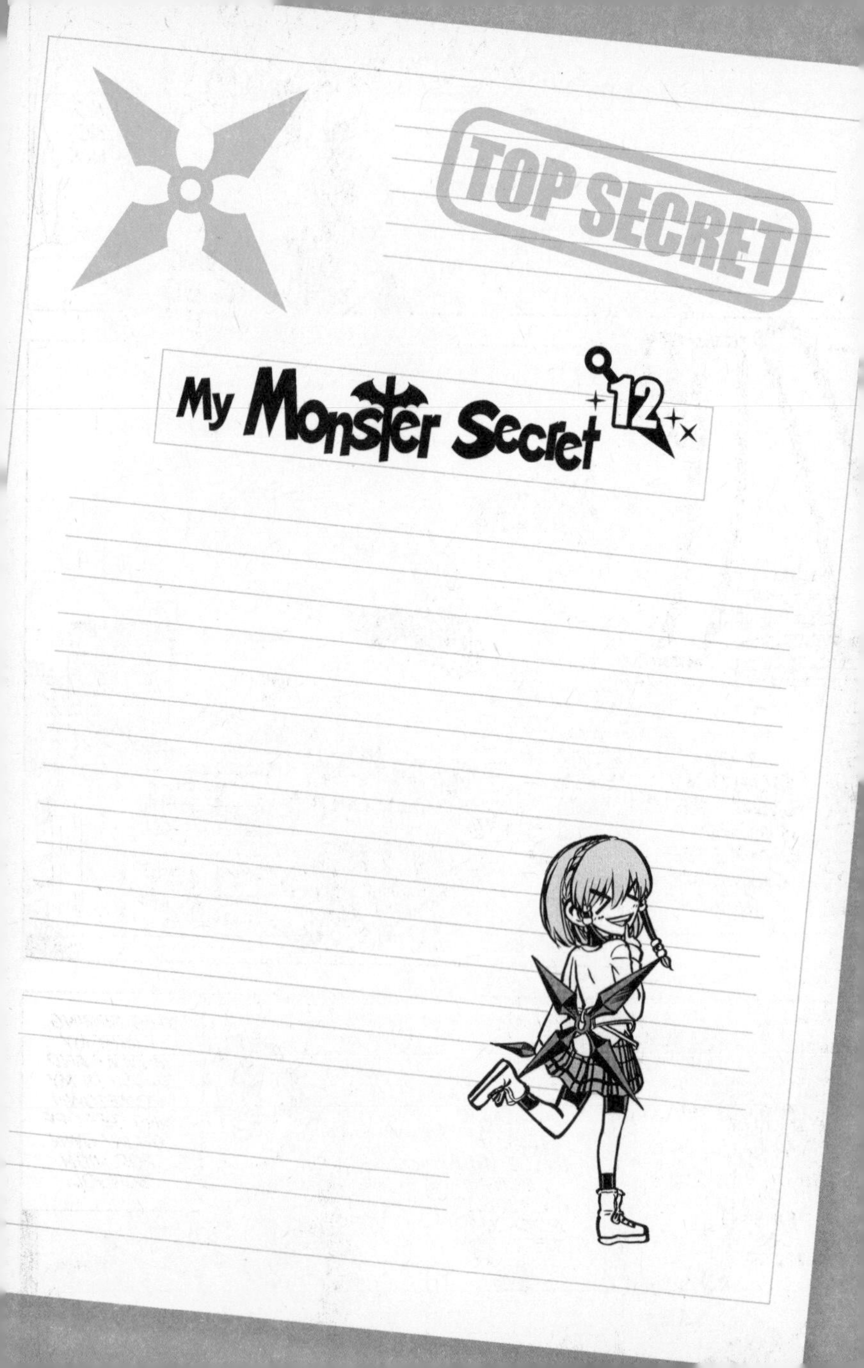

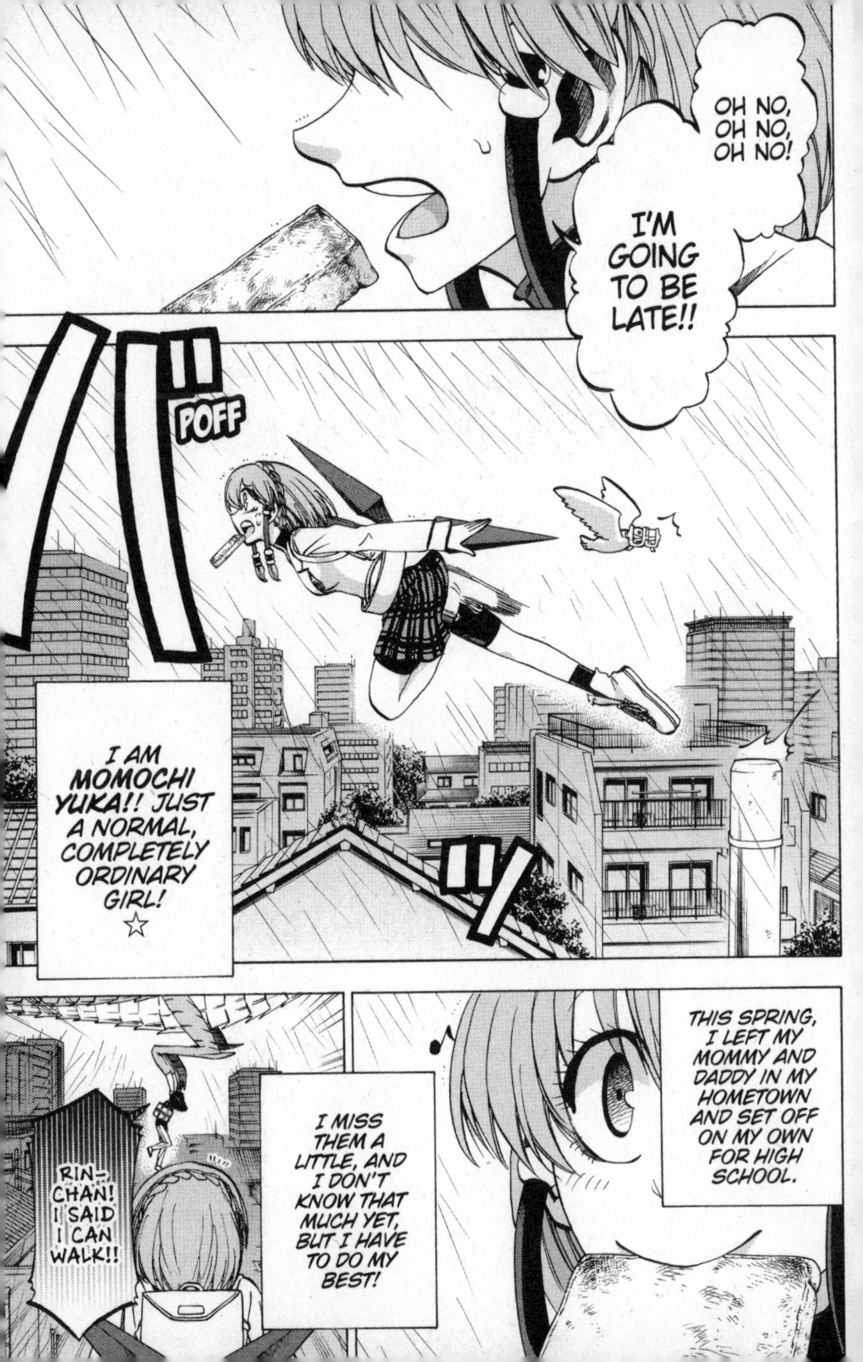
OH NO, OH NO, OH NO!
I'M GOING TO BE LATE!!
POFF
I AM MOMOCHI YUKA!! JUST A NORMAL, COMPLETELY ORDINARY GIRL! ☆
THIS SPRING, I LEFT MY MOMMY AND DADDY IN MY HOMETOWN AND SET OFF ON MY OWN FOR HIGH SCHOOL.
I MISS THEM A LITTLE, AND I DON'T KNOW THAT MUCH YET, BUT I HAVE TO DO MY BEST!
RIN-CHAN! I SAID I CAN WALK!!

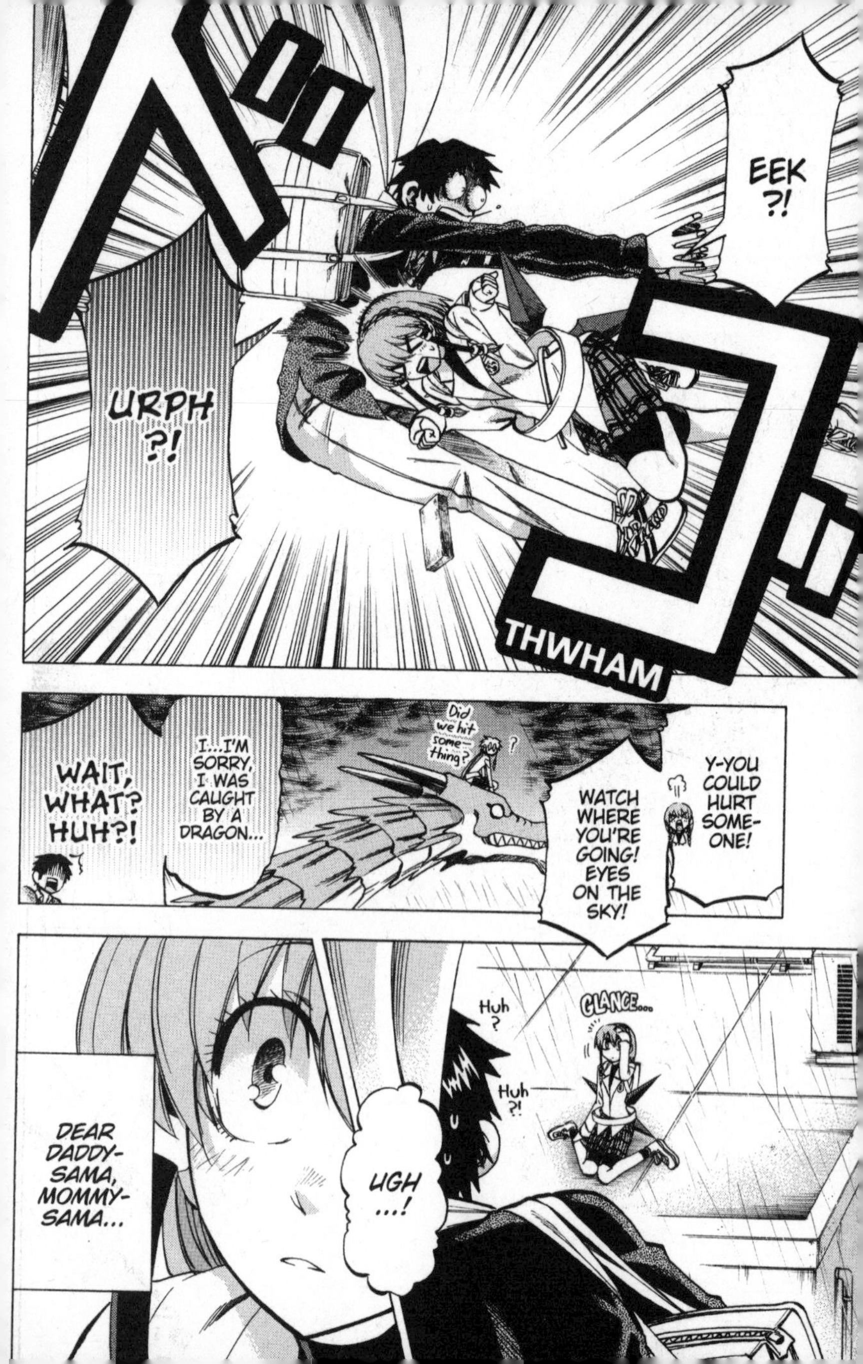

EEK ?!
THWHAM
URPH ?!
Y-YOU COULD HURT SOME-ONE!
WATCH WHERE YOU'RE GOING! EYES ON THE SKY!
Did we hit some-thing?
I...I'M SORRY, I WAS CAUGHT BY A DRAGON...
WAIT, WHAT? HUH?!
GLANCE...
Huh ?
Huh ?!
UGH ...!
DEAR DADDY-SAMA, MOMMY-SAMA...

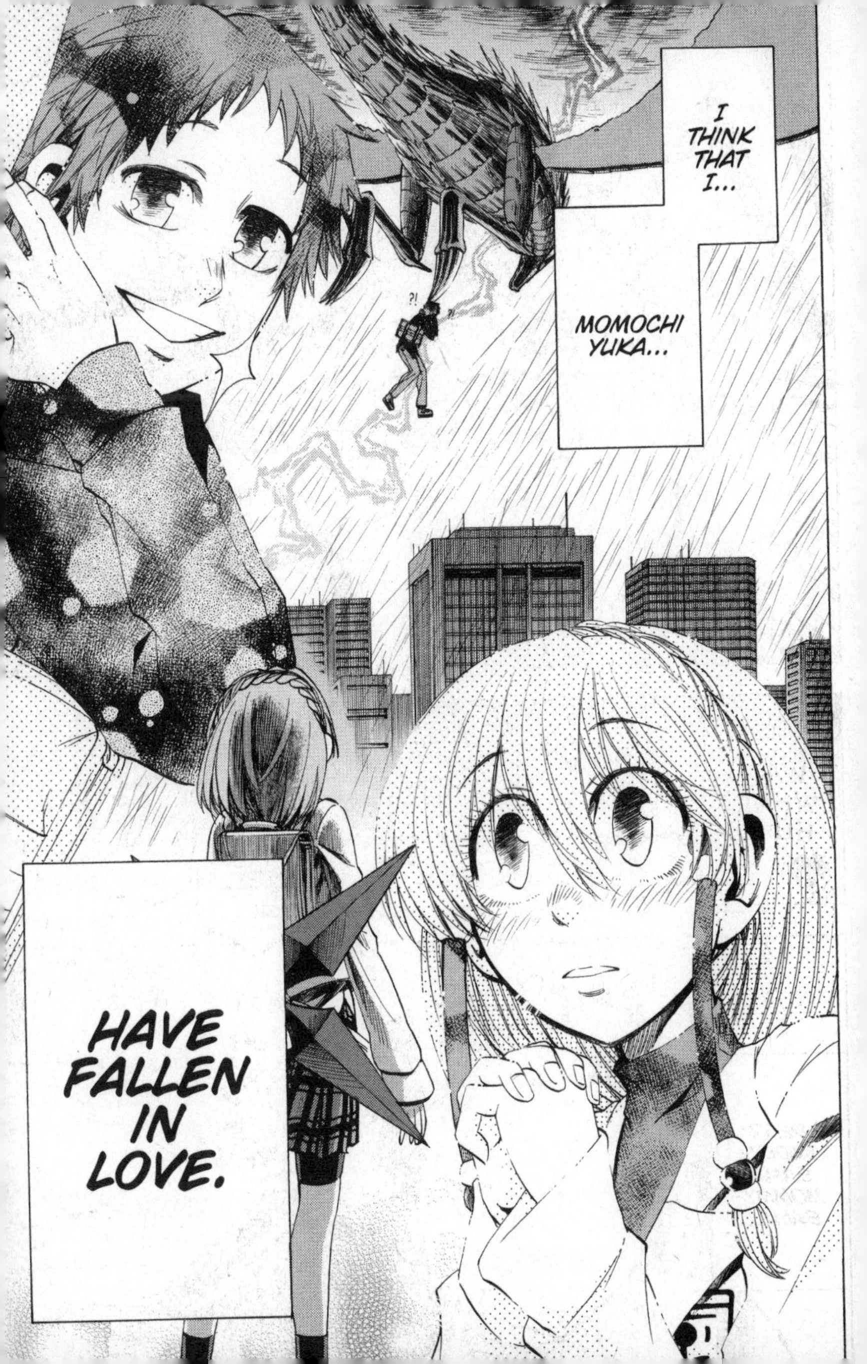
I THINK THAT I...
MOMOCHI YUKA...
?!
HAVE FALLEN IN LOVE.

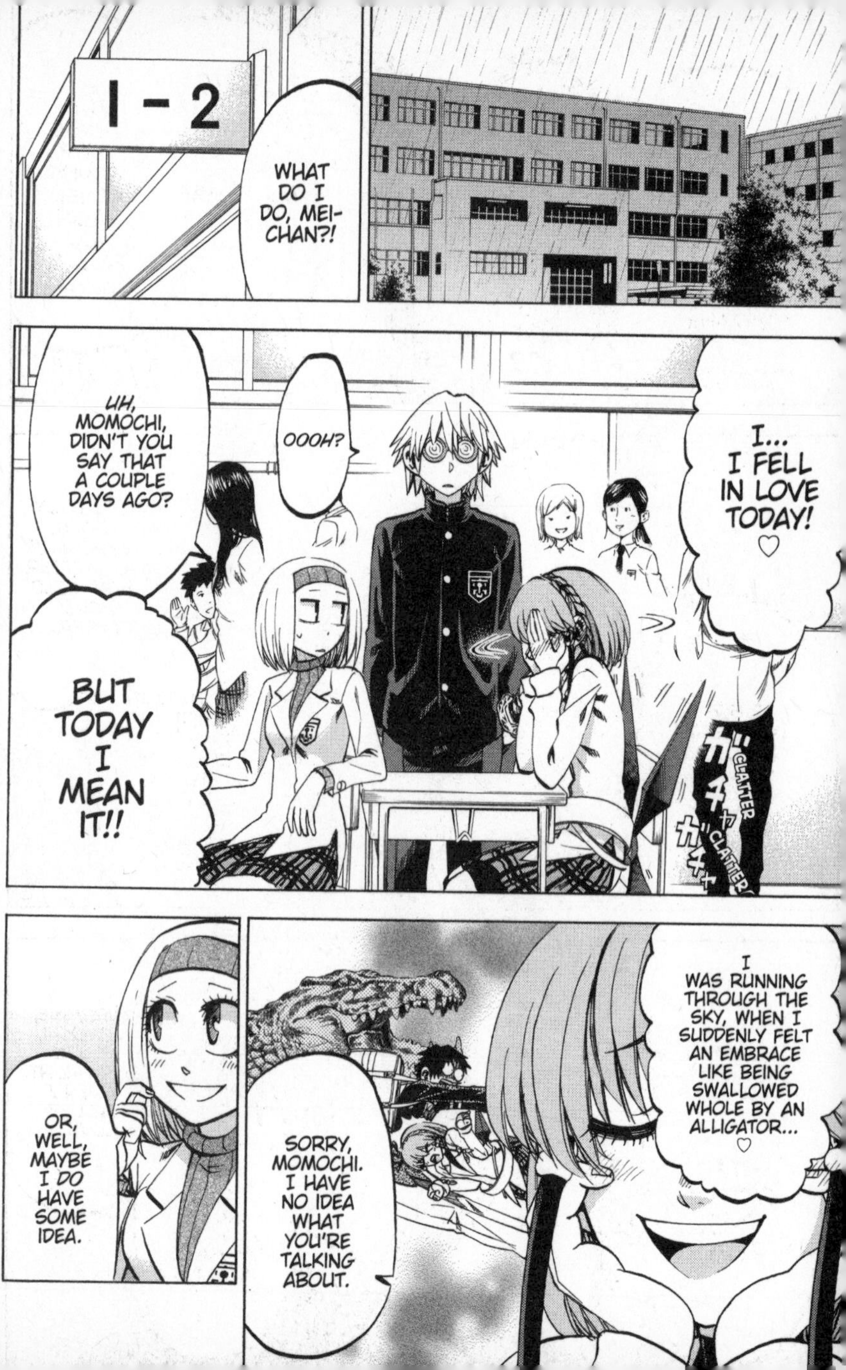
1 - 2
WHAT DO I DO, MEI-CHAN?!
I... I FELL IN LOVE TODAY! ♡
ガチャ CLATTER
ガチャ CLATTER
OOOH?
UH, MOMOCHI, DIDN'T YOU SAY THAT A COUPLE DAYS AGO?
BUT TODAY I MEAN IT!!
I WAS RUNNING THROUGH THE SKY, WHEN I SUDDENLY FELT AN EMBRACE LIKE BEING SWALLOWED WHOLE BY AN ALLIGATOR... ♡
SORRY, MOMOCHI. I HAVE NO IDEA WHAT YOU'RE TALKING ABOUT.
OR, WELL, MAYBE I *DO* HAVE SOME IDEA.

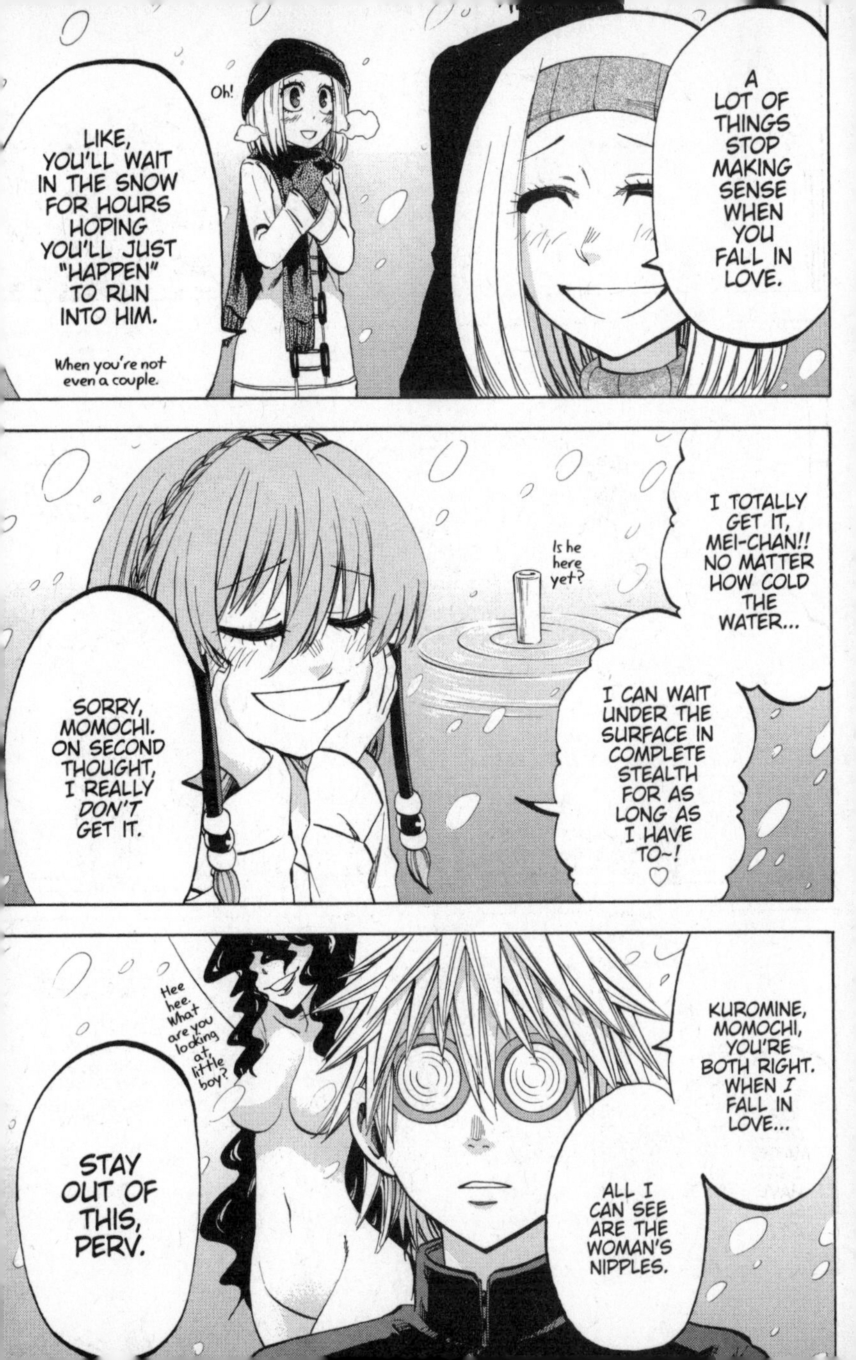
A LOT OF THINGS STOP MAKING SENSE WHEN YOU FALL IN LOVE.
Oh!
LIKE, YOU'LL WAIT IN THE SNOW FOR HOURS HOPING YOU'LL JUST "HAPPEN" TO RUN INTO HIM.
When you're not even a couple.
I TOTALLY GET IT, MEI-CHAN!! NO MATTER HOW COLD THE WATER...
Is he here yet?
I CAN WAIT UNDER THE SURFACE IN COMPLETE STEALTH FOR AS LONG AS I HAVE TO~! ♡
SORRY, MOMOCHI. ON SECOND THOUGHT, I REALLY *DON'T* GET IT.
KUROMINE, MOMOCHI, YOU'RE BOTH RIGHT. WHEN *I* FALL IN LOVE...
ALL I CAN SEE ARE THE WOMAN'S NIPPLES.
Hee hee. What are you looking at, little boy?
STAY OUT OF THIS, PERV.

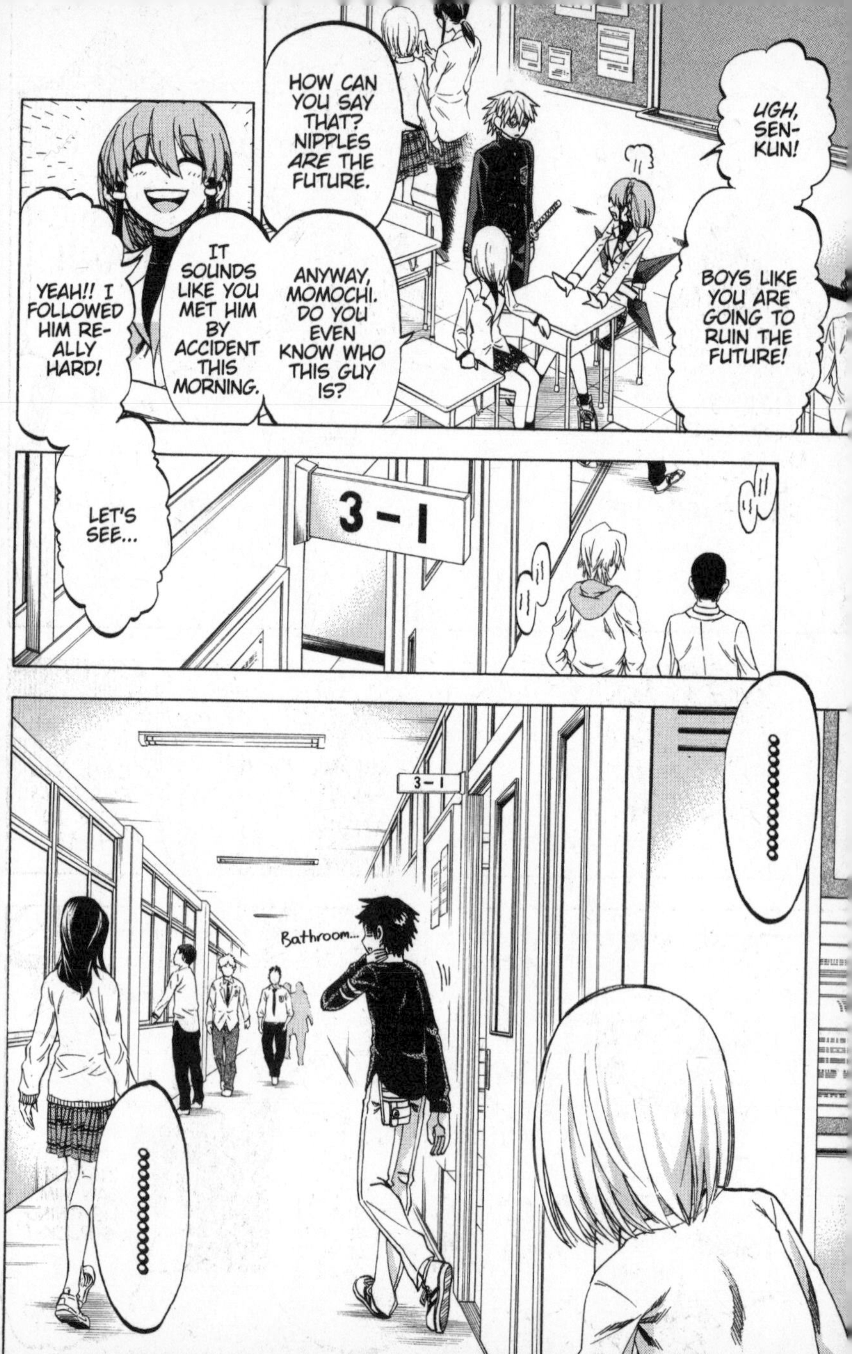
UGH, SEN-KUN!
BOYS LIKE YOU ARE GOING TO RUIN THE FUTURE!
HOW CAN YOU SAY THAT? NIPPLES *ARE* THE FUTURE.
ANYWAY, MOMOCHI. DO YOU EVEN KNOW WHO THIS GUY IS?
IT SOUNDS LIKE YOU MET HIM BY ACCIDENT THIS MORNING.
YEAH!! I FOLLOWED HIM REALLY HARD!
LET'S SEE...
3 - 1
....
3 - 1
Bathroom...
....

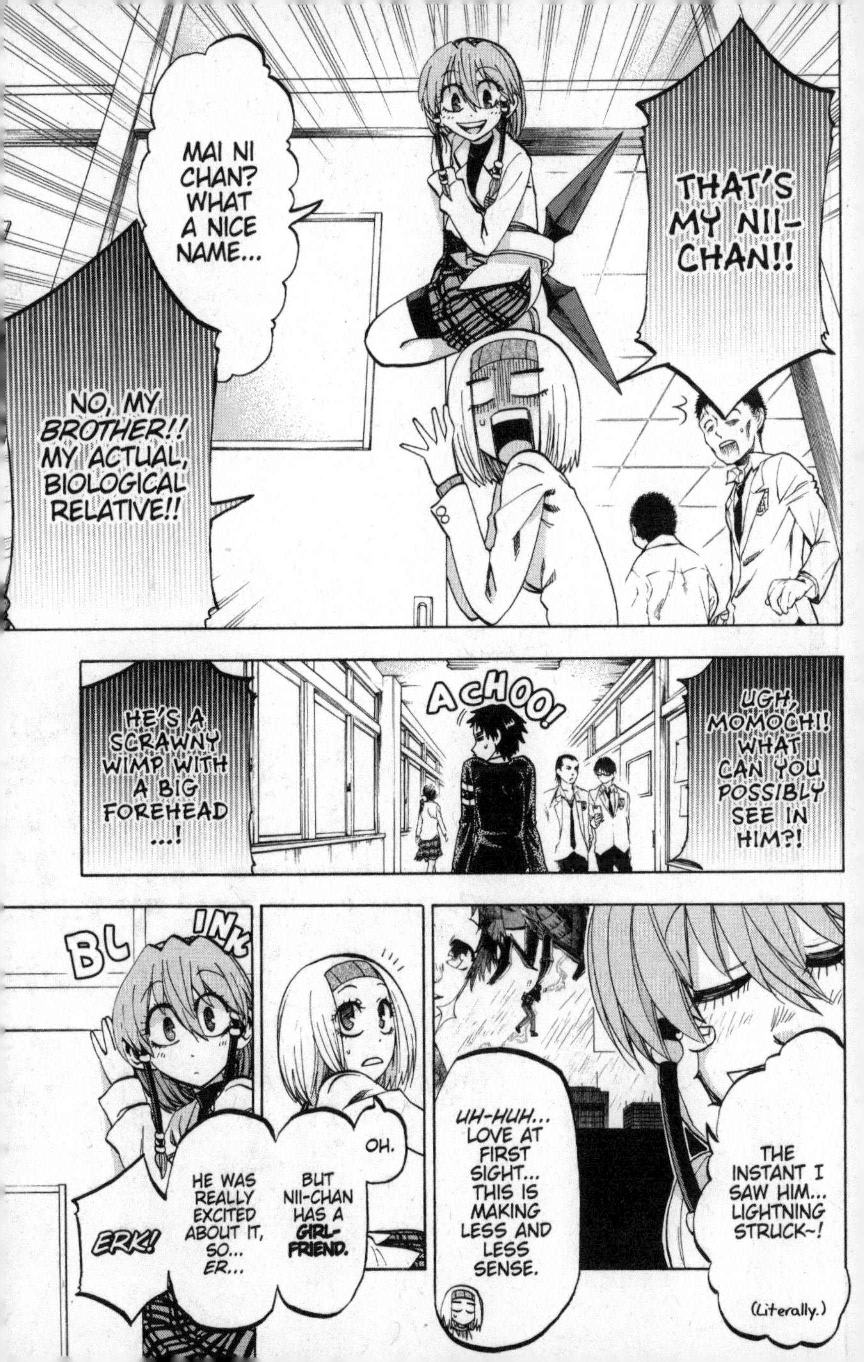
THAT'S MY NII-CHAN!!
MAI NI CHAN? WHAT A NICE NAME...
NO, MY BROTHER!! MY ACTUAL, BIOLOGICAL RELATIVE!!
UGH, MOMOCHI! WHAT CAN YOU POSSIBLY SEE IN HIM?!
ACHOO!
HE'S A SCRAWNY WIMP WITH A BIG FOREHEAD ...!
THE INSTANT I SAW HIM... LIGHTNING STRUCK~!
(Literally.)
UH-HUH... LOVE AT FIRST SIGHT... THIS IS MAKING LESS AND LESS SENSE.
OH.
BUT NII-CHAN HAS A GIRLFRIEND.
BLINK
HE WAS REALLY EXCITED ABOUT IT, SO... ER...
ERK!

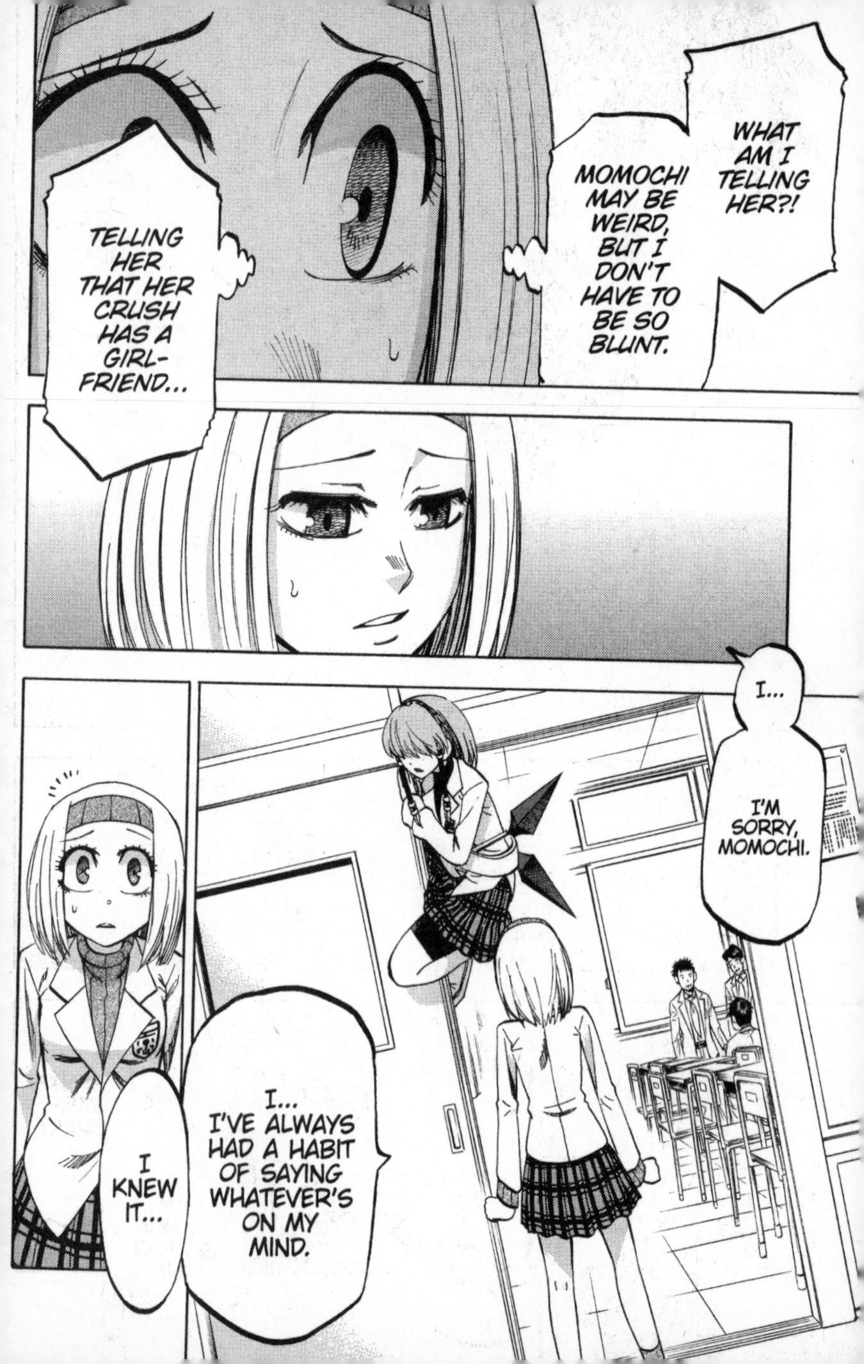
WHAT AM I TELLING HER?!
MOMOCHI MAY BE WEIRD, BUT I DON'T HAVE TO BE SO BLUNT.
TELLING HER THAT HER CRUSH HAS A GIRL-FRIEND...
I...
I'M SORRY, MOMOCHI.
I... I'VE ALWAYS HAD A HABIT OF SAYING WHATEVER'S ON MY MIND.
I KNEW IT...

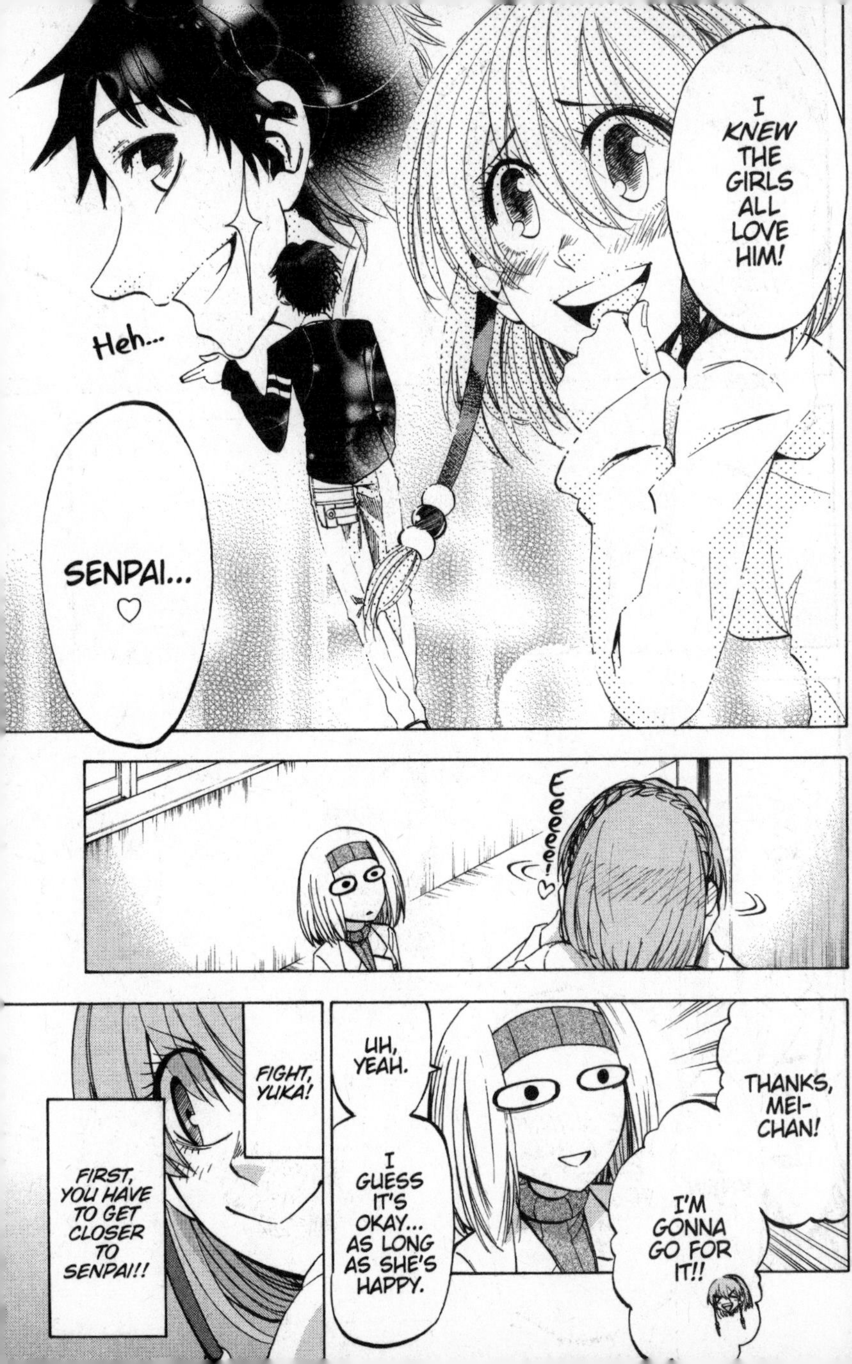
I KNEW THE GIRLS ALL LOVE HIM!
Heh...
SENPAI... ♡
Eeeeee!! ♡
THANKS, MEI-CHAN!
I'M GONNA GO FOR IT!!
UH, YEAH.
I GUESS IT'S OKAY... AS LONG AS SHE'S HAPPY.
FIGHT, YUKA!
FIRST, YOU HAVE TO GET CLOSER TO SENPAI!!

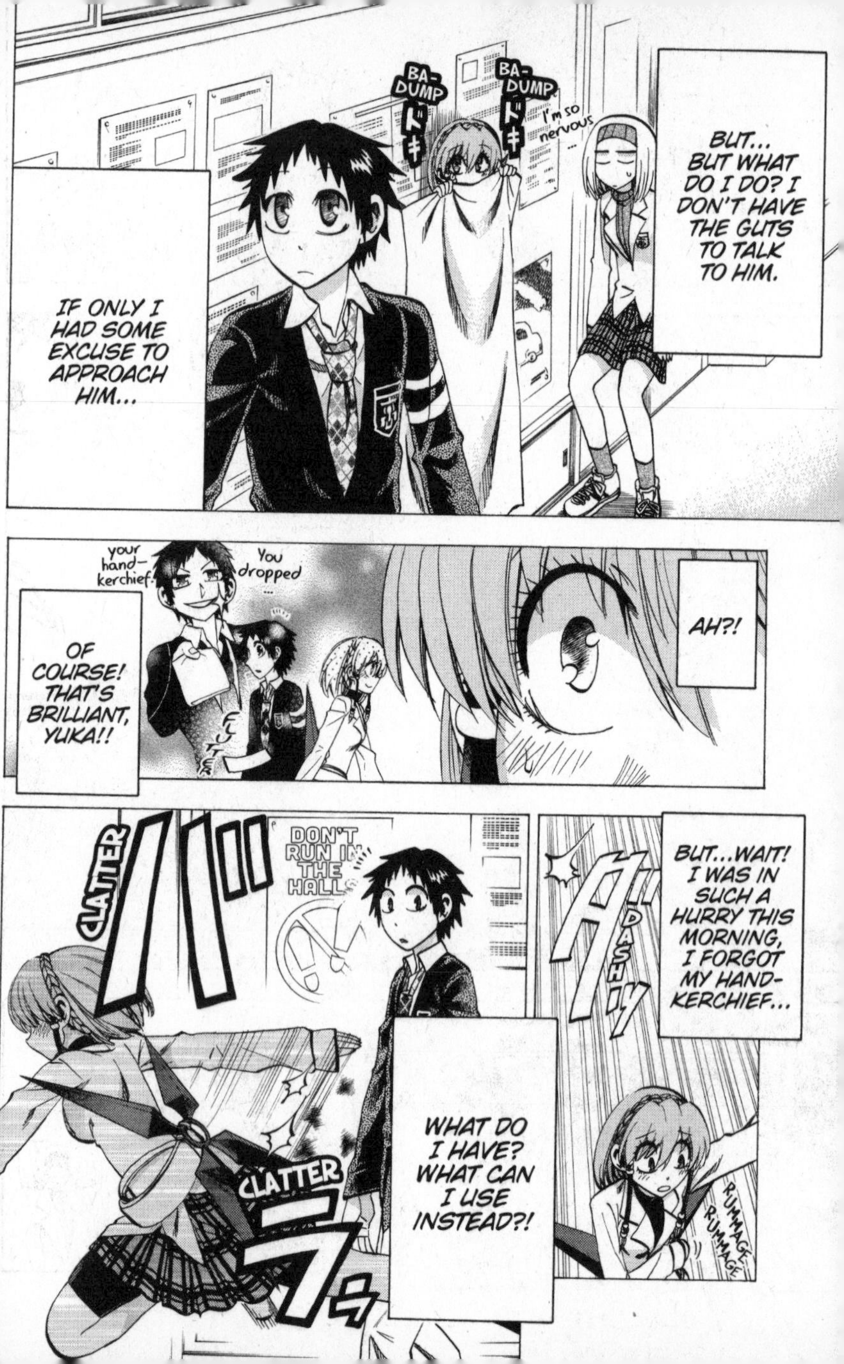
BUT... BUT WHAT DO I DO? I DON'T HAVE THE GUTS TO TALK TO HIM.
I'm so nervous...
BA-DUMP
BA-DUMP
IF ONLY I HAD SOME EXCUSE TO APPROACH HIM...
AH?!
You dropped...
your hand-kerchief.
FLUTTER
OF COURSE! THAT'S BRILLIANT, YUKA!!
BUT...WAIT! I WAS IN SUCH A HURRY THIS MORNING, I FORGOT MY HAND-KERCHIEF...
DASH
RUMMAGE RUMMAGE
DON'T RUN IN THE HALL
CLATTER
WHAT DO I HAVE? WHAT CAN I USE INSTEAD?!
CLATTER

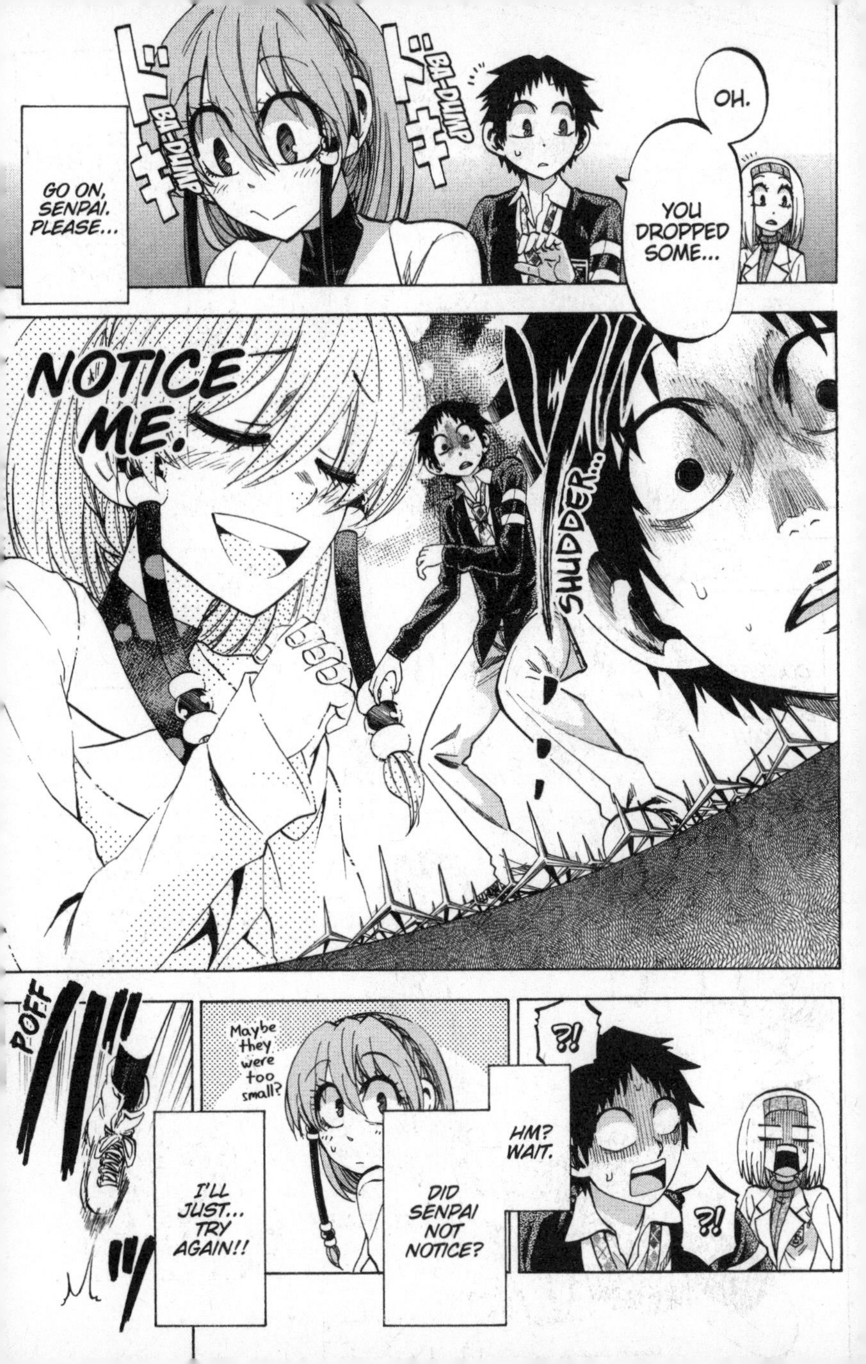
OH.
YOU DROPPED SOME...
ドキ
BA-DUMP
ドキ
BA-DUMP
GO ON, SENPAI. PLEASE...
SHUDDER...
NOTICE ME.
?!
HM? WAIT.
?!
DID SENPAI NOT NOTICE?
Maybe they were too small?
I'LL JUST... TRY AGAIN!!
POFF

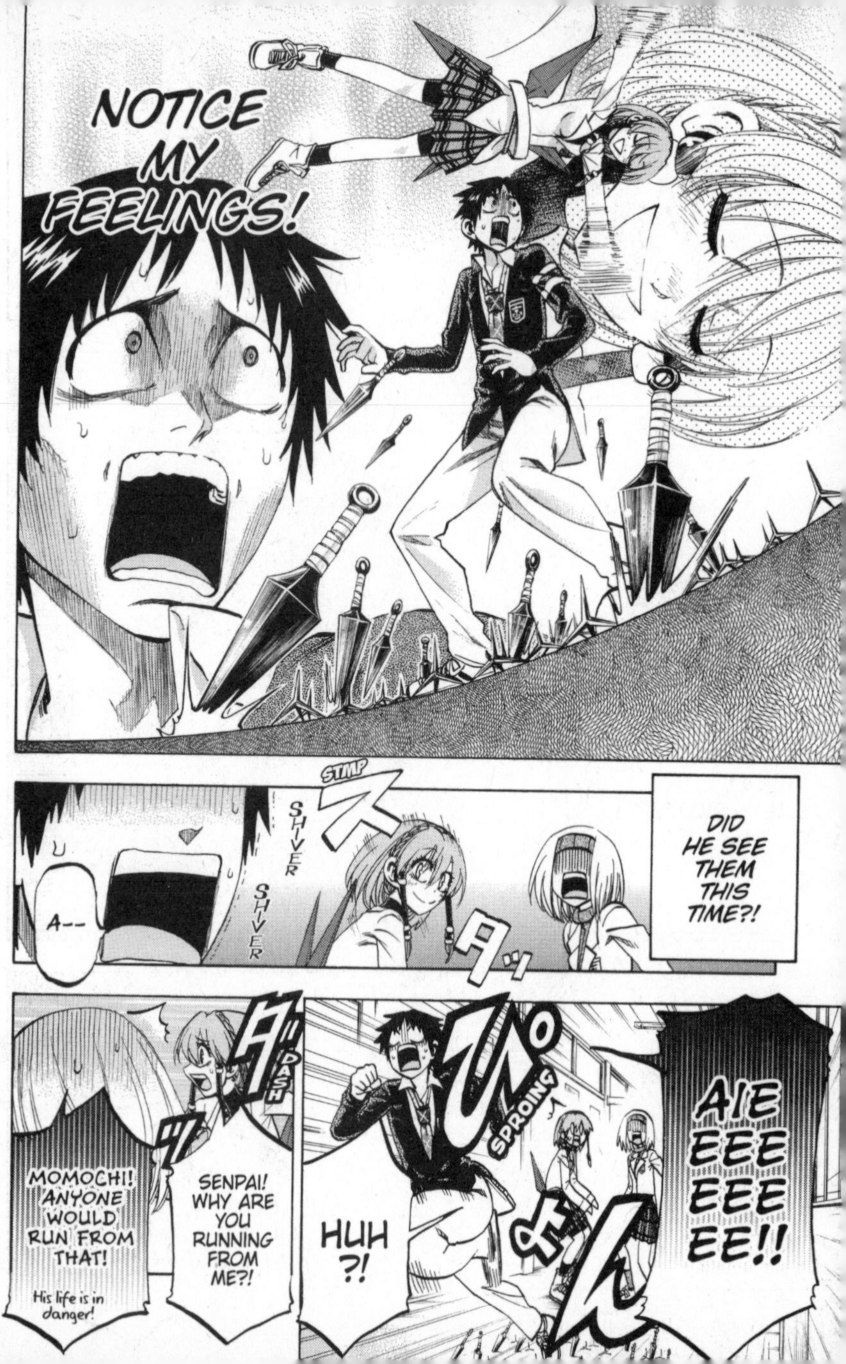
NOTICE MY FEELINGS!
DID HE SEE THEM THIS TIME?!
STMP
SHIVER SHIVER
A--
AIEEEEEEEEE!!
SPROING
HUH?!
DASH
SENPAI! WHY ARE YOU RUNNING FROM ME?!
MOMOCHI! ANYONE WOULD RUN FROM THAT!
His life is in danger!

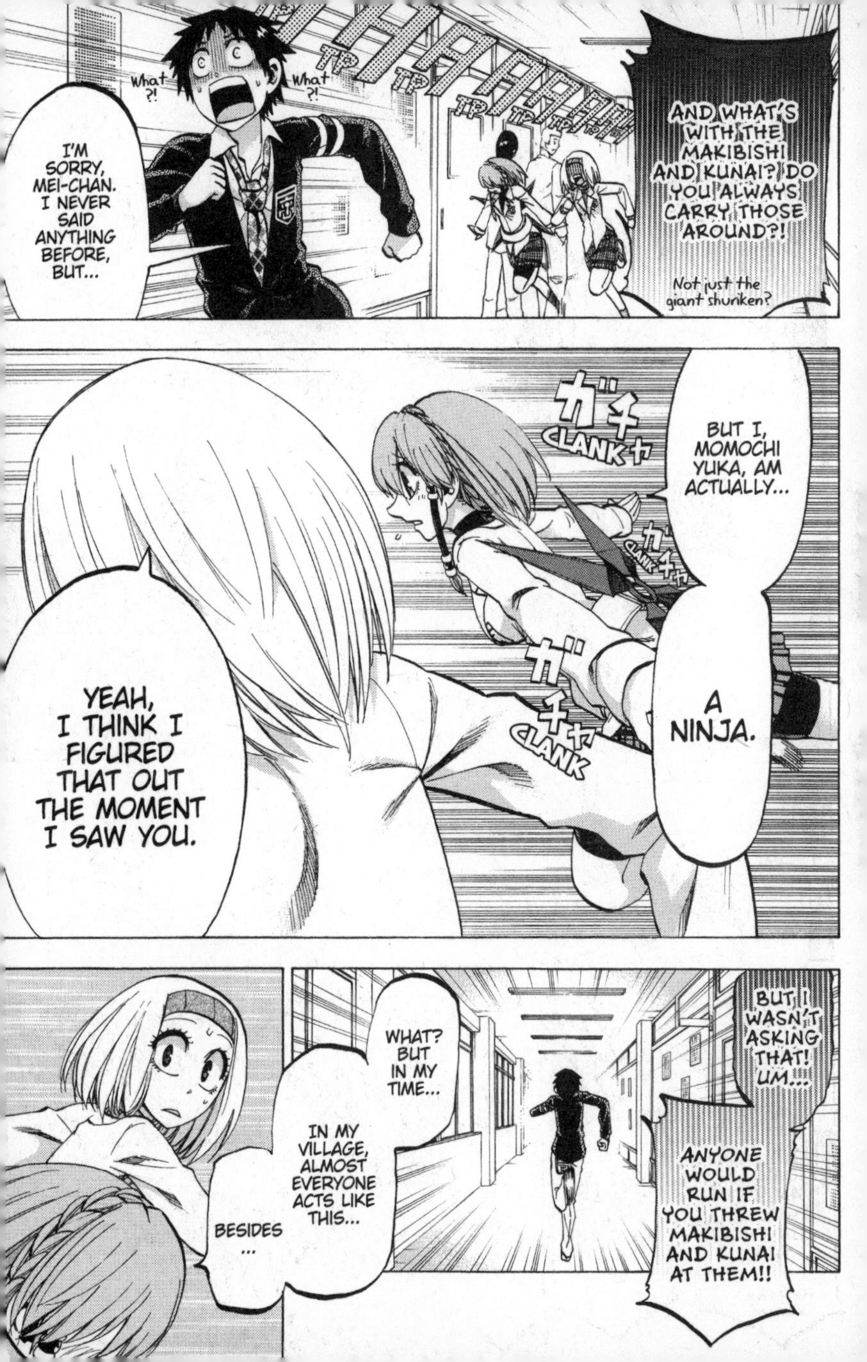
AND WHAT'S WITH THE MAKIBISHI AND KUNAI? DO YOU ALWAYS CARRY THOSE AROUND?!
Not just the giant shuriken?
What?!
What?!
I'M SORRY, MEI-CHAN. I NEVER SAID ANYTHING BEFORE, BUT...
BUT I, MOMOCHI YUKA, AM ACTUALLY...
CLANK
CLANK
A NINJA.
CLANK
YEAH, I THINK I FIGURED THAT OUT THE MOMENT I SAW YOU.
BUT I WASN'T ASKING THAT! UM...
ANYONE WOULD RUN IF YOU THREW MAKIBISHI AND KUNAI AT THEM!!
WHAT? BUT IN MY TIME...
IN MY VILLAGE, ALMOST EVERYONE ACTS LIKE THIS...
BESIDES ...

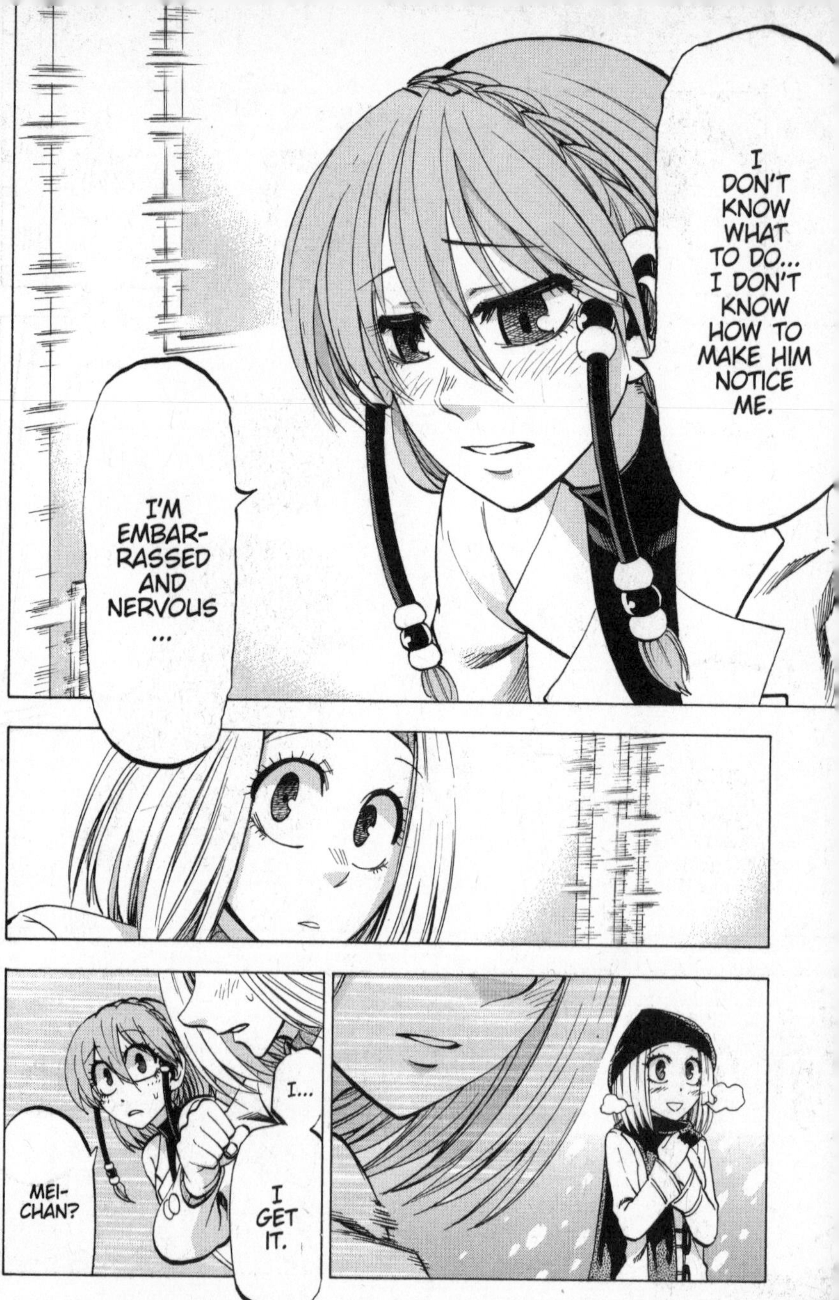
I DON'T KNOW WHAT TO DO... I DON'T KNOW HOW TO MAKE HIM NOTICE ME.
I'M EMBAR-RASSED AND NERVOUS...
I...
I GET IT.
MEI-CHAN?

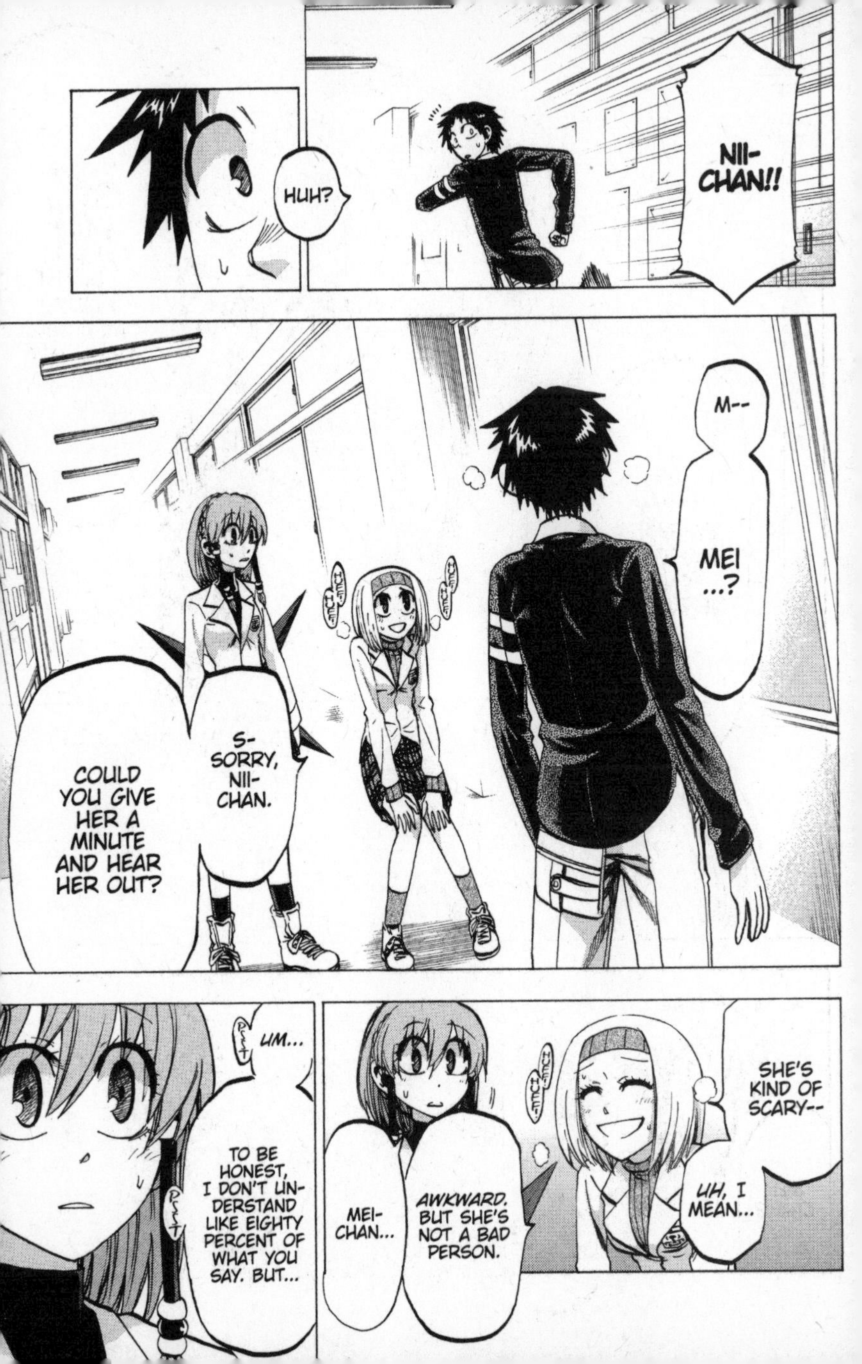
NII-CHAN!!
HUH?
M--
MEI ...?
S-SORRY, NII-CHAN.
COULD YOU GIVE HER A MINUTE AND HEAR HER OUT?
SHE'S KIND OF SCARY--
UH, I MEAN...
AWKWARD. BUT SHE'S NOT A BAD PERSON.
MEI-CHAN...
UM...
TO BE HONEST, I DON'T UNDERSTAND LIKE EIGHTY PERCENT OF WHAT YOU SAY. BUT...

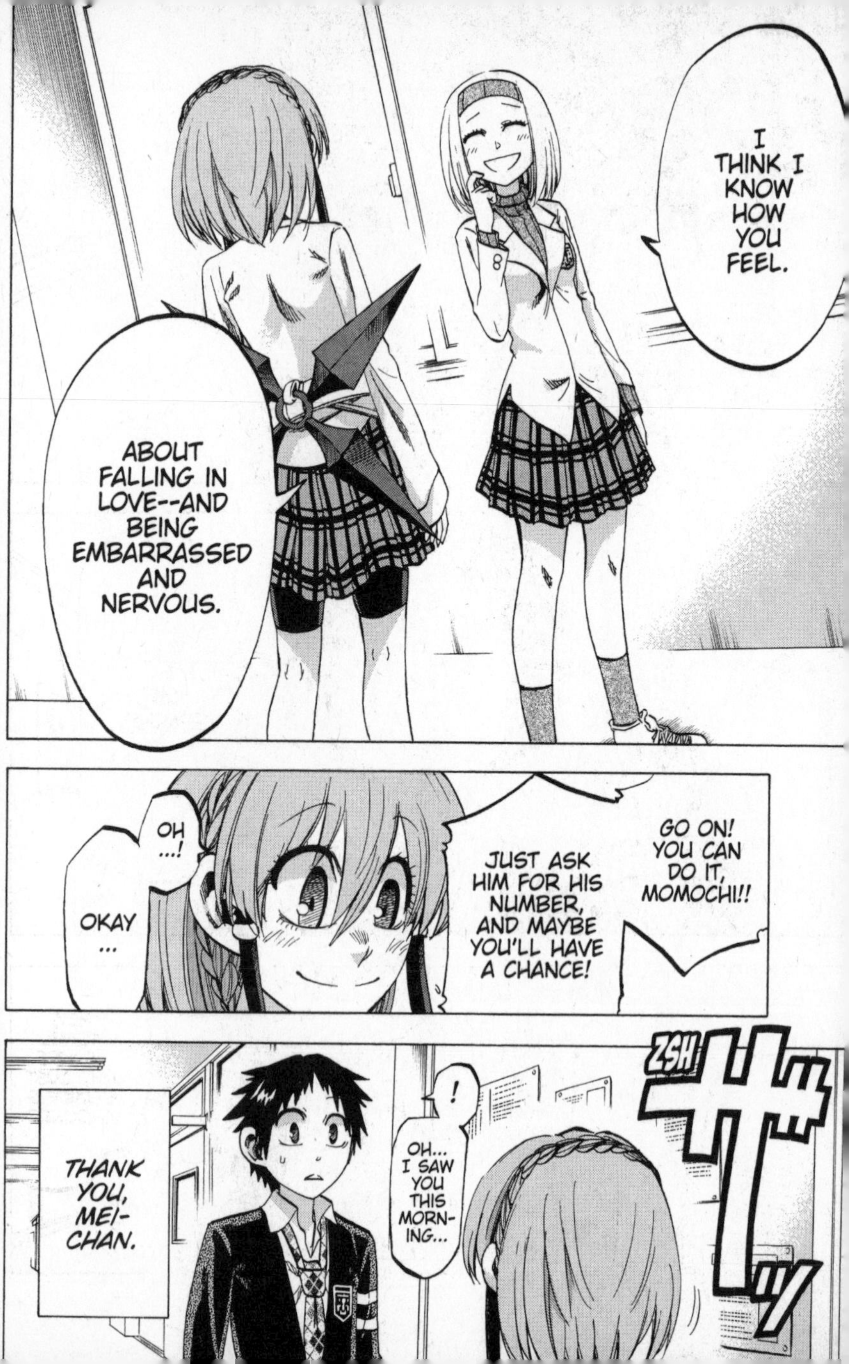
I THINK I KNOW HOW YOU FEEL.
ABOUT FALLING IN LOVE--AND BEING EMBARRASSED AND NERVOUS.
GO ON! YOU CAN DO IT, MOMOCHI!!
JUST ASK HIM FOR HIS NUMBER, AND MAYBE YOU'LL HAVE A CHANCE!
OH ...!
OKAY ...
ZSH
!
OH... I SAW YOU THIS MORN-ING...
THANK YOU, MEI-CHAN.

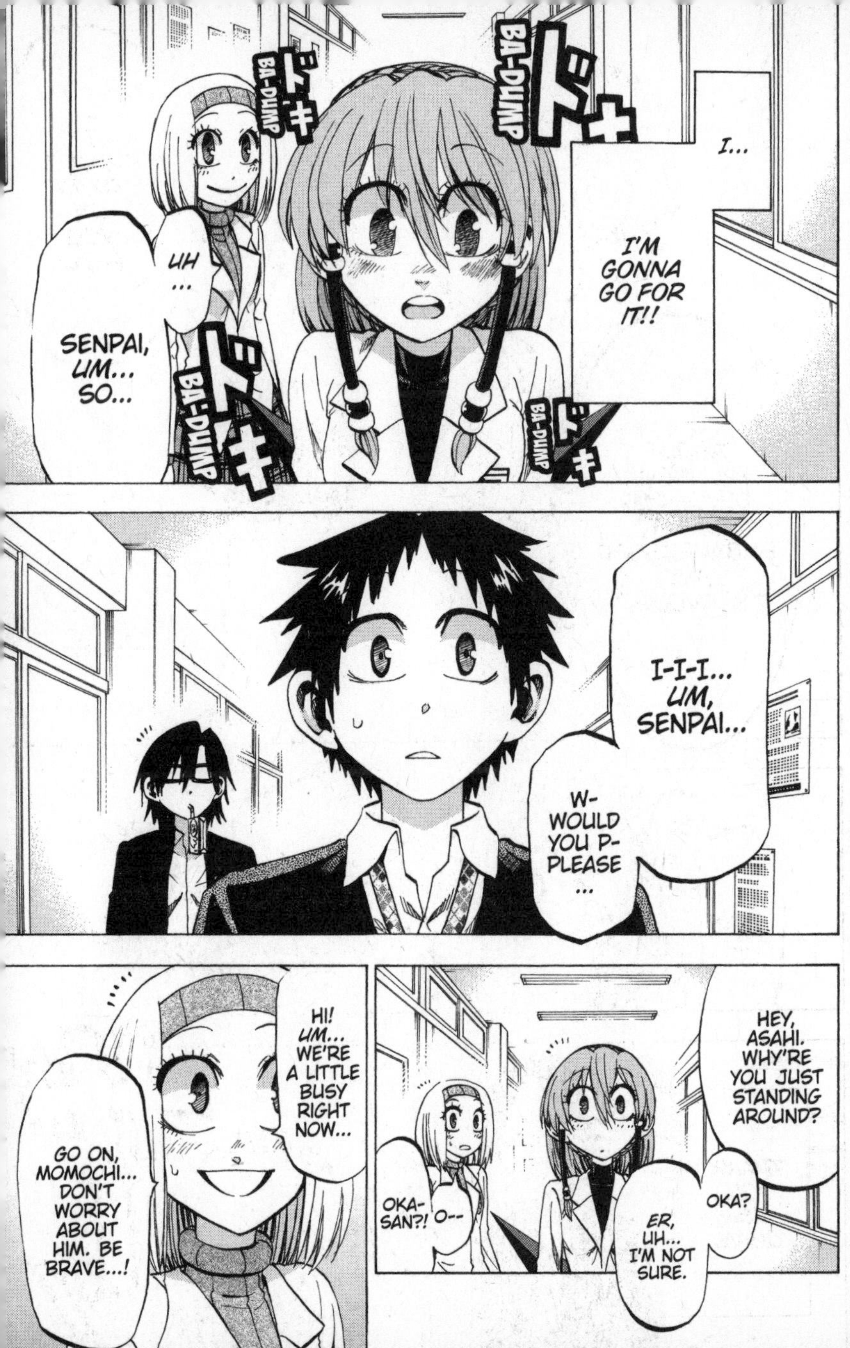
BA-DUMP ドキ
I...
I'M GONNA GO FOR IT!!
BA-DUMP ドキ
BA-DUMP ドキ
UH ...
SENPAI, UM... SO...
BA-DUMP ドキ
I-I-I... UM, SENPAI...
W-WOULD YOU P-PLEASE ...
HEY, ASAHI. WHY'RE YOU JUST STANDING AROUND?
OKA?
ER, UH... I'M NOT SURE.
O--
OKA-SAN?!
HI! UM... WE'RE A LITTLE BUSY RIGHT NOW...
GO ON, MOMOCHI... DON'T WORRY ABOUT HIM. BE BRAVE...!

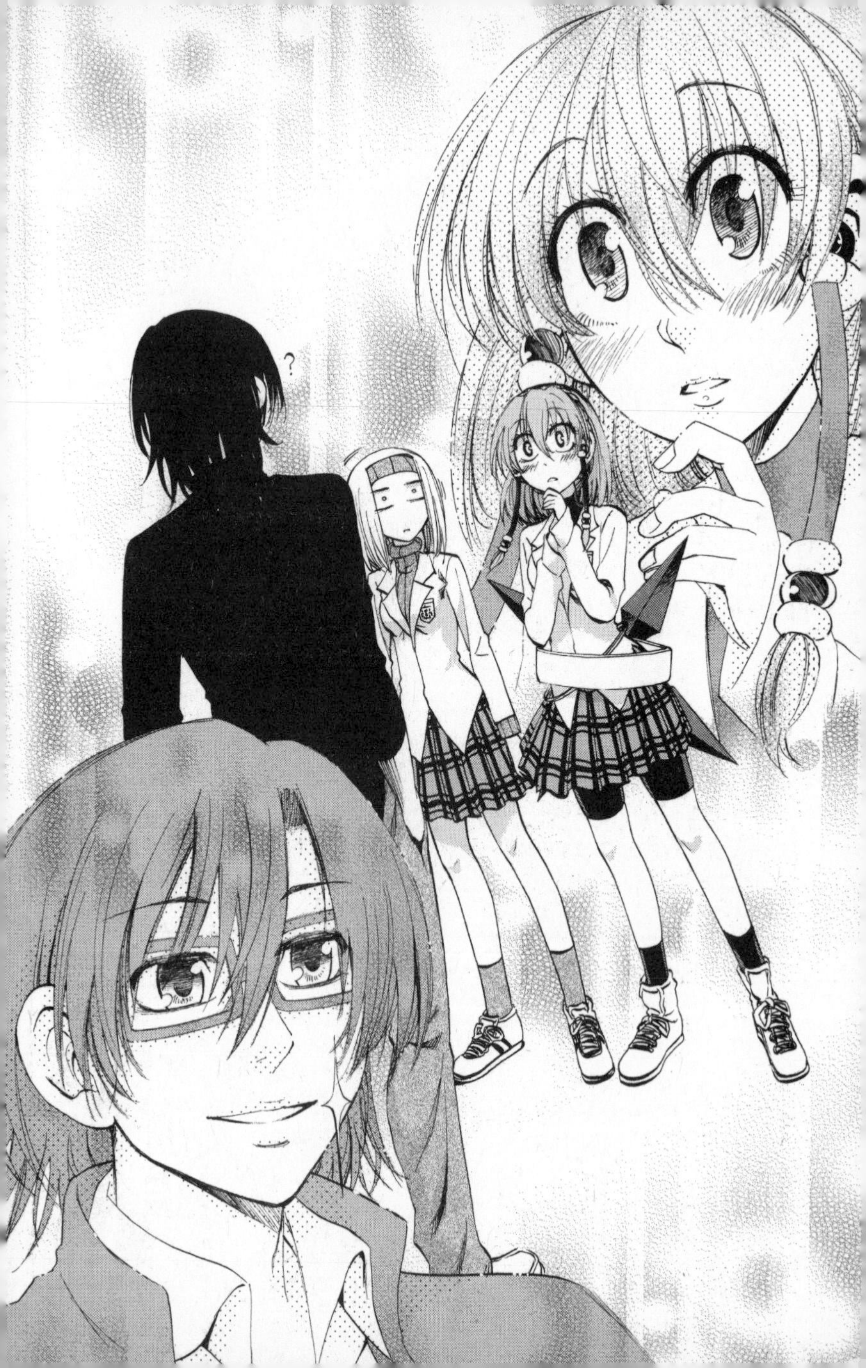
?

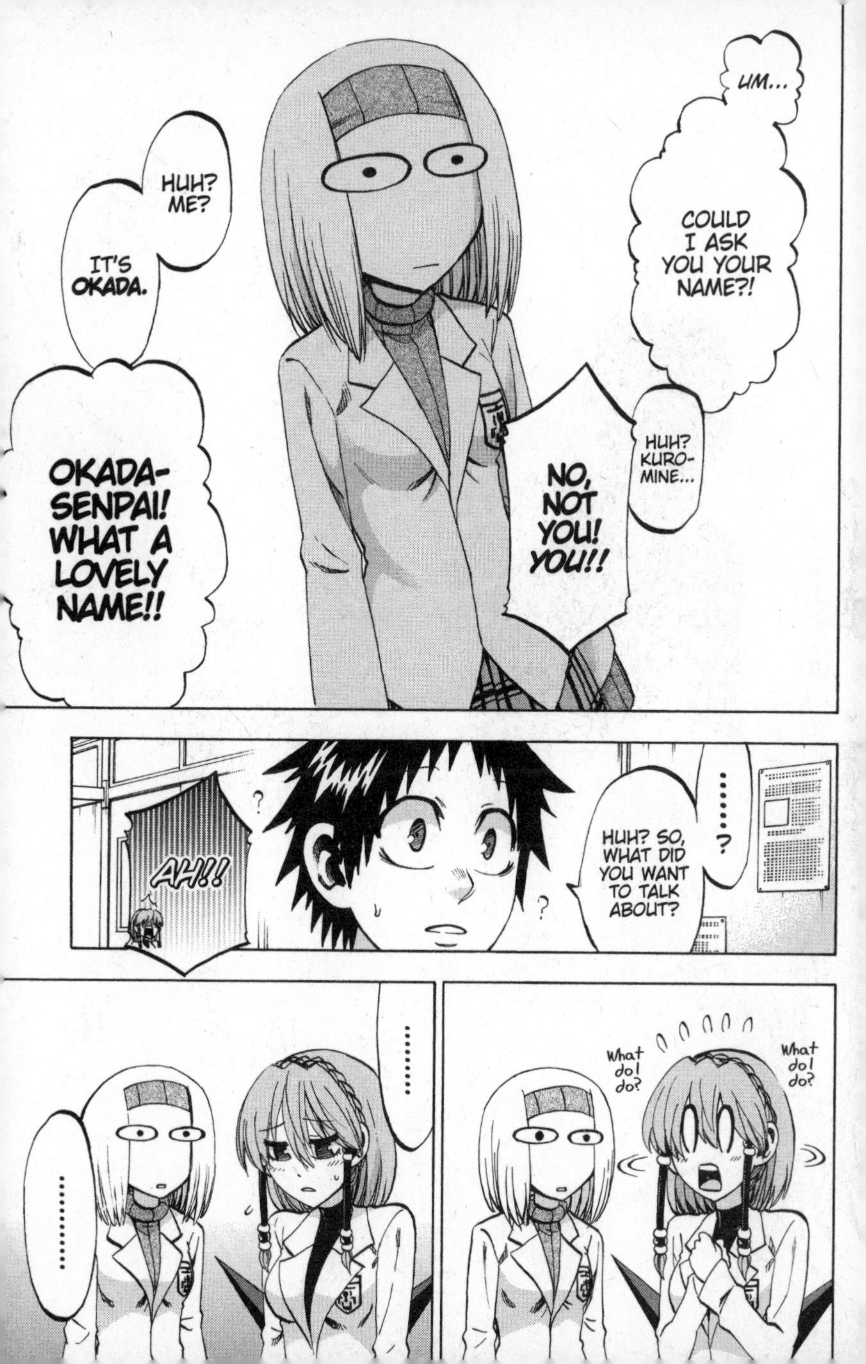
UM...
COULD I ASK YOU YOUR NAME?!
HUH? KURO-MINE...
NO, NOT YOU! YOU!!
HUH? ME?
IT'S OKADA.
OKADA-SENPAI! WHAT A LOVELY NAME!!
......?
HUH? SO, WHAT DID YOU WANT TO TALK ABOUT?
AH!!
What do I do?
What do I do?
....
....

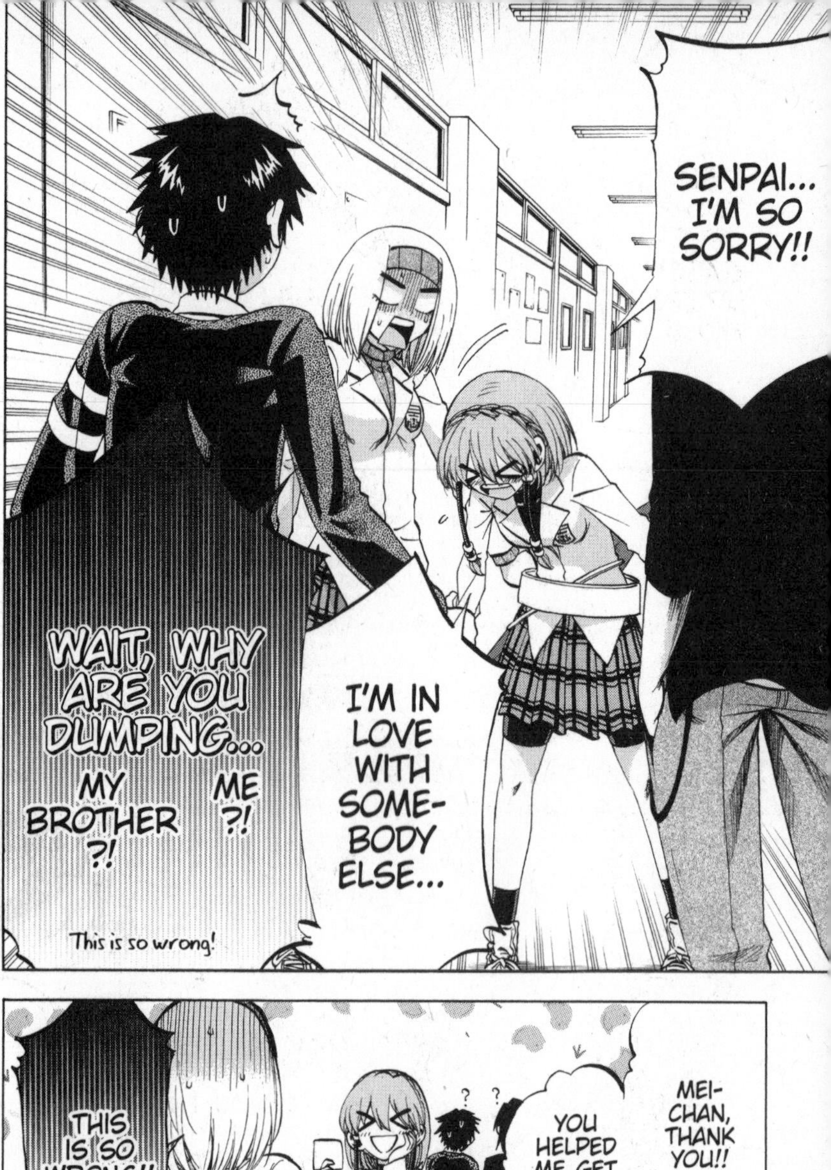
SENPAI... I'M SO SORRY!!
I'M IN LOVE WITH SOMEBODY ELSE...
WAIT, WHY ARE YOU DUMPING...
ME ?!
MY BROTHER ?!
This is so wrong!
MEI-CHAN, THANK YOU!!
YOU HELPED ME GET HIS CONTACT INFO!!
THIS IS SO WRONG!!

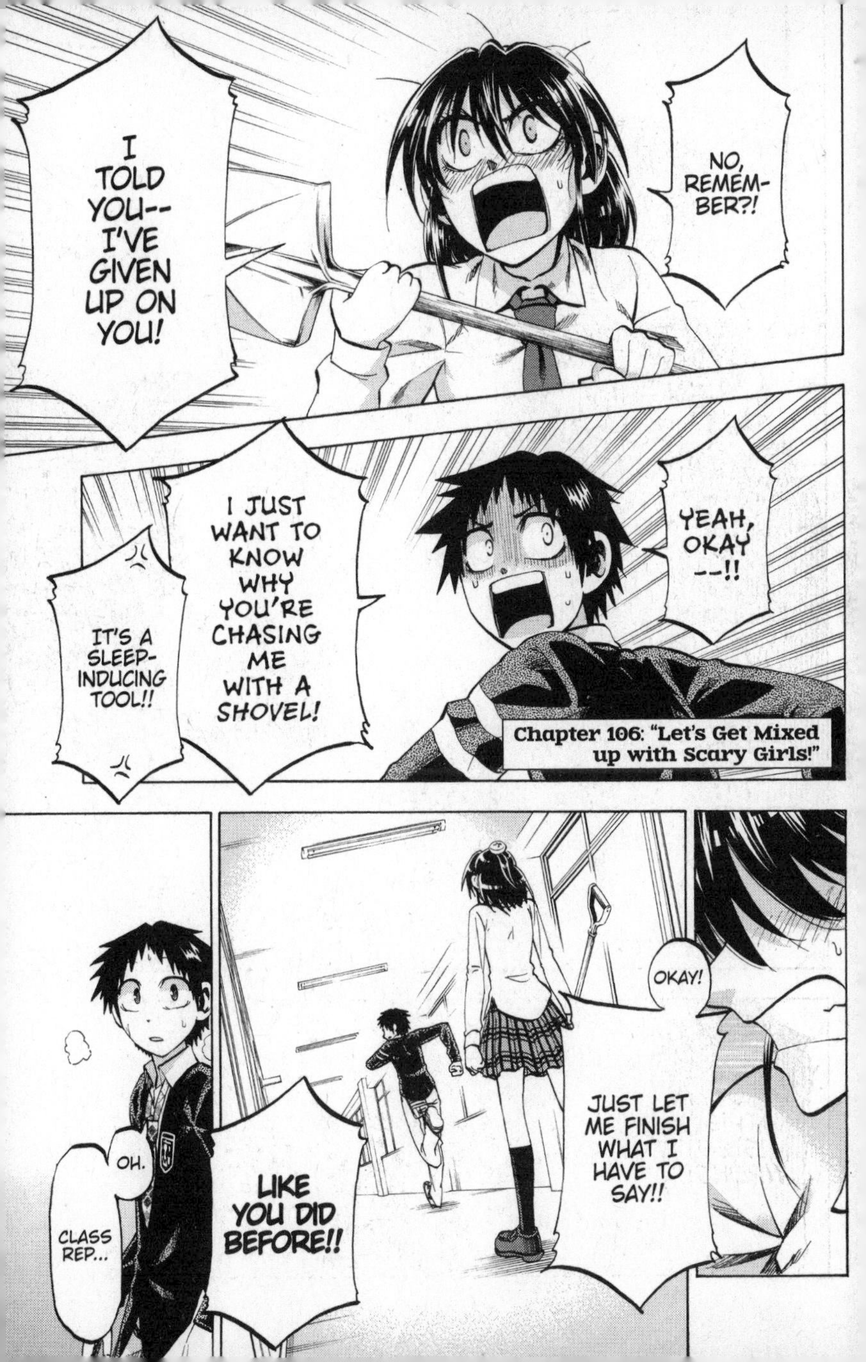
NO, REMEM-BER?!
I TOLD YOU--I'VE GIVEN UP ON YOU!
YEAH, OKAY--!!
I JUST WANT TO KNOW WHY YOU'RE CHASING ME WITH A SHOVEL!
IT'S A SLEEP-INDUCING TOOL!!
Chapter 106: "Let's Get Mixed up with Scary Girls!"
OKAY!
JUST LET ME FINISH WHAT I HAVE TO SAY!!
LIKE YOU DID BEFORE!!
OH.
CLASS REP...

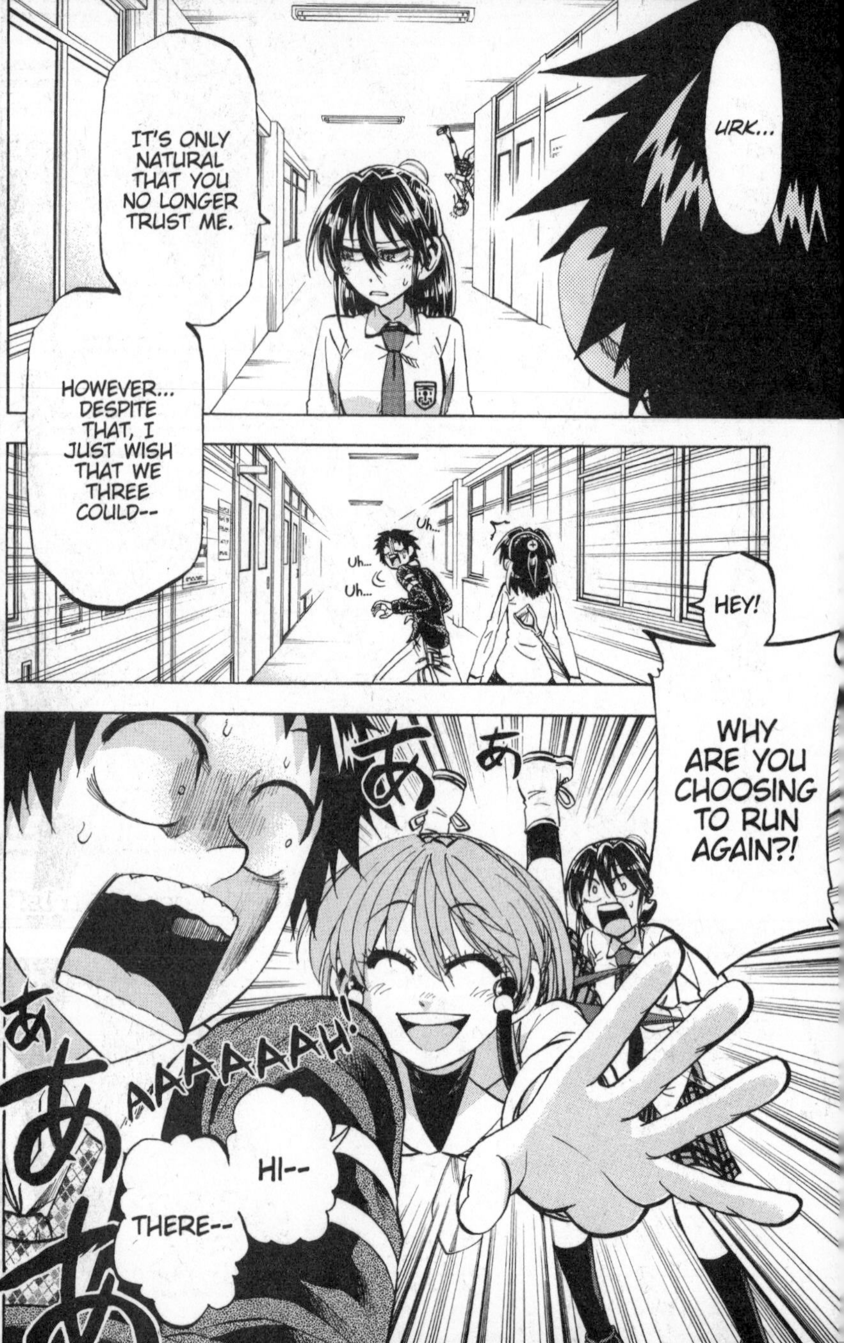
URK...
IT'S ONLY NATURAL THAT YOU NO LONGER TRUST ME.
HOWEVER... DESPITE THAT, I JUST WISH THAT WE THREE COULD--
Uh...
Uh...
Uh...
HEY!
WHY ARE YOU CHOOSING TO RUN AGAIN?!
あ
あ
AAAAAAH!
あああ
HI--
THERE--

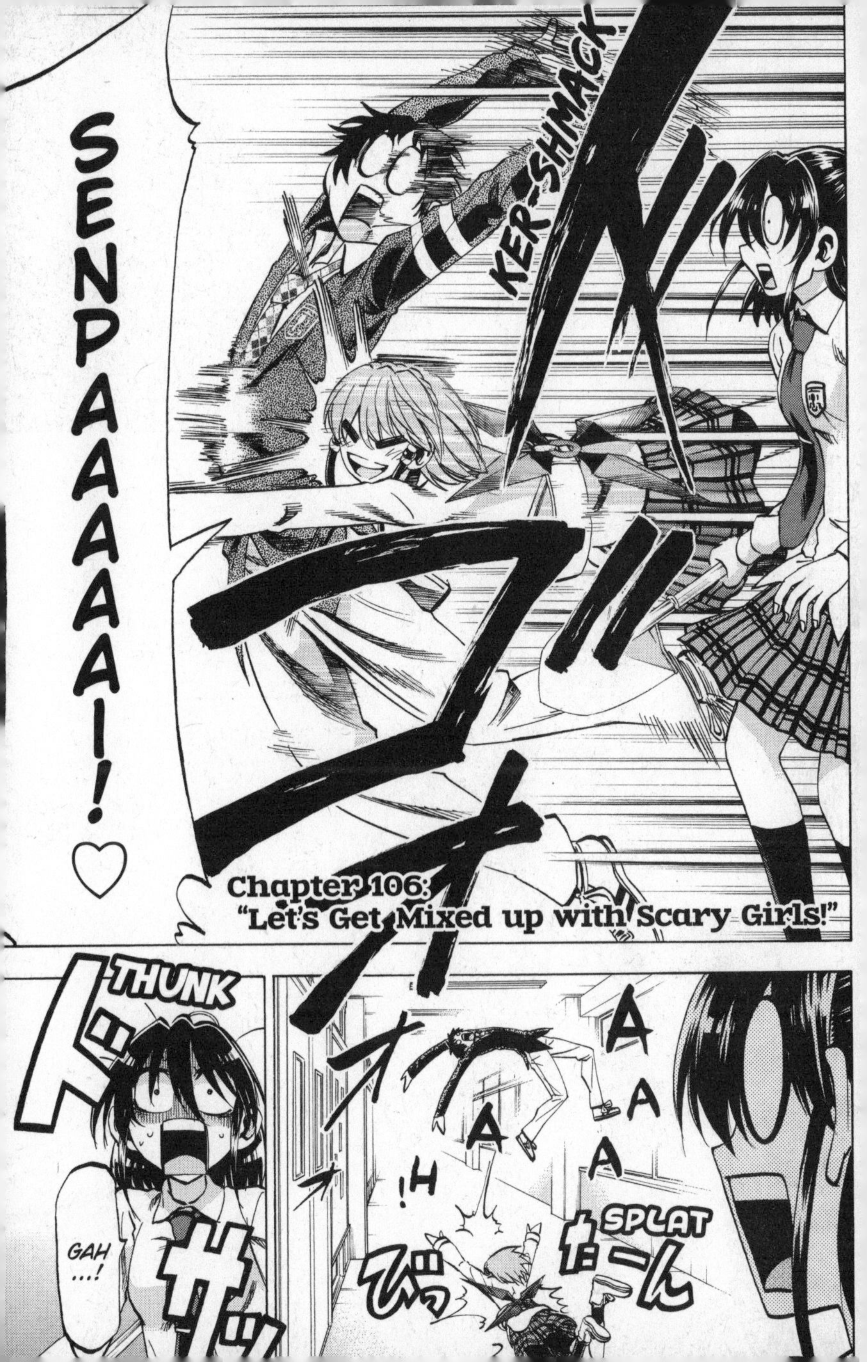
SENPAAAAAAI! ♥
KER-SHMACK
Chapter 106:
"Let's Get Mixed up with Scary Girls!"
AAAAH!
SPLAT
THUNK
GAH...!

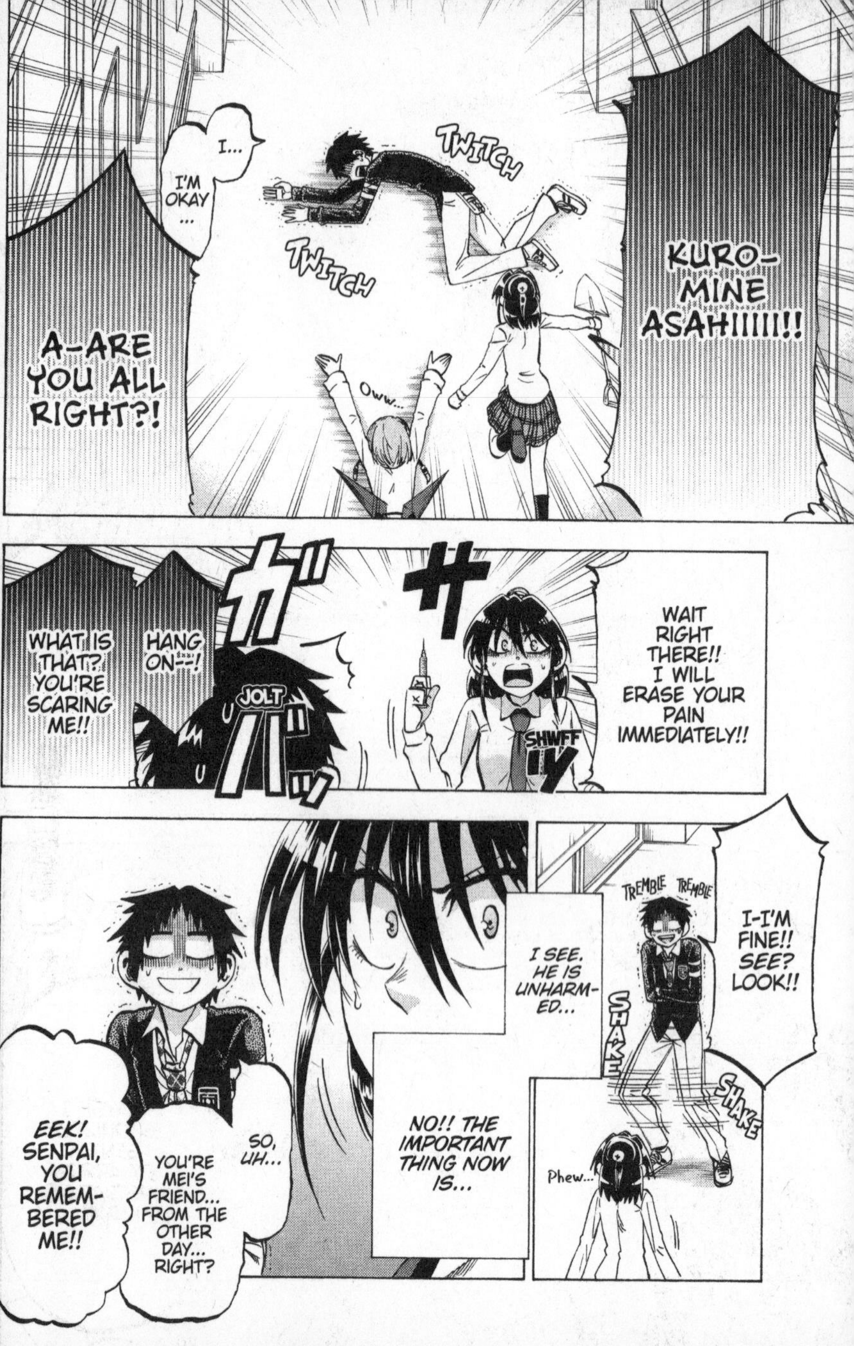
KURO-MINE ASAHIIIIII!!
TWITCH
I...
I'M OKAY...
TWITCH
Oww...
A-ARE YOU ALL RIGHT?!
WAIT RIGHT THERE!! I WILL ERASE YOUR PAIN IMMEDIATELY!!
ザッ
SHWFF
ガバッ
JOLT
HANG ON--!
WHAT IS THAT? YOU'RE SCARING ME!!
TREMBLE TREMBLE
I-I'M FINE!! SEE? LOOK!!
SHAKE
SHAKE
Phew...
I SEE. HE IS UNHARMED...
NO!! THE IMPORTANT THING NOW IS...
SO, UH...
YOU'RE MEI'S FRIEND... FROM THE OTHER DAY... RIGHT?
EEK! SENPAI, YOU REMEMBERED ME!!

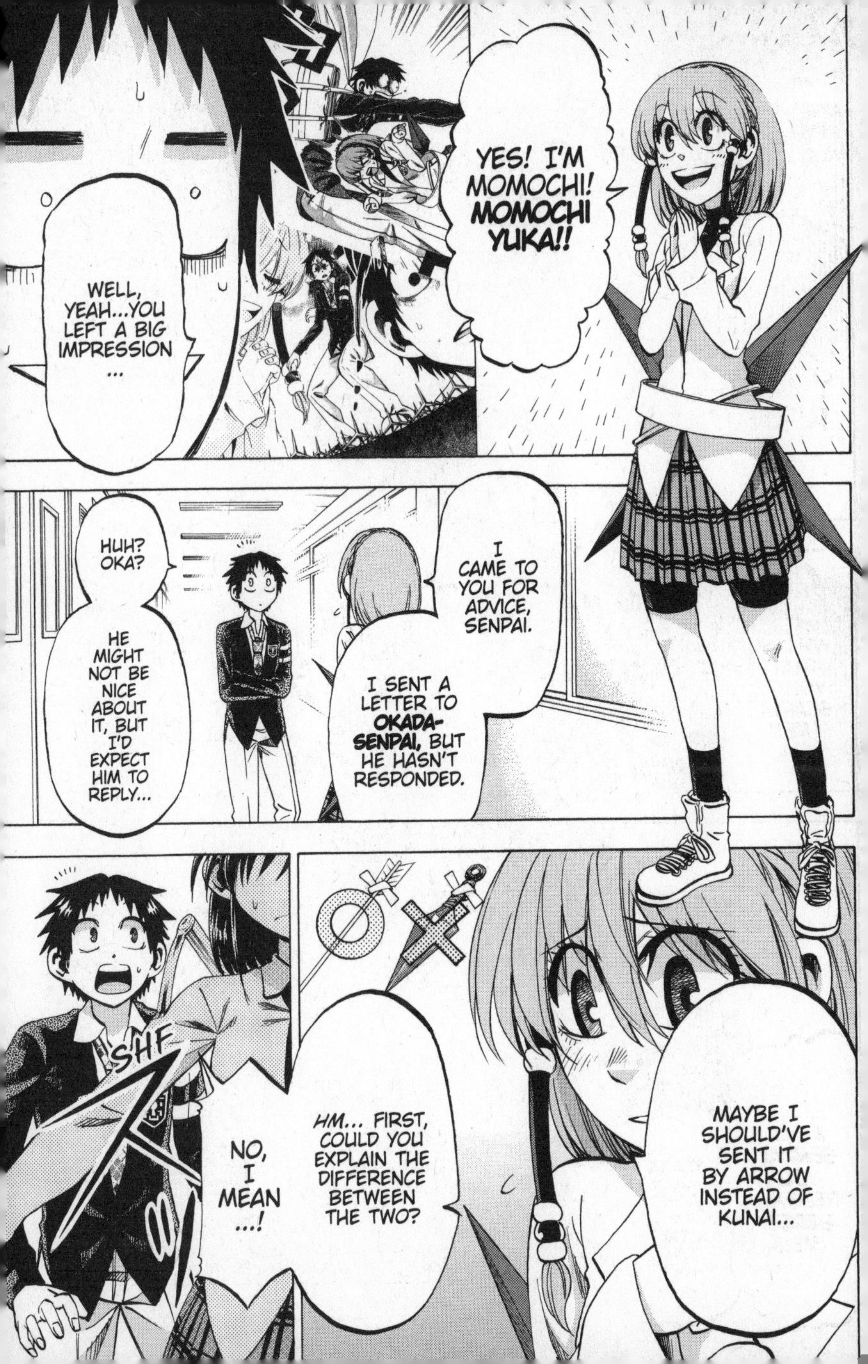
YES! I'M MOMOCHI! **MOMOCHI YUKA!!**
WELL, YEAH...YOU LEFT A BIG IMPRESSION ...
I CAME TO YOU FOR ADVICE, SENPAI.
I SENT A LETTER TO **OKADA-SENPAI,** BUT HE HASN'T RESPONDED.
HUH? OKA?
HE MIGHT NOT BE NICE ABOUT IT, BUT I'D EXPECT HIM TO REPLY...
MAYBE I SHOULD'VE SENT IT BY ARROW INSTEAD OF KUNAI...
HM... FIRST, COULD YOU EXPLAIN THE DIFFERENCE BETWEEN THE TWO?
NO, I MEAN ...!
SHF

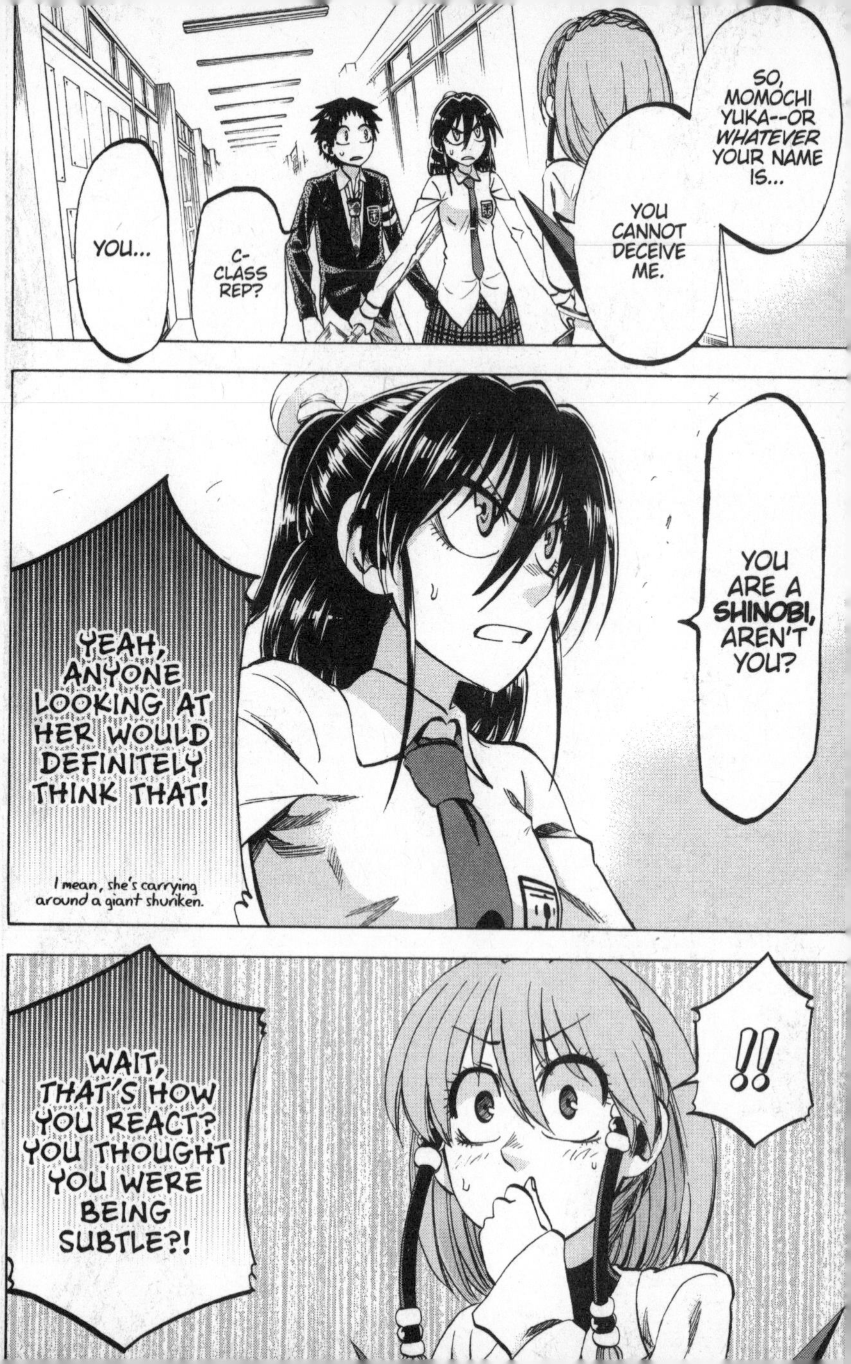
SO, MOMOCHI YUKA--OR WHATEVER YOUR NAME IS...
YOU CANNOT DECEIVE ME.
C-CLASS REP?
YOU...
YOU ARE A SHINOBI, AREN'T YOU?
YEAH, ANYONE LOOKING AT HER WOULD DEFINITELY THINK THAT!
I mean, she's carrying around a giant shuriken.
!!
WAIT, THAT'S HOW YOU REACT? YOU THOUGHT YOU WERE BEING SUBTLE?!

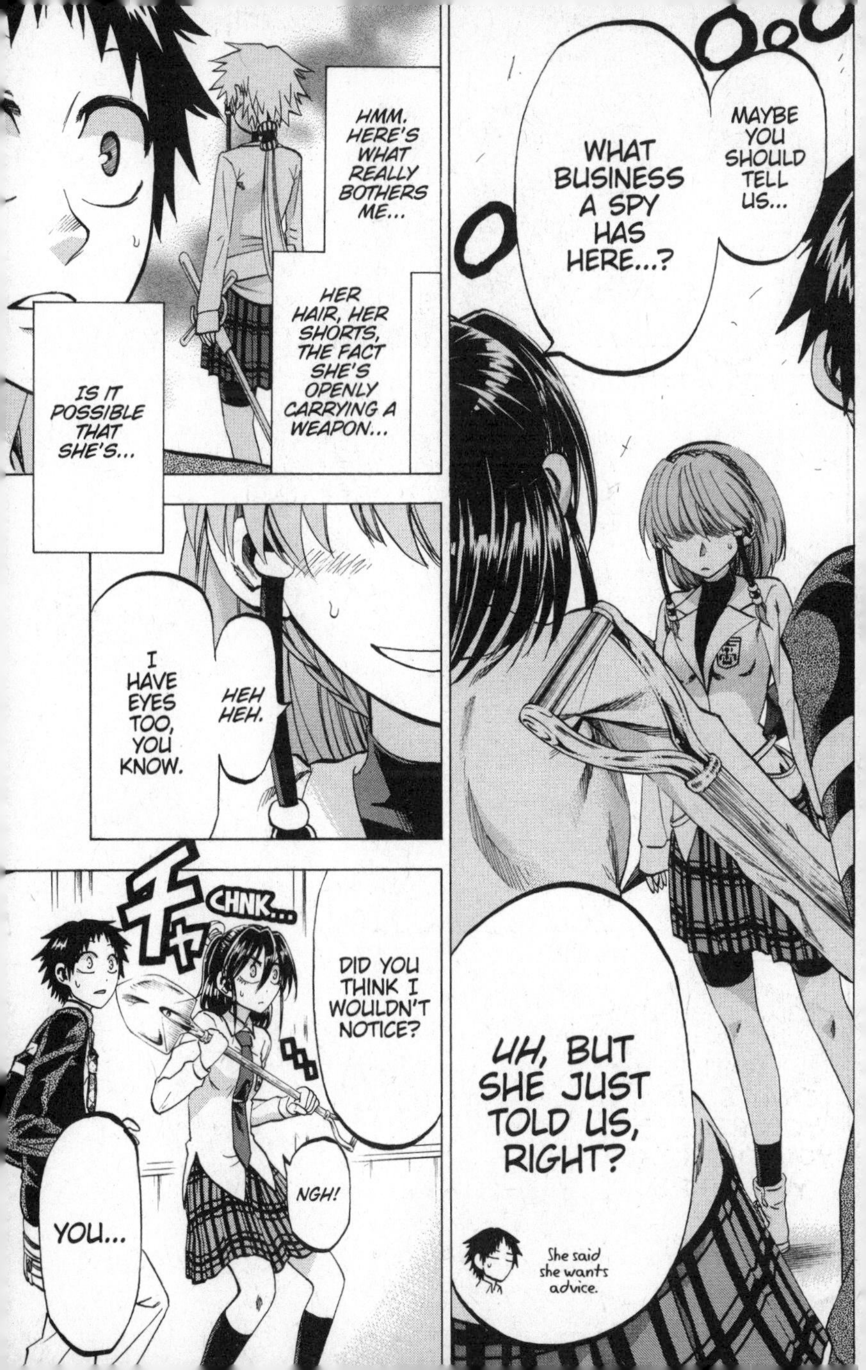
HMM. HERE'S WHAT REALLY BOTHERS ME...
HER HAIR, HER SHORTS, THE FACT SHE'S OPENLY CARRYING A WEAPON...
IS IT POSSIBLE THAT SHE'S...
HEH HEH.
I HAVE EYES TOO, YOU KNOW.
チャ
CHNK...
DID YOU THINK I WOULDN'T NOTICE?
NGH!
YOU...
MAYBE YOU SHOULD TELL US...
WHAT BUSINESS A SPY HAS HERE...?
UH, BUT SHE JUST TOLD US, RIGHT?
She said she wants advice.

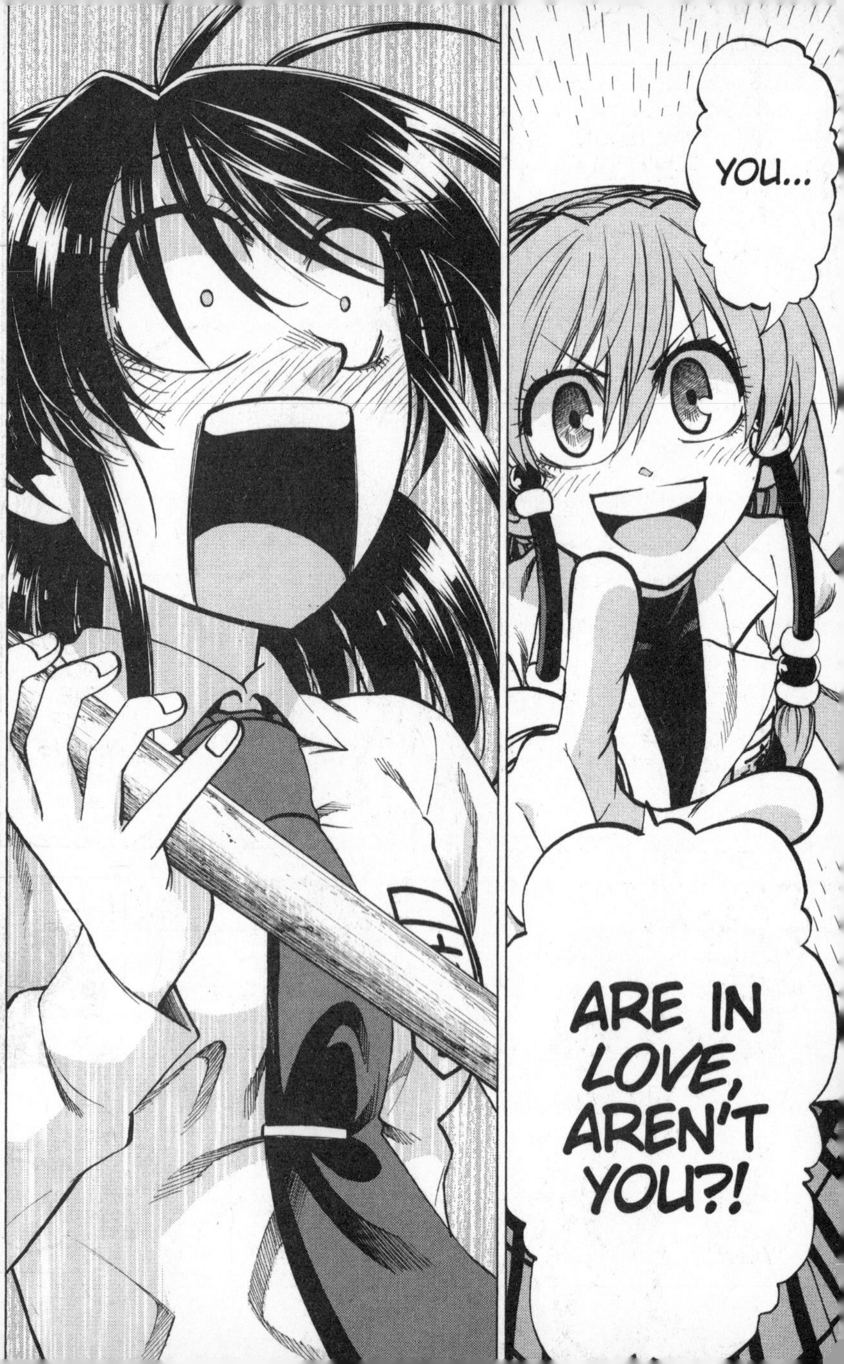
YOU...
ARE IN LOVE, AREN'T YOU?!

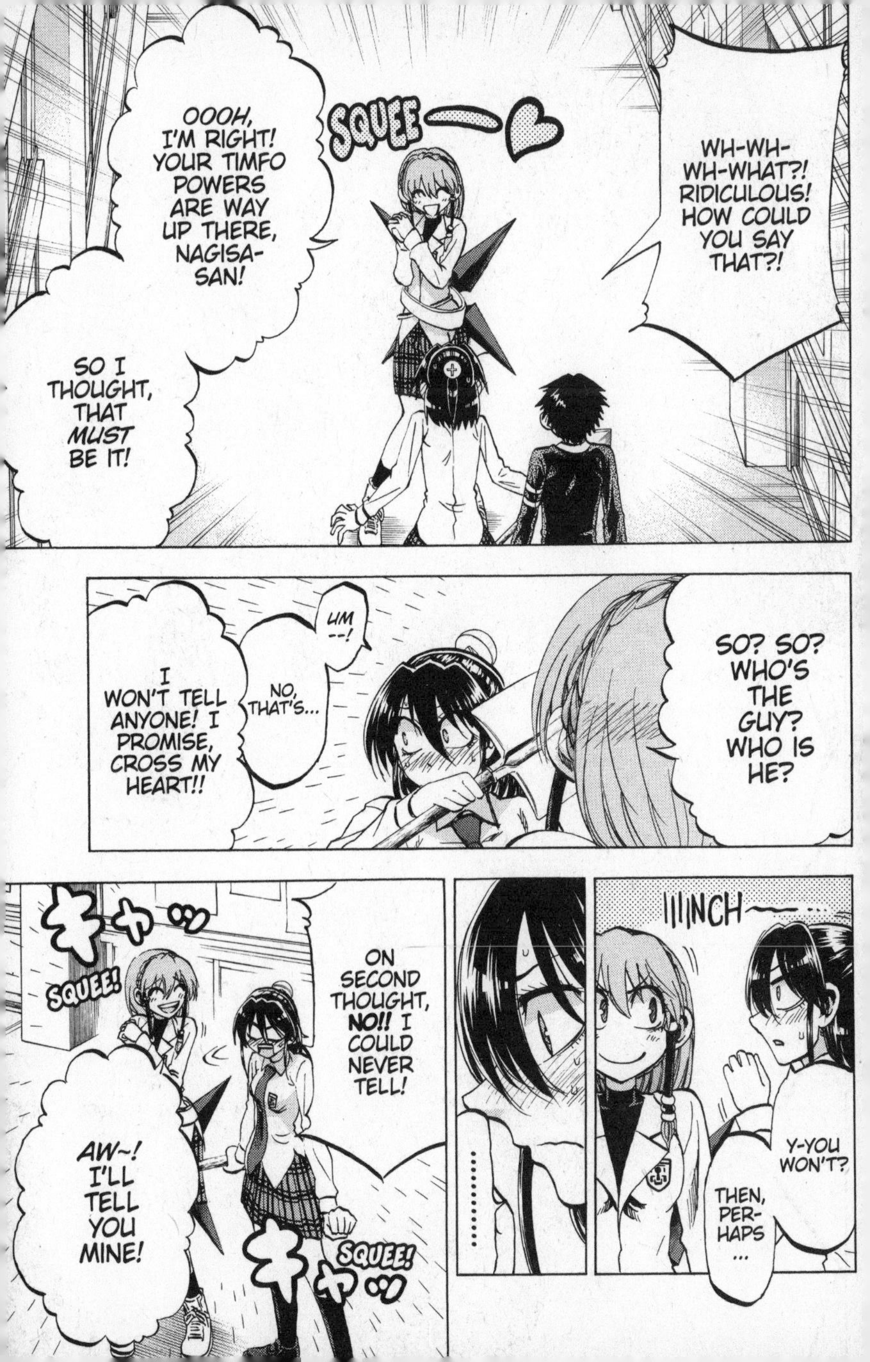
WH-WH-WH-WHAT?! RIDICULOUS! HOW COULD YOU SAY THAT?!
SQUEE
OOOH, I'M RIGHT! YOUR TIMFO POWERS ARE WAY UP THERE, NAGISA-SAN!
SO I THOUGHT, THAT *MUST* BE IT!
SO? SO? WHO'S THE GUY? WHO IS HE?
UM --!
NO, THAT'S...
I WON'T TELL ANYONE! I PROMISE, CROSS MY HEART!!
INCH~~...
Y-YOU WON'T?
THEN, PER-HAPS ...
......
キャッ
SQUEE!
ON SECOND THOUGHT, **NO!!** I COULD NEVER TELL!
AW~! I'LL TELL YOU MINE!
キャッ
SQUEE!

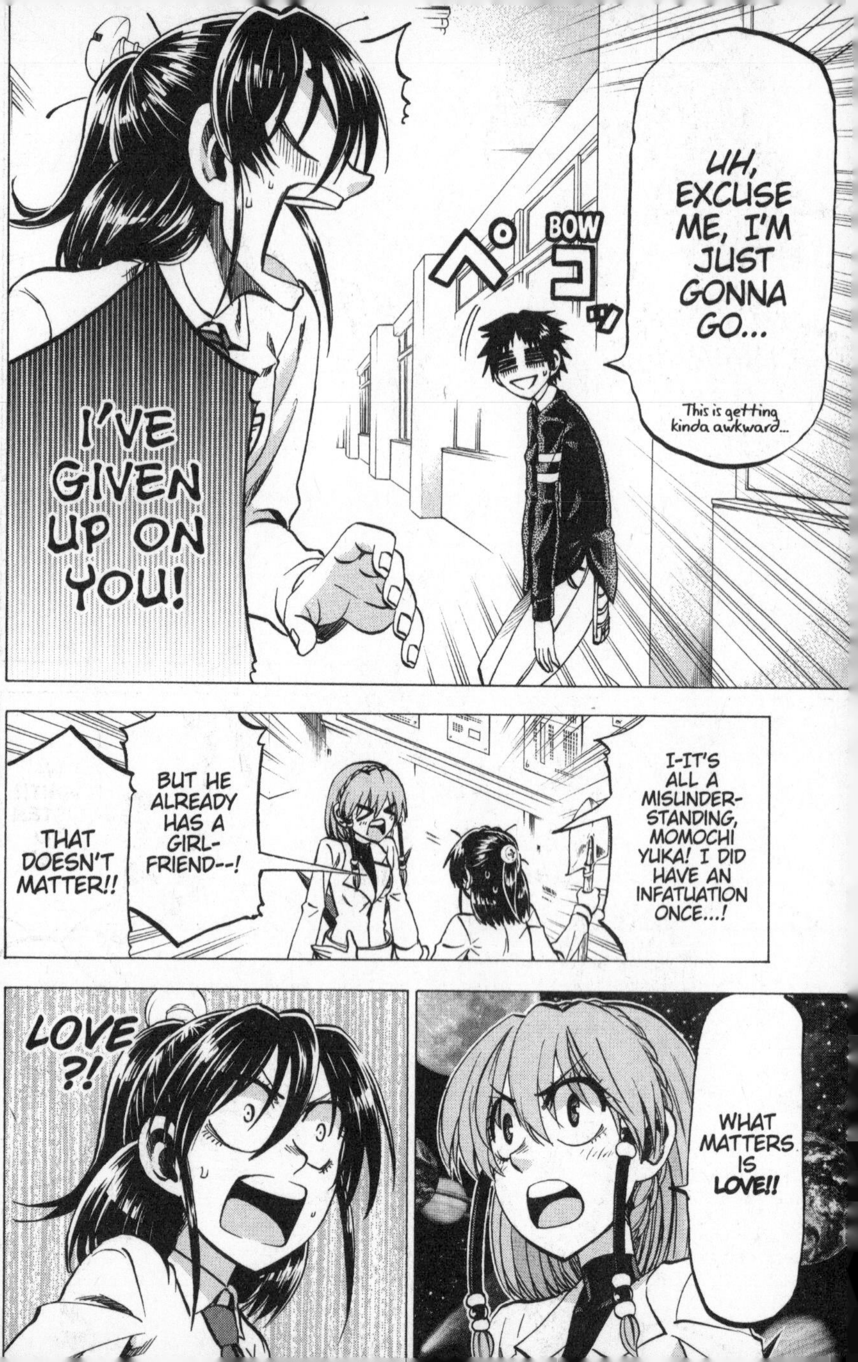
UH, EXCUSE ME, I'M JUST GONNA GO...
BOW
ペコッ
This is getting kinda awkward...
I'VE GIVEN UP ON YOU!
I-IT'S ALL A MISUNDER-STANDING, MOMOCHI YUKA! I DID HAVE AN INFATUATION ONCE...!
BUT HE ALREADY HAS A GIRL-FRIEND--!
THAT DOESN'T MATTER!!
WHAT MATTERS IS LOVE!!
LOVE?!

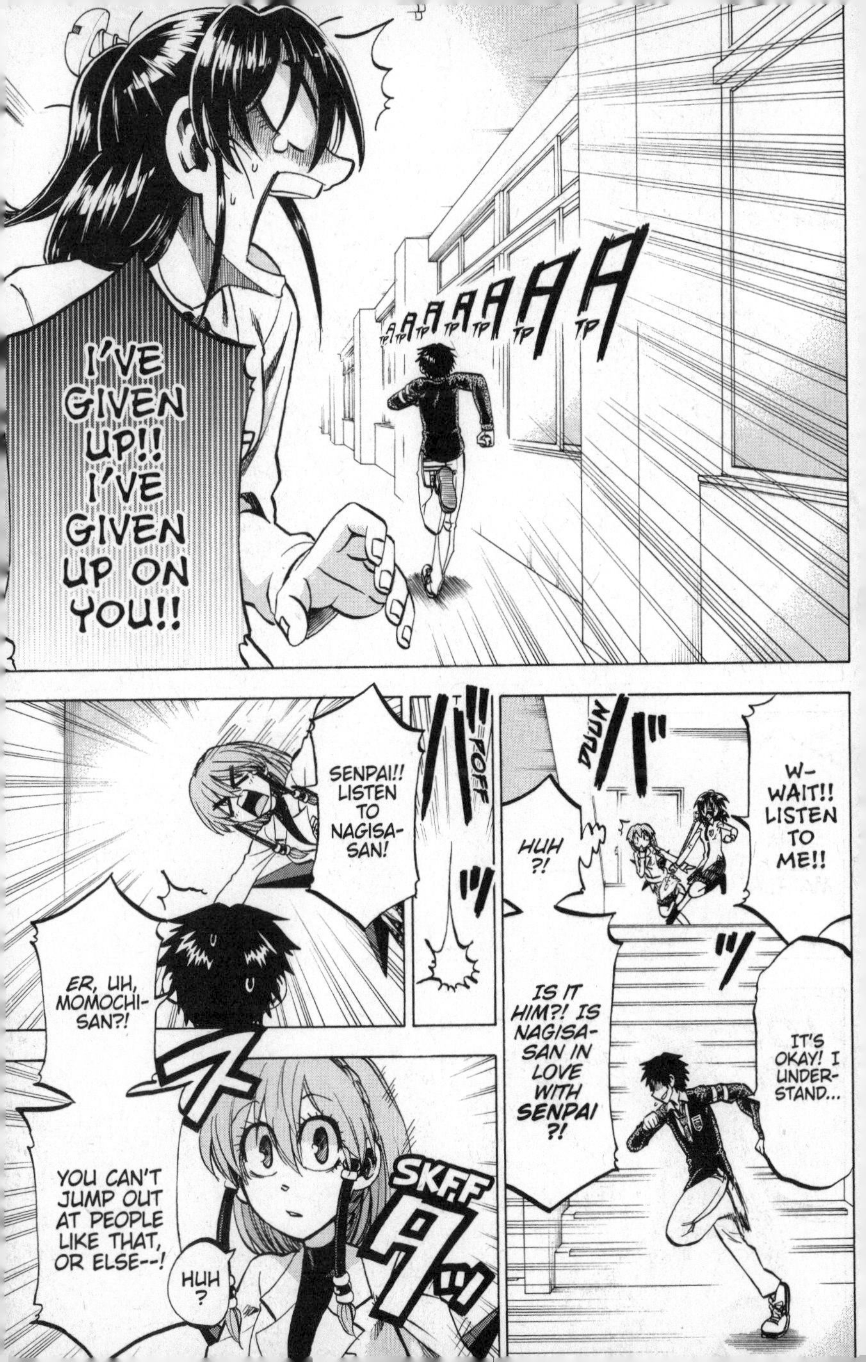
TP TP TP TP TP TP TP
AAAAAAA
I'VE GIVEN UP!! I'VE GIVEN UP ON YOU!!
W-WAIT!! LISTEN TO ME!!
DUUN
HUH?!
IT'S OKAY! I UNDERSTAND...
IS IT HIM?! IS NAGISA-SAN IN LOVE WITH SENPAI?!
POFF
SENPAI!! LISTEN TO NAGISA-SAN!
ER, UH, MOMOCHI-SAN?!
SKFF
YOU CAN'T JUMP OUT AT PEOPLE LIKE THAT, OR ELSE--!
HUH?

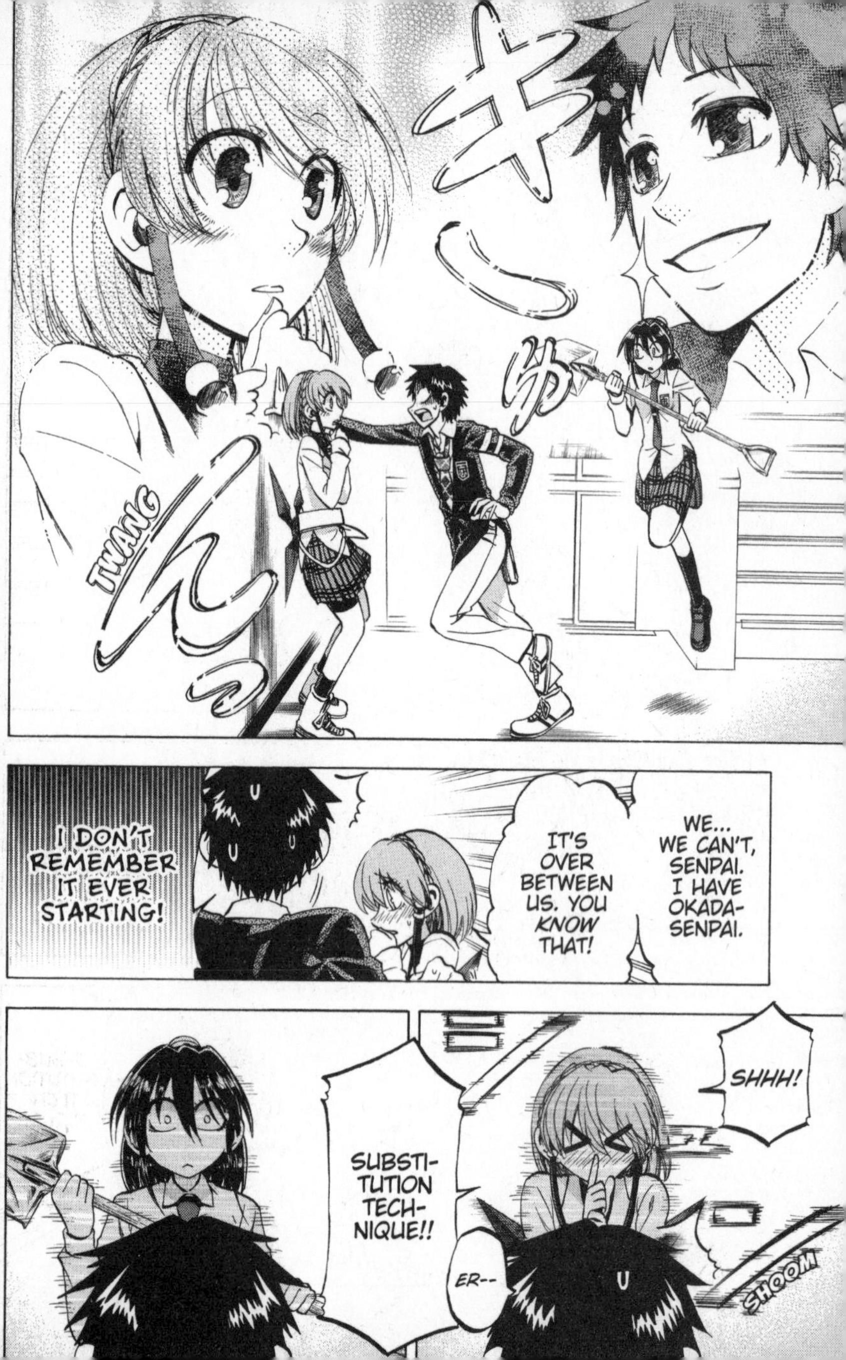
TWANG
WE... WE CAN'T, SENPAI. I HAVE OKADA-SENPAI.
IT'S OVER BETWEEN US. YOU KNOW THAT!
I DON'T REMEMBER IT EVER STARTING!
SHHH!
SHOOM
ER--
SUBSTI-TUTION TECH-NIQUE!!

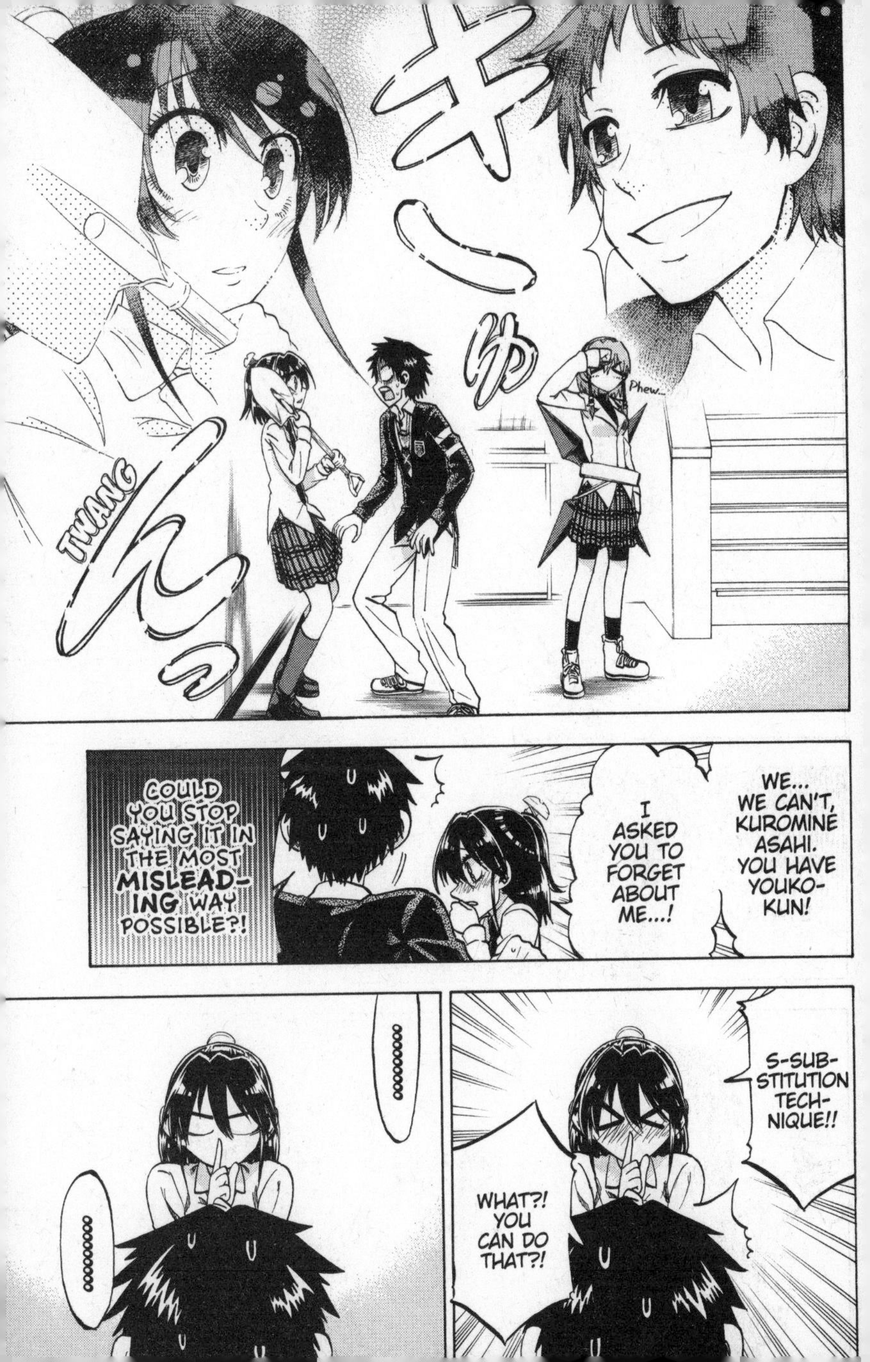
Phew...
TWANG
WE... WE CAN'T, KUROMINE ASAHI. YOU HAVE YOUKO-KUN!
I ASKED YOU TO FORGET ABOUT ME...!
COULD YOU STOP SAYING IT IN THE MOST MISLEADING WAY POSSIBLE?!
S-SUBSTITUTION TECHNIQUE!!
WHAT?! YOU CAN DO THAT?!
....
....

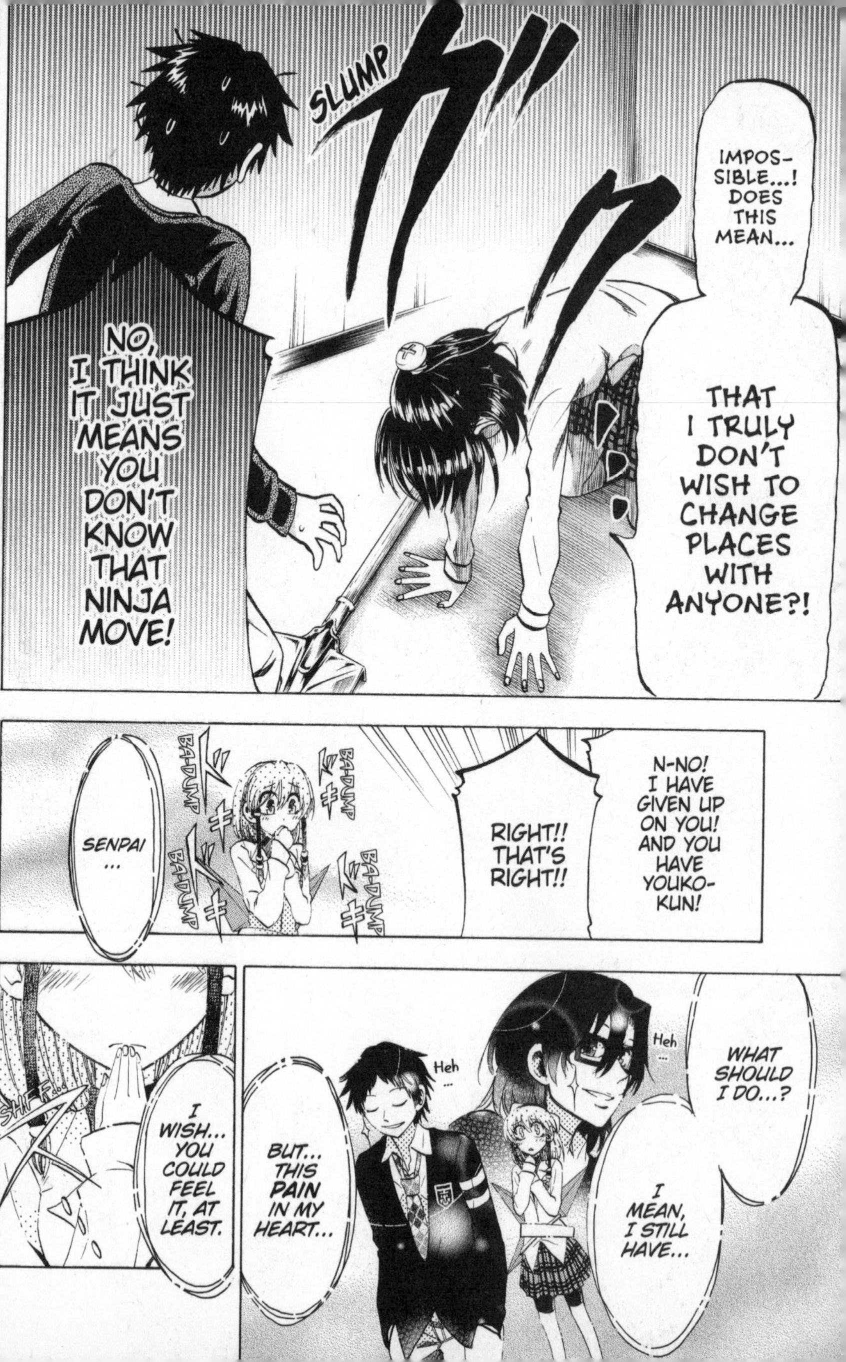
IMPOSSIBLE...! DOES THIS MEAN...
THAT I TRULY DON'T WISH TO CHANGE PLACES WITH ANYONE?!
SLUMP
NO, I THINK IT JUST MEANS YOU DON'T KNOW THAT NINJA MOVE!
N-NO! I HAVE GIVEN UP ON YOU! AND YOU HAVE YOUKO-KUN!
RIGHT!! THAT'S RIGHT!!
BADUMP
BADUMP
BADUMP
BADUMP
SENPAI ...
WHAT SHOULD I DO...?
I MEAN, I STILL HAVE...
Heh ...
Heh ...
BUT... THIS PAIN IN MY HEART...
I WISH... YOU COULD FEEL IT, AT LEAST.

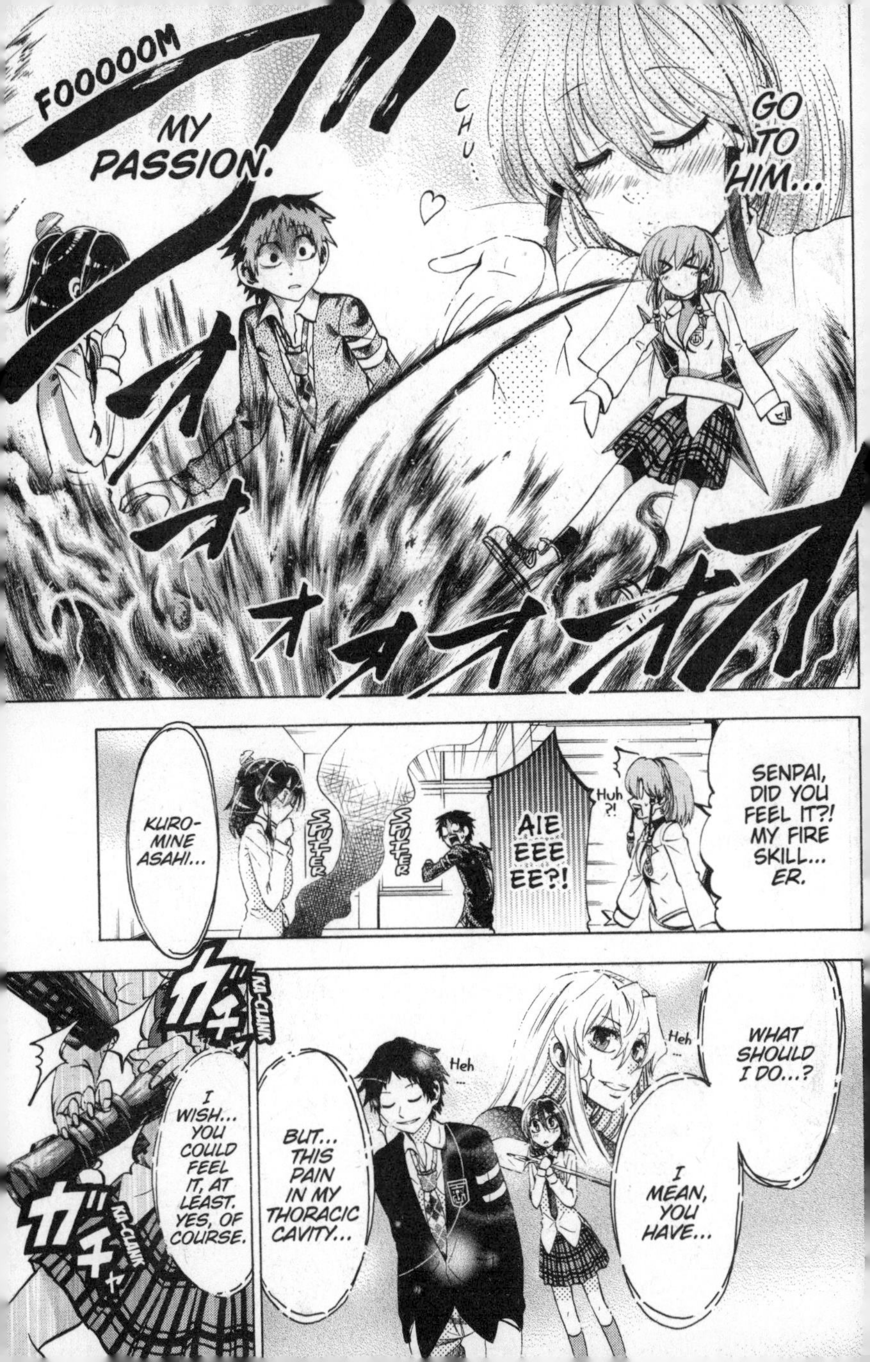
GO TO HIM...
CHU...
MY PASSION.
FOOOOOM
SENPAI, DID YOU FEEL IT?! MY FIRE SKILL... ER.
Huh ?!
AIE EEE EE?!
SPUTTER
SPUTTER
KURO-MINE ASAHI...
WHAT SHOULD I DO...?
Heh ...
I MEAN, YOU HAVE...
Heh ...
BUT... THIS PAIN IN MY THORACIC CAVITY...
I WISH... YOU COULD FEEL IT, AT LEAST. YES, OF COURSE.
KA-CLANK
KA-CLANK

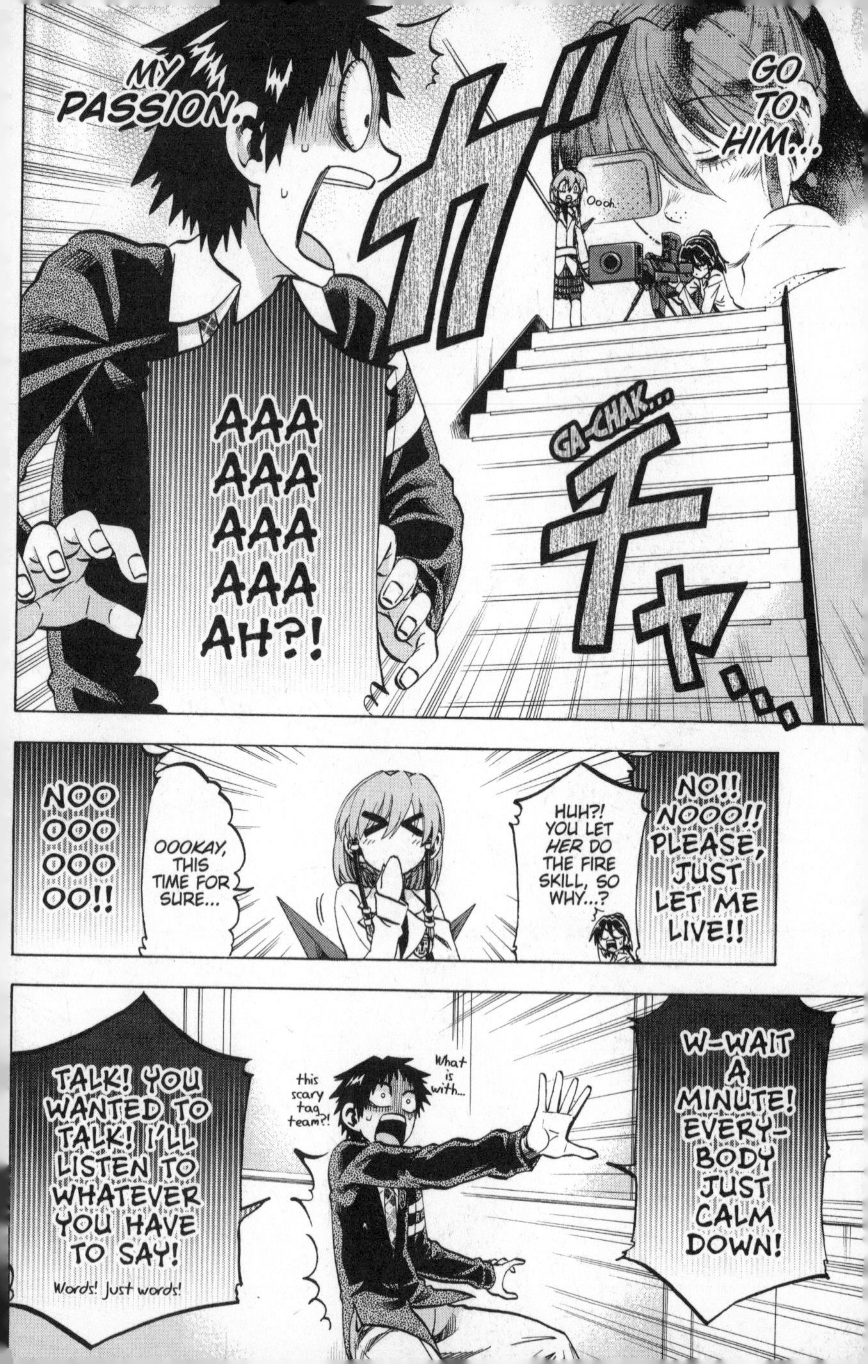
GO TO HIM...
Oooh.
MY PASSION...
GA-CHAK...
AAAAAAAAAAAAAAAH?!
NO!! NOOO!! PLEASE, JUST LET ME LIVE!!
HUH?! YOU LET HER DO THE FIRE SKILL, SO WHY...?
OOOKAY, THIS TIME FOR SURE...
NOOOOOOOOOOO!!
W-WAIT A MINUTE! EVERYBODY JUST CALM DOWN!
What is with...
this scary tag team?!
TALK! YOU WANTED TO TALK! I'LL LISTEN TO WHATEVER YOU HAVE TO SAY!
Words! Just words!

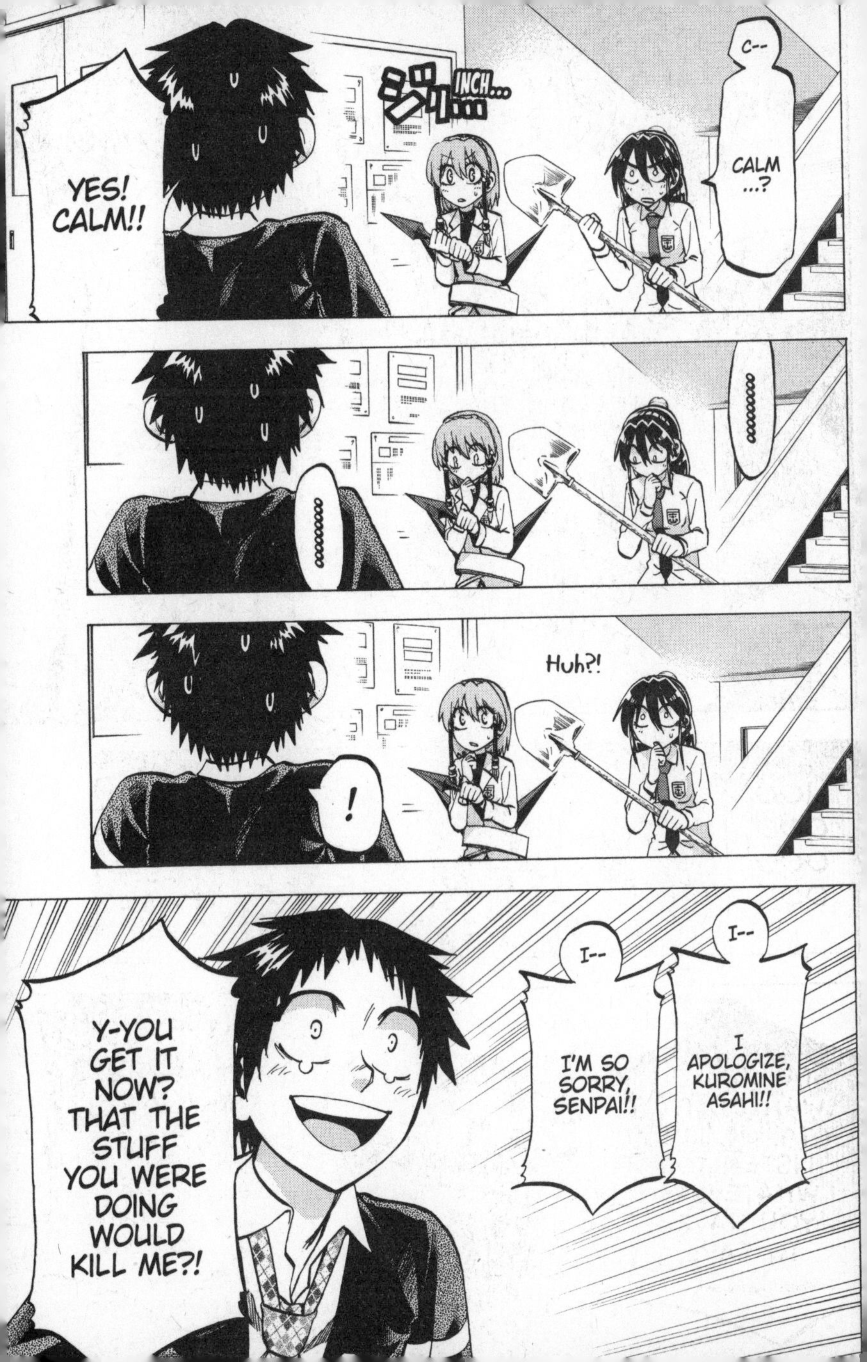

C--
CALM ...?
ジリ…
INCH...
YES! CALM!!
......
......
Huh?!
!
I--
I APOLOGIZE, KUROMINE ASAHI!!
I--
I'M SO SORRY, SENPAI!!
Y-YOU GET IT NOW? THAT THE STUFF YOU WERE DOING WOULD KILL ME?!

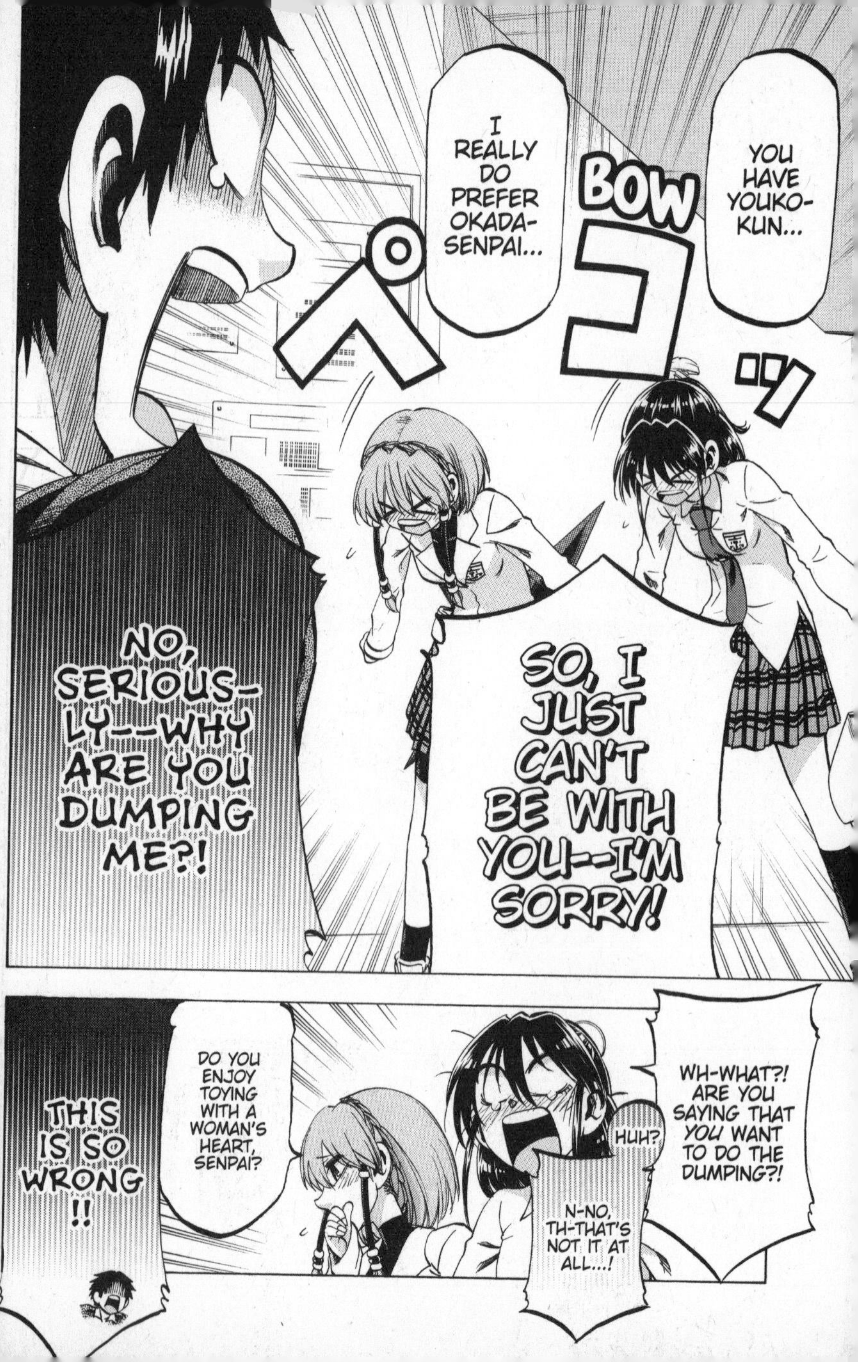
YOU HAVE YOUKO-KUN...
I REALLY DO PREFER OKADA-SENPAI...
BOW
ペコッ
SO, I JUST CAN'T BE WITH YOU--I'M SORRY!
NO, SERIOUS-LY--WHY ARE YOU DUMPING ME?!
WH-WHAT?! ARE YOU SAYING THAT YOU WANT TO DO THE DUMPING?!
HUH?
N-NO, TH-THAT'S NOT IT AT ALL...!
DO YOU ENJOY TOYING WITH A WOMAN'S HEART, SENPAI?
THIS IS SO WRONG!!

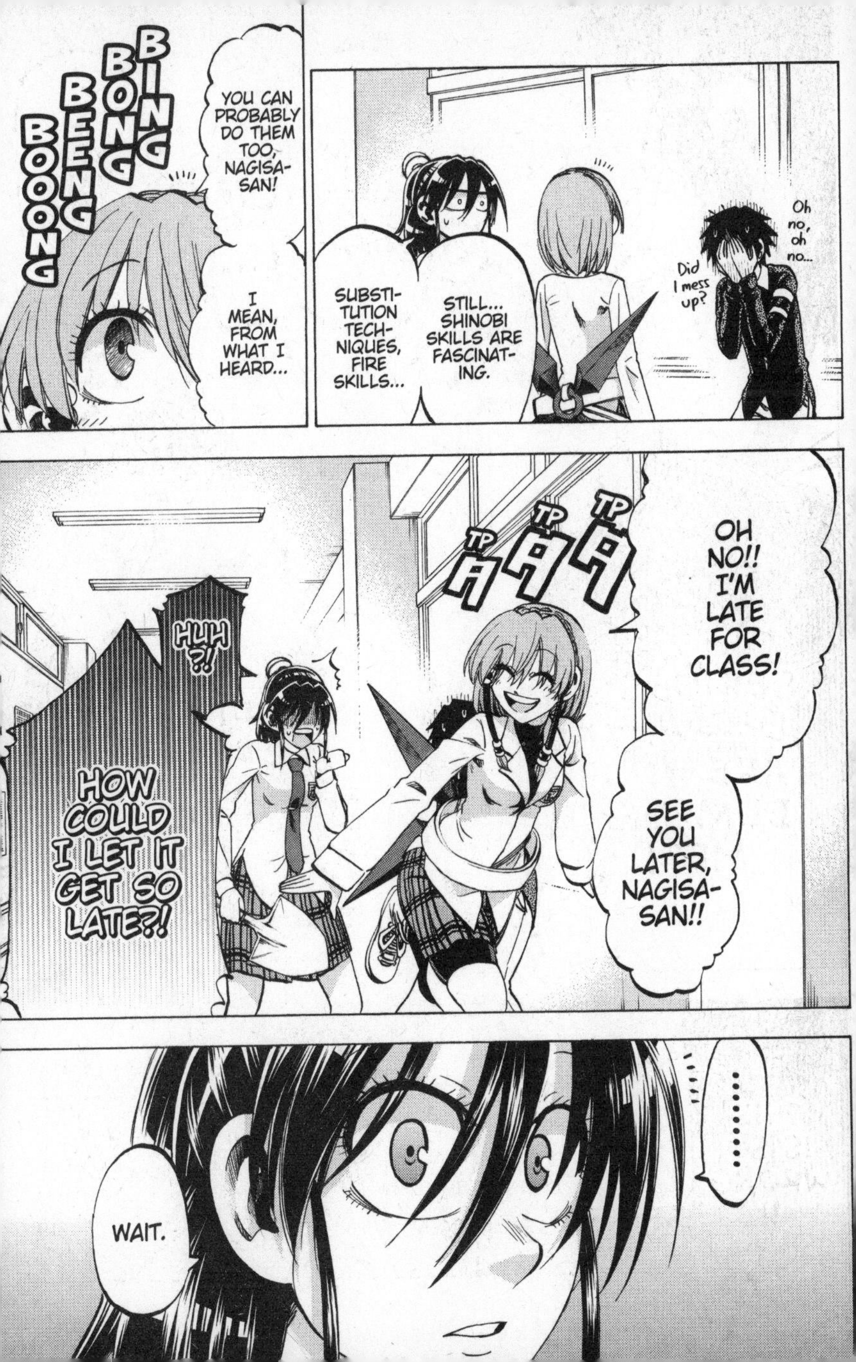
Oh no, oh no...
Did I mess up?
STILL... SHINOBI SKILLS ARE FASCINAT-ING.
SUBSTI-TUTION TECH-NIQUES, FIRE SKILLS...
YOU CAN PROBABLY DO THEM TOO, NAGISA-SAN!
BING BONG BEENG BOOONG
I MEAN, FROM WHAT I HEARD...
OH NO!! I'M LATE FOR CLASS!
TP TP TP
SEE YOU LATER, NAGISA-SAN!!
HUH?!
HOW COULD I LET IT GET SO LATE?!
....
WAIT.

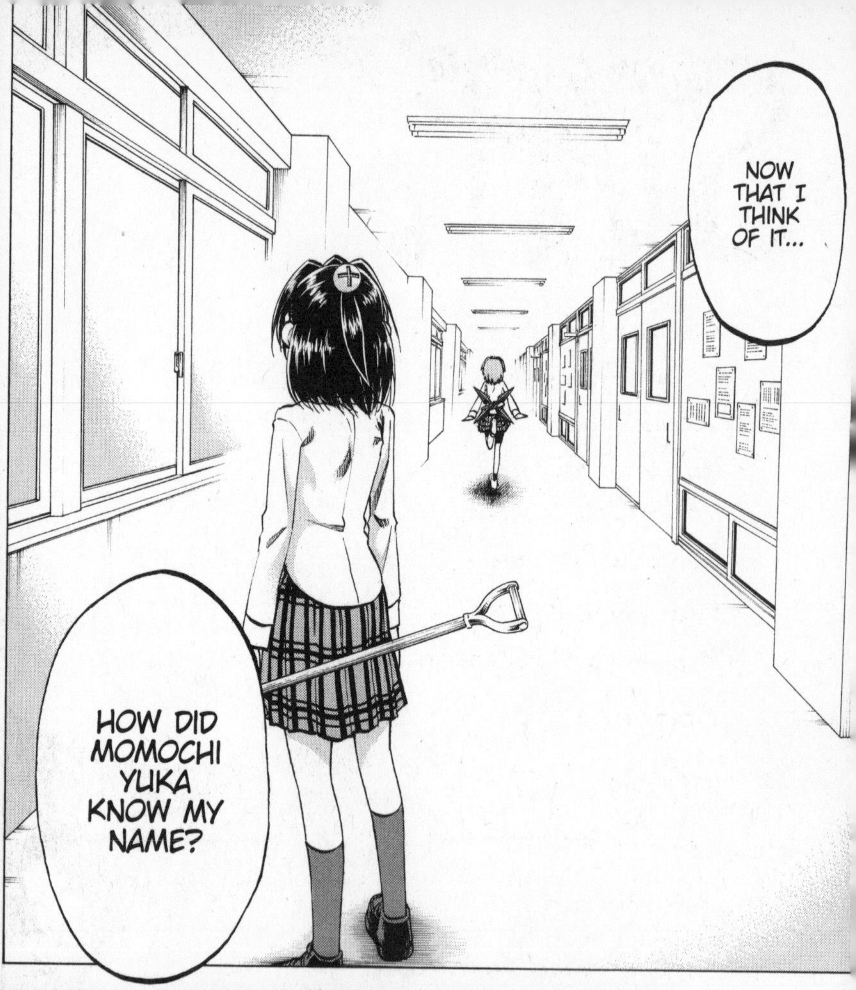
NOW THAT I THINK OF IT...
HOW DID MOMOCHI YUKA KNOW MY NAME?

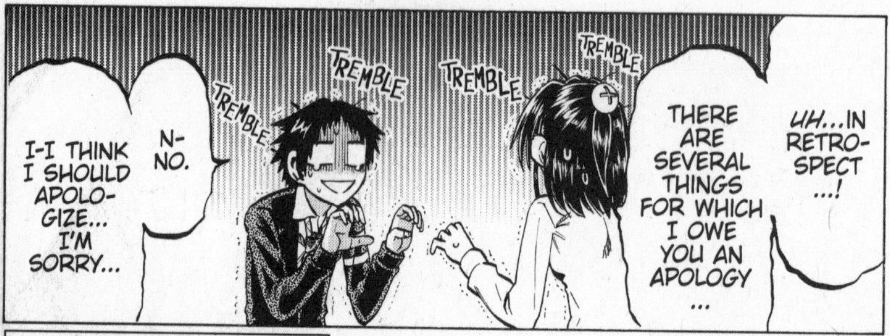
UH...IN RETRO-SPECT...!
THERE ARE SEVERAL THINGS FOR WHICH I OWE YOU AN APOLOGY...
TREMBLE
TREMBLE
TREMBLE
TREMBLE
N-NO.
I-I THINK I SHOULD APOLOGIZE... I'M SORRY...

My Monster Secret Volume 12/ End

STAFF.

- Garage Okada-san
- Shuumeigiku-san
- Suzuki Seijun-san
- Daifuku Mochiko-san
- Nakamura Yuji-san
- Hayashi Rie-san
- Mana Haruki-san
- Minemura Hiroki-san
- Mori Keiko

(in syllabary order)

SPECIAL THANKS.

- Adachi-san

Editor: Mukawa-san, Otsuka-san

Thank you to all of you holding this book right now and everyone who let me and this work be part of their lives.

Eiji Masuda

I am... 12

After "Like We Always Do"

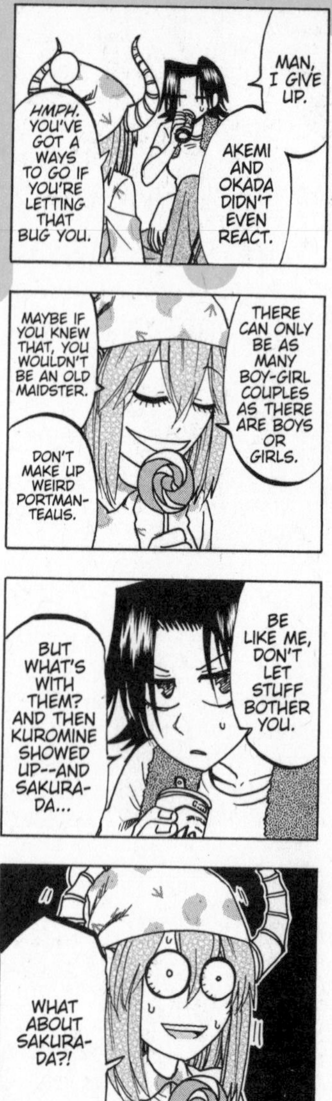

MAN, I GIVE UP.
AKEMI AND OKADA DIDN'T EVEN REACT.
HMPH. YOU'VE GOT A WAYS TO GO IF YOU'RE LETTING THAT BUG YOU.
THERE CAN ONLY BE AS MANY BOY-GIRL COUPLES AS THERE ARE BOYS OR GIRLS.
MAYBE IF YOU KNEW THAT, YOU WOULDN'T BE AN OLD MAIDSTER.
DON'T MAKE UP WEIRD PORTMANTEAUS.
BE LIKE ME, DON'T LET STUFF BOTHER YOU.
BUT WHAT'S WITH THEM? AND THEN KUROMINE SHOWED UP--AND SAKURADA...
WHAT ABOUT SAKURADA?!

After "Counsel"

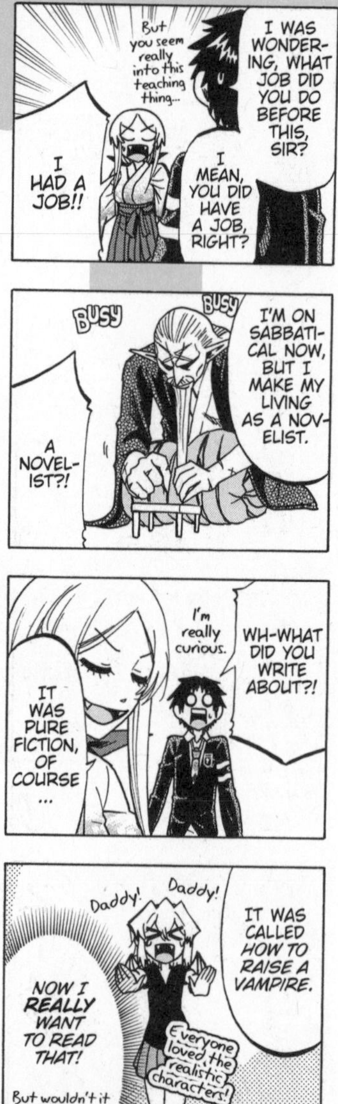

I WAS WONDERING, WHAT JOB DID YOU DO BEFORE THIS, SIR?
But you seem really into this teaching thing...
I MEAN, YOU DID HAVE A JOB, RIGHT?
I HAD A JOB!!
BUSY
I'M ON SABBATICAL NOW, BUT I MAKE MY LIVING AS A NOVELIST.
BUSY
A NOVELIST?!
WH-WHAT DID YOU WRITE ABOUT?!
I'm really curious.
IT WAS PURE FICTION, OF COURSE...
IT WAS CALLED *HOW TO RAISE A VAMPIRE.*
Daddy!
Daddy!
Everyone loved the realistic characters!
NOW I **REALLY** WANT TO READ THAT!
But wouldn't it be nonfiction...?

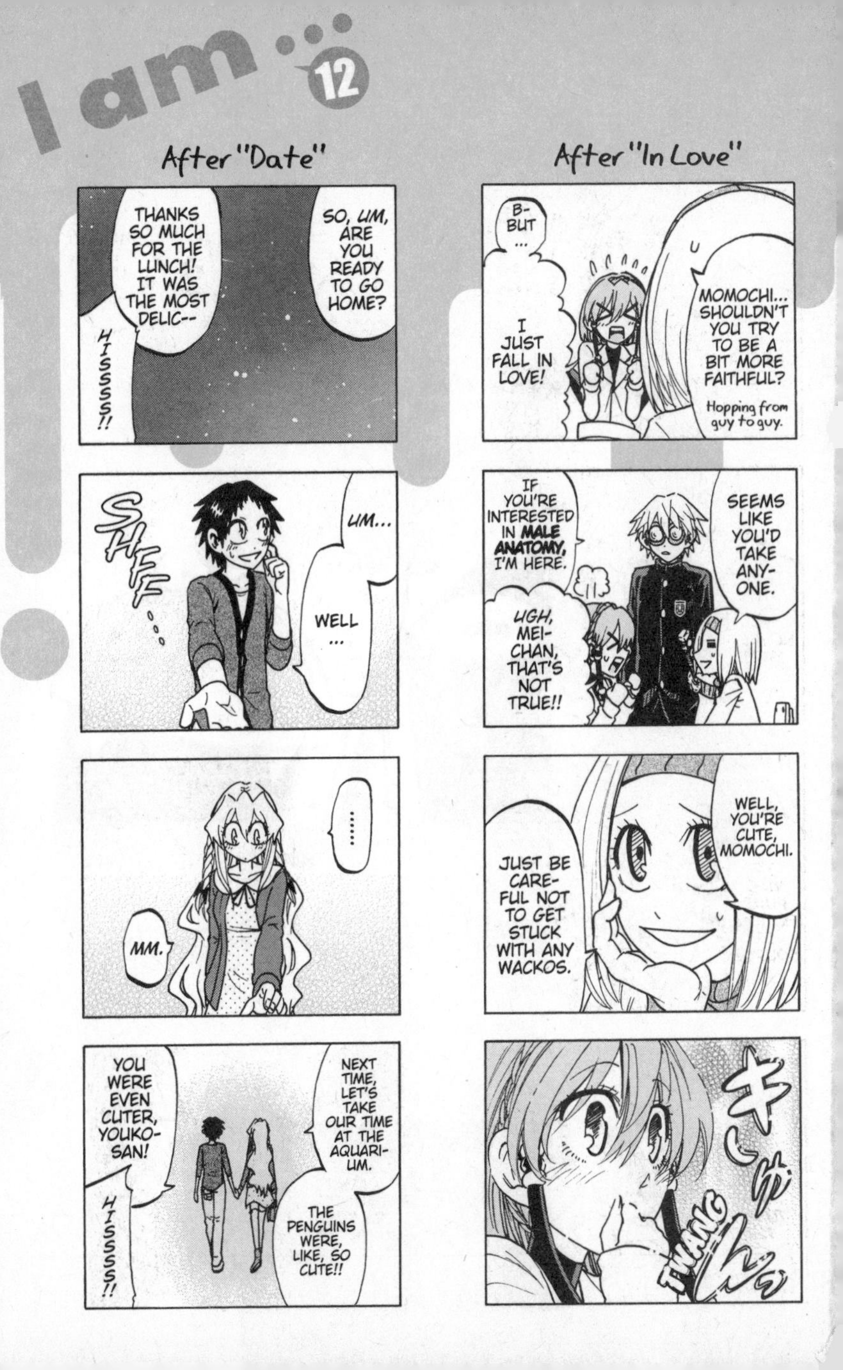
I am 12
After "In Love"
MOMOCHI... SHOULDN'T YOU TRY TO BE A BIT MORE FAITHFUL?
Hopping from guy to guy.
B-BUT...
I JUST FALL IN LOVE!
SEEMS LIKE YOU'D TAKE ANY-ONE.
IF YOU'RE INTERESTED IN MALE ANATOMY, I'M HERE.
UGH, MEI-CHAN, THAT'S NOT TRUE!!
WELL, YOU'RE CUTE, MOMOCHI.
JUST BE CARE-FUL NOT TO GET STUCK WITH ANY WACKOS.
TWANG
After "Date"
SO, UM, ARE YOU READY TO GO HOME?
THANKS SO MUCH FOR THE LUNCH! IT WAS THE MOST DELIC--
HISSSSS!!
SHFF...
UM...
WELL...
......
MM.
NEXT TIME, LET'S TAKE OUR TIME AT THE AQUARI-UM.
THE PENGUINS WERE, LIKE, SO CUTE!!
YOU WERE EVEN CUTER, YOUKO-SAN!
HISSSSS!!

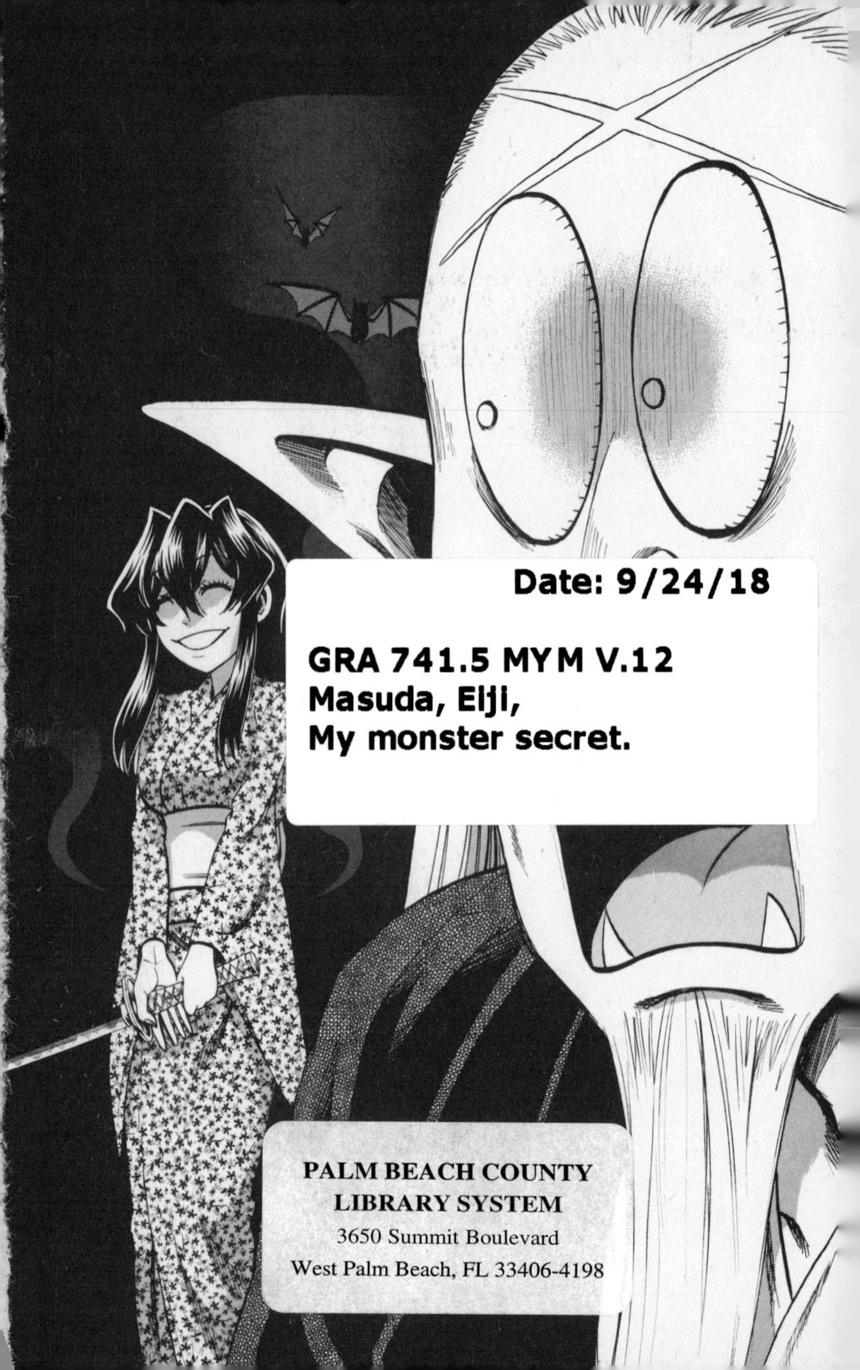